BOYS

LIKE

US

BOYS

LIKE

U S

*Gay Writers Tell Their
Coming out Stories*

EDITED BY

PATRICK MERLA

AVON BOOKS ◆ NEW YORK

VISIT OUR WEBSITE AT
http://AvonBooks.com

AVON BOOKS
A division of
The Hearst Corporation
1350 Avenue of the Americas
New York, New York 10019

Collection copyright © 1996 by Patrick Merla
Interior design by Kellan Peck
All photographs are courtesy of the author, except where otherwise noted.
Published by arrangement with the editor
Library of Congress Catalog Card Number: 96-20705
ISBN: 0-380-97340-5

Library of Congress Cataloging in Publication Data:

Boys like us : gay writers tell their coming out stories / edited by
    Patrick Merla.
        p.   cm.
    1. Gay men—United States—Biography.   2. Gay men—United States—Sexual behavior.
3. Coming out (Sexual orientation)—United States.   4. Gay men's writings, American.
I. Merla, Patrick.
HQ75.7.B69   1996   96-20705
306.76'62—dc20   CIP

First Avon Books Hardcover Printing: October 1996

IN MEMORY OF

Steve Abbott
Reza Abdoh
Hugh Allen
Peter Allen
Frank Arcuri
Reinaldo Arenas
Abel Rios Arias
Howard Ashman
James Assatly
David Craig Austin
Brett Averill
Charles Barber
Allen Barnett
Joseph Beam
Richard Benner
John Bernd
Jack Bissell
Jerry Blatt
Walta Borawski
William Bory
John Boswell
Alan Bowne
Joe Brainard
Arthur J. Bressan, Jr.
Donald Britten
Harold Brodkey
Howard Brookner
Chris Brownlie
Michael Callen
Bruce Calnan
Fred Cantaloupe
Warren Casey
Robert Chesley
Christopher Coe
Steve Corbett
Steven Corbin
Christopher Cox
Sam D'Allessandro
Nicholas Dante
William Dickey
Melvin Dixon
Tim Dlugos
Emmanuel Dreuilhe
Ethyl Eichelberger
Nathan Fain
David B. Feinberg
Robert Ferro
Michel Foucault

John Fox
David Frechette
Richard Friedel
Philip Galas
David Gilmore
Roy Gonsalves
Stuart Greenspan
Michael Grumley
Hervé Guibert
Richard Hall
Craig G. Harris
Stephen Harvey
Terry Helbing
Essex Hemphill
Bill Hennessy
Colin Higgins
Paul Hidalgo-Duran
Mike Hippler
Richard Horn
Jackson Hughes
Bo Huston
Arturo Islas
Paul Jabara
Robert Jacobson
Derek Jarman
Michael Jay
David Kalstone
Wayne Karr
Karl Keller
Kenneth Ketwig
Gregory Kolovakos
Harry Kondoleon
Mark Kostopoulos
Glenn Kramer
Barry Laine
Garey Lambert
Craig Lee
Stan Leventhal
David Lindahl
Charles Ludlam
Michael Lynch
Kiki Mason
Gerald Mast
Frank Maya
Peter McGehee
David McIntosh
Scott McPherson
Freddie Mercury

Ernest Matthew Mickler
Terry Miller
J. J. Mitchell
Lionel Mitchell
Paul Monette
Cookie Mueller
Jean-Baptiste Niel
William Olander
George Osterman
Craig Owen
Glenn Person
James Carroll Pickett
Henry Post
John Preston
John Read
Joel Redon
Marlon Riggs
Darrell Yates Rist
Craig Rowland
John Russell
Vito Russo
Assotto Saint
Rick Sandford
Martin M. Schaeffer
Jeffrey Schmalz
Howard Shapiro
Bill Sherwood
Randy Shilts
Kevin Smith
George Stambolian
Thomas Stehling
Otis Stuart
Alfred Sturtevant
David Summers
Paul Taylor
Carl Tierney
Alan Turcotte
Richard Umans
Paul Walker
Matthew Ward
George Whitmore
Mason Wiley
Jack Winkler
T. R. Witomski
David Wojnarowicz
Donald W. Woods
Thomas Yingling
Phil Zwickler

and countless other writers
lost to AIDS

ACKNOWLEDGMENTS

THIS BOOK HAS been decades in the making. Over that time I've built up more than a few debts of gratitude, which I now welcome the opportunity to acknowledge.

I want to thank the contributors to this volume, most of whom I met first through their writing, many of whom became my friends in the ensuing months and years in which we've shared good times and bad. I particularly thank Christopher Bram, Philip Bockman, Larry Kramer, Ed Sikov, and William Sterling Walker for their unfailing support. If Charles L. Ortleb had not hired me to edit his publications, I would never have been in the position to work with a good number of these writers; I thank him. I would also like to thank Dale Peck, who was unable to contribute to the anthology but steered me toward writers who did, and James Ireland Baker for his ready ear. And I thank Richard Labonté of A Different Light bookstore for his help in compiling the bibliography.

I owe debts to Christopher Cox, Maxine Groffsky, David Kalstone, J. D. McClatchy, and James Merrill which, quite simply, can never be repaid. Were it not for Edmund White, I would never have known any of them—and possibly never have had a career in publishing.

This book has had input from several editors who deserve to be named: Bill Goldstein, Tysie Whitman, Nan Graham, Ted Lee. And Charlotte Abbott— midwife, savior, paragon of patience.

My agent, Jane Dystel, is a wonder worker. No one could hope for a more valiant champion. She deserves a paragraph of her own, which I happily give her here.

ACKNOWLEDGMENTS

Likewise her associate, Miriam Goderich, indispensable colleague and friend who pushed me to make this dream come true and kept me on an even keel in sometimes troublous waters.

I give thanks to the Ann and Erlo Van Waveren Foundation and the Ingram Merrill Foundation for their financial support during difficult times if not for this project specifically, and to Lyn and Ned Chase for their encouragement and support, financial and moral.

Lewis Alban, Susan Barlow, Michael Donadio, and Larry Hertz played key roles in my own formative years. I'm thankful that three of them are still in my life and would welcome the reappearance of the fourth.

I owe very special thanks to Bette Midler. God bless her forever.

And Nicole Janssen, who literally saved my life and keeps me healthy.

Thanks to Chip Kidd for his wonderful jacket design, and to Kellan Peck for her elegant interior design.

Finally, I need to mention Barbara Confino, Dorianne Beyer, Eunice and Stephen Chalmers, Frances Chapman, Mary Lynn Fischer, Terry Foster, Dorian Rae Hannaway, Damien Jack, James Knight, Norman Laurila, Craig Lucas, Keith McDermott and Eric Amouyal, Barbara Novak and Brian O'Doherty, Bill Rose and Valden Madsen, and Nina Reznick—friends of the first rank, joys of my life.

NOTE

THE STORIES IN this anthology are arranged in chronological order and are meant to be read that way. The dates in the Table of Contents indicate the year(s) in which the primary events of each story occurred and are included for the reader's information. I asked the contributors to write personal essays which read like short stories. At least one, Edmund White, succeeded so well that the *New Yorker* published his, "Cinnamon Skin," as fiction. Samuel R. Delany's "Coming / Out" and Carl Phillips's "Sea Level," the first and last pieces in the book, are meditations on the nature of coming out, its changing meaning over time, its implications for the individual and society, and provide an apt "frame" to the collection. Except for Delany, I did not ask for contributions from writers (Felice Picano, Paul Monette, Martin Bauml Duberman, for instance) who have already told their stories in their own autobiographies or memoirs (see the Select Bibliography at the end of the book).

CONTENTS

CONTENTS

A LETTER TO THE READER

YOU MAY BE thinking the last thing on earth you need is another anthology of gay literature, and you may have long ago decided that you'd read the last coming-out story you ever needed to read. But take a deep breath and dive into *Boys Like Us*. Patrick Merla, one of modern American gay literature's true champions, has assembled a glorious crowd of talents—reflecting the diversity and accomplishment of gay writing today—and he's orchestrated their voices and stories as marvelously inventive, surprising, joyous, harrowing, and frequently lovely variations performed by master singers on a truly great theme, for the sounding of which polyphony is finally the best imaginable music. Coming-out stories frequently numb their readers with an airless solipsism, the individual asphyxiating in his hard-earned isolation. That's why this collection is so smart and so necessary. Its basic gesture is not narcissistic but inclusive and generous. I read *Boys Like Us* with growing excitement, as a sort of collective contemplation of the individual's journey toward a complex dignity and integrity. Here is a gathering of wildly divergent, brilliant personalities considering the processes, intentional and accidental, serendipitous and tragic, shaping that impossible, ineffable, personal and political singular object, the human Self.

—Tony Kushner

INTRODUCTION

IN THE EARLY fall of 1972, I was living in San Francisco, where I had moved to work for *Saturday Review* magazine as an assistant editor. I'd been brought on staff by Edmund White, a new friend who was soon to publish his first novel. Ed had already begun his other career—helping people whose talent he believed in—and several of our fellow staffers also owed their jobs to him. (In a sense, the present volume is a result of that generosity; but that's another story.) We were all dyed-in-the-wool New Yorkers (though only I had been born there) and still adjusting to this new laid-back city, so different from the in-your-face metropolis we were used to. Four of us had decided to try the famous pizza at the Sausage Factory, a restaurant on Castro Street so popular that a two-hour wait was not uncommon. We were well into our first hour when the conversation turned to coming out. (As Andrew Holleran observes, years ago "every new friendship in gay life entailed an explanation of How I Got Here.") Ed told an abbreviated version of his narrative in this book, then urged, "You should hear Stanley's story. It's really something."

Naturally, we asked to hear it.

As a student at a Midwestern college in the 1950s, Stanley had majored in drama and was close friends with his roommate. One day, the roommate revealed that he was in love with Stan. Stan rebuked him, telling him not to mention it again, they would pretend he'd never said anything. As proof of his goodwill, they would continue the kind of roughhousing that always had been part of their friendship. A few months passed. One day well before the end of the term, Stanley returned from class to discover his roommate packed and ready to leave school; he could no longer bear the pain of his hopeless unrequited passion, which was intensified, not lessened, by Stan's oblivious physicality. Had Stan arrived a few minutes later, he would have found a note in place of his friend. Realizing what he was about to lose, Stan was suddenly faced with his own true feelings. There was only one way to stop his friend from leaving: Stan took him in his arms—and to bed.

At least, that's how I remember Stan telling it. I was a romantic myself and Stanley a great beauty, so I've never gone back to confirm it, although I'm aware of how memory can affect things. I was so taken with Stan's story, I made it a practice afterward to ask other gay men how they'd come out.

"Coming out" is the central event of a gay man's life. It is at once an act of self-acknowledgment, self-acceptance, self-affirmation, and self-revelation intimately linked to how he views himself and how he interacts with the world. It can happen in stages, or be an instance of illumination in which a gay man recognizes who he is. It can be interior, a psychological sorting of facts and feelings, or an external act of identification to another person or persons. For most gay men, coming out involves all of these in one way or another. Because the individual's very identity is involved, and society in general makes such an issue of sexuality (as one writer notes, "heterosexuality is not always as easy as it looks"), the event is intimately linked to how the person views himself and how he responds to other people and the world. So much is at stake that the way in which a man comes out can reverberate throughout his entire life, whether the response to his disclosure is positive, negative, or neutral.

Were you to ask someone to tell you his coming-out story, it's likely he would describe some defining moment: the first time he had sex with another man (or tried to), the first time he realized he was gay, the first time he told someone else his secret. Gay writers, who have made their sexuality part of their artistic and public personae, are in a unique position to present this phenomenon in dramatic terms.

I returned to New York early in 1973 convinced that such stories would make a wonderful book. I planned to interview people and then edit the transcripts into first-person narratives. Many of my subjects would, of course, use pseudonyms.

I was unable to interest a publisher then. The Stonewall Riots had occurred only four years earlier, the Gay Liberation movement was still taking shape, and no one published books for a perceived gay audience, let alone a crossover market. By 1994, the time had finally arrived. And what changes had taken place!

No longer was it necessary for people to make up names to conceal their identities. Indeed, there was a large pool of gay authors who had proved by their success the existence of the market—novelists, short story writers, poets, playwrights, performance artists who knew how to tell a good story and could now do so as openly gay creators. As luck would have it, I had worked with many of them as an editor over the years, even discovered a few. They came from Maine, Massachusetts, Pennsylvania, Maryland, North Carolina, Virginia,

Florida, Louisiana, Texas, Oklahoma, Kansas, Ohio, Illinois, Michigan, California, the two Washingtons, Hawaii, and even New York.

I had an idea that if I placed their stories in chronological order and limited
the contributors to people born or raised in the United States, a kind of
historical picture might emerge. And it has.

Some things have changed drastically over the last fifty years, with luck
permanently. Where in 1961 a student at the University of Michigan must see
a psychiatrist to appease his parents, by 1976 an androgynous male student in
Los Angeles is mistaken for a "lesbian separatist from Ann Arbor." A graduate
student in psychology, "a Kinsey 6 who'd convinced his colleagues he was a
Kinsey 1," sits mute in New York's City College in 1968 while his sexuality
is described as a pathology; within a decade, there's a Gay Lounge at Columbia
University and students are wearing "Kinsey 7" T-shirts. Meanwhile, at Kenyon
College in Gambier, Ohio, a student is more concerned with being a virgin
than with being gay—a sure sign of the sexual permissiveness of the seventies.
In 1994, one writer speaks of a friend who can't "conceive of coming out to
himself because he had never been in the closet."

Some things haven't changed. A young man gets gay-bashed in 1990 Greenwich Village and worries about entrapment, just like the young man at a bar
in 1961 Toldeo, Ohio. A Norman, Oklahoma, seventeen-year-old in the mid-
eighties experiences the same self-hatred, guilt, and shame as did a thirty-
three-year-old late bloomer in New York twenty years before him—both of
them trying to be heterosexual and failing. Boys still have to hide their glances
at other boys, still must come to terms with being "bound for something
different from most of the guys" they know. Other people's identities still must
be disguised in these accounts, if not the writers' own.

The biggest change is tragic. AIDS hovers over many of these stories and
is the driving force in one. (Essex Hemphill died before this book went to
press, and I was unable to include Stan Leventhal's essay about having to give
up a promising career as a country-western singer/songwriter because he died
before completing it.)

I hoped that these pieces, gathered together, would "speak"—to one another
and the reader—in ways no single story alone could manage. I believe they do.
"Teenagers do not fetishize big cocks, hairy chests, powerful biceps, or blond
hair and thick necks; their desire is too general to respond to anything less
than eternal love, and their love is vague and powerful enough to ennoble any
body at all," asserts one writer. A thirteen-year-old responds, "I liked to lie on
his bed smelling his socks on his oversized feet. There were feet and there
were penises. There wasn't love." A twenty-year-old laments, "It seemed unfair
that so much should depend on technique. Wasn't love supposed to just happen, a spontaneous communion of like-minded souls?" While a fourth muses,
"I like to think that the conflicting jumbles of emotion, intellect, sex, and—
there's no other phrase for it—moral life actually do connect and can be
experienced most fully by two bodies speaking to and through each other."
One boy's mother doesn't want to hear it, another boy's mother asks him
point-blank if he's gay, a third is stopped from doing so by the boy himself.

Two young men—one middle-class and white and the other from a modest background and black—write to their fathers to tell them that their college theses deal with gay subject matter; one father accepts, the other rejects his son's decision.

One writer even provides a psychological deconstruction of his own story, an argument for a distinctly gay psyche that resonates throughout the other writers' pieces. And so on. It makes no difference that years and geography separate the speakers and they're not addressing each other.

Something of a cultural history emerges in these pages, as well. We watch tastes change along with the passing scene. In pop music, Judy Garland and Dinah Washington give way to Joan Baez and Judy Collins, who give way to Sly & the Family Stone, Big Brother & the Holding Co., Lynyrd Skynyrd, David Bowie, Donna Summer, Bette Midler, Adam and the Ants, Boy George, Skinny Puppy, Madonna. Plastic sunflower-head chandeliers blossom into lava lamps. The Vietnam War protests of the seventies become ACT UP street actions in the eighties and nineties. Tie-dyed T-shirts unfold into Patti Smith T-shirts, bell bottoms to designer jeans. Movies become videotapes (including porn). Boys receive condoms as going-away-to-college gifts.

While some things remain constant (pot, peanut butter), others are pervasive. Especially TV—references to which appear in virtually every story from the late sixties onward (soap operas, sitcoms, *An American Family*, *The Brady Bunch*, *How the Grinch Stole Christmas*). And the influence of movies. One writer speaks of his "wide-screen moment," while another remarks on how "finding a man didn't automatically place me in a condition of cinematic bliss."

Two of these pieces reveal the source material later used in novels and thus serve as object lessons on the art of writing fiction; a third has the added gossip value of the presence of a Broadway star. Yet another provides details omitted from the author's published memoirs. Some are romantic, a few are funny, many are sad. I find them all moving.

Here are rueful lessons learned ("It is one thing to come out; it is quite another to get the person you really want") and hard-earned wisdom: "It seemed so easy finally to be a sexual being, so deliciously simple." "Being gay was not itself the problem. Everything *else* was the problem—the pressures, the opprobrium, the future, the double life." "This is what God wants me to do, what's right for me." "I put my hands all over him, took in a sudden rush of air, and became the man I was meant to be." "I'm not exactly sure what will happen, but I feel safe, suspended in the grace of knowing that right now I want it to happen. More than a part in a play or a place on the dean's list. More than anything." "Like a drop of ink let fall into a glass of water, being gay was a small part of the whole, but imbued everything."

And more.

—Patrick Merla
February 1996
New York, New York

COMING / OUT

Samuel R. Delany

"COMING OUT" HAS acquired extraordinary significance in the gay community since the Stonewall Riots of 1969—so much significance that many of us might even say that coming out "defines" the difference between being gay and an older, pre-gay notion of being homosexual. During those (post-Stonewall) times in which, if you hadn't "come out of the closet," many gay men and lesbians felt you had somehow betrayed them, that you couldn't really "define yourself as gay," and that you had not "accepted your gay identity," I found myself faced with a paradox: Much of my critical enterprise over the last thirty-five years has been devoted to showing that such "defining" or "identifying" events—when, as a reader, you first became aware of science fiction; when, as a child, you realized you were black, gay, or an artist—simply do not "define" anything.

In the gradual, continual, and constantly modulating process of becoming who we are, all events take their meanings, characteristic or uncharacteristic, from the surrounding event field in which they occur. While certainly they contribute to what we are or are becoming, single events simply do not carry the explicative strength "definition" denotes. This is not to say some events aren't more important than others.

Recently I had a discussion with a woman who, some years back, had been a catcher in a circus aerial act. "Well," she said, "I see what you mean. But I remember the moment my partner fell. It completely changed my life. We were in the middle of a performance in Las Vegas. I didn't drop her—I'm rather touchy about that. She was swinging around, hanging from a hand loop

1

attached to the trapeze. To steady her, I was fronting the bar—my term for balancing horizontally on my pelvis on a still trapeze bar. We were just getting ready for the finale. The loop broke and she flew out, still on her side—and went down. She landed on the concrete, almost thirty feet below. No, she wasn't killed. But she shattered her elbow, broke her arm, and bruised herself from head to foot. From that moment on, I just couldn't be an aerialist again. I formed another act with my boyfriend immediately, where he was the catcher this time. I guess it was to prove to myself that I *hadn't* changed. But three weeks later, after three more performances, I quit." She sighed. "I missed the circus for the next ten years. But my life just wasn't the same after the accident as it was before."

"I didn't say that what happens in a single moment can't *change* your life," I told her. "I said that it doesn't *define* your life. What made that moment have the meaning for you that it did was your previous years of training as an acrobat, as an aerialist, the circus tradition. It was the medical emergency that followed, the severity of your partner's injuries, the response of the people around you—all that makes such an occurrence as overwhelmingly significant as it was. The fact that you did go up again, and also that you missed the circus for so long, once you left, shows how much *wasn't* changed, in spite of the very real change that *did* occur."

It's a subtle but important difference. She agreed.

All the incidents I'm going to recount—none so dramatic as my aerialist friend's adventure—changed my life. But they changed it in small, distinct ways. None of them marked a before or after point, distinguishing absence from presence. Rather, each is notable because it *was* a point of change, a point where what was present before was still present, only in rearranged form.

I.

My second summer camp was as wonderfully rich and pleasant as my first had been nightmarish. The boys in the senior camp area were housed just beyond a small hill, called the Knoll, in a clearing in the trees called the Tent Colony. To one side was a plank-walled, black-brown shack with a slant roof: the boys' john. Inside were two wooden-stalled showers, two wooden-stalled commodes, sinks, and urinals. Outside, just left of the door, against the creo-soted planks and above a splatter of gravel, the steel basin (that let the water fall out the bottom onto the stones) leaned askew. A water fountain's gaunt spigot thrust up from it, with an ancient spring knob to turn it on.

Around a twenty-five- or thirty-yard clearing, set in pairs, were the wooden platforms and frames over which, for the summer, orange or olive drab canvas tents were put up to house the young male campers: two tents for Bunk Five, two tents for Bunk Six, two tents for Bunk Seven, two tents for Bunk Eight, and, finally, completing the circle on the other side of the john, two tents for storage of extra beds and mattresses. At least that was the ideal arrangement, but sometimes the vagaries of enrollment moved things around. The other interruption to this pattern was geographical: The far corner of the colony dipped down steeply, so that the Bunk Seven tents were practically out of sight of the others.

The summer the Korean War ended, 1953, began with a major disappointment. I and some of my friends were assigned the same tents for Bunk Six as we'd had the year before for Bunk Five—beside the john. The camp's logic (and folklore) was that the younger you were, the closer they wanted you to the bathroom. The extra eight- or nine-yard walk across the worn grass and gravel was to be a mark of our one year's seniority, our new maturity—and now it had been denied us. We sulked as we put away our clothes in the wooden cubbies beside our beds, newly made up with olive drab army blankets.

Two days after our arrival, however, on a windy and rainy July 3, after we'd hiked down in our rain gear to the recreation and dining hall for breakfast, while we were eating our oatmeal and pancakes the weather blew up into a major windstorm. In our green ponchos and yellow slickers, we crowded to the doors to stand at the top of the long wooden steps and gaze out, laughing and daring one another to go down to the cinder-and-gravel path, on each side of which branches snapped and quivered as torrential gusts sheeted the silvery, swimming-pool-sized puddles before the deluge salted them over again with froth.

The rain stopped. The wind lessened.

But when we got back to the Tent Colony and the six of us in the old Bunk Five tent started across the clearing, we saw something wrong.

A tree had blown down across the tent's roof and smashed the two-by-four that held up the peak. Our counselor, Roy, announced that we should stay a good twenty feet away from it. One obstreperous, small, and angry camper, Noah, began to argue that he had valuable things in there that needed to be taken out. Now! Though I didn't say it, I felt much the same. My violin was in there. The rest of us argued with Noah: Suppose the tent collapsed further while he was inside? No one *should* go in, at least till the fallen tree was removed.

"Now *don't* go in there!" were Roy's last words as he sprinted away toward the Tent Colony entrance to get some assistance.

The moment he was gone, Noah uttered a harsh "Fuck *him!*" and marched up to the half-collapsed tent. He pushed inside the skew orange flap, emerging a few moments later with his microscope, a box of slides, and his camera.

"You're crazy," a bigger, more stolid camper named Dave declared. "You know that? You're really crazy."

"Well, I just didn't want anything to happen to *these*," Noah retorted, "while they were fooling around with the tree."

Once the order was breached, however, we all drifted closer to check things out.

Bathtubs of rainwater filled the bellied-down canvas. A few leaves floated in it. The tree itself had lodged securely. None of the tent canvas was actually torn, except for a six-inch rip at one corner where the weathered wood had

3

pushed through. A short, heavy, sensible kid named Billy shoved first at this part, then leaned on another. Nothing budged. Beneath the canvas, the shape the broken two-by-fours had fallen into was stable.

"I'm going to look inside, too," I said.

I stepped up through the front flap. Inside, weighted with all that water, the canvas pressed on top of my bed, held up by my cubby beside it. Through the fabric watery light deviled the shadows. The canvas smell seemed far more intense than it had in the past two nights we'd slept there. Flush with the weighted fabric, part off and part on my cubby top, sat my violin case.

Crouching down and holding the edge of one, I squat-walked between two beds to see that the cubby corner had punctured the case's bottom. I tried to nudge the case free. With hundreds of gallons of water above it, though, it wouldn't move.

In what condition, I wondered, was the violin?

Outside, I went down the platform steps. In a few minutes, Roy came back with the camp director and Mr. Herdmen, from the neighboring farm.

In the next hour, with a block and tackle, the tree was removed from the tent roof and it was decided that our group would relocate, along with one of the other bunks, to what last year had been the Bunk Seven tents, down in the depression at the Tent Colony's corner—even farther from the john than the Bunk Six tents! The remaining Bunk Five tent would be used for storage, and the old storage tent would now become the counselors' "day off" tent. It was a vindication and a reward Nature had engineered to compensate for the camp's shortsightedness.

Throughout the rest of the morning there was much dragging of trunks and remaking of beds. In the collapsed tent, the water was pushed out of the canvas, so that it roared and splattered down the side, over the tent ropes. I got my violin case out, took it to my new tent, and, on my new bed, opened it.

The violin's bridge was broken. A seven-inch crack split the front.

I lifted the instrument from the blue plush lining. The right-angle cubby corner had gone through the case back and punctured the red-varnished wood. Short of major repair, it was unplayable.

The day's relocation meant Roy had to be down at the camp office a lot. The wind settled. The sun came out. The morning grew warmer. And, in our new tent out of sight in the dell, we were left unsupervised.

It was stolid Dave who suggested, "Hey, let's all gang up on somebody and have a fight!"

"Yeah, sure!" declared Noah. We all felt the thrill of possible victimization—like a great Russian roulette game.

"Yeah, but who's it gonna be?" I asked.

"We're gonna gang up on . . ." In the middle of the tent floor between the bunk beds, Dave turned slowly. ". . . him!" He pointed to short, heavy Billy.

Who cried out, ". . . Hey!"

Relieved, the rest of us threw ourselves on Billy, who began to shout. "Come on—cut it out! Now, stop it! Stop!"

It was also Dave who yelled, "Let's make him suck our dicks!"—a camper who, before or afterward, I never had any reason to think was other than straight.

"Yeah!" agreed Joel, another big camper, now in the midst of the fray.

Like me, Joel wore glasses. Like me, Joel was black. Like me, Joel was light enough that you might not have noticed it. It was signaled only by the broad nose and the tight curl to his brown hair, above a bony, even horselike face that, on someone older, could have spoken of a truly interesting character. In addition, Joel was a very bad nail biter.

Once Dave had articulated the game's sexual goal, over the first thirty seconds I became aware of the increased avidity, a level or two higher than anyone else's, with which Joel threw himself into it. In the crush of the six of us, pushing protesting Billy to his knees between the iron-frame steads, without even looking Joel grabbed first Dave's hand, then mine, to thrust it against his gray khaki crotch. Within, his penis was hard. Dave just yanked his hand away and went on struggling with Billy, but I squeezed—and rubbed. And kept rubbing, till first Dave, then Joel, then Noah, then I pulled our flies open to push our cocks at Billy's grimacing face as he tried to twist away. Joel's and mine were strainingly erect.

Quickly it was over. Billy was released, with all—except Billy—laughing. I remember watching him carefully. More than anything else, his attitude was annoyance. There was no major distaste, horror, or degradation. But then, the "cocksucking" had only been a ritual touch of our penises to his mouth. Only Joel and I had tried to push within Billy's pursed and tightened lips.

"That was really *stupid!*" Billy said—three times.

Moments later, Roy was coming up the tent steps, and the incident—like several during those first days—simply vanished in all its bodily traces, as much from Billy as it did from Dave, Joel, and the rest of us.

I DON'T KNOW when I determined to speak to Joel about the subject, but sometime in the following week or ten days, I decided that I would, the next time we were alone together. One afternoon we were walking up to the pool, thirty or forty yards away from any other campers.

"Joel," I said, "do you remember when we had the fight where we all made Billy suck our cocks?"

"Yeah," Joel said. "Sure."

"We really *liked* that, didn't we? I mean, I could tell—you and me, we liked it a lot more than the others did."

"Huh? Yeah, I guess we did."

"I could see it. I mean, I liked it, too." Then I said: "I think that's because we're homosexual."

Though I had read it, looked it up in the dictionary, and searched it out of the indexes of any number of books, this was the first time I'd spoken the word *homosexual* to another person.

"Oh," Joel said. "Yeah. I guess so. . . . I figured that." He let out a sigh.

I sighed, too. "It's funny," I said. "You and me. We're both homosexual. We're both Negro. . . ."

"Well," Joel said, after a considered moment. "I'm only *half* Negro. It's just my father."

I was a little surprised. A shade or so lighter than Joel, I'd never thought of myself as anything other than black. But then, he'd been raised by a white mother. I'd seen them together the previous year's Visiting Day. From some chance conversation, when I'd asked him why his father hadn't been able to come up, I'd learned Joel's dad had left the family so long ago Joel didn't even remember him.

"Yeah," I said. "But in this country, that doesn't mean anything. Legally, you might as well be all Negro."

"Yeah," Joel said. "I thought about *that*, too."

"We should probably be friends," I said. " 'Cause we may have a very rough time. A lot of people don't like people like us, when they find out."

"Yeah," Joel said, "I know."

It sounded as though that came from experience.

Before we reached the pool, we had agreed to be friends—then had practically nothing to do with each other for the remainder of the summer.

Three years later, when I entered the Bronx High School of Science, I learned that Joel had also arrived there as a freshman. None of our courses overlapped, though, and a certain anxiety, connected largely to what I was learning about what society thought of such sexual pursuits, kept me from seeking him out. By my junior year, however, experience had sedimented within me both more self-consciousness and more social awareness. I decided to find Joel, to say hello again, to see how he was doing, and, yes, to reminisce about old times at summer camp. I asked a girl named Maddy if she remembered him. She did. But after three or four days, it became clear that he no longer attended the school. I even hunted up people who had gone to elementary school with him. None of them had any news.

In the thirty-seven years since, I've run into dozens of people from my high school days. Now and again I've heard news of dozens more. But, though I've often asked after him, I've never encountered Joel or any information about him.

II.

There's a reason heterosexuals do not usually ask each other "When was the moment you realized you were straight?" That's because the fixing of such a moment would mean that there was a whole block of time prior to it when you *didn't* know you were straight. To know you are straight is to know you are normal. Thus, to the extent that such ignorance is itself a form of knowledge, not to know you were straight would signify a time when you were dangerously close to *abnormal*. Not only is that an uncomfortable idea for homophobic reasons, it is also intuitively "off." One learns one is attracted to whatever attracts one—males, females, whatever—more and more over a period of time. The only times straight men are asked "When did you first become interested in girls?" or straight women asked "When did you first become interested in boys?" are when the overarching rhetorical enterprise is to trivialize and delimit male heterosexuality vis-à-vis some other social field, such as labor or familial relationships, or to trivialize female heterosexuality vis-à-vis male heterosexuality.

The rhetoric of singular discovery, of revelation, of definition, is one of the conceptual tools by which dominant discourses repeatedly suggest that there *is* no broad and ranging field of events informing the marginal. This is true of science fiction versus the field of literature, art as compared to social labor, blacks as a marginal social group to a central field of whites, and gay sexuality as marginal to a heterosexual norm. That rhetoric becomes part of the way the marginal is trivialized, distorted, and finally oppressed. For what is wrong with all these seemingly innocent questions—which include, alas, "When did you come out?"—is that each tends to assume that the individual's subjective field is the same as the field of social statistics.

Sexual interests, concerns, and observations form a broad and pervasive field within every personality, as broad in me as it is in you, as broad in the straight man as it is in the gay woman. When we speak of burgeoning sexuality, that's the internal field we speak of—not the social field defined by what percentage of us are gay or straight. The discourse behind that same rhetoric of singularity is, of course, the discourse which believes that a single homosexual event can make an otherwise straight person turn gay—or that the single proper heterosexual experience can "cure" someone gay and turn him or her straight.

As a prelude to more incidents, then, that preceded my "coming out," I've put together a list of some twenty-two incidents involving sex that happened to me between age seven (1949) and age fifteen (1957), including the '53 incident with Joel. The twenty-two are not exhaustive. They are the ones I remember. A reason I remember them is because each taught me some specific lesson. (Probably I've forgotten the sexual incidents which only repeated or confirmed these lessons.) Together they limn the *range* of sexual events against which any *individual* event among them signifies; thus they delineate at least part of the field of my childhood sexual awareness.

To help them register *as* a field, however, I'll speak about them for a few paragraphs in statistical cross section, rather than as specific occurrences, or even in terms of particular meanings drawn from them.

Only one of the twenty-two—the earliest, during my second year at my first summer camp, with a somewhat older girl, herself wildly misinformed about sex—involved anything like pain or abuse.

Eight of these twenty-two events occurred in rural settings.

Three occurred in suburban locations.

Eleven occurred in New York City, where I lived the vast majority of my life throughout those years—far more than the fifty percent the statistical deployment of the events suggests.

Seventeen involved bodily contact with other youngsters.

The other five involved clear and strong desire on my part for such contact.

Seven of them were fundamentally heterosexual.

Finally, fifteen of them were fundamentally homosexual, so that, with experience to back me, I was fairly sure by the age of eleven my own sexuality was largely gay—though I was curious enough about the other kind.

Virtually all real sexual behavior in the pre-fifteen-year-old lies outside socially acceptable—but by no means outside socially determined—boundaries. Freud and Foucault both have reminded us that the family *is* the social unit that most confines and constrains children's sexual behavior. The "normal" model for all of us in the West, even the most resolute heterosexual, is to begin our sexual life *outside* the socially acceptable, as children, and only with time to enter it more and more.

Immediately and absolutely I bow to the assertion that the various meanings I took from those early incidents were determined by a range of intersecting and intercritiquing pre-existing discourses—discourses which allowed me to read, which stabilized in my memory, which constituted for me the events themselves. But because of that "intercritique" one of the important meanings I quickly inferred from my experiences was that what is said about sex often does not cover the case.

GENERALLY SUMMER CAMP was a series of sexual surprises. The afternoon of my very first day in Bunk Five, a young camper from Florida explained to the bunk that the way to have the best summer was if the big boys (like him) regularly fucked the asses of the smaller boys (like me)—and proceeded to use an interested and willing me to demonstrate how it was done. Five years later, on my very last night in camp, half a dozen of us were cavorting in the altogether after lights out in the bunk next to our own when the flashlight of the returning counselor flickered across the porch screening. Big, rough Berny, whose foreskin was as long as his four-syllable Italian last name, lifted up his covers and whispered, "Quick, Delany! Get in!"—and I slid in to be enfolded by his arms, my naked body pulled against his, where his cock, already rigid, began to rub against my belly.

In that same landscape, between these first and last moments, fell some half-dozen more of those twenty-two incidents that constitute the field of my childhood sexuality. One of the oddest was when, in my third year of camp, I noticed a boy hanging toward the outside of the circle of campers and counselors that we formed every morning before breakfast for Flag Raising. When he thought himself unobserved, Tom would dig in his nose with one thick finger or the other and feed himself the pickings. Watching him gave me an erection. There was little specificity to the desire, neither to emulate nor to share, though if he had offered me some I would have accepted, pleased by the bold self-confidence and inclusion of his gesture. (At five, in school I'd been roundly embarrassed out of the same habit by public ridicule, led by Miss Rubin: "If you are hungry, young man, I'm *sure* we can arrange for you to get something to eat. But *stop* that!") My response was to make every effort to befriend Tom and, once the friendship had been secured, to explain to him that I had no problems with the habit I knew must have caused him, now and then, at least *some* social pain; he should feel free to indulge it whenever we were alone together. He did, at first with some trepidation, though less as time went on. We ended up taking long walks through the woods, holding hands (another nail biter, he), talking of this and that. While he dug and ate, we wandered along beneath the leaves, pushing aside brush, crunching twigs, and climbing over logs, I in a haze of barely presexual ecstasy.

The same years contained three fairly enduring (for weeks in each case) heterosexual experiments which, while they were pleasant enough physically (all three involved everything, as they say, except penetration), nevertheless registered with a complete emotional flatness and a lack of affect, save the immediate frisson of trying something new—a flatness and lack whose prevailing sign is the lack of detail with which I recount them here. (The four girls' bunks occupied two bunkhouses outside the Tent Colony on the other side of the Knoll across from a red-and-white barn, gray inside and housing a Ping-Pong table and an upright piano, called, rather eccentrically, Brooklyn College.) Although the word *love* was spoken repeatedly—and, I suspect, sincerely—by the young women (and even a few times by me, to see how it tasted on my tongue), my silent judgment was that if this was all that accrued to these "normal" adventures—very much socially approved of by both the male and female counselors—they just weren't worth it. In two cases, the lessons learned were among the more negative ones I took from these early explorations. One affair ended with a fight between me and a rival named Gary over the affections of a young woman who could not, or would not, make up her mind.

"You decide which one of us you like better," Gary and I agreed, "and the other one will go away."

"But I don't want to hurt anyone's *feelings!*" the young woman lamented repeatedly behind Brooklyn College, while Gary and I growled, repeated our request, then shoved, repeated our request once more, then—finally, to avoid any hurt feelings—bloodied each other's noses.

A feminist critic to an earlier account of this incident suggested: "Perhaps she wanted you both and was as stymied in her ability to get outside the status quo response as either of you." It's possible. Probably we were all social dupes. The other girl, the other boy both may have been acting under the impetus of an always excessive heterosexual desire. But if some idealized social norm *is* villain in the piece then I represent it—since, though I sincerely liked the girl and equally sincerely disliked the boy, I found both without sexual interest: My actions were determined purely *from* my knowledge of social norms and had none of the creative energy, enthusiasm, or invention that sexual desire can sometimes lend.

I've no clear memory of what any of us did afterward. I don't think much of it was with each other. (Possibly she wanted neither of us. She was in tears when it was over. I suspect that means she was furious.) Leave such pursuits, I decided, to the girls and boys who got some sense of soaring, of safety, of security out of them—or at least got the rewards from creative social manipulation that honest sexual interest always adds to a situation. But all my heterosexual experiences have grown from opposite-sex friendships that have gotten out of hand, spurred on by a vague sense of social approbation, whether at camp or in the dozen years after.

Another incident returns me to New York City, the spring in which I went from fourteen to fifteen (though I don't recall which side of my birthday it fell on). By that time, I'd learned (again, I don't remember how) that New York's Forty-second Street and Broadway area was one of the centers of the city's furtive homosexual activity. Sunday morning, when I was expected to go to church and then choir practice, I decided to visit.

I'd contemplated the journey for days. But how or why, that particular Sunday, I knew when I woke that *this* was the day I would make the trip, I couldn't tell you—though I recall the silent, tingling excitement, all morning, through breakfast down in the kitchen, through shaving at the upstairs bathroom mirror, through putting on my white shirt and tying my red tie.

In gray suit and tan overcoat, I left my Harlem house to walk up Seventh Avenue, turn left at 133rd Street, stop for a shine at Lewy's sagging green-painted plank stall, then continue down the street, even angling across the macadam between the cars toward the church's back entrance, now and again wondering if any of the three horse bettors chatting with Lewy inside his shoeshine parlor would notice that this morning I did not turn in to the parish house entrance that would have let me into the church, but continued down the street toward Eighth Avenue. No, I figured, they would all be too busy speculating on the track events that went into the day's number—at least, I hoped so.

Three or four Harlem blocks I knew to every inch, but my father was strict about where I was and where I was not allowed to go. As little as a block away from my own house lay vast areas of the neighborhood I'd simply never seen. At the unfamiliar corner of Eighth Avenue and 133rd Street I turned north, thankful for my knowledge of the city's grid. Though I traveled to high school every morning using the 135th Street/St. Nicholas Avenue subway stop, this morning's decision had sent me there by a wholly new route, by new barbershops, new eating places, new accountant offices, new record shops, new funeral parlors (far smaller than my father's or Mr. Sterritt's back on Seventh Avenue). Finally, at the familiar 135th Street station, across from the rising slope of St. Nicholas Park and under a sky without cloud, I took the steps at the downtown side (instead of the uptown kiosk across the street, as I would have done on a school morning).

I came up, some few minutes before nine A.M., at Forty-second just in from Eighth Avenue. In those days, Forty-second Street was an all-night affair, with its dozen-plus movie houses open till four o'clock in the morning and reopening four hours later, at eight A.M. On weekdays, that is. Opening time was ten A.M. on Sundays, I found out when I wandered up to a closed ticket window.

Across the street and up at the other end of the block, Grant's (where one could get hot dogs, hamburgers, and fresh clams at the sidewalk counter) had a few people lingering before it. Directly across from me, someone wandered into the Horn & Hardart automat while someone else wandered out. But there was certainly not the constant and lively flow of pedestrians that I'd seen on my last Saturday afternoon or Friday evening visit with whatever friend or cousin.

This was my first visit alone.

Across the street, its neon lights wan in the chill spring daylight, Hubert's Museum was open. I went to the corner, crossed, and decided that was as good a place as any to explore. On the front window, hand-painted letters declared "Hubert's Flea Circus"—a sign that easily could have been twenty years old.

I went inside—was the Sunday morning admission fifty cents?—and down the black stairwell, at the bottom pushing through the orange curtain. In a little room, someone was already waiting. When two other people joined us, the guide/guard (wearing a uniform cap but otherwise in street clothes) said they usually waited for six customers before they started. But it didn't look as if they were going to get six any time soon. So we four were ushered in to see, first, behind a rail up on a kind of stage, the Fat Lady, who told us how heavy she was, how much she ate daily, then, grinning, leaned over the rail to hand us her statistics on little paper slips. We went on to see the Alligator Man and the Dog-faced Boy; the guide apologized that the Siamese Twins were off that morning.

I don't remember which exhibit we were watching, but, with my overcoat open, I was standing at the front, both my hands on the wooden bar. Then, on my left hand, I felt something warm.

I looked down—and up.

A young black man in a sports jacket and cap, perhaps just twenty, had slid his dark fingers over mine and was smiling at me. I knew this was exactly what I had come here for. But I was much too surprised to smile back. I pulled my hand from under his, turned back to whatever was on the stage, but did not step away.

Moments later we were ushered into the room with the flea circus—a round, glass-covered table beneath whose transparent pane the fleas pulled a small cart, jumped over a hurdle, wore bits of colored paper for "costumes." Maybe six people could fit around it at any one time. I made a big show of watching, deciding quietly that, when we went upstairs, I'd speak to the young man— that is, once the others had left.

Only, when I looked up—the show was over, we were asked to go upstairs— he was gone. Apparently because I had not responded, he'd decided he'd better leave.

Back on Forty-second Street, I looked for him. But he must have hurried away—perhaps gone into the automat. Or just sprinted across to the subway.

It was almost an hour till the movies opened. After walking up and down the block another twenty minutes, I went to the subway and rode home.

BY MY LAST year of high school, my friends were divided into two categories: those who knew I was "queer"—the working-class term in general use back then—and those who didn't.

Those who knew included Marilyn, Judy, Gale (friends of mine now in college, a year or so ahead of me in their education), and a young man in a number of my high school classes named Radolph. Though blond and gray-eyed, Radolph had been born in Central America. His hair was *extremely* long—a half or even three-quarters of an inch longer than any other boy's in the school. In the pre-Beatles fifties, that was as good as having a two-foot ponytail. There were always whispers about how Radolph looked like a girl. His features were delicate. He was very smart. Like me, he enjoyed music and the arts. I was certain he must be queer.

There was *nothing* about him I found sexually attractive.

But I'd also realized that, since entering high school, the easy, polymorphous bisexuality rife among my friends in elementary school and summer camp had dried up almost completely. I had moved into a space where a stricter and stricter code of heterosexuality was taking over—and where, if I wanted to have any sort of satisfying sexual outlet, I'd have to work at it.

Several times I'd invited Radolph to my house. A couple of times I'd gone over to his. On his next visit to my place, after a few minutes of moody silence during which he asked me what was the matter, I told him that I was homosexual—and wanted to go to bed with him.

I was very surprised when he explained to me (1) he just wasn't *like* that; (2) this was the second time, not the first, that someone had felt this way about him; and (3) though he liked me and wanted to be my friend, he really hoped I wouldn't find it too upsetting or frustrating if he didn't share my sexual feelings. But (4) knowing how serious the matter was, he promised that he would not reveal my secret.

To which I said, "Yeah . . . sure. Okay," actually with some relief.

We remained friends. And now I had, though oddly acquired, a male friend with whom, however guardedly, I could mention, now and again, my desires for other men, which—intellectually, at least—he seemed to find interesting.

III.

I first heard the words *camp, closet,* and *coming out* all on the same afternoon in July 1959. I was seventeen and had gotten a juvenile role in an aspiring summer stock company whose directors had had the ingenious notion of basing us in New York City. They'd rented a little theater one building west of the St. Marks Baths, on the south side of St. Marks Place near the corner of Third Avenue. (The iron steps that led up to the lobby are still there today, though the space is now a secondhand clothing store.) After our theatrical company was long gone, the theater became the performance space for Ed Sanders, Allen Ginsberg, and the legendary Fugs. When we got it, however, the place was in appalling condition. In true summer stock style, cast members were requisitioned by the set designer, his assistant, and the two directors/producers to paint the entire theater—lobby, auditorium, and stage—once some minimal carpentry work had been done.

The set designer and his male assistant were lovers—had been lovers, they told us all that afternoon, for some ten years. I was the only person in the volunteer paint crew under twenty-one and much was made of it, to my embarrassment. I'd been taking ballet lessons for the previous three months and had a hopeless crush on the only straight student in the class, a twenty-three-year-old aspiring actor with a wonderful bearlike body who had been instructed by his acting coach to take ballet lessons to "learn how to move." We were becoming friends, but I'd taken a lesson from Radolph: There was as much chance of our becoming lovers as there was of this thick-thighed, stout-bellied fellow's becoming a dancer. I'd never gone back to Forty-second Street and, despite the banter and repartee in the Ballet Theater's men's changing room (and, frankly, there wasn't much), in many ways I was as naïve about the social side of homosexuality as it was possible for a New York City youth to be.

From the joking that went on among the actors painting the theater lobby that afternoon, I learned that "coming out" meant having your first homosexual experience. And what you came out *into*, of course, was homosexual society. Until you had a major homosexual experience, you could be—as many younger, older, straight, gay, male, or female folk have always been—a kind of mascot to homosexual society. But it took some major form of the sexual act itself to achieve "coming out." And fooling around with your bunkmates after lights out, I was informed, was *not* major.

The origins of the term were debutante cotillions, those sprawling, formal society balls where, squired by equally young and uncomfortable cousins, brothers, or schoolmates, young ladies of sixteen or so "came out" into society. By now I'd been an escort at a couple of those, too—Harlem variety: the presentation march down the hall's red central carpet, two seventeen-year-old or eighteen-year-old gentlemen on the arms of each young lady, the listless rehearsals in echoing ballrooms, the quivering orchid petals, the nervous parents, the rented tuxedos.

During that afternoon's painting, I first learned what "a camp" was—the color scheme the directors had chosen for the theater (peach, gold, and azure), for one. I also learned that "to camp" (and the gerund "camping") denoted dressing up in drag and, by extension, acting in a particularly effeminate manner, either in private or in public—flouting the notions of the straight world by flaunting the customs of the queer one. The noun form was the base form: "Oh, my dear, she is such a camp!" ("she," in such cases, almost always referring to a male). Etymologically, of course, "camp" was an apocopation of "camp follower." Camp followers were the women, frequently prostitutes, who followed the armies across Europe from military camp to military camp. Since the military have always had a special place in homosexual mythology, and presumably because the advent of a large group of young, generally womenless men was as good an excuse as any for cross-dressing among the local male populace so inclined, the then-new meaning of the term—"to go out and camp it up"; "to have a mad camp" (and "a *mad* camp" was the phrase most commonly in use)—gained currency in England during World War I and had been brought back to the United States by American soldiers. Calling something "a camp" followed the same linguistic template as calling a funny experience "a riot." Indeed, the two were often synonymous.

The same afternoon, I learned that ordinary day-to-day homosexual argot had a far more analytic way of dividing up people by sexual preference than any but the most detailed psychiatric jargon. There were queers exclusively interested in "seafood" (sailors). There were "toe queens" (foot fetishists) and "dinge queens" (white men interested only in blacks) and "snow queens" (from a popular brand of ice cream, black men only interested in whites) and "speed queens" (from a common clothes-washing machine, a gay male addicted to amphetamines). There were "leather queens" (the S&M crowd) and "size queens" ("There are two kinds of queers, my dear. There are size queens—and there are *liars!*") and "chubby chasers" and "chicken queens" (those who went after young children). And "closet queens." However mildly pejorative each term was, it represented an active perversion. A closet queen was someone who *liked* doing it "in the closet"—that is, who enjoyed the fact that friends and others didn't know.

I don't know how much my discovering a group of gay men who used these terms and expressed themselves with this slang had to do with it, but four months later, in October, when the plays and playfulness of the summer were over, I "came out."

In many ways it was a repeat of something I'd already done, though not for three years.

ONCE MORE ALONE I went down to Forty-second Street, on a Saturday afternoon. This time I walked directly to the largest theater on the strip, the New Amsterdam, and, once inside, took a seat midway back in the orchestra. It was a busy day, and soon people were sitting on both sides of me. The film was a Western in which I had no interest but which I made myself watch.

After fifteen minutes, on my right I felt a leg move against mine. I remembered what had happened with the guy in Hubert's Museum and resolved not to let this one get away, no matter who it was.

I pressed back. Soon a hand was on top of mine; it moved over to my crotch. I felt around between *his* legs. He was stubby and hard. When I looked, he was a dumpy guy in his middle or late forties, with glasses and white hair. Finally, tentatively, he leaned over to speak. "Can you come home with me . . . ?" He had a strong accent.

"Yes!" I declared.

We got up together and left the theater. He lived in Brooklyn, he explained. Brooklyn was a long way away; but I was determined.

On the subway, sitting inches apart, we had a spare conversation. The man was Israeli. He'd been in the country not quite a year. I also realized, as we rode over the Manhattan Bridge, he was very nervous.

A block from his house, I listened to his complicated instructions. He would go in first and leave the door open for me—if it was all right. If someone was around, he would lock the door—he was sorry. But if the door was locked, then I would simply know the coast was not clear and I had to go home.

If the door was *not* locked, I was to come up to the third floor and knock softly on the apartment door there. Even inside his apartment we would have to speak quietly. . . .

The door was open. In a stairwell covered with cracked yellow paint, I walked up to the third floor. I knocked—softly. The door opened, wide enough to show half his face. For a moment he looked as though he was not sure who I was. Then, the quick whisper: "Come in . . . !"

He lived in two grungy rooms, the first of which was both kitchen and living room (with *very* blue walls). He took me into the second. We sat on his bed and put our arms around each other. I was excited enough by doing it with a stranger that I came the moment we lay down. (It remains my single experience of a premature orgasm.) Because I felt guilty for coming so fast and because I still had an erection, I tried to be obliging while we took our clothes off—he never removed his undershirt—and we labored to an orgasm for him.

"Okay," he whispered as soon as he finished. "You gotta go now."

"Couldn't we rest just a little?" I asked, even as I slid on my pants. I'd worked hard to make him come, and I was tired.

He took a deep breath. "You wanna rest a little . . . ?" He didn't sound happy. "But I don't think it would be good in the same bed." He got up and, carrying the clothes I hadn't yet put on, took me into the living room/kitchen. "I rest in there. *You* rest in here—on the couch."

"Okay. . . ." I sat down on the sagging yellow couch and stretched out.

He hurried back inside. A moment later, I heard a kind of *ratchet* and looked up. There was a full key-and-lock mechanism on the bedroom door.

I stretched out again, possibly even tried to sleep. After a little while—it may have been only minutes—I got up, went around the couch, and knocked on his door.

There was no answer. I tried the door. Yes, he had firmly locked it against me.

Suddenly I got a sense of the despairing idiocy of the whole thing.

"Hello . . . !" I called through the door. "Look, I'm going home now."

He didn't answer. Maybe *he'd* fallen asleep.

"I'm going to leave now. Good-bye."

I put on my shirt and my shoes, got on my jacket, and went outside into the hall and down the stairs.

A YEAR LATER I'd had many more sexual experiences, many of them on Forty-second Street, many of them on Central Park West. If you'd asked me to evaluate my coming-out experience against these others on a scale of one to ten, where five was average/acceptable, I'd have given it a two. Frankly, it doesn't often get much worse. But the unpleasant ones are the most informative, and I'd learned from it how much sheer anxiety certain men connected with the sexual encounter—and how much anxiety they were willing to put up with to have sex in spite of it.

Eventually I described the experience in a long letter, complete with an attempt to sketch the man's face, intended for my friend Gale, which I never sent her. Rather, I kept it. A year later, when I read the letter over, I was astonished by how many stock phrases of despair and disgust I'd used, as though the vocabulary for describing the incident had been loaned me by some true-confessions magazine (that didn't exist) devoted to degrading homosexual encounters. The experience had *only* been a two, after all—not a one or a zero!

Another bit of fallout from the whole business is worth mentioning.

I talked about the experience endlessly to Marilyn, to Judy, to Gale. I also talked with them of the much more pleasant encounter, only a few weeks later, with a Puerto Rican pharmacist who'd picked me up on Central Park West and given me detailed instructions on how to give and take anal sex. He lived in a friendly brownstone off the park whose tenants were all gay and most of whom I'd met over a three-day stay. I told them about the twenty-three-year-old postal worker who'd driven me to his apartment in Brooklyn—quite as anxiety-ridden and neurotic as the Israeli, but at least he was one of the most physically gorgeous men I've ever been to bed with, before or since. I told them about the odd experiences with Cranford and Peter and the incredibly hung black man, just out of jail, who'd taken me to the Endicott Hotel. ("He came walking up to me, stopped right in front of me, with a big, friendly smile, and said, 'Hi, there. What you out lookin' for tonight?' And I said, 'I don't know! What do you . . . have?' And he said, 'Oh . . . 'bout eleven inches—'!" Gale threw her hands over her face and cried, "No! No—*really?* Oh, my god. Really? No, don't tell me this. Yes, *tell* me!")

Other friends—mostly male—I simply didn't consider broaching the subject with. One of these was my good friend Bob.

I don't think I've ever known anyone who had more hostility toward his parents, both of whom were fairly elderly—his father a doctor, his mother an administrator in the New York public high school system. A grandmother lived with them who reputedly had quite a bit of money (millions was the rumor among the tenants at Morningside Gardens housing cooperative, where we'd both lived throughout my high school years). Bob claimed that his parents' only interest in letting his grandmother live with them was her money. From what I'd seen of his parents and his grandmother, this sounded patently unfair. But to visit their apartment with Bob was soon to witness a shouting match between child and parents of a vicious intensity I've never encountered, before or since, at *any* social level.

Bob's sexual history was equally strange. The first time he'd masturbated, he explained to me, he'd been twelve or thirteen, sitting in the tub finishing a bath. The orgasm had occurred underwater. Soapy bathwater had backed up his urethra and sperm duct; within a day or two infection had ensued. Afraid to tell his parents about it, he'd let it go till it reached an incredibly painful state. He'd had to be hospitalized and come near having to be castrated. He'd never masturbated again.

Almost exactly a year after I came out, my father died. It was October 1960. At the month's end I moved into Bob's 113th Street apartment in the St. Marks Arms (no, it had nothing to do with St. Marks Place) and immediately, unbeknownst to Bob, started a low-key, pleasant, desultory affair with a white guy from the South who lived down the hall from us named Leon.

At about the same time, Judy and Bob had gone out on a few dates together, and Judy had told him of my Forty-second Street adventure. One evening, when I came in and stepped into the living room, full of Bob's ham radio equipment, where both of us slept, he switched off his microphone, turned around in his T-shirt, and stood up, somewhat uncomfortably, blond hair awry, bare feet on the cluttered rug. Pulling at his T-shirt, he began. "I've got something very important to say to you, Chip. You don't have to say anything back. Judy told me that you . . . did something. Down on Forty-second Street. You know what I'm talking about. We don't have to say exactly what it was—no, don't say anything now. . . ."

I was dumbfounded. I had no idea *what* he was talking about. The incident I'd related to Judy had occurred almost a year ago, and there'd been a goodly number of others since, on Forty-second Street and elsewhere. Only as he went on did I realize it was last year's "coming out" that he was talking about.

". . . But I don't want you to do anything like that ever again! That's very important. You have to promise me—no, we're not going to talk about it. But you have to promise me that—see? I don't want you to try to explain it. I don't want you to say anything about it at all—except that you promise me you'll never do it again. And now I've accepted your promise"—all I'd done was raise an eyebrow when finally I'd realized what he was referring to—"and now it's over. We'll never mention it anymore. It's all been taken care of. I won't—I promise you. And you won't. Because you've promised me. That's all there is to it." Nodding his head, he turned back to the radio.

I was left to get a soda from the icebox, sit for a while, read, then finally leave the apartment to go down the hall and drop in on Leon—and, between bouts of lovemaking, tell him about what Bob had said, decry how self-righteous he'd been, but suggest we'd better be careful, the two of us. . . .

One night seven years later I was leaving my mother's and ran into Bob, who was now married to a pleasant young black woman with whom I had gone to elementary school. With a surge of old friendship he invited me to come up and say hello. He and his wife were living in another Morningside Gardens apartment filled with strange contraptions: mechanical Gypsy fortune-telling booths of the sort that had lined the walls of Hubert's Museum; odd musical instruments contained in glass booths, such as the Tango Banjo or the Duo Arts Player Piano or the Violano Virtuoso (a player violin built in 1916, also in a glass booth, with mechanical stops and an automatic bow that played songs programmed into it). Bob had restored them all, and had become an expert on them—though they made his apartment look like the storage room in a carnival. The notes I took on the evening, right afterward, provided a scene in the novel I was then writing, *Nova*.

A year or so later, Bob took his own life somewhere in the Caribbean.

IV.

When I was seventeen and my friend Judy was eighteen, one evening I left my parents' Morningside Gardens apartment to visit a coffee shop around the corner on Amsterdam Avenue and settled into the phone booth, so Judy and I could have an uninterrupted hour-and-a-half conversation. Judy had been a child actor and was now a dancer. She knew lots of gay men, some of whom (Freddy Herko, Vincent Warren, James Waring) she'd introduced me to. I remember my surprise when she said (the first of half a dozen women who would later tell me the same), "I always wanted to be a man so I could go to bed with other men. I've often wondered why *anyone* would want to go to bed with a woman, anyway." The comment was offered as support from a young woman to a younger gay man. But even in 1959—pre-Stonewall, pre-Women's Liberation, pre-Martin Luther King—I could hear in it a profound and troubling dissatisfaction with the *whole* situation of women in this country.

Marilyn, Judy, and Gale are a trio of names anyone who has looked at my memoir, *The Motion of Light in Water* (1988), will remember as repeatedly sounding out, singularly and together, through the course of my late adolescence and early manhood. In August 1961 Marilyn became my wife. We lived together for thirteen years and have a wonderful daughter who has always known her parents are gay. (In 1984, when she was ten, my daughter sat on a panel of children of gay parents at the Lesbian and Gay Community Services Center in New York, discussing the situation and answering questions. All those children agreed that it's best to let your child know as early as possible. The sooner they know, the less traumatic it is.) When we were first married, I remember how, at eighteen, Marilyn seemed to delight in using gay terms and gay slang in front of our straight friends, to make jokes or to pass comments to me behind their backs or over their heads. Several times when we were alone I asked her not to. It seemed as though she wondered what was the fun of being gay if it wasn't a special club that allowed you to have it over the ordinary people. But in that need to be special I sensed the same dissatisfaction with the ordinary situation of women that I had sensed in Judy's statement on the phone a year or so before.

Racism, anti-Semitism, sexism, and homophobia are intricately related—only secondarily because of the overlapping categories of oppressors. Despite their range of specific differences so many of their mechanics follow the same patterns, from the direct inflicting of economic and social damages to blaming the victim and the transcendental mythicizing of the victim's "world." Marriage brought that analysis quickly to articulation (the tale is told in *Motion*).

I must mention here, if only as a gloss, all the help, support and friendship

I've had from women in learning to understand these mechanisms—from hours, months, years of personal discussions, questions, and insights to (at the institutional level) the many volumes of feminist and social analysis I've been lucky enough to have them push at me, without which my understanding of the mechanics of oppression, from racism to homophobia, would have remained in another, far more impoverished ballpark. Judy and Marilyn remain my friends to this day. And happily I would welcome a reunion with Gale. All three eventually took greater or lesser joy in lesbianism, but being gay is not a matter of being in a special club. In this country it's a beleaguered situation that one must learn to negotiate as best one can.

I don't think I've ever been that much into control. But I did want to be in control of who knew and who didn't know I was gay. In the homophobic social field that obtained pre-Stonewall (and, indeed, since) it was still—as it had been with Bob—a little too disorienting when people found out on their own. As our current society is discursively constituted, that is still one of the things that creates tension in the relations between some gay men and a range of women.

IT'S A PHILOSOPHICAL paradox:

Differences are what create individuals. Identities are what create groups and categories. Identities are thus conditions of comparative simplicity that complex individuals might move toward but (fortunately) never achieve—until society, tired of the complexity of so much individual difference, finally, one way or the other, imposes an identity on us.

Identities are thus, by their nature, reductive. (You do not need an identity to become yourself; you need an identity to become *like* someone else.) Without identities, yes, language would be impossible (because categories would not be possible, and language requires categories). Still, in terms of persons, identity remains a highly problematic sort of reduction and cultural imposition.

Through the late sixties a sensation-hungry media began rummaging through various marginal social areas for new and exciting vocabulary. In almost every case, once a new term was found an almost complete change in meaning occurred as the term was applied to more or less bourgeois experiences and concerns. "Rap" had already been appropriated from the world of down-and-out amphetamine druggies ("rapping" was initially the term for the unstoppable, often incoherent cascade of talk from someone who'd taken too much of the drug); "camp" had already been borrowed from gay slang, largely in the wake of a popular 1964 *Partisan Review* essay by Susan Sontag ("Notes on 'Camp'"), after which it all but lost its meaning of "cross-dressing" and became a general synonym for "just *too* much." Spurred on by June '69's Stonewall Riots and the rapid formation right afterward of the Gay Liberation Front, the term "coming out" over the next eighteen months changed its meaning radically.

Gay Liberation proponents began to speak about "coming out" *of* "the closet"—the first time either the words or the concepts had been linked. (Till then no one would have thought of asking the closet queen to give up his closet any more than they would the toe queen to give up his toes—save in the smug, peremptory tone in which all perversion was decried.) In the media this metaphorical extension soon displaced the denotative meaning ("coming out" *into* gay society, having one's first major homosexual experience). A good number of people—myself included—who were under the impression we had come out years ago, now realized we were expected to come out again in this wholly new sense.

The logic of coming out—in this new sense—was impeccable. Sixteen and seventeen years before, the House Un-American Activities Committee, along with its hounding of Communists, had been equally vigilant in its crusade against homosexuals. HUAC's logic was that homosexuals were security risks because we were susceptible to blackmail. Said the Gay Liberationists, if we're "out," nobody *can* blackmail us and nobody can accuse us of being black-mailable. So let them all know who we are, how many of us there are, and that we're proud to be what we are.

Like many gay men, I found myself seriously asking, "Just how out am I?"

In 1961, I'd gotten married.

As far back as 1964, I'd decided—when I'd spent a few weeks in Mt. Sinai Hospital's mental ward—that if anyone ever asked me was I queer or not, I would never even consider lying. Was that a kind of coming out? Only it was five years before Stonewall and in a pathologized situation. And though I'd made the decision (and stuck to it), years had passed without my having to confront the question directly and test my resolve.

In 1967 I'd published a story, "Aye, and Gomorrah . . ." in which a future perversion is a clear analogue of homosexuality. The story won a Nebula Award for best science fiction story of the year. I was sure most of the tale's readers would assume I was gay. In 1968 I'd written "Time Considered as a Helix of Semi-Precious Stones," a story about homosexual S&M which went on to win both a Nebula and a Hugo. I was pretty sure any reader who'd had any doubts about my sexuality after the first story would have them cleared up by the second. Was I afraid of being found out? Yes. In no way do I mean to imply I partook of some particularly heroic social bravery. That I was gay had been one of the greatest factors in determining me to commit myself seriously to writing and the arts in the first place: Even in my early teens I knew the worlds of theater, dance, and literature were far more tolerant of such deviancy as mine, whereas what happened to gay men and women in more "central" areas of endeavor were the sort of tragedy and social ostracism portrayed in Lillian Hellman's *The Children's Hour*, a play I'd read in high school.

At least one straight science fiction scholar, who did not meet me till more than a decade later, has told me: "I knew you were gay by 1968, though I don't know *how* I knew. Nor do I remember who told me." I'm sure he did, too. The only people in America who wrote even vaguely sympathetic portrayals of gay men and women in 1967 and '68 were—it was a foregone conclusion—gay themselves. In science fiction, the only gay characters not written by gay authors were those such as the evil Baron Harkonen and his equally evil nephew, Fayd Ratha, in Frank Herbert's *Dune*, monstrous villains who Died Horribly in the end.

By 1969, the year of Stonewall, it was common knowledge throughout the science fiction field that I was gay. Marilyn and I were then living together about half the time. (When Stonewall occurred, we were in San Francisco.) The other half we spent following our own amatory pursuits, with neither of us really set on establishing any sort of permanent relationship—which was not proving to be an easy solution for either of us.

As a result of Stonewall and the redefinition of coming out, I had to consider that while I approved vigorously of coming out as a necessary strategy to avoid blackmail and to promote liberation, there seemed to be an oppressive aspect of surveillance and containment intertwined with it, especially when compared to the term's older meaning. Before, one came out *into* the gay community. Now, coming out had become something entirely aimed at straights. Its initial meaning had been a matter of bodily performance. (It involved *coming*.) Now it had become a purely verbal one. Despite its political goals, *was* this change really as beneficial as it was touted to be? Since it had been a case of displacing a term rather than adding a term, hadn't we lost something by that displacement?

We heard the phrase more and more; it became almost a single word. The straight media began to take it over. (That was the time when the "silent majority" was coming out of the closet of its silence. A few months later, fat people were coming out of the closet of their fat, and smokers were coming out of the closet of their smoking.) I found myself wanting to stop people every time they began to say the phrase—to slow them, startle them with a slash struck down between the words, make them consider what each word meant separately, remind them of all the possible meanings—historical, new, and revolutionary—that the two could be packed with, either apart or joined.

There was a closet of banality, overuse, and cliché I wanted to see "coming out" come out of!

In 1975 I taught my first university class as a visiting professor. I told my students I was gay within two weeks. In the gay press the fact had appeared often enough that there seemed no reason to let it move through a new group of young people as a more or less confirmed rumor. I'd heard too many horror stories about gay teachers who did not come out to their students and who had been accused by neurotic young men or women (who knew, of course, their teacher's secret) of playing favorites because of sexuality. The problem is taken care of when everything is aboveboard, when they know, when I know they know, and when they know I know they know—because I've told them.

In the mid-seventies I received a harsh criticism from a gay friend because a paragraph that appeared in the back of a number of my books mentioned that I was married to the poet Marilyn Hacker, that we had a daughter, and that Marilyn had won the National Book Award for Poetry. Not only was I trying to gain prestige through Marilyn's reputation (ran my friend's accusation), I was falsely presenting myself as a straight man, happily married, with a family, even though Marilyn and I no longer lived together. The paragraph had been written perhaps a month before we'd last separated. I'd used it, initially, because it was true when I wrote it. My reason for mentioning the National Book Award I'd felt to be wholly altruistic. Though it is the highest, or one of the highest, awards for poetry in the United States, the fact is, a year after you've won it, hardly anyone can remember—even people presumably concerned with such things. (Can *you* name the last three years' recipients?*) I'd thought by putting it in my biographical squib I might keep the fact of Marilyn's award before a *few* people's eyes just a little longer than usual.

That's how I'd intended it, and that's how Marilyn had taken it. (At about that time, Marilyn applied for an interim teaching job at Columbia University. When the junior professor interviewing her told her the possible salaries and asked how much she would seek, she named the highest figure. He laughed. "For us to give you that much," he said, "you would have to have won a National Book Award or something." Recounting the story to me later, Marilyn said: "It was so much fun to be able to smile at him demurely and say, 'Well, actually . . . I have.' He turned quite red.")

I'd already made one desultory attempt to change the paragraph even before my friend objected, but it had gone astray in the Bantam Books office. Now, true, Marilyn and I *were* living apart. I had a permanent male lover. So I wrote another biographical paragraph and turned it in to my publisher, only to learn that a new printing of my science fiction novels had just been ordered mere days before—with the *old* squib! It was another year and a half before I could correct it. However innocent my transgression, the criticism had its point and I felt I should respond to it.

V.

In 1978, for the first time, at the World Science Fiction Convention in Phoenix, Arizona, a panel on "gay science fiction" was placed on the official World Con Program. I was asked to sit and agreed readily.

The four panelists included Frank Robinson (author of the 1956 science fiction classic *The Power*), Norman Spinrad (our token straight), and me. When the program committee asked for permission to tape the proceedings, I was a bit surprised that the young woman on the panel flatly refused. She would not participate if there was any chance of its getting back to her family. For a week before the panel I, too, had been electrically aware that this would be the first time I'd sit in front of an audience and talk about being gay.

That audience turned out to be standing room only and comprised of more than three hundred people. It was wonderfully invigorating. For me its high point came when Robinson told about what Theodore Sturgeon, already a hero of mine, had had to go through in 1953, during and after writing his seminal story on a gay theme, "The World Well Lost." When Sturgeon submitted the

---

* A. R. Ammons, 1993; James Tate, 1994; Stanley Kunitz, 1995.

story to *Fantastic*, editor Howard Browne not only refused to publish it but launched a telephone campaign among all the field's editors never to publish anything by Sturgeon again, and, further, threatened to see that anyone who published *that* particular tale would be ostracized from the SF community. Feisty little hunchbacked editor Ray Palmer broke the nascent boycott and published Sturgeon's story in *Universe Science Fiction*, where it became an immediate classic.

After the panel had taken place, I was astonished how quickly I became "Samuel R. Delany, the gay science fiction writer" in the straight media. (Though my 1967 and '68 stories had gotten me invited to sit on the panel, they had produced no such effect.) An interview in the *Advocate* followed, and several articles appeared in the *Village Voice*. Any newspaper mention of me—even in the *New York Times Book Review*—seemed obliged to tag me as gay (and black), and if the article was by a straight reporter, the tag usually appeared in the first sentence. After only a little while, the situation began to seem vaguely hysterical, as if, through an awful oversight, someone might *not* know I was gay. I didn't mind. But from time to time it got a bit tired, if not excessive.

In the late seventies, when my daughter was about four, I helped establish a Gay Fathers group with two other men—a bank vice president and a musician teaching at Columbia University. Over the next two years the group expanded to include more than forty fathers and twice that number of children. I was surprised to learn that, just as I had, these men all had told their wives-to-be that they were gay well before the wedding; though often neither husband nor wife was quite sure what, exactly, that would mean once marriage took place.

In those same years, a collection of gay businessmen presented a program at an East Side gay club in which they asked three gay male "role models"—Quentin Crisp, an openly gay officer on the New York City police force who had been much in the news of late, and me—to take part. During the fresh-faced blond cop's presentation, I remember, he said, "You know, there've been half a dozen articles about me in the *New York Times* in the last year—but the truth is, I'm not out to my mother."

I wanted to hug him. I'd never spoken about being gay to anyone in my immediate family, either.

I remember visiting my mother in 1985 while her downstairs neighbor Mrs. Jackson, having dropped up for a visit, enthused to me over a recent *Village Voice* article in which, yes, I'd been identified as gay in the first sentence. Did my mother know? I don't see how, during those years, she could have missed it. Still, we'd never talked about it.

Perhaps a year later my mother took me to see William M. Hoffman's moving AIDS play, *As Is*, which she'd already seen once and been impressed with enough to see again. She'd wanted me to see it. Was this her way of letting me know she knew? We talked only about the play, not about ourselves.

Along with pieces on the burgeoning tragedy of AIDS, I was reading many articles by gay men about the problems they had getting their families to accept their lovers. My family, however, was always immediately and warmly accepting of any man *I* ever lived with. My family problems began when we broke up; *my* folks seemed unable to accept that the relationship was finished.

"Why don't you ever bring over X, Y, or Z these days?"

"I told you, Mom. He moved out. We don't live together anymore."

"Oh, well, where *is* he living? Maybe I'll call him up and invite him for dinner next Sunday. He always used to enjoy my Sunday biscuits so much. . . ."

Would my coming out to my mother solve such a problem? (Several times I'd had to remind her that Marilyn and I really *were* divorced.)

In the mid-eighties, I was regularly giving lectures in which the personal examples I cited came from my life as a gay man. One November evening I was lecturing to a large audience at the main branch of the New York Public Library. Halfway through my talk I realized my sister was sitting some rows back—next to Mrs. Jackson. When the question-and-answer period started, I saw among the audience a dozen other well-tailored black women, also close friends of Mom's, who'd come to the lecture together and were sitting to one side.

When the lecture was over, Mrs. Jackson brought my sister up and explained, "I realized that Peggy had never heard you talk. You've always been such an eloquent speaker, I decided to bring her here to hear you lecture as a birthday present." A minute later, my mother's friends gathered, each of them congratulating me on one or another of my points.

I was truly happy to see them. But I left the library that night muttering, "Well, if I wasn't out before, I am now!"

In 1987 I began writing a memoir, focusing specifically on changes in attitudes toward sex—especially gay sex—from 1955 through the sixties. I resolved that, once I finished the text, I *would* have the by-now-fabled coming-out talk with Mom. Since our separation, Marilyn had been exploring her lesbianism and had finally opened the subject with my mother, only to find—to her surprise (but not really to mine)—that it had *not* gone well. My mother felt such things were better left behind closed doors and not spoken of. Now, because of the nature of the book I was writing, I felt that such a direct conversation—the first and most important that so many advocates of coming out encouraged—was imperative.

Some two weeks before I finished the manuscript, in a Village restaurant on the way to the Public Theater with two old friends, my mother suffered a major stroke, as a result of which she lost all powers of language, both of speaking and of understanding. She survived in that state for the next eight years.

Once the book was finished, I had a conversation with my sister. It turned out to be easy, brief, and all but superfluous.

I never did get the chance to come out to my mother.

The truth is, though, it's not a major regret.

*　　*　　*

MANY TIMES I'VE asked myself just when and if (in the post-Stonewall sense) I *did* come out.

Although I approve of coming out and believe it imperative at the statistical level, it's still not a question I've an easy time answering.

Did I do it when I was eleven, walking from the athletic field with Joel?

Is it what I did at nineteen when, on the platform of the D-train, I asked pregnant Marilyn, whom I would shortly marry, if she was *really* aware that I was homosexual and told her that, even if we married, I didn't see how that was going to change? (She laughed and said, "Of course I am. You've taken me cruising with you, for God's sake!")

Did I do it in the mental hospital when I explained to the group of psychiatric residents interviewing me that I didn't think my homosexuality had anything to do with any problems that had brought me there?

Did I do it when I took my three-, four-, then five-year-old daughter on outings with the Gay Fathers and our kids to the Upper Central Park ice-skating rink, where my daughter laughed and had fun with the other children? (As I wobbled across the ice, a large black woman in a sweeping purple coat, far steadier on her blades than I, asked, "Excuse me, but who *are* you all?" I explained, falling into her arms, "We're a group of gay men, here with our children . . . !") Or did I do it at the Staten Island Zoo, where I answered the same question for the young woman taking our kids around on the donkey ride? "When are we going with the *daddies* again?" my four-year-old demanded just before we left. Everyone laughed. And "The Daddies" became our group's unofficial name.

Did I do it when I sat on the panel in Phoenix and spoke about the realities of being a gay SF writer?

Will coming out be something I shall do in three weeks, once I start teaching again at the University of Massachusetts and (again) tell the anonymous hundred faces in my lecture class I have to look at this tale or that from the point of view of a gay man because, after all, I *am* gay?

Or, finally, is it something that I, like the gay policeman written about so widely in the *Times*, can *never* really do—because I never came out to Mother?

I wonder today if, instead of considering coming out—in the new sense *or* the old—a point effect that separates a *before* (constituted of silence, paralysis, and fear) from an *after* (constituted of articulation and bodily or linguistic freedom), the discontinuity between the absence and presence of an identity, it might be better to consider coming out an aware attitude, a vigilant disposition, an open mood (or even a discursive apparatus) that could beneficially inform all our behavior and discussions involving the sexual, and even, at some points, for any number of considerations, contain its presumed opposite—*not* coming out to someone—as long as the reason involved choice and not terror, not intimidation, not victimization, nor any of the range of attitudes that can fall under the umbrella effect of oppression. (On those, I'm afraid, we *still* have to come out; and if it's too scary to do it by yourself, organize a full-scale demonstration: That's one of the things they're for!) But the fact is, coming out (in the post-Stonewall sense) was something that many of us had begun to do, here and there, without the name, years before Stonewall. Stonewall only focused and fixed its statistical necessity as a broad political strategy. We need to remember that if the human material—not to mention the simple bravery so many have shown and continue to show in our still-homophobic society—had not already been there, the strategy would not have been any-where near as successful as it was.

Many people have made the point: One does not come out once. Rather, one comes out again and again and again—*because* the dominant discourse in this country is still one of heterosexist oppression and because it still controls the hysteria to *know* who's gay and who's not. Heterosexuals do not have to come out—indeed cannot come out, because there is no discursive pressure to deny their ubiquity (and, at the same time, deny their social contribution and the sexual validity of their growth and development, the event field of their sexuality) and to penalize them for their existence. This is the same discourse that constrains coming out, for all the act's utopian thrust, to a condition of heterosexist surveillance. And though perhaps my coming out with the anxious Israeli was an incident that my interested friends could subsequently use to identify me as someone who had, indeed, actually come out, or though my coming out publicly in Phoenix meant that the straight media could now define me regularly as a "gay science fiction writer," though I would not relinquish either experience, and value what both taught me (for both are part of the *field* of experiences that have articulately demonstrated to me that the human boundaries of sexuality can be far more humanely placed than they have been), though both showed me much and changed my life in ways I can only cele-brate, I cannot claim that either *identified* or *defined* anything of me but only parts of my endlessly iterated (thus always changing) situation.

Firmly I believe that is how it should be.

1953, Camp Woodlawn

CINNAMON SKIN

Edmund White

WHEN I WAS a kid I was a Buddhist and an atheist, but I kept making bargains with God that if He'd fulfill a particular wish I'd agree to believe in Him. He always came through, but I still withheld my faith, which shows perhaps that rationality is not reasonable. I suppose the only result of these futile exercises was that I ended up believing that this God I didn't believe in must care about me, which only added to my vanity as well as to my feeling that because of my hardheadedness I was dangerously isolated even from Him.

One of these miracles occurred in April 1954, when I was fourteen. I was living for a year with my father in Cincinnati (my mother, a psychologist, thought I needed the proximity of a man, but my father ignored me and, curiously, seemed uninterested in teaching me baseball or tennis, the sports in which he excelled). My father and stepmother were going to Mexico for a holiday that would not, alas, fall during my spring school break. Nor was it probable he would have invited me even if I had been free, since my father lived by the rule book and the divorce agreement specified nothing about vacations. I was up in Chicago for a long weekend with my mother and sister. In the dark, I fell on my knees beside my bed and prayed that I'd be invited to come along anyway. The next day my mother received a telegram from my father that suggested I join him in Cincinnati the following day for a three-week car trip to Acapulco. He advised my mother that he'd already asked my teachers for advance assignments I could work on during the trip; he would supervise my homework.

My mother had a phobia about speaking to my father, and after twenty-

27

two years of marriage to him she spent the remaining thirty-five years of his life without ever so much as hearing his voice. If vocal communication was forbidden, the exchange of cordial but brief tactical notes or telegrams was acceptable if it occurred only every four or five months. My mother's generation believed in something called "character," and it was established through self-discipline. Anyway, my mother suggested I phone my father long-distance, since court etiquette forbade her to do so.

The next day I took the seven-hour train to Cincinnati; it was called the James Whitcomb Riley, after the Hoosier Poet ("When the frost is on the punkin," begins one of his odes). At the end of each car were not scenes of rural Indiana, as one might have expected, but, rather, large reproductions of French Impressionist paintings—hayricks, water lilies, Notre Dame, mothers and children *en fleurs*. . . . This train, which I took twice a month to visit my dad when I was living with my mom, or to visit Mom when I was living with Dad, was the great forcing shed of my imagination, for I used it as a stage for trying on new roles. No one knew me. I was free to become anyone. I would tell one startled neighbor I was English and visiting America for the first time, putting on an accent so obviously fabricated and snobbish it would invariably provoke a smile. I told another seat partner I had leukemia but was in remission. Another time I said both my parents had just died in a car crash and I was going to live with a bachelor uncle. Once I chatted up a handsome young farmer, face immobile under its burn, T-shirt incapable of repressing the black hair sprouting up from under it, and the next week I started writing a tragic opera named after him, *Orville*. It was a Midwestern story of violence, incest, madness, all inherited, but my pleasure came from offering a prolonged musical compliment to this chance acquaintance. Or I'd be drawn into one of the great American pastimes, biblical exegesis, although I would shock my Fundamentalist seat partner by suddenly announcing that Christian hermeneutics was only an idle hobby for me since I was actually a Buddhist.

On this trip, my imagination was busy enough with the thick guidebook on Mexico I'd checked out of the public library. I read everything I could about Toltecs, Aztecs, and Mayans; but their astrology bored me, their bloody attacks and counterattacks became a blur, and one century blended into another without a single individual to step out of the plumed hordes—not until the tragic Montezuma (a new opera subject, even more heartrending than Orville, whose principal attribute had been that he smelled of Vitalis hair tonic and, more subtly, of starch and ironing, a quality difficult to render musically).

My father and stepmother rode in the front seat of his massive Cadillac; the car was new, shiny pale blue metal and chrome on the outside, oiled dark blue leather and shag carpet inside, and I had so much space in the back seat I could stretch out full length, slightly nauseated from the cigars my father chain-smoked and his terminally dull monologues about the difference between stocks and bonds. While we were still in the States he'd listen to broadcasts of the news, the stock report, and sporting events, three forms of impersonal excitement I considered as tedious as the Toltecs' battles.

Or as my constant hard-on. As I lay in the back seat, knocking my legs together in an agony of unreleased desire, I could feel my stiff little cock rubbing against my taut stomach. My head filled with daydreams vague and randomly rotating as the clouds I could see up above through the back window. In those days, the speed limit was higher than now and the roads just two-laned meanders; there was no radar and no computers, and if a cop stopped us for speeding my father would just tuck a five-dollar bill under his license and instantly we'd be urged along on our way with a cheerful wave and a "Y'all come back, yuh heah?" Then my father would resume his murderous speed, lunging and turning and braking and swearing, and I would hide so I wouldn't have to witness, white-knuckled, the near disasters. As night fell, the theme song from the film *Moulin Rouge* was played over and over on station after station, like a flame being passed feebly from torch to torch in a casual marathon.

I abandoned myself to cloud-propelled dreams of love: melting ecstasy, heavenly embraces, ethereal intimacy. People are wrong to imagine teenage boys want to shoot their loads; what they want is a union of souls which will only incidentally result in a tangling of arms, thighs, loins. Teenagers do not fetishize big cocks, hairy chests, powerful biceps, or blond hair and thick necks; their desire is too general to respond to anything less than eternal love and their love is vague and powerful enough to ennoble any body at all. And if I loved a particular man (Orville, say), it wasn't as though I loved all men. No, we would be friends for life, not horrible, rodentlike queers.

We stopped in Austin, Texas, to see my grandfather, who was retired and living alone in a small wooden house he rented. In those days Austin was just the impressive Capitol building hovering over a wide, dusty street of single-story feed stores wavering in the heat; my grandfather would walk down the street, tipping his hat toward white friends and calling out to Negro acquaintances by their first names. My stepmother took a picture of my father, grandfather, and me. We all three had the same name; in true Southern fashion, my father had a Roman numeral, "II," after his name and I a "III."

I don't remember much about my grandfather, except he told endless "nigger" jokes, which he collected in self-published books with titles such as *Let's Laugh*, *Senegambian Sizzles*, *Folks Are Funny*, and *Chocolate Drops from the South*. He also wrote a book called *Mental Arithmetic*. He was the retired dean of students at a women's college, but was still called Dean White. He made fun of me for saying "Cue" Klux Klan instead of "Koo"—an organization he'd once belonged to and accepted as a harmless if stern fraternity. He was as dull as my father, though in a different register; my father was all facts, all business, misanthropic, his racism genial and condescending, though his anti-Semitism was virulent and reeked of hate. My father had constructed his life so that he'd have as little contact as possible with other people. He liked women, but regarded them as silly and flighty and easy to seduce; they excited men but weren't themselves sexual, although easily tricked into bed. Men he despised, even boys.

We were freaks. My grandfather was gregarious but disgustingly self-absorbed, like his son a monologist, who started each new intolerable riff with the drawled words "Did you hear the one about . . . ?" He was the definition of self-satisfaction, and people rolled their eyes whenever they saw him coming, knowing they'd be stuck with him for an hour as he picked his big yellow teeth, smacked his smiling lips, snipped, licked, twirled, lit another cigar, and exhaled "Hm-*hmn*" in witless affirmation of what he'd just said or was "fixin' " to say.

My stepmother was "cockeyed and harelipped" (my mother's description), although the truth was she simply had a lazy eye that wandered into and out of focus, depending on how tired she was, and an everted upper lip that rose on one side, like Judy Garland's in the movies whenever she hits a high note. Kay read constantly, anything at all; she'd put down *Forever Amber* to pick up *War and Peace*, trade in *Désirée* for *Madame Bovary*, but a day later she couldn't remember anything about her latest novel. An escapist, she read rapidly for the plot. My father, who'd never finished a book, would always say, when the subject of literature came up, "You'll have to ask Kay about that. She's the reader in this family." He thought novels were useless, even corrupting; if he caught me reading, he'd find me a chore to do, such as raking the lawn.

My father liked long-legged redheads in high heels and short nighties, if his addiction to *Esquire* magazine and its illustrations was any indication, but my stepmother was as short and dumpy as my mother, though less intelligent and less high-minded. She'd been brought up on a farm in northern Ohio by a scrawny father in bib overalls and a pretty, calm, round-faced mother from Pennsylvania Dutch country who said "mind" for "remember." ("Do you mind that time we went to the caves in Kentucky?") Kay had done well, fatally well, in elocution class, and even now she could recite from memory mindless doggerel and children's stories, anything she judged to be "real cute" (her highest praise), with ringing authority, the sort of steely diction and hearty projection impossible to tune out. She could paint, sort of, and did watercolors of little Japanese maidens all in a row or kittens or pretty flowers; her love of art led her to be a volunteer at the art museum, where she worked three hours a week in the gift shop run by the Ladies' Auxiliary. Oh, she had lots of activities and belonged to plenty of clubs, such as the Ladies' Luncheon Club and the Queen City Club and the Keyboard Club.

My stepmother had spent her twenties and thirties being a shrewd, feisty office "gal" who'd let herself be picked up by big, bored businessmen out for a few laughs and a roll in the hay with a good sport. She always had a joke or a wisecrack to dish up, she'd learned how to defend herself against a grabby drunk, and she always knew the score. I'm not sure how I acquired this information about her early life. Probably from my mother, who branded Kay a Jezebel, an ugly woman with secret sexual tricks, like Wallis Simpson. After Kay married my father, however, and moved up a whole lot of social rungs, she pretended to be shocked by the very jokes she used to deliver. She adopted the endearingly dopey manner of the society matron immortalized in Helen E. Hokinson's *New Yorker* cartoons. Dad gave her an expensive watch, a brooch she pinned to her lapel. It was a bow of white and yellow gold, the knot set with a beautiful lapis lazuli. The watch dangled, upside down, from this bow, so that only Kay could read it. Her skirts became longer, her voice softer, her hair grayer, and she replaced her native sassiness with an acquired innocence. She'd always been cunning rather than intelligent, but now she appeared to become naïve as well, which in our world was a sign of wealth; only rich women were sheltered, and only the overprotected could afford to remain unworldly. Just as in China bound feet proved that one never had to walk unaided, so in our entourage female innocence showed that a suffocating father had handed his daughter directly over to an overbearing husband. As my real mother learned to fend for herself, my stepmother learned to feign incompetence.

Such astute naïveté, of course, was only for public consumption. At home, Kay was as crafty as ever. She would speculate out loud for hours about other people's motives and piece together highly unflattering scenarios based on the slimmest evidence. Every act of kindness was considered secretly manipulative, any sign of generosity profoundly selfish. She'd quiz me for hours about my mother's finances (turbulent) and love life (usually nonexistent, sometimes disastrous). She was, of course, hoping Mother would remarry so Dad wouldn't have to pay out the monthly alimony. My sister was disgusted that I'd betray our mother's secrets, but Kay bewitched me. We had so few entertainments, we spent such long, tedious hours together in the stifling Cincinnati summer heat, I'd been so carefully sworn to silence by my mother, that finally everything came out, I told all. I was thrilled to have a confidence to betray, a promise to break.

Kay and my father fought all the time. She'd pester him to do something he didn't want to do or challenge him over a trivial question of fact until he'd explode: "God damn it, Kay, shut your goddamn mouth, you don't know what the hell you're talking about and I don't want to hear one more goddamn word out of your mouth! I'm warning you to shut it and shut it now. Got it?"

"Oh, E.V.," she'd wail (his nickname; our middle name was Valentine), "you don't have to talk to me that way, you're making me sick, physically sick, my heart is pounding, and, look, I'm sweating freely, I'm soaked right through, my underarms are drenched, and you know—my high *blood* pressure." Here she broke off and began blubbering. She had only to invoke her blood pressure ("Two hundred and fifty over one hundred and ten," she'd mysteriously confide) in order to win the argument and subdue my red-faced father. I pictured the two of them as thermometers in which the mounting mercury was about to explode through the upper tip. Kay constantly referred to her own imminent death, often adding, "Well, I won't be around much longer to irritate you with my remarks, which you find so *stupid* and *ignorant*." During our trip, these disputes would become more violent and frequent.

My father filled his big house with Mahler throughout the night; he went to sleep at dawn. Either his music or his snoring formed a sound barrier against Kay. Anyway, the more socially successful she became, the less she conformed to his hours. They scarcely saw each other. Of course, she'd still cook him his pound of bacon and six fried eggs for breakfast at dusk and leave him a cold three A.M. steak and clammy fries on the sideboard, and a mushy chocolate sundae in the fridge. At dawn, she would be sipping a wake-up coffee while he put pats of cold butter on chocolate-covered graham crackers. Then he headed out to walk his dog, Old Boy, through the dew-heavy grass, before turning in.

During the hot Cincinnati days, while Daddy slept in his air-conditioned room, Kay and I would spend the long, idle hours talking to each other. I bit my nails; she paid me a dollar a nail to let them grow. When they came in, I decided I wanted them longer and longer and shaped like a woman's; Kay promised to cut them as I desired, but each time she tricked me and trimmed them short while I whined my feeble protests: "C'mon. I want them long and *pointy*. . . . Kay! You *promised!*" I would dance for her in my underpants; once I did an elaborate (and very girly) striptease for her. As I became more and more feminine, she became increasingly masculine. She even put one leg up and planted her foot on the chair seat, hugging her knee to her chest as a guy might. I felt I was dancing for a man.

Perhaps she watched me because she was bored and had nothing else to do. Or perhaps she knew these games attached me to her with thrilling, erotic bonds; in the rivalry with my mother for my affections, she was winning.

Or perhaps she got off on me. I remember that she'd give me long massages with baby oil as I lay on the Formica kitchen table in my underpants. She must have noticed I'd spring a boner. Her black maid watched us and smiled benignly. Her name was Naomi and she'd worked for Kay one day a week ironing before Kay married, and afterward had moved in as a live-in, full-time employee. She no doubt remembered Kay's earlier incarnation as a roaring girl and wondered how far she'd go now.

In fact, she went very far. Once, when I told her I was constipated, she had me mount the Formica table on all fours and administered a hot-water enema out of a blue rubber pear she filled and emptied three times before permitting me to go to the toilet and squirt it out.

But my whole family was awash with incestuous desires. When my real mother was drunk (as she was most nights), she'd call out from her bed and beg me to rub her back, then moan with pleasure as I kneaded the cool, sweating dough. My sister was repulsed by our mother's body, but I once walked in on her and my father in his study in Cincinnati. She must have been fourteen or fifteen. He stood behind her chair, brushing her long blond hair and quietly crying. (It was the only time I ever saw him cry.) Later, she claimed she and Daddy had made love. She said she and I'd done it in an upper berth on the night train from Chicago to Cincinnati once, but I can't quite be sure I remember it.

When I was twelve, Kay was out of town and Daddy took me to dinner at the Gourmet Room, a glass-walled dome on top of the Terrace Hilton. The restaurant had a mural by Miró and French food. Daddy drank a lot of wine and told me I had my mother's big brown eyes. He said boys my age were rather like girls. He said there wasn't much difference between boys and girls my age. I was thrilled. I tried to be warm and intuitive and seductive.

NOW, AS WE approached the Mexican border, Kay started teasing me: "I hope you have on very clean underpants, Eddie, because the Mexican police strip-search every tourist, and if they find skid marks in your Jockey shorts they may not let you in." My father thought this was a terrific joke, and with his thin-lipped smile nodded slowly and muttered, "She's serious, and she's a hundred percent right."

Although I worried about how peccable my panties might be, I half hoped brown-skinned, mustachioed guards in sweat-soaked uniforms would look at my frail, naked body and undies. At the same time, I was convinced I'd never been uglier. I had a brush cut Kay had forced on me ("You'll be hot if you don't get all that old hair out of your face"), and my white scalp showed through it. I wore glasses in enormous black frames and looked like an unappealing quiz kid without the budding intellectual's redeeming brashness. I was ashamed of my recently acquired height, cracking voice, and first pubic hairs, and posed in front of the foggy bathroom mirror with a towel turban around my head and my penis pushed back and concealed between my legs. In public, I'd fold into myself like a Swiss army knife, hoping to occupy as little space as possible.

At the border, disappointingly, the guards waved us through after querying my father about the ten cartons of Cuban cigars in the trunk (Dad had to grease a few palms to convince them the cigars were for his own use, not for resale). We drove down the two-lane Pan American Highway from the Rio Grande through an endless flat cactus-studded desert into the mountains. Kay encouraged me to wave at the tiny, barefoot Indians walking along the highway in their bright costumes, their raven-black hair hanging straight down to their shoulders. Sometimes they'd shake their fists at our retreating fins, but I seemed to be the only one in the car who noticed.

From the highway, we seldom saw villages or even houses, although from time to time we noticed a red flag that had been tossed into the top of a mesquite tree. Daddy said the flag signified that a cow had just been slaughtered. "Since they don't have refrigeration," he informed us through a stinking cloud of cigar smoke, his tiny yellow teeth revealed in a rare and sickening smile, "they must sell all the edible parts of the animal and cook them within a few hours." I don't know how he knew that, although he had grown up in Texas, worked summers as a cowboy, and undoubtedly had known many Mexicans when he was a kid. What struck me was his equanimity in contemplating such shameful poverty, which would have disgusted him had we still been in the States; in Mexico, he smiled benignly at it, as though it were an integral part of a harmonious whole.

My father had a passion for traveling long hours and making record time. He also had huge, ironclad kidneys. Kay had to stop to pee every hour. Perhaps her blood pressure medicine was a diuretic. "Anyway," she whined, "I don't understand why we have to rush like this. What's the hurry? For Pete's sake, E.V., we're in a foreign country and we should take a gander at it. *No es problema?*"

Before her marriage, when she was still just my father's secretary and "mistress" (my mother's lurid, old-fashioned word), Kay would have said "For Christ's sake." If she'd replaced Christ with Pete, she'd done so as part of her social beatification. "Take a gander" was something she might actually have said when she was a farm girl in northern Ohio, but now she said it between gently inverted commas to suggest she was citing, with mild merriment but without contempt, an endearingly rural but outdated Americanism. Like many English-speaking North Americans, she thought speaking a foreign language was an occasion for humor, as though no one would ordinarily do so except by way of a joke. *"No es problema?"* was her comic concession to the mishap of being in Mexico, the verbal equivalent of a jumping bean.

Her parodic Spanish irritated Dad, who could speak it no better than she but who had convinced himself he was an expert since he'd studied the language back in high school in Denton, Texas. He'd say, modestly, "I don't know any French or German. Spanish is my language," though this claim was more a hands-across-the-border token of neighborliness than an assertion of linguistic competence. He'd say, *"Habla usted inglés?"* and *"Sí"* or *"No"* or *"Gracias"* and *"Buenos dias,"* and spell out with pedantry the English equivalents to these flashy expressions. He'd say, " *'Buenos dias'* isn't exactly 'How are you,' though it *could* be used in a pinch to mean that, just as in English we wouldn't ever really say 'Go with God'—*'Vaya con dios'*—when we mean 'Good-bye.' "

Halfway to Mexico City, we stopped at a beautiful old colonial-style hotel that had what it proudly advertised as the world's largest porch, which wrapped around it on all four sides. Meek Indian women were eternally on all fours scrubbing tiles the garnet color of fresh scabs still seeping blood. That night, Kay and Dad and I went past banana trees spotlit orange and yellow, and a glowing swimming pool that smelled of sulfur. *"Pee-you,"* Kay said, holding her little nose with her swollen, red-nailed fingers.

"It's a sulfur spa, Kay," Dad explained. "The Mexicans think it has curative powers."

We entered a roomy, high-ceilinged cave in which a band was playing sophisticated rhumbas. The headwaiter, broad and tall as a wardrobe, wore a double-breasted jacket.

"Uno whiskey," Dad said once we were seated, showing off for our benefit. "Y two Coca-Cola *por favorita."*

"Sí, señor!" the headwaiter shouted before he reclaimed his dignity by palming the order off with lofty disdain on a passing Indian busboy in a collarless blue jacket.

All the other guests at the hotel appeared to be rich Mexicans. No one around us was speaking English. The most attractive couple I'd ever seen were dancing an intricate samba, chatting and smiling to each other casually while their slender hips swiveled into and out of provocative postures and their small, expensively shod feet shuffled back and forth in a well-rehearsed, syncopated trot.

Suddenly, Daddy and Kay looked impossibly sexless in their pale, perspiring bodies. Daddy was decked out in a pleated jacket with side tabs that had opened up to accommodate extra girth; I think it was called a Havana shirt. The marimbas lit a crackling fire in my blood, a fiery longing for exactly this Mexican couple before me, their bodies expert and sensual, their conversation light and sophisticated, a vision of a civilized sexuality I'd never glimpsed before. Outside, however, the heavy sulfur smell somehow suggested an animal in rut, just as the miles of unlit rural night around the cave made me jumpy, made me think of an animal held at bay. Nowhere to go, and the nowhere pungent with smoke from hearths, the cry of cocks, the shadowy forms of distant mountains.

In Mexico City, we stayed in a 1930s hotel on the Reforma. In those days, there were only two million people in "*México*," as the citizens called their beautiful city with a proud use of synecdoche. Although people would swarm over our car at each stoplight, proffering lottery tickets, we simply closed our windows and sailed through them down the spacious boulevards. We saw the Ciudad Universitaria under construction outside town, with its bold mural by Diego Rivera—a lien on a bright future, a harbinger of progress. We visited the Museum of Modern Art and ate in a French restaurant, Normandie, a few blocks away. We ascended the mountain to the fortress castle of Chapultepec, where the rebellious Mexicans had overthrown their Austrian rulers, the lean Maximilian, the pale Carlotta. The baroque cathedral impressed us with its statues of the Holy Family looking like Indians and its entryway sunk into the soil under the weight of time and stone. We were poled in barques through floating gardens and climbed the Aztecs' step pyramids.

We went everywhere with one of Daddy's business associates and his wife; after I corrected this man ("Not the eighteenth century," I snapped, "that was in the *sixteenth*"), Daddy drew me aside and said, "Never contradict another person like that, especially someone older. Just say, 'I may be wrong but I thought I read somewhere . . .' or 'What do I know, but it seems . . .' Got it? Best to let it just go by, but if you must correct him, do it that way. And by the way, don't say you *love* things. Women say that. Rather, say you *like* things."

I had always been proud of noticing and criticizing everything said by fatuous adults. Now I was appalled to learn that my father had been vexed by things I said, expressions I was utterly unaware of. I was half flattered by his attention (so he was looking at me, after all) and yet I was also half irritated that he was pushing me toward his ideal of masculinity.

We went to Cuernavaca and saw the flower-heavy walls of mansions, then to Taxco, where Kay bought a very thin silver bracelet worked into interlocking flowers. The heat made her heavy perfume, Shalimar, smell all the stronger; its muskiness competed with my father's cigar smoke. Only I had no smell at all. Daddy warned us to look for tarantulas in our shoes before we put them on.

In Acapulco (then a chic beach resort, not the paved-over fast-food hellhole it was destined to become), we stayed at the Club de Pesca. I had a room to myself on a floor above my father and Kay. The manager had baskets of soft and slightly overripe fruit delivered to our rooms; after a day, the pineapple smelled pungent.

One night, we went to a restaurant in a hotel on top of a cliff and watched teenage boys in swimsuits shed their silk capes and kneel before a spotlit statue of the Virgin, then plunge a hundred and fifty feet down into the waves flowing into and out of a chasm. Their timing had to be exact, or else they'd be dashed on the rocks. They had superb, muscled bodies, tan skin, glinting religious medals, and long black hair slicked back behind their ears. Afterward, they walked among the crowd, passing a hat for coins, their feet huge, their faces pale behind their tans, their haughty smiles at odds with the look of shock in their eyes.

The popular song that year in Mexico was *"Piel Canela"* ("Cinnamon Skin"), an ode to a beautiful mulatto girl. Among the people we knew in the States, any reference to color was considered impolite, although everyone told racist jokes in private; here, apparently, a warm brown color was considered an attribute of beauty. In the afternoon, on the beach, young water-ski instructors stretched their long brown arms and legs, adjusting themselves inside skimpy swimsuits, dazzlingly offering lessons to pale tourists, both male and female. It was clear we gringos had a lot to learn from them.

A South American singer and movie star, Libertad Lamarque, was staying in our hotel. When we rode up the elevator with her, she was wearing a tailored white linen suit and had a snowy white Chihuahua on a leash. It turned out her room was next to mine. I became friendly with her daughter—I don't remember how we met. Although Libertad was in exile from Perón's Argentina, her daughter still lived most of the time in Buenos Aires, where she sang American ballads in a nightclub. One night, she volunteered to sing "You Go to My Head" at the Club de Pesca—yes, that must be how I met her. I went up to congratulate her and was surprised to discover she scarcely spoke English, though she sang it without an accent. (I was a terribly forward kid, always tackling famous people. I'd made Jimmy Durante and Lauritz Melchior and Kate Smith give me autographs, and, once, in a New York restaurant, I'd chatted up Jerome Hines until he invited Kay, Daddy, and me to sit in his box at the performance of *The Magic Flute* the next night at the Old Met in which he sang the role of the high priest.)

Libertad's daughter must have found me amusing, or perhaps docile, or a convenient alibi for her midday mid-ocean pastimes. She invited me to go out on her speedboat late the next morning; after dropping anchor, she and her handsome Indian driver kissed and embraced for an hour. I didn't know what to do with my eyes, so I watched. The sun was hot but the breeze constant. That night, I was so burned Kay had to wrap me in sheets drenched in cold water.

Kay was terribly nice to me as I moaned and turned for two days and nights in wet sheets. A local doctor came and went. My fever soared. In my confused, feverish thoughts, I imagined I'd been burned by the vision of that man and woman clawing at each other on the varnished doors that folded down over the speedboat's powerful motor.

The man who had accompanied Libertad's daughter on the piano was a jowly Indian in his late thirties. Perhaps he smiled at me knowingly or held my hand a second too long when we were introduced, but I honestly can't remember his giving the slightest sign of being interested in me. And yet I became determined to seduce him. My skin was peeling in strips like long white gauze, revealing patches of a cooked-shrimp pink underneath. My mirror told me the effect wasn't displeasing; in fact, the burn brought out my freckles and gave me a certain raffishness. Perhaps soon I, too, would have a cinnamon skin. Until now, I'd resembled a newly shorn sheep.

One night at ten, my well-sauced father, atypically genial, sent me off to bed with a pat on the shoulder. Instead of undressing and going to sleep, I prepared myself for a midnight sortie. I showered in the tepid water that smelled of chlorine and pressed my wet brush-cut hair flat against my skull. From my chest I coaxed another strip of dead skin; I felt I was unwinding a mummy. I soaked myself in a cheap aftershave made by Mennen redolent of the barbershop (witch hazel and limes). I sprinkled toilet water onto the sheets. I put on a fresh pair of white Jockey underpants and posed in front of the mirror. I rolled the waistband down until it revealed just a tuft of newly sprouting pubic hair. I danced my version of the samba toward the mirror and back again. I wriggled out of my undershorts, turned, and examined my buttocks. I kissed my shoulder, then stood on tiptoe and looked at my chest, belly button, penis.

At last, my watch told me it was midnight. I dressed in shorts and a pale green shirt and new sandals and headed down to the bar. My legs looked as long and silky as those of Dad's pinups. I stood beside the piano and stared holes through the musician; I hoped he could smell my aftershave. He didn't glance up at me once, but I felt he was aware of my presence.

He took his break between sets and asked me if I wanted to walk to the end of the dock. When we got there, we sat on a high-backed bench, which hid us from view. We looked out across the harbor at the few lights on the farther shore, one of them moving: A one-eyed car or a motor scooter climbed the road and then vanished over the crest of a hill. A soft, warm breeze blew in over the Pacific.

It struck me that some people lived their whole lives beside the restless, changeable motions of the ocean, rocked by warm breezes night and day, their only clothing the merest concession to decency, their bodies constantly licked by water and wind. I who had known the cold Chicago winters, whose nose turned red and hands blue in the arctic temperatures, whose scrotum shrank and feet went numb, who could scarcely guess the gender, much less discern the degree of beauty, under those moving gray haystacks of bonnets, mittens, overcoats, and scarves—here, in Mexico, I felt my body, browned and peeled into purity, expand and relax.

The pianist and I held hands. He said, "I could come up to your room after I get off at four in the morning."

"I'm in room six-twelve," I said.

I looked over my shoulder and saw my very drunk father weaving his way toward me. When he was halfway out the dock, I stood up and hailed him.

"Hi, Daddy," I said. "I just couldn't sleep. I decided to come down and relax. Do you know Pablo, the pianist from the bar?" I made up the name out of thin air.

"Hello, Pablo." They shook hands. "Now you better get to bed, young man."

"Okay. Good night, Daddy. Good night, Pablo."

Back in my room, I looked at the luminescent dial on my watch as it crept toward two, then three. I had no idea what sex would be like; in truth, I had never thought about it. I just imagined our first embrace, as though we were in a small wooden boat floating down a river by moonlight. Pablo and I would live here by the sea; I'd learn to make tortillas.

I woke up to the sound of shouts in the hall. Oh, no! I'd given Pablo not *my* room number, 610, but that of Libertad Lamarque, 612. I could hear her angry denunciations in Spanish and Pablo's timid murmurs. At last, she slammed her door shut and I opened mine. I hissed for him to come in. He pushed past me, I shut the door, and he whispered curses in Spanish against me. He sat on the edge of the bed, a mountain that had become a volcano. I knelt on the floor before him and looked up with meek eyes, pleading for forgiveness.

I was appalled by the mistake in room numbers. In my fantasies, love was easy, as easy as waltzing in a costume drama, a blessed state that required neither skill nor aptitude but was conferred on—well, on *me*, simply because I wanted it so much and because, even if I wasn't exactly worthy of it, I would become so once love elected me. Now my hideous error showed me that finding a man didn't automatically place me above mishaps and in a condition of cinematic bliss.

Pablo undressed. He didn't kiss me. He pulled my underpants down, spit on his wide, stubby cock, and pushed it up my ass. He didn't hold me in his arms. My ass hurt like hell. I wondered if I'd get blood or shit on the sheets. He was lying on top of me, pushing my face and chest into the mattress. He plunged in and out. It felt like I was going to shit and I hoped I would be able to hold it in. I was afraid I'd smell and repulse him. He smelled of old sweat. His fat belly felt cold as it pressed against my back. He breathed a bit harder, then abruptly stopped his movements. He pulled out and stood up. He must have ejaculated. It was in me now. He headed for the bathroom, switched on the harsh light, washed his penis in the bowl, and dried off with one of the two small white towels that the maid brought every day. He had to stand on tiptoe to wash his cock properly in the bowl.

I sat on the edge of the bed and put my underpants back on. The Indian dressed and put one finger to his lips as he pulled open the door and stuck his head out to see if all was clear. Then he was gone.

A couple of years later, when my dad found out I was gay, he said, "It's all your mother's fault, I bet. When did it first happen?" He was obsessed with such technicalities.

"I was with *you*, Daddy," I said, triumphant. "It was in Acapulco that time, with the Indian who played the piano in the Club de Pesca."

A year later, after he'd made another trip with Kay to Acapulco, he told me he'd asked a few questions and learned that the pianist had been caught molesting two young boys in the hotel and had been shot dead by the kids' father, a rich Mexican from Mexico City. I never knew whether the story was true or just a cautionary tale dreamed up by Daddy. Not that he ever had much imagination.

Recently I was in Mexico City to interview Maria Felix, an old Mexican movie star. She kept me waiting a full twenty-four hours while she washed her hair (as she explained). I wandered around the city, which was reeling from a recent earthquake. The beautiful town of two million had grown into a filthy urban sprawl of slums where twenty-four million people now lived and milled around and starved.

I returned to my hotel. My room was on the fifteenth floor of a shoddy tower. I had an overwhelming desire—no, not a desire, a compulsion—to jump from the balcony. It was the closest I ever came to suicide. I sealed the glass doors and drew the curtains, but still I could feel the pull. I left the room, convinced that I'd jump if I stayed there another moment.

I walked and walked, and cried as I went, my body streaked by passing headlights. I felt that we'd been idiots back then, Dad and Kay and I, but we'd been full of hope and we'd come to a beautiful Art Deco hotel, the Palacio Nacional, and we'd admired the castle in Chapultepec Park and the fashionable people strolling up and down the Reforma. We'd been driving in Daddy's big Cadillac, Kay was outfitted in her wonderfully tailored Hattie Carnegie suit, with the lapel watch Daddy had given her dangling from the braided white-and-yellow gold brooch studded with lapis lazuli.

Now they were both dead, the man I was traveling with and I were seroposi-tive, the city was dirty and crumbling. Mexico's hopes seemed as dashed as mine, and all the goofy innocence of that first thrilling trip abroad had died, my boyhood hopes for love and romance faded, just as the blue in Kay's lapis had lost its intensity year after year, until it ended up as white and small as a blind eye.

HE'S ONE, TOO

BEING A CHRONICLE OF
SEXUAL LIBERATION, MY OWN

Allan Gurganus

for Edmund White

IN FALLS, NORTH Carolina, in 1957, we had just one way of "coming out." It was called getting caught.

EVERY FEW YEARS, cops nabbed another unlikely guy, someone admired and married—a civic fellow, not bad-looking. He often coached a Pee Wee League swim team. Again we learned that the Local Man Least Likely to Like Boys *did!* In our town of 2,200, this resulted in confusion unto nausea.

Our *Herald Traveler* was usually sedate ("Recent Church Goings-on of Fun and Note"). It now encrusted the front page with months of gory innuendo. Circulation beefed right up.

And into jail, they chucked the hearty, beautiful Dan R——, my boyhood idol.

IT TOOK ME weeks to learn why they'd removed him completely as a carpet stain. I was nine and prone to hero worship. I suffered a slight stammer. I lunged at outdoor activities; accidents happened—often to bystanders. Archery from my tree house discouraged neighbors' backyard cookouts. I felt that 1957 *required* its boys to enjoy a major sport.

Soon as Dan got grabbed, my parents halted newspaper home delivery. I pedaled my Schwinn uphill to the public library. I spotted a stack of local papers set—unusual—on a shelf above kiddies' reach. I dragged over three *Who's Who*s, one stool from Circulation. Then I hid in shadows, safe among 1921's unasked-for *National Geographic*s. I read about the public fall of my secret friend.

(I once hooked Dan R——. Showing off my fly casting, I snagged his furry forearm. Even bleeding, the guy never blamed me. He joked: I should think of him as my first "big one," the lead "rainbow" in a long, good, lifetime's catch. —I did.)

My index finger now traced the nine weeks and sixty column inches of Dan's descent. I read of his capture, for deeds I'd considered doing, with him. I felt exactly as sick as excited.

This would become a familiar flash point for me and my kind—everything we want is everything most others find the most disgusting.

What's daylight to us? that's sewage to them.

Your hope, their shame. I was, at nine, confused. I am now forty-eight.

ODD, AUTHORITIES NEVER arrested our town's obvious ones. Maybe in being flagrant, those boys knew best how to hide. The vice squad failed to book Falls's supple florist; comically self-informed—he defined everything as "buttery," "heavenly," "icky," or "Velveeta." Cops spared our insinuating, gifted organist; didn't Melvin play for the Baptists at ten, the Methodists at eleven? Also left unjailed, Falls's admired if chunky mama's boy librarian.

These ones, born "out," went genially overlooked thanks to good behavior. They hailed from decent families; they told welcome if unrepeatable jokes to generations of mayors' wives. They were clever from surviving. And—if their humor was weekend excessive—their lives stayed weekday useful to Falls, N.C. "The Boys" would be called that well into their senilities. The Boys accepted who they'd been assigned to be.

True, they might flaunt their sexuality's effervescent side effects, but they had the sense to do the sex deed (if do it they must, and you guessed they probably must) well out of state. Sure, they got teased, and daily. Did they even hear the rednecks' sidewalk chorus—"SisterMan," "Miss Sump Pump," "NellieBelle," "Velveeta"? Yes. But otherwise no one bothered these vamping mutant versions of Falls's "good old boys."

"The Boys are inseparable," ran one tired local joke, "except with a crowbar."

An artistic aunt of mine spoke fondly of these three best pals; she bought the floral arrangements of one, marveled at the Sunday Wurlitzer crescendi of another, and—from a third—received (under the library counter) steamy bestsellers concerning tobacco-growing oversexed hillbillies.

"Judging The Boys against our town's gray businessmen, why, there's just no contest, is there? It'd be like comparing, oh, a cuckoo clock, say, with some wall-mounted round thing, just any ole modernish GE school clock. You can get the time from both, but the cuckoo one'll give you real *fun* every fifteen minutes. Never scared of a little drama. Whereas the other is just putting in his time . . . just *up* there."

THE MARRIED FELLOWS that our cops caught were just trying to outwit their molten (uncontainable) secret. Failing that, many hoped simply to outlive it. Couldn't you slowly lose the central urge toward men, the way your waistline painlessly eventually dispersed?

Your wife, your kids, sat inches away; and who would know that, while this service station attendant shot white foam across your car window, as this punk (whose cap read "Fill 'Er Up, Mister?") toyed with your floppy windshield wiper, who'd ever need know that you studied such drenching—not to catch a smudge on green glass—but to observe, through it, the beautiful brown ligaments in a perfect, working, young, male, arm.

Desperation for actual sex with living men led some of our brightest locals (ones with law degrees, ones passionate for clever Civil War battle strategy) direct into the crudest traps.

And the very nanosecond queer news got out, these guys fell forever.

II.
A Man's Man

I so admired Dan R——. He golfed with Dad. They often partied. I guess he must've sold insurance or real estate (I never saw him actually working).

Dad's friends arrived at our house, en route to their games. Our home stood in sight of the club's first hole. Foursomes gathered on our porch, drank there, paced, awaiting today's tardy partner.

Their beloved hostess was Mother, Falls's best-informed young wife. She remembered the nuances of each man's favorite drink ("Exactly three extra baby onions, please").

"Don't know how you keep so many standing liquor orders in that lovely head, Helen," guys flirted with a woman whose IQ was 159.

HOORAY! HERE CAME Dan's sporty Plymouth wagon, "cream" and electric blue (white interior). Seeing me, he always honked, *Shave and a haircut*. His sound piled into our drive, activating everything. In Dan's car, young lawyers, young doctors, joshing. Behind them, leather golf bags of saddle-shoe two-tones. Bags, lumpy as boys' marble sacks grown huge, chucked atop each other like some shoulder-padded orgy—dumb, male, goodwill at rut.

Dan never swore, he rarely broke the speed limit. This husband and father and soon-to-be-caught queer served as deacon for that new brick Methodist church—the one near U.S. 43? beyond the carpet discount hut? yeah, that one.

Jocular, adored, and nearly too handsome, Dan was saved by not quite knowing it. That let you stare, let you draw maybe four inches closer than you'd risk with some dude aware of his exact market value. Dan, so visible to others, seemed half blinded by his own inviting innocence.

People rubbed shoulders with him—"for good luck," they told themselves (if they noticed doing it at all). I noticed their doing it. At nine, I wanted to.

HIDDEN IN MY tree house above his parked wagon—I gazed down upon this man; my admiration felt almost patriotic: It weakened me, but for ideal reasons.

The floor of my crow's nest was one closet door, sacrificed in recent expansion; my father had nailed it up a maple at roughly lighthouse height. Just one closet's width held me aloft. It gave a good if sneaky overview, but offered no real living space. Suspended by rope, I kept a net sack full of ice-cold Cokes. A three-legged stool dangled. I pulled things closetward only when needed.

Today, Dan, seeing one stray line, fished a dollar bill from his wallet. Grinning, he tied it on, jerked three times. I knew to tug his green up into mine. I saluted over the ledge and, alone, sniffed dampish folding money. Its ink smelled more black than green. The smell hinted at wadded white bread, billfold's rawhide and, not Jockey shorts, but Dan's second-day-wear boxers, possibly plaid. Eyes closed, I inhaled mainly Dan, worth hundreds.

Friendly below me, he stood no more than five foot six. And yet, like certain compact guys, he appeared a giant, shrunk—someone monumental rendered wittily portable, more concentratedly male for that. He was the most perfectly made, if shortest, of my father's crowd. These men were immodest ex-soldiers of a won war. They acted as pleased with themselves as with their unearned trust funds.

Dad's group called itself the Six Footers Club. Dan needed six more inches to qualify. These six inches caused lurid jokes I never tired of overhearing.

Men! So simple in beasty anxiousness about their size relative to other guys' vitals' sizes. "Is it large enough?" cannot be called the subtlest question in the world, but it sure remains a biggie.

DAN, THE SIX Footers' mascot and pony beauty, again got teased about his runtiness and profile. A tree house was good for such eavesdropping. I knew that—between guy-drink two and guy-drink three—the smut would start. I waited.

Country Club North Carolina: Most days after five P.M. from 1949 to 1969 meant bottoms up, three good stiff ones downed in an hour and a half. (Not sissy white wine, either. The hard stuff.)

Men watched our driveway for the last of today's foursome. He'd soon roar up after closing some deal or suturing shut the victims of Falls's latest teen car wreck. Our house had a horseshoe of parking lot, plus hammocks and the open bar.

Mom, perfectly dressed, with a master's degree, hovered, warmly impersonal. Indoors, two black, uniformed maids did her heavy lifting. Dad's friends lounged and goofed right under my treetop.

After jawing through money news, after gossiping about sewage bond issues, after the mind-numbing hit parade of their last game's best shots, "So Dan surprises us, choosing his three iron . . ." they finally got dirty on me.

Stripped to shorts, my eyes half shut, breathing Dan's dollar, nose to nose with George Washington, I'd been ready.

They mentioned certain looser secretaries—those days always named Donna—and who Donna'd "done" now, sometimes three in a hotel room at one time. Smut hushed when Mom reappeared wearing a Dior flared skirt, carrying the silver tray that—some summers—seemed jewelry fused direct to her hand's red nails. As she swept indoors, trash restarted mid-syllable.

I never tire of hearing deep-voiced, long-legged guys bray through the six key words in human reproduction. Holy Man-tra!

WHAT DID A youngster hear, those corny days of sexed-up '57? Often simple dick jokes of the kind that boys my age enjoyed.

"Hey, Dean," remarked our youngest bank president, ever, "summer sure has bleached your hair. Or you been dipping into one of Jeanie's Clairol bottles? So tell us, Big-time Lawyer Man, is it true blondes have more come?"

Tree high, I kept still.

"I'm not answerin' that directly, sir. But you can state your question direct into my Bone-o-Phone, Phil. Put Mouth Against Tip of Receiver and Inhale Hard . . . right *here*." Much *yuks*. Above them, half stiff in seersucker shorts (shorts whose very fabric's name gave me a minor-major boner), I listened in a trance of premonition, dread, desire.

AT ANYTHING OFF-COLOR, Dan grew shy and pebble-kicking. The Six Footers admired him as "too straight an arrow." When he literally blushed, they seemed not unexcited, watching somebody so handsome redden, laugh, then hide his face behind two palms while bowing forward.

Quiet, he reigned at their group's dead center. If any Packard or golf cart broke, Dan was first under its hood. The joke ran: He could fix an engine without getting any oil on him. Dan wore his snug, pressed clothes like some proud, poor boy—quietly defending his one good school outfit.

People included young Mr. R——, though his family wasn't *from* Falls. He was token Elsewhere. Dan seemed more mysterious and attractive, being uninitiated. Locals took him aside to explain the genealogy behind some recent land deal—some webbing of tribal traits and 1790 betrayals so complex, you could see he hadn't a clue. It didn't matter. Around here, nobody new ever truly *knew*. Two hundred and fifty years were involved; strangers could never catch up with that many genes and so much ownership.

Dan R—— (no last name, please, though it's thirty-odd years later) showed one immodesty. He had a charming, actorish way of planting knuckled fists onto his hips. He had this lovely way of letting his well-made head fall back as he laughed. He laughed often and—if the things he said were the things that, at church, on fairways, they *all* said then, Dan said them in so ripened a baritone, and with such banal complete conviction—it made him seem even more a man.

Originality has never been required for admission to a country club. Originality would soon lose this guy his membership.

MY DAD WAS himself a chopper and clown on the links. His own ambitions for his game made him far less good at it. Dan R—— played golf to relax. Golf worked my father's every nerve. "That darn Dan." Pop shook his head. "Guy consistently shoots in the low seventies." My father watched the younger man's natural swing; Dad's groans sounded close to Lust, not the simpler vice of Envy.

"I swear, Dan. I keep telling the pro . . . person can't *learn* it. Guy either gots it or he don't, and, Dan? you're loaded with factory options, dammit. Maybe bottle it? for us mortals, pal? Sell me a six-pack at cost, what say?"

"Well, thanks, Richard. I do really usually try hard, I do. And sometimes, I admit, I'll get m'balls to set down at least *near* where I wanted 'em."

Be careful what you wish for, Dan R——.

IF THIS WERE fiction and not the blunt, hyperpictorial, and unlikely truth, I would assign "the Dan character" some personal peculiarities. These would separate him from his leggy, same-ish junior partners' crowd. Maybe I'd make him a bit accident-prone? or give him some slight endearing limp, a major stammer. Fact is, he was too able-bodied.

He was plain and good, and as visible everywhere as Wonder Bread was then. "Builds Young Bodies Twelve Ways." (I felt built by every vitamin Dan's company and little gifts provided me.)

FROM MY TREE house, through field glasses, I stared down on a Dan foreshortened. His beer-loving pals had already begun the tragic waist-high unraveling that gets most guys. From my perch, they looked like stacks of pebbles, largest on the bottom and the smallest, pinkest, right on top. Dan's build still reversed this.

From overhead, his brown locks and foursquare shoulders eclipsed narrow hips. Just shoe tips showed. I'd memorized the hair cocooning his ridged forearms. Back when I put my fishhook in poor Dan, I touched arm fuzz growing haywire, all directions. Hair sprouted every color, blond, brunette, and Lucy-red—mixed, like the pelt of our brindled boxer dog.

I'd never seen Dan shower at the club; I didn't dare, but liked knowing *I could've.* I feared he would be burred across with many-colored patches. The taut chest and high butt—speckled, furred thanks to helpless handicapping manliness. Odd, that his perfection almost made you pity him.

From my closet perch, through binoculars, I now bird-watched a friendly compartmented bulge in the front of young Dan's ironed chinos. From direct overhead, you could see its smiling sickle curve. He always "dressed" his due right, like some driver signal's courteous extended arm.

"What you seein' from up there, John Jay Audubon?" Hands on his hips like a goalie, daring you to score, Dan stared right up into my suction-attention.

"You . . . look"—I felt caught—"close."

"Excellent glasses, hunh, buddy? German, I bet. One thing's sure, those Krauts flat-out knew their optics."

No other friend of my father's took any time with me. Passing, guys might rub my blondish hair but always the wrong darn way. Puppylike, I growled. They never noticed.

Dan did, laughing. "You're too much, little buddy."

III.
Wanted, Dead or Alive

Then Dan was not. Not in Papa's golfing party. Nowhere near our home, the couples swarming for Friday night bridge, arriving solemnly intent as if planning new Normandy beach landings. Something'd happened.

I, a watchful boychild, with the man-sized interest in him, retreated to my tree house, soon overheard tag ends of stifled driveway conversations. "Never in a million years'd guess . . . him . . . one . . . those."

My favorite had descended from such visibility. That same year he'd headed our Community Chest charity drive. Dan was often shown in the paper, grinning beside a giant plywood thermometer. The hand of his arm—muffed as in downy shredded wheat—touched painted mercury. Mercury shot up as cash poured in. He smiled a hopeful grin one-sided; he rolled his eyes to urge our town toward generosity—a salesman's readiness to look however foolish for a sale.

I myself gave forty-seven cents.

Though the same picture appeared week after week, I still scanned it for small message differences.

NOW, NO PHOTOGRAPHS, no word. Missing In Action, one electric-blue Plymouth (its pale interior startling as a white sock around the calf of some dark, older boy). My parents having purged our house of any telltale *Herald Traveler*, I grew so jumpy/bold from missing Dan, I blurted during dinner, "Wwwwhat ever happened to . . . ?" (I didn't even need to finish . . . they'd been waiting.)

Mother stiffened from Casual to Regal. Using her linen napkin, she blotted her mouth, then—napkin stretched between her fists—studied it as if my question had just made the cloth go beautifully bloodstained.

Dad cleared his throat, public speaking, "Someday, I'll explain, son. Once I figure it out more myself. There are certain men, often not the ones you'd expect ... Dan went and tried something that ... Dan's left us, basically. Nobody understands it. Pass the turnips, son, and take more or you'll never make the Six Footers Club. Mighty good turnips tonight, Helen, crispier. Son, I know how much you, all of us, feel so attached to, but ... Fact is, son? around our town? what Dan tried? it's the one thing a man cannot come *back* from. . . ."

This passed for clarification. I simply nodded, swallowing it whole. I would need to bike to the library. I understood I was not meant to know ... how bad it was, whatever Dan had chanced. . . . Did Everyone's Great Shame come from his having attempted it, or his longing for something Dan really truly wanted but never even nailed?

He ceased being. He ceased being, as Mom put it (her joke, not mine) "The Heartthrob of our Community Chest."

Monopoly had one card we dreaded most: GO TO JAIL. The worst part, you could only sit, could just admire the others' hopping happily forward, snatching up your better hotels. Eventually, your fellow players stopped even addressing you; you could watch them from up close forever, but could not get OUT.

IV.
Book Me Passage on The Fellow Ship

When Mom complained about the hours Dad squandered getting even worse at golf, he reminded her: The happiest times of his whole life had been spent at war, with other loud good boys in mobs and squadrons. "Helen, I need my weekly fellow ship time." The Fellow Ship. Guys spoke of it often, as being golden. As something craved nearly as much as women were, by all real men. Me, too. I heard about a local high school athlete winning "a full Fellow Ship to Duke" and envied him his crowd onboard, the jolly boyish voyage upriver clear to the steepled campus.

At age six, I made The Fellow Ship a pirate craft, longer than wide, a carved dragon's head snarling at its rapier tip, a barge almost too pointedly male to ever float on nebulous female water.

At nine, I pictured a torch-bearing Viking boat, its rowers shirtless doctors and lawyers, its cargo leather monogrammed golf bags, its destination the Links of America, but its true goal: grab-assing, the dirty guesses about who that slutty little Donna wouldn't "do" dry.

At the prow, hands on hips, lit unevenly by violent orange torchlight, shirtless yet bandoliered with those leather thongs Kirk Douglas wore in *The Vikings*—stood Dan, Captain of The Fellow Ship of choice. His deep voice calling, "Stroke, fellows. Stroke it good, pals o' mine. Pull hard, because The Fellow Ship is for us *baad* boys only. Pull hard, good men, because you *can*."

I imagined my tree house closet was a Fellow Ship franchise. Or at least its outrigger offspring, The Boy Raft. Sometimes, among maple leaves, I took off my seersucker shorts. Because I could. Who'd know (robins excepted)? I let the breeze be my buddy, my coxswain.

There was a new verb, used mainly in churches then. Mother found it vulgar. "To fellowship." For me, that latent active word sounded like a pillage itinerary, some oarlock means of transport, and my own future port in Paradise.

*   *   *

PROMINENT YOUNG EXEC
ARRESTED EXPOSING SELF TO YOUTH
(AT PENNEY'S TOILET)

Dateline: Raleigh—A 33-year-old Falls resident, recent chair of our town's most successful Community Chest Drive ever, a four-time winner of the Broken Arrow Amateur Golf Tourney, did not probably know how much his life would change while in Raleigh, this Saturday past, on family business. It was a day of record-breaking heat, but otherwise no different from most days.

The week before, having already been elected Rotarian Young Man of the Year for 1955, he was made it for '57, too! His lovely wife had taught third grade. His three bright children are themselves valued members of their own playground community. But, within one hour of arriving in that shoppers' haven, Raleigh, Dan R—— was handcuffed and already on his way to prison.

Arrest came swiftly for the young local church and business leader.

Chief Executive Officer with J & L Realty/Insurance of this city Dan R——, of 211 Elm Avenue of Falls, was caught in the Men's Room of Raleigh's new J. C. Penney's Department Store. According to authorities, he was apprehended while "making sexual-type-suggestion-advances" to and "having sustained manual contact with the privates of" a 15-year-old boy "at the urinals of the new Penney's rest room facility, 2:32 P.M., Saturday."

The father of the boy propositioned chanced to occupy a booth in that very rest room. He was planning to take a faulty camera to the repair shop there in Big Elk Mall. The father also happened to be an off-duty detective (still carrying his service revolver).

The resultant photographs are, according to a reliable source who asked not to be identified but has closely examined them, "conclusive and damning." No sooner had flashbulbs cooled than the father made a dramatic arrest. He then paraded the suspect in handcuffs the full length of Raleigh's newest luxury shopping facility, Big Elk, Browse 'n Buy Mall, Lake Boone Trail (Road). The photos are now in the hands of Capital police, said Raleigh Sheriff's Department spokesman Red Furman. He would only indicate that young Mr. R—— was being held for "Corrupting A Minor," "Soliciting," and "Indecent Exposure." Other charges are being considered. A printed statement on this case ended, "The snapshots prove past any shade of doubt—*some touching was definitely involved.*"

Mrs. Dan R—— would make no statement when reached by telephone at home after not answering their door during this reporter's twenty minutes of knocking.

Reverend Elmo "Mo" Haines, of New Hope Road Methodist, is pastor to the once-popular young couple. His only comment ran, "This is just not the Dan I know. Dan rates among the finest young gents I have fellowshiped with or ministered to, ever. I'm sure there is an explanation, though I don't yet know what it's going to be. But we're all ready. We do just pray for the R—— family, and for Dan especially. Despite this being such a true and total shocker, we remember that, in the end, all things work together for the Glory of God."

V.
Stakeout: Crime Scene Pix

There was once a brand-new J. C. Penney store. It dignified an early shopping mall in glamorous Raleigh. It was built prior to four-lane highways. Achieving the state capital meant a tough three-hour drive from manicured and clubby Falls.

While Dan's children made fast work of their Jumbo-Tub popcorn in the dark Mall Theater (then known as just the Cinema Twins, not yet today's extravaganza of bad choices), the R—— kids' dapper father—with time to kill—purchased golf balls (used and new, old for practice, new for real forkeeps games).

Finding he'd secured himself two whole hours by his lonesome (unusual back home), maybe Dan scoped out the mall's haltered adolescent girls. They drifted to and fro across the vast space, always tacking at obliques in bright attracting "schools" of three to five. Not unlike the pet store's neon tetras glorifying aquarium windows of that shop exotically stinky.

IT IS OUR rarest luxury, sufficient time alone. Odd how we forget, it is a "hall pass" we so crave. Solitude becomes especially precious to a father of three this overtaxed and hectic with blood drives, land closings, putter practice, sidewalk edging, carpooling kids from dressage to clarinet lessons. Today, atypically wifeless (her asthma acted up each August), today briefly unhooked from children, Dan must have felt like some once-clunky plug-in appliance suddenly retooled to be, the miracle of 1957, "A Portable."

Alone at last, free of wall sockets, maybe he probably got so doggone horny. Maybe it crunched his lower body like his wife's worst cramps coming on all at once, doubling her over. Was it a nausea of displaced attraction? What made Dan feel this strengthening weakness for some action *now*?

If the female genitalia can be considered (in certain magical functions) a plug-in device, the male ones remain perversely, indeed sinisterly, portable—extruded, independent, air-able, always primed for the latent test drive.

They'll get a guy—unchaperoned—into all kinds of freelance trouble, quick, even at a fluorescent mall. What to *do* with a healthy set of portables, at two-thirty P.M., at Big Elk Browse 'n Buy, before the baby-sitting Disney animation ends?

Maybe surely Dan endured the driven sexual thoughts of a young man—in so tumid an August—just at the peak of his need to implant. Maybe these two hours among attractive strangers helped Dad admit to a more unsettling itch. It was an itch you couldn't even name, much less sate, slake, or properly dig at in reputation-conscious yard work Falls.

Itches can go unscratched only so long. Watch.

VI.
He Grows Up, Anyway

Soon as I got older, I got out.

It's 1970 and I have just bought a batch of spring flowers. Not a single dollar bunch, but three I've artfully merged. That's a notable percentage of my weekly food money. I now take night courses at Harvard. I sell art reproductions at the Coop. I am studying painting and have allowed myself to be in love. With a. Man.

He's ten years older, four inches shorter, Japanese American, also a painter, watercolor mostly, a fellow Gemini. It seems ordained. A Columbia grad, he once published a prose poem in the *Saturday Review*. It concerned the first winter snowfall in a gray city—imagistic if not controversial.

All this impresses me, but what matters most, his kindness, his deft water-color hands, the sense of shelter his basement apartment provides. It is so full of cloisonné and mirrors and screens—gold-leafed cranes flying. Our sex depends on adolescent friction and it smells of Johnson & Johnson baby products, both clear and pink ones. His laughter contains all the lucid giddiness hidden in puns, unguents, and champagne. A buzz available anytime I can get him giggling, which is most anytime.

I've rearranged this bouquet, rewound it in green tissue paper. Then I bind it all with one argyle shoestring tied in a bow, looking jaunty, semibutch. I wear brown suede bucks and my good old blue-and-white seersucker suit. I'm riding Boston's Lechmere subway line out toward Brookline. I'm hand-delivering flowers to the first man I can say I truly love.

I am a boy, and I am a healthy boy, twenty-three, and I do not look the way unimaginative people believe a queer one must dress or sit.

I have shoulders now, and a real jaw, and can appear somewhat lifeguard-worthy. I have grown up to be a complete and manly man, I could be my Dan R——'s own son. His Beloved First Mate on The Fellow Ship. A member of the Six Footers Club, I sometimes manage the look of old money, though I myself lack any.

Today is April and our subway car has climbed free of its tiled tunnel and now spills along the center of the street and the driver has (illegally, with glee) opened all the doors to let spring breezes in.

Seated across from me, three white-haired pretty ladies are visiting, well-kept. They look like girls who sat down to play bridge one day in 1920 and, after many laughs and a legion of rubbers, rose with difficulty, shocked to stand up old. But—even so, all during aging by accident—they've basically had a lovely game. Even their dresses—chosen at separate homes—show complementary pastels. You feel their lives' essential agreement. Now I see they are smiling back here at me.

I have been deep in my own young man's vernal sexual and romantic thoughts, I've been staring down at jonquils and one ratty peony, busy sniffing French lilacs. I'm gazing so hard at three dollars' worth of flowers, rapt with such inhaling joy, it must look as if I'm going to drop my pants and—here and now—fuck these blossoms good.

Wondering what the ladies want, I grin back, mild. I love my grandmother and the artistic aunt who once compared our pathetic swishy hometown Boys (so unlike strapping *moi*) to pert "fun" cuckoo clocks. If possible, I plan to like these Boston ladies—beaming, placid, entitled.

Nudged by the others, one powdered one nearest me leans off her seat's rattan, points to blooms and smiles. "For your girlfriend."

SHE DOES NOT ask, but tells.

I know I am only required to nod. Even a shrug, a grin, will do quite nicely, thanks. The one thing they'd like more? Overt baritone confessing. "Yes, ma'am—fer my Melanie. We're to wed come June, ma'am. She teaches third grade and she's as good as she is beautiful. She's taken such super care of my mother who's an invalid with one shriveled leg but a great disposition and Ma already loves Mellie like a daughter. Melanie put herself through school by making the best darn marmalade, ever. Think she'll like these posies?"

I understand what these nice ladies want.

I am being asked to reinforce the natural order, their own middle-class romance with middle-class romance. I imagine how they see me, a boy pretty, young, and tender as the flowers he's paid dearly for. They note my pressed suit, but cannot smell its aura of Niagara spray starch. I washed this seersucker thing in Woolite, dried it on towels spread across my tenement's tar roof, then ironed it myself, unable to afford both dry cleaning and nosegay.

"For my boyfriend."

I say it louder than I even planned. The tram driver checks his rearview mirror. Ladies' faces shift. I haven't spoken "boyfriend" to hurt them, to teach them, or to scold them.

I just want some of my complexity known (since they asked). There are stemmed and petaled layers of complexity, involving the weird unexplainable innocence of all this, of simply He and Me and Us in the World. Is pleasure such a threat? Is a little privacy too much to ask? It all seems, to me, as innocent as the phrase "for my boyfriend."

Itself, a bouquet.

The ladies look hard at one another, some glum muttering. Their leader checks back, describing, debating. An argument's in progress. Do I fuckin' *need* this? Why do I keep *doing* this to myself? Which means, of course, Why does the world keep doing this to me and my kind? Dan, among us. How much pain can be inflicted for one species of involuntary joy?

Then something happens. It again proves how complicated, the world. Shoulder to shoulder, they're all smiling back at me, anyhow; their leader lady nods.

They have—through knowing each other so deeply, through a basic lack of experience with anyone "out," through some abiding belief that every good-looking boy on earth is really created for one equally fine gal—decided that "boyfriend" can't possibly mean *that*.

They opt for thinking I don't know quite how my statement might be misread by other minds, ones far dirtier than theirs. They decide male friendship is nice but not so important as actual love. They choose to feel I am too fresh-looking and ethical-seeming. I'm visibly from far too good a Caucasian family (I could almost be a son of theirs). And they're going to go ahead and enjoy all this . . . me, the flowers, seersucker, spring. They are going to pretend I didn't really say that. I didn't really mean that I was . . . one.

Despite them, thanks to my mission, Brookline's center street tram line smells improbably of woods abloom, citric-scented wildflowers in late April. Despite these three Boston Athenas indicating what I'm *not* to do, the town still feels whimsical, this Northern spot I came to come out in. Its central lake in its emerald park has boats shaped like giant swans. Even here, Wagnerians hold sway.

So I get away with it again. I am not arrested. And when I rise to leave, my honey-colored hair ruffled by breeze, as I pull the cord, and hold my floral tribute, bridal before me. The ladies wave. Their leader mutters fondly, automatic, as if speaking nonsense syllables to some dear grandchild, "Toodles. Enjoy."

I never marry.

VII.
Walk Your Own Stiff Plank, Sir

It is two-twenty-eight P.M., August 7, 1957, in a pastel department store, and it's about to happen because Dan has got to pee.

Through Hi-Fi Stereo, past Glassware and Rec Room Needs, he wanders into the men's room at our state's flagship J. C. Penney store.

I admit, out in the open: I wish I'd been there then. I wish I could have saved him from the high price of desire fueled by decades' sickening secrecy: the erectile trend is further crazed by late-summer heat of Carolina. Barring my helping Dan out or my feeling Dan up, I guess I wish I coulda just watched. . . .

People later praised the two-way mirror. Some Falls gossips swore that's how cops caught Dan, and on movie film. Others claimed that this unlikely toilet had become a secret breeding place for capital-area inverts. (If, of course, they *could* breed.)

My own belated adult guess is that: A restless Dan chanced into the absolute right bathroom on the absolute worst day.

If only he hadn't already seen *Snow White* four times. If only it hadn't been 1957, when you could freely park your kids in any movie house.

There were many reasons Falls condemned its ever-popular Dan R—— overnight. The following is one:

DAN'S CHILDREN CAME out, of the Cinema, blinking, scared after seeing the witch's poisoned apple eaten. They felt spooked by so spiky a green villainess. (Always, in fables and life and in Disney movies, Evil's more photogenic than any sappy virgin dumb enough to bite an apple so obviously laced with chemo. An apple this good-looking dares you *not* to eat it. So you really shouldn't.)

Dan's kids, perhaps with buttons of popcorn strayed into their fine silver-blond hair, were first surprised, then shocked, next hurt—not finding Dad.

"He said meet right *here*, right? And at four. I'm sure."

Imagine them staring at the mall's terrazzo flooring—still influenced by the movie's wishfulness. Just because they wanted it, couldn't their dad break through this paving, hands on hips, head tipped back, and, rising, laughing?

The kids felt mainly ready for the long nap home in the back of their Plymouth wagon still-new smelling, somehow male-smelling. Cross, then bored and—when an hour'd passed—irked with a first hiccup of completest fear, the youngsters finally sent their oldest brother on a mission. "Go and scout out that darn dad of ours, Dan Junior. The car's still parked, so he's here, okay. Hope he's not sick or somethin'. But, naw. Dad's never sick."

If, in Falls, these kids had been stood up, some other parents—friends of Dan's and Julie's (his wife)—would have spied the familiar pretty R—— features. They would have noted the kids' worry. They'd have noted how children of such different ages—usually quite eager to appear not *with* each other—clung together now. But, see, this mall stood in faraway cosmopolitan Raleigh, and life was harsher there and faster and so crowded. And no one knew them.

Only later—during the mall's lock-up around ten-thirty P.M., only then did a black security guard find three children sleeping, roughly spoon-fashion, behind one huge imported palm tree. Like kids from some Grimm tale, lost in the enchanted woods, they'd stolen back among the decorative plantings nearest where Dad said to meet this afternoon at exactly four. Six and a half hours later, discovered tucked behind the fountain, back by its transformer where the rushing water's clear recycling tubes were coiled and snuffling like Mother's asthma, three kids waked. They felt sure Dad had found them. Smiling, they turned.

But no, uh-oh, it was a worried Negro guard, chancing half a smile. And the kids understood they were all in so much trouble. They'd spent their last coins on further Milk Duds. They didn't know how to phone Mom collect long-distance. And if they had, they might be getting Dad into real hot water. See, without even understanding why, they already knew to be ashamed.

The R—— kids attended Methodist Sunday school; bruise-colored consciences were forming. Starter cultures of the ethical and, when need be, the self-punishing. At home, everything usually worked on schedule; so—when it didn't—somebody got blamed.

The mall guard seemed to be half eating his foot-long walkie-talkie. People were being called, the lost kids' father's full name uttered. Then Dan's children heard a minor stir. The walkie-talkie picked up one downtown cop, "Oh, him? Yeah, we've got him. Guy's already been printed, guy's been booked. Good riddance to bad rubbish, hunh?"

"Booked, what fo'?" the kind guard asked. Then Dan's kids, eyes large, hands laced around each others' necks and shoulders—they all knew first, knew first what their father really was.

THE REST OF it interests me because I am one, too.

Like Dan, who was locally noticeable and then became hyper-visible en route to being totally unseen, I am trying once again to make myself more opaquely and superstitiously visible an invert. I am trying, through this story.

I am fairly smart and a decent actor, and I've had sex with women without soliciting immediate reviews, or expecting ladies' awe at my versatility; and I can pass. I know that.

If I'd married, and stayed put in Falls: I would now teach art history at a local junior college. I'd have a smart if no-longer-slender wife named Alice, and the one son, Kyle, five—a prodigy-brat-joy.

I didn't. So I don't.

Still, I think of what the authorities did to Mr. Dan, who slipped that once, then slipped into the searing spotlight before falling so utterly out of view. And—incidentally—out of the life of a kid who liked to look at him, loved just being near him.

When Dan took his own lucky kids to visit Shiloh Battlefield, he brought me back a greenish musket ball. It looked old as Rome. It tasted of salt. I still have it.

Recently, a famous men's magazine asked for some of my fiction. I told the editor I planned mailing him a good new story about a gay sailor, stuck on a ship off Vietnam. The editor whistled. "Oh, boy. I hoped you'd be professional. You planning to rub our noses in it, hunh?"

I wanted to tell him, "I bet if I were Toni Morrison and you phoned to ask me for a story, and I sent you one about my fellow black people, you sure wouldn't use the term 'rubbing our noses in it,' I betcha."

Rubbing *our* noses in it? Isn't that how you train a puppy who keeps shitting in your house? You jam his little black nose in his brown illegal leavings. That'll eventually cure him. Besides, your getting to legally punish him (for his own good and the Oriental rugs') will certainly make *you* feel better, before cleaning up his mess again.

THEY SURE RUBBED Dan's nose mighty hard; they broke it, rubbing it in.

Did I say so to the gentleman editor? No. I never even sent that story out, to anybody. He'd already jinxed it, see?

Still, I forgive myself. You learn to. You go crazy otherwise. But know what? It's so damn tiring. I'm no natural hero. I just want to do my work, eat okay, have a place to live, and get laid once every month. Okay, twice a year.

I pretend I don't mind outing myself daily. (There's one huge reason not to be a black person in the U.S.A. now: You've got to *talk* about that all the time, if only out of enlightened self-defense.)

I claim I don't mind the risk of getting marginalized. I keep putting my hands on my hips, like some Errol Flynn pirate, acting proud to be so wild and so well paid for it. I throw my head back and laugh to prove I just don't care who knows. I care.

I pretend it doesn't cost me every single bloody time I remake the point, every time I bust again toward full prison-break Out. But In keeps sealing over, the hymen grows back so damn quick. And once you are Out in the Open once more, old threats feel fresh and jagged. Loud sounds make you jump. If you have, in your day, checked out a few boys' butts, you'd best watch your back full-time.

It's not enough to have healthy, Six Footers Club self-esteem; you'd best be Superman, and just to break even. You cannot marry your true love. Your idea of daylight is their idea of sewage. Make love, risk jail.

You're starting over absolutely every day. You'd best know why you bother. Assuming nothing, it can sure take major traction. You need psychic four-wheel drive, for life.

Q: To whom shall you, the cuckoo clock's pet cuckoo, explain your calorie-requiring Self-Outings every fifteen minutes?

A: Explain it to Yourself. You will become, in the end, the world's hardest party to convince. You'll soon sound like your own conservative, protective, loving wife. Her familiar voice will grow un-brave, so quick to tell you, "For God's sake, let the others protest. Relax for once, Little Ms. Firebrand. Stay home tonight. Stay *in*."

SOME DAYS I *feel like a 185-pound shrimp, peeled and left at noon on a huge white plate in some Courthouse Square downtown—drifting car fumes, gawkers, pigeons pecking.*

Too nakedly glistening. And, since nobody's ever seen one this size, they ignore it. "If it's been left out here in this heat, bound to've gone bad by now, anyway. Don't look at it."

AT LEAST I haven't made Dan's endgame mistake. I am still free to make others, better ones, slipups more mine. At least I'm not the married man with three kids waiting. At least the first time I tried something, I did not get nabbed, exposed and fined, imprisoned. Instead, up front, I *say* I am one (the principle of inoculation: a little of it, taken on purpose, cures you, if you survive).

I emerged from hiding a decade after 1957. And I get to remain free. If only under my own recognizance.

DAN, CAUGHT IN public, at a Raleigh urinal, had not been wise as The Boys. These buddies survived Falls only because they took their unusual appetites elsewhere. The good ship Fellow Ship sailed The Boys across state lines. And if they'd docked in Raleigh to seek adventures around mere malls, these experts at hiding would have known the safety code for bathroom pickups.

You go into a booth, you don't risk public detection as poor Dan did, standing out in the open. You take your classic position on the pot, then tap your foot, setting up a signal that shoes to either side of yours can acknowledge or ignore. By the time you peek under the partition—or through a burrowed portal called, in terminology both profane and sacred, the Glory Hole (no Fellow Ship should be without one, above decks)—you have received a Morse code marriage proposal, tap dance pre-nups from the soles next door. Everybody's implicated, notes on scrolls of toilet paper passed. "What you into doing?" has given total strangers more up-front candid sexual info than most wedding couples know about each other. Physical description, list of fave sex acts, signed, sealed—prior to first touch, a veritable contract. If society makes your lust illegal, you might as well subvert those laws efficiently.

Men! What won't they do to get some? And guys seeking guys are spared all female indirection, all the ladies' emotional subtlety, decency, and marriage mill formality: Guys'll just stick it through the hole, get "done" in the time it's taken you to read this page. It's honest, if illegal.

The Boys judged Raleigh a bit too close to home. No telling which Falls preacher or city manager you might run into. And besides, the men you snared at Penney's would be suburban, too married, far too penitent for The Boys' intended caliber of fellowshiping.

No, weekends they traveled direct to the Ships of Many Fellows, also known as the Atlantic Fleet.

They leaned coastward—eventful weekends at run-down tolerant Norfolk hotels nobly named: The Monticello. In formerly grand Deco lobbies, reconnoitering with other small-town escapee florists named Hiram, Buford, and Earle—"*Avec une 'e'* please, Mary"—they drank treacherous if Windex-colored drinks titled after ports far more exotic than Norfolk.

Then The Boys, feeling Out, wandered Water Street; two aircraft carriers, six thousand young salts, were in.

A little drunk, The Boys still talked inherited Spode.

A lot drunk, they trawled the sailor bars, and—come morning—phoned each other's hotel rooms to brag in inches.

HOW, AT AGE nine, could I announce to the world that I preferred, I think, fellow sailors on The Feller Ship? My tendencies and character were probably visible to anyone with eyes. The Boys surely guessed about me long before I did. (Just, as I later learned, they'd "spotted" the unlikely Dan before Dan probably knew.) Instead they taught me lore about their jobs. They acted kind, familiar, courtly; but they never "told me" about myself in a rude way, never took advantage of a ready, wistful kid, as many Republicans will tell you they *all* do—correction, *we* all do.

Coming out to my parents was literally tougher than going on record in *People* magazine. Telling them was like saying I had some news: I'd been arrested at J. C. Penney's pee trough, and why? Because, the other good news was . . . They dared me to tell them. Short of clamping a hand over my mouth just as I formed the syllable, they did everything to actively prevent me. They knew, all along, of course. But maybe they remembered the dreadful fate of our friend, ridden out of town for reaching toward an apple too perfect, too easily achieved, too good *not* to be pure poison. The very sleeping potion makes the fruit's red shine so.

They kept asking which girls I was dating most, how impending an engagement, howbout the promise of grandchildren, when? Which likely family names for that first boy?

These were people who'd dropped a suddenly depraved young Dan. Is it any wonder I feared blurting? And they feared hearing? I told them gently at first: "I'm married to my work." "Don't expect me to go out with the daughter of your next-door neighbor, that plump but pretty-in-the-face personality girl you keep mentioning, the art teacher at the public school. I am not erotically interested in women, period."

That seemed sufficient. I didn't want to be a guy who'd brutalize his parents in the guise of coming clean.

VIII.
Tell It to the Judge

What went on at the urinal of the brand-new J. C. Penney's at that early mall still holds me. It holds me in part because I remember how beautiful Dan's forearms were as he pressed both his fists, knuckles downward, onto the farthest points of his fine hipbones.

The arms were wound in every color, including—near the right wrist—a sprinkling of first silver. I recall the way his dark eyebrows sent a translucent chevron (ambassadorial) to negotiate those black woolly dashes into staying perpendicular above so very Roman a nose. How blue Dan's jaw was where he shaved so often, how it looked like tempered steel—a dented icebreaker chin, its metal neatly folded (oh, to rub my nose in *that*).

I WANT TO wander back in time. I'd shinny down my tree house rope, and—with me magically advanced in age to become a guy, say, thirty, and Dan still thirty-three, maybe we'd adjourn to the shower room of the club, no, to his family's Plymouth wagon, but parked on midnight Lovers' Lane, his daughter's stuffed dog toy wedged under the front seat. And I would interview Dan; and maybe later, touch him. "There, there, pal. They can't hurt you now. We're safe out here. Safe 'cause this we're in is a fantasy of mine. It's the one place they can't go, can they? Except for your being the first of my several beloved married men. Oh, well . . . nothing's perfect, not even our escapism." And I would ask Dan when he first knew he was, one.

I would ask him how—before his regionally publicized Raleigh arrest—he'd managed it, living locally with all that competent wildness crammed so far, far down in him? At one Adjustors' Convention in Houston, did he not try some room service hankypank with a red-suited winky bellhop, a Tex-Mex kid as interested in the tips as the kicks? Had Dan thought about doing it with another man every minute of his life, or only quarter-hourly, male-male sex rearing its circumstantial head like that comic, startling, makework clockwork cuckoo bird?

Did he, as with so many before him, coach a swim team of teenage boys and make the occasional spot check of the shower rooms, but not so often as to be conspicuous and always with a clipboard in his hand, always faking some set-faced chore as he swung into the showers, gruffly barking, "Anyone seen Smitty? Got to get Smitty's darn parents' signatures or we're not going to have a bus for our away games. You seen Smitty, Butch? No? Well, dry the heck off, and quit popping towels at guys, down there, savvy, bud? Cover yourself, look at you, grabassing bucknaked drippingwet. Grow the heck up, m'pal, okay? Umkay."

HOW OPENLY DID the young boy, in snug blue jeans, entice an itchy, married Dan, who led the Community Chest so well and made the red part of the plywood thermometer go redder, faster than any other fund-driver, ever? How did my hero fall prey to some pimply if pretty boy? And did authorities insist the boy's policeman father fill some monthly quota of morals charges? Or was this simply off-duty sport, done on spec, for the glory?

Dan's court-appointed lawyer would place most blame upon Dan's tempters. On both the young son and his hidden father, readying the camera. What overcame Dan as his own children sat intrigued by seven small men in love with one brunette wearing an outfit that looked made via cookie cutters; each dwarf named for his own comic vice/shortcoming? (Mightn't there have been a little "sensitive" one called, not Sneezy, but . . . Velvety?)

Shall we blame that blazing August's having twenty-four nonraining days? Or was it Dan's depressed asthmatic wife? Was it Julie's unwillingness to "let him" lately, given Dan's solemn rigor at it every Friday—and this bad recent humidity? What drove young Dan to eye, then sidle nearer and finally touch, the secret, if offered, velvety parts of a younger and seemingly more innocent fellow male, fifteen?

All this they discussed at the hearing. It was reprinted in our local *Herald Traveler*, barely euphemized. I sat in the silent library's shady stacks, backed against the *Geographics'* egg-yolk yellow and egg-white whites. I sat reading some and crying some and reading more, in painful little sips, and not understanding how—between the lines—I understood all this so well.

They showed Dan's picture, once the trial started. It was early, a locally made portrait taken just after he arrived in town, so hopeful (the top studio of Falls's two), the file photo they'd used for all his awards as Young Man of the . . . whatever. All the drives and that big banquet he'd meant to end world Muscular Dystrophy. A well-intended guy, not yet thirty-four, smiling in his white, overlaundered shirt and with such teeth, and the starchy, believing whites of his overlaundered (unsuspecting) eyes.

IX.
This Town's Not Big Enough for Both of Me

Six weeks after Dan's arrest, three weeks through his jail term, his wife still lived in Falls. She repacked, hiding as well as you could in a town this small. No further church attendance. She had groceries delivered to her back door till her husband—released from his imprisonment ("Unnatural Acts" "Liberties Taken With A Minor" "Indecent Exposure")—could travel wherever they'd picked to settle next. He would get a new job—if without too many letters of rec.

Till Dan sent for the loved ones, his kids were kept indoors. When Julie R—— dodged into some store, seeking milk, she wore a kerchief and dark wing glasses. Most people avoided her. A few confident veteran clerks did speak (if only about the weather), and later they asked others for brownie points at having treated her as a regular human being. "After all, *she's* not the one's been going on all fours in J. C. Penney's boys' rooms. See the bags under her eyes, even behind those glasses? To find that out about the father of your sons—poor thing, crushed-looking. . . ."

Dan served a seven-week sentence. Though he'd golfed with every white-shoe-firm lawyer in Eastern North Carolina, not one stepped forward to help. And he—shamed—just accepted the court-appointed choice, a kid from Ohio fresh out of a so-so school and nothing special.

We never saw Dan again.

I, I never saw. Him.

(When in airports, grown, waiting for the rental car line to dwindle, I'll still thumb through local phone books, checking under R——. No luck to date. What *would* I say to him? Is he still with his wife? Or maybe splitting the rent with some younger man? Alone? Alive?)

My dad played eighteen holes a week with him for six years, but that was neither mentioned nor admitted. Dan, once considered indispensable, seemed—overnight—not just dead but unmissed, except in certain tree houses.

I would aim my bike toward the R—— home, its FOR SALE stake tilted, cockeyed, out front. Sudden weeds everywhere. A split-level brick rancher with mature evergreen plantings, it looked like most other homes on the block; it was a Duke of Clarence. Myself a little pedant, I knew the model home names of every suburb in biking distance. Musket ball in my pocket for luck, I stayed seated on my bike, stopped before Dan's nice unsold home. I regretted having snubbed his three skinny kids at the club pool.

Every car approaching from behind made the bristles of my crew cut stand on end, tentacles predicting him. Sure he'd keep an implied appointment with his "little buddy," as he'd called me. But the sun set. It got cold. Dan never arrived.

One month later, I expected I would miss him less, not more. But it was more. So, with a certainty peculiar to the insane, I biked direct to a hanging "colonial" sign: "J & L Realty/Insurance—Reaching Out To The Community."

Wearing shorts, barefoot, I approached a gargoyle secretary powdered in hopes of looking younger. She did not. She gaped at my question, rose, wedged half behind a frosted door. "Boy, no shoes, asking ways to find Dan R——. Seems upset. Thin, well-spoken . . . nervous."

"How young?"

The lady tipped back, smiled, disappeared. "Maybe around ten?"

"Oh, dear God. Now they're coming in here to *us*. Where will it end? Payments is where."

A man veered out, his hand extended, the smile enforced as a laminated name tag. "Can I be of help? What do you need with him, son?"

"Nobody knows where Dan went. I miss him."

The secretary stepped one high heel back, but the executive bent forward, considered touching me, then thought so much better of it, his right shoulder spasmed. "We have no address. Even if I wanted to trace him, which I don't, I could not. Who are your parents? Have you told them any of this? Because you're going to need help with it. More help than we can give you here, son. This is a workplace." The big phone rang and two adults practically giggled, both lurching toward one black receiver. She beat him to it.

"Who is your father?" he asked. "Tell us who your people are."

I turned so slow, I padded out, bare soles sloppy on cold lino, soles gingerly across hot pavement. Then I pedaled off so quick, swallowing all the air, eyes burning. I knew then. I could not afford to find him.

X.
Hard Evidence

The boy Dan "touched" was the attractive youngest son of the heavyset arresting officer. It later came out: This lieutenant tended to place his fifteen-year-old on nonschool days at better-known public urinals. This ploy rarely worked, since the intended victims enjoyed communal word of mouth expert as their not-unprideful oral sex. Raleigh queers were long since onto *that* little trick and morsel. They did acknowledge as how the cop's kid looked a bit like James Dean, and—why lie?—he was extremely well hung for a boy who'd only shaved the once, for Easter service. They nicknamed this troubled smoldering boy the James Dean Decoy,

Bait Meat, and,

best perhaps,

the Trojan Hose.

They knew to run from the sight of him (only some jerky married out-of-towner—hiding from his own kind and their helpful information—would've gone *near* that infamous young beauty holding his infamous older-looking beauty).

THE LIEUTENANT ENCOURAGED his son, once stationed at busier urinals around our state's capital, to unhasp his all and, having unzipped, to, what?

I find imagining this father-to-son pep talk a very tough assignment. It may be the hardest thing to know. Eros: a magician's implement bent on disappearing everything put in it.

I understand Desire better than the Desire to kill Desire with a Desire of superior force, superior because fatal. To use your kid as other fellows' ship direct into prison. To me this seems as Martian as I might appear to any cop willing to dangle his boy as fishing bait— literally, dangle. "Son, just maybe think of, oh, say, Marilyn Monroe. Then, nature being nature, what happens'll happen, and don't mind letting the old one near you see your 'whatever' . . . 'peek,' whatever. . . . Not to be scared, either. 'Cause Dad's right back here. You just get the evildoer started and, by God, Dad and the long arm of the law'll do the rest."

I have myself experienced joyous moments in public rest rooms, commingling and looking at, and more. Some moralists would say that Dan should not have touched a boy that age, even if the kid seduced him. Some readers will not have got this far because I seem to be pulling for the wrong side.

IT IS A medical fact:

You can kill a starving man by feeding him too fast.

AS I WRITE this, trying to reconstruct the start of Dan's arrest, I'm still turned on somewhat. The impending tragedy adds wallop to a humid scene in this large men's facility—four sinks, six stalls, eight urinals, all down the carpeted hall past Customer Services and Handy Layaway.

Perhaps this bathroom became so popular because its unoiled entryway door squeaked—because the foyer entrance is obscured from the urinals and booths—because this gives its friskier patrons two seconds' warning. (That's of no use, naturally, if a secret photographer is lurking behind the only closed door, stall number five.)

I know all this because, at twelve, I insisted we go see a movie at this very Raleigh mall. Soon as my parents left me alone to watch Fred MacMurray and some irrelevant flying sheepdog, I slipped out, rushing straight to Penney's.

I found the sign still saying Customer Services, Layaway. I felt sad on discovering the crime scene abandoned. I paced off everyone's deeds. My already-adult dick out, I was crying some, feeling now nauseous, now aroused, titillated at acting it all out, at letting my part take all the parts.

The life of the erotic must have consequences. Sexual urges can be exactly as memorable as they feel savage, precisely as pleasurable as they must look— to the uninvolved—pagan and utterly animal.

A kid with his pink staub in hand, face smiling, eyes drowsy, mouth gone slack, and waving his all around (as ordered), turned into a deadly fishing lure; and the Dad, wearing a trench coat to make this stakeout look more movielike, waiting in the stall to pounce on you. (Between clients, do father and son talk ball scores, trying to fake normality and pretend that such safaris constitute everyday policing?)

DAD IS ABOUT *to leap and photograph.* At home he has the complete incriminating snapshots stuck into a store-bought album that came stamped with the words "Our Best Memories . . ." When he's feeling discouraged about his other work on the force, some nights late, he'll get them out and peruse the terrified faces depicted and feel . . . achievement? a quickening? The father knows that, when lurching forth, he must look only at the culprit. This'll give Junior time to hide whatever just made the malefactor (on first seeing it) jump so, made him grow so immediately culpable when, invited to reach out, he does so, *flashbulb.*

Booth's metal door is kicked wide open. First bulb fires off, blinding in a mirror four sinks long, and another one is caught . . . red-handed, red-whatevered. The yelled legalities, barked sounds so loud on tile, and silver handcuffs flashing out. They're soon cinched onto a fellow whose dick is yet quite free. The culprit's dick is yet left sticking out, it's unable to change gears that fast, belonging to a human beast, if a decent Rotarian one. Hairy wrists are bound in metal bands, but the sturdy papa hard-on is yet poking forth so far that— even the cop, a fellow male after all—lets the pederast try and wedge it back in, before the officer pulls his perp through the bustle of our leading Penney's store, past Meeting Your Kitchen and Bathroom Needs, Up To 40% Off, Everything Must Go, where shoppers will be perplexed enough to see a handsome young man—head nodding shamefaced forward—bound in cuffs, and really shouldn't have to deal with such a boner on him, too.

It's tough forcing yourself back into your britches while wearing the cuffs that've already cut reddened slices into downy wrists. Best to either deal with your zipper or your handcuffs, but both at once is pretty much a killer.

XI.
The Fellow Ship Docked Below Fourteenth Street

Somehow, I've lived, grown, flourished, and fled Falls, by many, many states and jobs and beaux, and somehow, it's 1990: The newest of my escape hatch tree houses is called Greenwich Village.

We speak of a lovely Saturday night in spring, and I'm carrying sixty dollars' worth of rubrum lilies, careful that their red-black pollen not stain my pristine clothes.

I am bound for a party whose parchment invitation insists overartfully, "Come as you would be, and as you *are*, but, if possible, tonight, in white, dear."

So, feeling good after a day of writing fiction that spawned four actual living kicking sentences, I am gussied up in white bucks, white ducks, a pale tie, and off-white shirt—and I'm feeling nautical but nice when I hear a passing hot rod yell one word that I, in a naval mood, believe to be *"Farragut!"*

I get hit full-face. Two Jersey-flung paper cups, one full of warm beer, the other all cold orange crush, and I am so soaked.

I hear loud laughing as they roar off. I'm left here gasping, bent double. The shock of it has knocked the wind clear out of me, but nothing worse. I set the flowers on a stoop. Take stock. There's a small cut on my forehead. Could one piece of flying ice have managed that?

"Everything's fine. No harm done," I tell myself. But I am so stained and sogged. I smell like someone else's four-day binge. I look down at the lightning bolt of orange sogged from chest to my once-white crotch. I realize—even if I dash back home to change—I have nothing white left to wear.

One block north, I dodge into an alley. These lilies are trembling so, like living things. I guess they are. I hide against the hoodlums' coming back for me. I know, through friends beaten or worse, that these boys—if they get off a "good one"— tend to circle the block and swerve back for further fun. I imagine fists next time, or hammers. This season, they've favored hammers—the gay-bashing fashion accessory of choice. Innocence, my own, makes me wonder how they even *knew* I *was* one. Duuhh! (Probably, I overdid. All the Wildean lilies, right?)

Caught, I'm moved to explain to them, I don't usually walk around all in white like Mark Twain, who claimed to be straight. Shamed, I consider just skipping the party. Maybe I'll go late, when a spotless entrance will matter less. I pull out the sogged invitation, double-checking the address.

We'd had White Parties all year. "Come As You Are" ones had recently been done to death. I now reread tonight's prissy, funny, self-defensive "theme":

> COME AS YOU WOULD BE, AND AS YOU ARE,
> BUT, IF POSSIBLE, TONIGHT,
> IN WHITE, DEAR.
> R.S.V.P.

And, vowing to tell every-fuckin'-body how I got so orange and wet and why I smell of Hoboken brewery, I soon make myself into something of a party hit. Our specialty: a brand of bravery as flashy as some new perfume's name. Cheap yet necessary, it's a comic art that only other survivors will recognize. I am become a tale of woe transcended—I am my own sole excuse. I am the opposite of apology. Maybe I courted grief by being too far "out"? Do I make myself look overeager to be knocked way, way back in again? I don't seek to become a nose-rubbing-in Target, believe me.

I have not been tortured fully. I am in good health, and have had hundreds of lovers, and I've never been arrested, yet. My heart's been broken but that's pretty normal, right? I am not sick, nor do I think of myself as "sick." My parents still ask for credit, having somehow heroically accepted my "lifestyle choices." They still remember my birthday. But they swear I've rubbed their noses in it.

Mother took me aside one year after Dan was driven from town, when she saw me still gloomy and jumpy about the speed and injustice of his going, and—trying to help, I'm sure—she said, "There's something we never told you about Dan, when you were younger and all?" I felt scared, seizing her white wrist, begging for news. "He was not exactly smart, Dan. He had other qualities that made up for it, and sweet as the day is ... but not like your father or our doctor-lawyers, he was sort of always along because of his charm and the way he looked and his ... not reTARded, just not all that swift and ..." She saw my face and added, "I'm not sure why I'm telling you this. Maybe trying to make it easier for you to ..." And I knew, in that absolute way we, this hooked genetically, so knew each other, Mom was about to say "Get Over Him," but stopped. See, that sounded too much like a boy-girl romance. "Maybe I'm trying to make it easier for you to forget him, son." It was the wrong thing to have said. This close against my face, she saw that.

XII.
The Captain Hook

I once literally hooked literally all of him. It proved addicting. This was the year those others caught, then vanished him.

He had stationwagoned over to pick up Dad for further golf: *Shave and a haircut.* Dad, fighting his latest financial reversal, was late. Those guys never tired of golf. Maybe the dick jokes helped? I owned a new green Wilson fly-casting rod. I'd been practicing alone a lot.

I felt I was getting pretty darn accurate. I could place my weighted silver hook just about where I wanted it. (Be careful what you aim for.)

Dan discovered me tossing my line at a chalked blue ring on the side of our white garage. Waiting for my father, Dan had come seeking me. On our white-frilled porch, his partners milled, swilling vodka, massacring baby onions.

"Why not cast her my way, pardner? You're gettin' good at it, I see that plain. Here, maybe try and put 'er about *here?*" Dan had spied a red plastic ring. It was the chew toy for Tuffie, our boxer. Dan lifted it free of a boxwood bush, then held red out, an exact right angle to his body. His jaw so square and blue, his face so blankly direct, he looked earnest as some model in a Red Cross diagram for Boating Safety. I felt weakened by appreciation, patriotic.

Dan squinted in April sunlight. With his face screwed up, you saw how he must've looked as a boy, winsome if underfinanced, rawer. He was not like me. He'd been born poor. Part of his sexiness came from some lasting smell of that. I once believed that dogs were the daddies, cats were the moms. I once thought all women were rich and men born poor. Go figure.

Today Dan wore fresh-pressed chinos, deck shoes, a plaid short-sleeved shirt. He smiled across sixty feet. Distance reduced him to trout size. But his hundred-watt attraction remained a lure, immense. I readied my aim. I took a bowlegged stance. It was my own approximation of the Male. I posed, tough, fifty-six whole pounds.

Dan's pals played raucous Twenty-one on our side porch; they gossiped hard. (Some young country boy who worked at Aetna had just got engaged to Donna!) Big drinks' ice cubes clinked. I readied my rod, checked all my interior devices. It was a day of birdsong, temperature in the seventies, a day as gold as blue.

Studying Dan's pale inner arm held direct off his torso, I so wanted to touch him. "Here she comes, Dan. On your mark . . ."

I aimed. I recall the thumb release of line. "Go!" The reel sang its precise ratcheting, pure play-out. April!

(Later, during sex, I'd recall this giddying suspension. A man feels his release "go off," you feel the aim-out pleasure unspiral into air, your reel line is moving, about to mainline joy throughout your groin, then flooding every cell of you. You know it's literally coming, *you* are. You know that nothing on the earth— not even a jealous macho God—can stop it now, your gusher, eureka!

The Fellow Ship fullsteamahead!)

MY SILVER LINE lifts a C shape of rolling light, midair. Settling. Then I feel the snap of my hook find something hard/good—a surface firm yet yield-ing—springy, live, worthwhile. There's much game "play" in it. And, even as I realize I've hit, not the red ring, but one pale human wrist (not the left, holding a target, but Dan's other one), some excitement, some malice unac-countable, makes me jerk it anyway. Gotcha, motherfucker!

Snagging the arm of a man who's always been only kind to me, is a response so male, so savage, automatic—it scares me sick. The Sports Gene! "*Owww-eesh!*" Dan howls. (Might this not be Dan's exact sexual release cry?)

My rod drops to grass. I speed toward my prize. Even in pain, even after studying the wound I've caused, Dan is easing down. He's kneeling on our lawn. Readying himself, because, at my level, *he* plans to comfort *me!*

I follow line to him. Filament burns a hole in the center of my chubby fist. He's before me, guessing how upset I'll be. The guy prepares a grin. He means, even in his shock, to protect me from embarrassment.

On knees, Dan is just my own height fully standing. This close, his head appears enormous as a puppet's, its handsomeness gone jagged as Sherlock Holmes's hat and pipe and shoebill nose. He receives my running weight with a little grunt. He shields me from seeing his bleeding arm. Cardplayers have heard Dan's holler. Two lean off the porch. "It's nothing," Dan's baritone calls, warming my neck and ear. The one good arm cradles me against him. It pulls me closer to my target, home direct between a squatting hero's opened knees.

Tuffie's chewed red plastic ring is now suspended—bull's-eye—just above my friend's clumped crotch. Other men are toasting us with bourbon, laughing, calling all their usual usuals.

(In polite Falls, you never say what's gone previously unsaid. If something has not yet been spoken, it probably never needed saying. So:

"Caught you a big one, hunh, kiddo? Six inches shy of a six-footer, best just throw him back, what say?")

Trying to keep our dealings private, Dan smiles at me, apologizing for those clods. His fibrous arm flips over, accidentally showing me white skin, powder-blue marbled veining, and one long spittle of opaque red leaving the silver beak of my own hook. That surgical hook puckers a two-inch sample of someone's bacon-fat flesh. "Noo," I cry. The barb looks too big to ever cut quite out of him.

We're bound together for good, flies tied. I nuzzle, sobbing, "Didn't mean to, to *you*, Dan . . ."

I feel half faint, daylight overdoing it and drenching me, accusatory. I'm pitched even deeper in a pliant vise between Dan's open sinew thighs.

Mother, seeing my latest tangled mess from her kitchen window, will soon come running. As ever, perfectly supplied, she'll hold a silver tray supporting Merthiolate, pedicure scissors, cotton balls plumped fast and hostessy into a silver salt dish (Grandmother Halsey's, 1870 or so). Plus Dan's favorite drink—a light Cutty and water. (I heard "Cutty *Shark*," I liked knowing that its label showed The Fellow Ship.)

Dreading others' seeing us, hating how pain alone permits our union, I cry "Soory" into splayed legs. They remain wide open. I've run right into their V-shape shelter, a berth. I now wedge farther between.

I am sobbing, he holds me fast. I am getting to touch good fur on one arm I failed to hook. I find that, in his pain, Dan doesn't much notice how I hold him. So, sick with boldness, I tip against the inner fabric of his much-washed pants.

Mid-thigh, I read the Braille outline of sexual parts, his. They're presented plain, canine in guilelessness, grapelike in gentle plentiful cascade. The very symbol of abundance, Mr. Dan's nearby portables.

Birds, disturbed by his wounded cry, go again all song. I hear mother clanking in the kitchen, assembling emergency gear. And me? I'm just crazed enough by guilt and proximity. Using bloodshed as my excuse I find nerve to cup my open right hand lightly—light as light itself—against them, against all his. Just overtop, no pressure. I simply do it, crying as distraction.

First Dan only holds my shoulders, staring at my freckles. Then my pleasure—stirred, overambitious—leads me to tighten my clamp on him, his. My reach exceeds my grasp. I see his face change, slow.

(Meanwhile, back at the crotch, my subtle squirrelish fingers register: My Dan today wears no underdrawers, unusual in Falls in '57. My palm can tell: Unlike Dad and me, my Dan here, is not circumcised [born poor].)

I see concern fold the brow of a squatting man who clutches a child, holding, unexpectedly, that dude's own central credentials. No "Ooops." No "Errr, would ya please let 'em aloose, son?"

Instead: Dan himself glances down between Dan's own mighty legs. Definitely checking on a little scoop-shaped paw now curved against his right-dressed member. Beneath my grasp, it all feels as spongy as a round home loaf of sandwich-sized Wonder.

He still half pretends not to notice. No one near the house can see what's going on. Dan, metal-blue jaw, gives me one sleepy, dubious half smile. In it, amused recognition, some pity maybe, much fellow feeling, a father's patience for his own kid's guileless curiosity. Oh, The Fellow Ship. Dan says, "Well, little buddy . . ."

He makes no move at all to close his legs or shift my hand. But—being Protestant—I know to remove my hand, for him. Enough. For now.

The moment I let loose, he laughs about my hooking him. "No sweat, buddy. Hurts about like a mosquito bite, tops. Just shows how many you're gonna land ahead. You got some touch on you, know that? Just did what they say do, in the books: 'Concentrate, "spot" your trout, then flick 'n hook.' "

Oh, God, here comes Mother wobbling on high heels and carrying that clanky, glinting tray. "I hurt you," I apologize, partly bragging. Mom hostesses me aside. Soon I've inchwormed up into my tree house. I am coughing with sobs, staring down at my gentle, bloodied trophy.

Mother, like some comic waiter, keeps the silver tray level at all costs. Kneeling, ministering, she offers Dan his Cutty first.

(1957, Carolina, the Golden Age of Silver Trays.)

I yell down, "I didn't know it hurt. To fish. Hurt the *fish*, Dan."

"Don't blame yourself. You've got the sporting touch. . . . You'll land hundreds more ahead, and rainbows, too. Glad to be the first in line—a great long catch o' keepers, pal. Your only problem is, your aim's *too* good. Every man should have such trouble. Definitely no more crying, umkay, m'buddy-ro? Promise your Dan?"

"I pwwo-mise, . . . D-D-D-Dan."

How could you not love such a fellowshiper? Had Dan talked to me in code? Did he even deeply mind or notice as I—leisurely, entranced—felt his dick's noble heft? And did Dan allow me or prevent me or invite me? Who'd *had* whom?

EVEN TODAY, WHEN I hear the phrase "child molester," I think, not of One Grown-up Who Molests Children, but of some kid who diddles unsuspecting innocent adults, grown-ups who glaze over immediately, going child-passive.

I'm told that the victim adults—racked with equal parts guilt and interest—sometimes never get over it.

Dan? I count on that.

Inside your right wrist, even with the lights out, can you not still touch a little scratchy signature of scarring?

XIII.
Over and Out

I "came out" in whatever room was left, after Dan—whatever space remained to stand up in. That zone proved no larger than one store's men's room, one stall of it, a tree house, one closet door laid horizontal, opening downward, but only onto spine-cracking gravity.

Me? born guilty as any Calvinist sinner (guilty prior to even getting it up once, much less forcing myself on another male).

I struggled past the threat of local arrest. I didn't even feel safe in Norfolk. I needed four to six state borders between me and Home before I tried anything. It was way out of town, up north in Boston, before I dared unzip for any reason beyond legal peeing (and even after that, I scrubbed these pecker-handling paws but good). I'd been well trained in pain—pleasure was a night course I would have to teach myself. (Not to brag, but I found I had a certain latent talent for it.)

Alone with my first, I had to know for sure that the person who seemed to want me to reveal my lower body to him was not just doing this to please his dad, one alcoholic copper father, waiting, with a reel-to-reel recorder underneath this very bed.

Dan R—— failed to become what authorities intended—a reason for me to hesitate. Sure proof of why to keep it forever sealed up in your pants. Instead, my Dan—who let a worried nine-year-old boy lightly touch his crotch "for luck"—became a reason *not* to hesitate sexually, ever. Dan's real crime wasn't the one they creamed him for. His true sin was earlier postponements (all the joy a man so splendid, skilled, and energetic might've given other men).

Fear led to his lurching, damning recklessness. He is still my hard-on polar north. Hands on hips, he's innocent even of his own scary magnetic looks, the teeth too white, the face too decent not to have a lot of patsy in it—given a world as mean as ours.

Sometimes . . . I believe my artistic aunt was maybe all too right. Those days, you know what I feel like?

I am a mechanical cuckoo. Lots of laughs. I got built, a charming Tirol timepiece that I myself did not design. A clock is both my castle and my cage; I guess you could say I have the penthouse.

But I'm really just the mechanism's star-quality *Hello, Dolly* doodad. My loud mandatory appearance announces each hour's timely high points. Odd, I never do get over my stage fright. Every quarter hour of human history, I brace, required again to act cocky and jaunty and artistic, decorative. And yet, it's odd, I feel completely unprepared, each time. I am both star and target.

I get popped out anyway, my nose rubbed in the blinding light, I'm terrified even during my most cheerful chirping.

Otherwise, rocked back on the governing coil, my beak tips rest just against two round shut swinging doors, I feel most grateful for usual darkness. They named this whole clock for my carefree two-note song.

But, truth is, I am usually "in." My tree house closet is shut. Then I don't have to think of how I look, or which latent assassin is waiting out there this go-round. I prefer not thinking of it much each day. But, four times hourly, I'm totally and publicly "out," outed. It feels self-conscious and short-lived as someone sticking his own tongue out. You can't ever really say much that way, can you?

Even when you hear me sing, *tweet-twitty-twit*, even when you set your watch by me (and do, by all means, 'cause I'm so reliable), even as you smile over your shoulder on hearing my musical comedy again, even when I seem all charm, pure velvety buttery goodwill—truth is, I'm not singing.

It's a shaped scream.

THANKS TO DAN, I can't afford to ever comfortably abstain. Not with a two-hour layover between trains in Milan, and after meeting somebody kind and at least half attractive, someone whispery and nodding, with a borrowed apartment just a three-minute walk from this terminal, some guy so visibly willing not to let time go, not to let this pleasure pass. I remember Dan. I go with him.

I expect eventual arrest. I am never fully safe in this my country. Times, I seem to live scot-free, I'm healthy, I'm allowed against all odds to exist in my own way, and to write this toward you, fellow innocent. If I were not gay, I would be supporting Alice and Kyle and meeting at this moment with the search committee at the college—afterward, stopping by a busy but dangerous rest area on the interstate—and I would not have written this and, therefore, for whatever it's worth, you would not be reading it.

XIV.
Last

Coming out, I managed. *Staying out* is hard.

A day in the life?

I came out at seven A.M. today—I did so just by tucking one cream-colored silk hanky in my blazer pocket. To me, it didn't look fey, it just looked right, necessary. By three this afternoon, I was having a late lunch with two co-workers. Who told a gay-bashing "Hear about the pit bull with AIDS?" joke, one I really might've/should've protested. The lunch had been so heavy and I'm getting over a hellacious summer cold, and I just couldn't find the energy to make a scene, to force the point again, and act so nunnishly doctrinaire. Didn't want to make another dreary plea for tolerance, yet again, Killjoy.

Walking back to work alone, I saw a truly great-looking boy. And—before I quite censored myself properly—I'd tossed an appreciative stare at this blond, aproned clerk. He stood spraying down the eggplants displayed before our corner greengrocer. And he offered me some visual encouragement—top lip curling back, a toughening of his flippant stance—but then, three seconds later, reverse, he flipped me the finger and muttered, "You fuckin' *wish*."

I crossed the street, my face neutral, spirits silenced. I was sure he'd chase me, or holler an insult (the actual name of what I am). I felt sure he'd at least aim his rubber hose at me. The Trojan Hose. At the very least, he'd ruin my best suede shoes.

See, friend, I came out at seven A.M. today. And, at around two-forty-eight, I went back in.

Tentative, I reemerged around three-forty-three, until that aproned blond flipped me the bird and threatened me at three-forty-four, till he drove me to tiptoe boldly back in yet again where many men have gone before. By five-ten, feeling stronger, I risked it again . . . but then . . .

In the dream I am still nine. Not "out," but up my tree house. There's been a lynching, or some act of piracy in Falls. It's late, just before dawn. Our neighborhood echoes with men shouting, "Not in here. He over there? Found yet?" Manhunt.

I'm huddled, flannel pajamas, on my closet door. When I notice torchlight, I discover you, Dan, tied to the tree above me.

In the filmic way of dreams, a voice announces, "Women look finest in candlelight. Men are best seen lit by torch."

Torches smoke all around us up here, the maple leaves sizzle. Somebody has bound you fast. Your chest is as glazed as a Viking ham, drenched in salt spray or blood or honey. Varnish shows ribs' every perfect fold, the bulk and hollow. But there are hooks in you. Lures with wet feathers, savage broken lines from years ago. Your hands are tied behind you around the tree's main trunk. I fight to release you. Your eyes are aimed up, sainted, lost. My fingers prove too small. The knots seem permanent, grown barky as the tree.

Far below, voices keep mapping the search for you. You wear only a white towel around your waist. As I stare past it, toward your face, I see that something immense bulks underneath the terry cloth. I say, "Dad, are you okay, can I help here?" but I mean "Dan." I give you many chances to object as, slow, I touch your thighs. Finally, with you in such pain and beauty, I don't await an invitation; I tell myself that what I do is just First Aid; I reach under your towel, I unfasten it.

Lit by orange light in my tree, I understand that they have hurt you. Where I expected your manhood waiting, springy, perfectly cheerfully complete, they've slid a giant fishhook. It has been stuck all the way between your legs and I see its barbed tip gleaming in the flame. It's perfectly down-curved. I see how cleverly it's made, so it will go right through, but never get back out.

And looking up at you, I touch the hook they've hooked you with, so cruelly, Dan. Depriving you of such a right. Kneeling in a state of worship, sobbing, kinship, lust, I find it's warm under my palm. Now, finally unshy, I kiss your thighs and crane up nearer it. I am your fellow fellow. I place my mouth to it. I find the taste is ketchup, metal, Milk Duds, bitter money, milk, and salt and sugar mixed.

. . . The taste is equal pleasure, equal pain. I wake. The first thing I know is: I am no longer nine. You're still gone. They caught you out.

DAN, ARE YOU alive? Might you really read this? If so, please, please drop me a line care of the publisher. I'm older. I've learned what to do—for pleasure, after pain. I've got questions. About that kid, the cop's blond son, how good did he look? How much did he do to draw you those few urinals closer (into camera range)? I think I know a lot about you. But it's just based on those first nine years you honked at me. And paid attention. And sent bills on strings up my tree. Did you suspect I was one, too? Did you know that *you* were? Was I funny then, or somewhat sweet? Or even pretty, in my longing looks both up and down? Listen to me, this old, still fishing for compliments! Jailbait. I just want to check in.

HE'S ONE, TOO

YOU DIDN'T SEEM to mind a fellow's drawing close against you, even as you bled. His little mitt nested on worn pants just above your crank. Your grin was relaxed, secure, if fairly tired. (Did you already guess what it would cost us?)

Still Ideal Captain of My Fellow Ship, my first "rainbow," "big one," at times I feel so sound and lucky. I myself never got caught, never did get sick. My very occupation is to tell the truth—as much as will still sell.

I feel I owe you everything, Dan. Times, it seems they did my damage all to you.

I bet you're still in the world. Your youngest kid finished college, what? twenty years ago. You are barely seventy. That, increasingly, is not all that old. I'm forty-eight already. The hair on your arms must be mostly silver now, not unattractive. I sense you ended up in Arizona, maybe Colorado, somewhere dry out there.

Are you still her husband? Or by now splitting house payments with another guy? But, no, I picture you as living alone. I picture a blue car, your climbing into it, driving to some modest restaurant, coming back home, stretching, putting hands on hips, going back inside.

DESPITE MY THERAPY and the wish to think well of myself, I am still a subdivision of desire. Here I choose to end it.

I am the horny guilty husband, noticing one sullen blond boy slouched at the urinal three down; I move his way, beckoned by his head wave, and one slow wink, and something that he shows me.

I am the blond boy, aware of my poisonous beauty, ready for Dad to pop out of that green stall with a black camera in lieu of his pink face. For now, I'm mostly a youngster enjoying the weight of my blood-stocked dick. I am feeling the full power of being male, which means, in an odd way, being fatal for others.

And, alas, I am also, alas, the tortured ex-Marine cop, forty pounds over his Parris Island weight, a major smoker, rifle collector, registered Republican with fifteen long years till retirement, a disappointed man who—having built rabbit-catching boxes as a boy, finds entrapment lots more fun than giving speeding tickets. He is also a guy whose own sexual fantasies let him display his son (nearly as pretty as he once was). He does it in order to catch the vermin he sees swarming everywhere, the shameless weirdos who'll be the death of this Great Land, the queers that he knows want, most obsessively of all, *him*.

Sure, he might have drinking probs and the so-so marriage and no further prospect of promotion anywhere near even assistant chief, but at least he's not *that* far gone. He is the detective about to detect. Sick behavior like.

Mine. Like Dan's. And I keep silent, in a stall already unlatched for kicking open at lethal speed. I prepare the necessary flashbulb I'm about to insert into its reflector socket. I hear whispering. Good boy, my son is waving the perpetrator closer. I prepare the flashbulb. The glass sphere's metal tip I dampen with my tongue. I am ready, now, I breathe, I kick toward desire illegal. The blast in a tile space this small is a cannon going off. I holler "FRee-eeze!" at heat. And I capture, for eternity, the Older Me just as I touch the healthy prong of Me Young. And, armed with pictures of me molesting myself, I am going to have to turn me in. Otherwise, admit it—I'd be less than a whole man.

Hey, Dan? Missed you.
Find me, sir.

Yaddo, 1975

FISHING PRACTICE

Philip Bockman

ABOVE THE SOUNDS of screaming and laughter and the blare of the jukebox playing Dinah Washington's "What a Difference a Day Makes," I could hear the telephone ringing loudly behind the bar. On the stage at the far end of the room, Lotta Love, her six-foot-five, nearly naked black body glistening under the hot lights, stopped lip-synching, straightened her blond wig during the violin interlude, and yelled, "If that's my father, tell him I'm not here!" It was the standard joke at Toledo's favorite gay bar, that autumn of 1961, which someone would always quip whenever the phone rang. The crowd laughed, as usual, then cheered and applauded Lotta, who ate it up so eagerly that she almost missed her cue when the interlude ended and Ms. Washington launched tremulously into the second verse.

"It's for you, honey—yeah, you, Phil baby!" Big Penny the bartender pointed at me over the heads of the people jammed together along the bar. She always pointed with her thumb, keeping the fingers of her right hand curled in a fist, ready, as she put it, "to punch somebody out if I need to." She handed me the receiver with a serious look, whispering as I took it from her, "It's your father."

"Oh, come on," I protested. "That's just a joke."

But Big Penny's face remained serious. She raised her painted eyebrows ominously and shrugged her shoulders.

I held the receiver tight against my ear, straining to hear over the noise in the bar. The voice on the line was carefully controlled. It sounded far away and oddly expressionless, compared with the laughter around me.

"Son? This is your father. I'm in your room at the university. Come back here right now. Please don't waste any time. I'll be waiting for you."

Stunned, I listened to my own voice answering dutifully, mechanically, as if I were merely lip-synching, like Lotta: "Yes, Dad. Okay. I'll get there as soon as I can."

It was about an hour's drive from Toledo to the University of Michigan. Usually it was a fun ride, since I always took a carful of other students with me. My lemon-yellow Studebaker had even been dubbed the "Fairy Ferry." But now the thought of making that drive alone ... and to meet Dad—Dad! What did he want? How had he gotten the number of the bar? What had he found out?

It was so strange to hear his voice in a place like this. It took me a minute to fully believe it had happened. Then suddenly I felt cold. Doom clutched at my stomach. I motioned to Penny to give me another vodka tonic, which she produced with a sympathetic smile, God bless her—Penny whose nonfisted free hand served her underage clients unquestioningly, providing us with an endless flow of motherly concern, free advice, and, if we wanted it, oblivion.

I gulped down the drink and my mind began spinning. I tried to focus on the scene in front of me: the roomful of people laughing and chattering, dancing and making out; smoke hanging like wisps of cloud over the sunset glow of the red lights; the figure of Lotta Love, tirelessly gyrating to the beat of "Do the Mashed Potato" on the stage, though most of her audience had taken up the dance and were no longer paying attention.

A hand holding a beer bottle reached toward me from between the faces of two boys who were dancing very close together. It was Earl. He pushed his way between them and puckered for a kiss. His lips were hot and sweaty and I withdrew from them quickly.

"You'll never find a new husband if you kiss like that," he warned me with gentle sarcasm. "Why are you standing here all by yourself, anyway?"

I told him about the phone call. He stood with his mouth hanging open, blue eyes uncomprehending under the delicate strands of his blond bangs. It was strange to see him at a loss for words. It was so uncharacteristic. Earl was the first gay person I'd met at school. He had introduced me to the others—including Bob, with whom I'd fallen instantly in love. Our affair had been brief, but I still kept one of Bob's love letters tucked away behind the bottom drawer of my built-in dresser at home, so I would always remember the feelings he'd had for me.

Far from being jealous, Earl had set himself up as my "gay mother," a mentor who would watch over me and keep me out of trouble. It was Earl who had taught me to carry a hundred dollars on me at all times, in case I was arrested by an undercover cop, and Earl who had urged me to memorize the telephone numbers of my gay friends and never write them down. Most pertinently at this moment, it was Earl who had warned me never to tell anyone I was gay.

"My god," he said, "how did he know to call you here? He must have found out somehow." He stared at me with a look between horror and pity. Then his voice rose in a lilting bravado. "Well, you must deny it, of course! You must talk him out of it, whatever you do! My god! This is terrible!"

Silently, I agreed with him. I did not want Dad to know. In that era nearly everyone thought of "queers" as sick and depraved, drooling perverts who preyed on innocent children. I could not imagine what it would be like to have Dad think of me that way. But there was more—much more—at stake than my father's good opinion.

Earl brushed his long hair up onto his forehead. In the near darkness, his eyes seemed to have lost their sky-blue brilliance, their buoyant cheerfulness. Reflections of the red lights flickered in them as he asked in a hushed voice, "Are you scared?"

We gazed at each other. I found myself thinking about the night not long before when three heterosexual teenagers had somehow managed to get past the mafioso bouncer at the door of the bar. Rushing in, they'd grabbed me, pushed me down, and raised their metal-cleated boots over my face. Just in time, Big Penny had come out swinging, bloodying one's nose and knocking the others' heads together with a resounding crack. Everyone had stopped dancing, but when she returned from tossing them into the street there was no cheering, no applause, not even a wry remark. The bar was silent, except for the jukebox. Terror had broken through the laughter—the camp humor and the brittle wit by which we sought to distract ourselves from the fragility of our existence.

Our only protection was secrecy. We even had a password, by which we identified ourselves in those days when very few dared to be "obvious": "I'm a friend of Dorothy's." If people didn't get it, you knew they weren't gay. A gay person would answer, "I am, too," with a knowing smile. Perhaps we chose this reference to *The Wizard of Oz* because Judy Garland sang songs with which we identified, ballads of hope and despair, love and rejection: the contradictions of our double lives.

The music suddenly seemed overwhelming, pounding in my ears. Someone had turned up the jukebox. I thought of all the good times I'd had here and in the homes of the men I'd met, nights of laughter and passionate conversation, endless discussions of philosophies and experiences. Shared bodies. Shared dreams.

The place seemed to grate on me now. A kick line was assembling on the stage to the rhythm of "I Wish That I Could Shimmy Like My Sister Kate." Yes, it was fun. But would it do for a life, I asked myself—a life in exile from the rest of the world?

Although my head had cleared, I felt confused as I reached for a hug from Earl and he wrapped his arms around me. I loved Earl deeply. He was my best friend, my gay mother, my fellow outlaw. There was no way I could ever give all this up. On the contrary, I wanted to affirm it, proclaim it loudly. Yet at the other end of the hour's drive ahead of me there was something else I wanted, too—wanted more consciously, more painfully than ever before. What would I do when I got there? What would I say to my father?

The night air did little to revive me. I swerved onto the narrow country highway without checking for oncoming traffic. Flooring the Studebaker, I plowed along the pavement under the dark sky full of stars, scarcely caring whether I lived or died. I found a good station on the radio and turned it up full blast. They were playing the ubiquitous Dinah Washington. The significance of "What a Difference a Day Makes" dawned on me like the punch line of a bad joke, and I tried to sustain a laugh; but it kept turning, in spite of me, to tears.

Through my tears I watched the speedometer edge past eighty, ninety, a hundred, stopping only when it could climb no farther. A wave of drowsiness washed through my mind and my eyes clouded. I didn't see the truck until it flashed its brights and blew its horn. What was it doing on my side of the road, coming straight toward me?

A few seconds later I awoke as if from a dream. Somehow, miraculously, I had managed to swerve, and the white line reappeared in front of me. The sound of the truck's horn diminished like the whistle of a passing train. I jerked my foot off the accelerator and clutched the steering wheel in my sweating hands. "Oh, my god," I gasped out loud. "What am I doing? What's happening to me?"

I had always enjoyed driving down unlit country highways at night, finding it strangely comforting, like being borne along in a kind of portable womb, protected by the plush familiarity of the sweet-smelling upholstery, safe against the dangers of the unknown into which I ventured so eagerly. At nineteen I thought of myself as a rebel—even an outcast—who had left behind the stulti-fying conformity of my parents' way of life in the winding streets of their neat little Grand Rapids suburb. But I'd never really left it behind. It had been easy to reject, knowing it would always be there. Now, as I contemplated confessing, "Yes, I'm a homosexual," I realized that those four words could banish me from that world forever. The night sky with its millions of stars had wrapped me like a blanket when I was a child; now it seemed remote and indifferent, more like a pall. Nothing could protect me if I uttered those words. If I crossed that line, there would be no going back.

Yet somehow I had always known it was inevitable. I had first sensed I was different at the age of six, when I had gone to see a Tarzan movie with my eight-year-old neighbor Joey. Coming out of the theater, Joey had exclaimed, "Gee, that Jane is really sexy, isn't she?" Startled, I felt as if he'd put up a barrier between us for the first time. I'd always thought our closeness was inviolable. Night after night, in his upstairs bedroom under the eaves, we'd explored each other's bodies, kissed each other's lips, tormented each other with a tingling ecstasy.

Having no word for it, I was nevertheless in love, and had thought Joey was, too. As he blithely stated his delight in another—female!—body, I realized it was not the same for him. Like all the other boys in the theater (I thought then), Joey had been focusing on Jane, while only I had waited breathlessly for every glimpse of Tarzan's glistening muscles. I was alone, my feelings unacceptable. And I knew instinctively that I could never reveal them, not even to Joey. I felt condemned as I spoke the required words: "Yeah, I thought Jane was sexy, too."

Now, as the road signs reflecting in the headlights began to proclaim that I was nearing Ann Arbor, I remembered the deadly seriousness in Earl's voice as he'd kissed me good-bye at the door of the bar and warned me to think of the consequences. Yet I could not make up my mind.

If I denied it, I thought, I was betraying myself. If I admitted it, I was betraying Earl, too. Whatever I did, I couldn't win. A hundred times I weighed the dismal alternatives, growing more and more anxious as the university buildings began to slink past and finally the snug, sleeping houses of Forrest Street appeared.

Turning into the driveway of the run-down Victorian mansion where I rented a room, I switched off the lights and sat for a moment looking at Dad's black Chevy on the other side of the drive. Feeling like a terrible coward, unworthy of the man who had tried so hard to raise me to be like him, unworthy as well of Earl's devotion, and of the love I'd shared with Bob in this very house, I sadly concluded that no, I could not tell him. I would insist that it was all a misunderstanding. I would appeal to him to continue to believe in me. I would say anything I had to say to get out of it. I couldn't bear the thought of his disgust.

Dad sat in my overstuffed chair, reading one of my textbooks. He closed the book slowly, pausing as if to finish a paragraph, then placed it gently on the table under the brown-shaded lamp. As I approached, he leaned back, but did not look at me. His pale gray eyes seemed weary behind his reading glasses, the white flecks in his hair more numerous than I remembered.

"We'd better get going," he said hoarsely, still not looking in my direction. He gathered up his jacket and preceded me out the door.

If my drive from Toledo had been excruciating, it was nothing compared with the drive to Grand Rapids, sitting next to Dad in the front seat of the Chevy. He wouldn't speak, beyond a few words in response to my worried questions.

"How did you get the phone number?"

"A friend of yours."

"What did you want to see me about?"

"That can wait."

"Does Mother know about this?"

"Yes, she does."

And so on. Finally I stopped asking, and we rode the rest of the way in silence.

When we got home, Mother came down to greet us. She was wearing her nightgown with a robe over it, complaining that her back was hurting her. Dad volunteered to make sandwiches.

"Sandwiches?" she snapped irritably. "Don't be silly. I've got everything ready. I just have to heat it up. It'll only take a minute. Sit down, both of you." When Dad started to object, she cut him off firmly. "I'm not helpless, you know."

After that no one dared to say anything. We ate self-consciously under the plastic sunflower-head chandelier. I'd always hated the tacky kitchen with its green and orange flower motif, but now I kept following the patterns of leaves and daisies on the shiny tablecloth, miserable with the thought that I might be banished forever from the warmth of that awful chandelier and all the love this stifling room suddenly seemed to represent—the love that had struggled to congeal in this glaring circle of light for so many years.

Mother would not let us help with the dishes. Dad sat with one arm across his stomach and the other propping up his chin. I feared that any minute now he would issue the opening statement of the argument—like so many other arguments that had taken place here in this room, only much, much worse, reverberating with all those previous interrogations: Why were you out so late? Where have you been? What have you been doing that you can't tell us about? We've tried so hard, we're so proud of you—everyone thinks so highly of you—all the neighbors will be wondering. What do you want them to think? But when he finally spoke, it was only to suggest that we go to bed and talk in the morning.

I awoke to find him sitting on the edge of my bed. He must have been there for a long time, looking at me. "What does this mean?" he asked, holding a letter in his shaking hand, suppressing tears with a great effort. I recognized the fine blue handwriting. I'd read and reread it so many times. It was my love letter from Bob.

I was shocked, feeling frightened and betrayed. Mother had a habit of going through my wallet, but I realized now that in one of her relentless search-and-destroy missions against all dust and dirt she must have dismantled my dresser and found the letter.

I looked into Dad's teary eyes. So she had put him up to this, left him to do the dirty work. I remembered the distaste with which he used to spank me with a willow branch on my bare bottom at Mother's insistence. All those years he had carried out her orders, never once coming to my defense against her notion of what I "needed." And here he was now, doing it again—hating it again.

I felt sorry for him. I hesitated a minute, wishing to spare him—wishing to spare both of us. But I'd lain awake most of the night thinking about it, and I'd made up my mind. I couldn't face going back to two separate worlds. I had to take the risk. I had to let go of the lies that had damned me.

I swallowed hard and said, "You probably have all kinds of misconceptions about what it means. Society knows nothing about us. We live in secret. But I want to share my life with you. I want you to know who I am. I'm a homosexual."

It was the first time I'd ever told someone who wasn't gay. It felt strange—especially saying "homosexual." But I couldn't say "gay"; no one but gays knew what it meant in those days.

Dad's lower lip hung down in amazement, then twisted with disgust. The word *homosexual* hung oddly in the small space between us, as if I'd said *fuck*, another word forbidden in our household. Tears rolled out of his gray eyes. "Oh, god!" he breathed hoarsely. "You know, those guys get together and—" He jerked his head from side to side, as if to shake away some awful vision. The intensity of his pain filled me with anguish. This, then, was the price of crossing the line. I asked myself if it was worth it, half wishing I could take it back. But the deed was done, irrevocable.

He cried for a while, his face in his hands. I was deeply shaken. What must he think of me? His idea of queers was probably not much different from that of the boys in the locker room, who regularly insulted each other with this worst of all possible curses. From a religious standpoint, he must certainly consider me a sinner. And he would surely be disappointed that I would not be carrying on the Bockman name, of which he was so proud. There would be no marriage, no grandchildren. Worst of all, there was his terrible vision— of two men getting together and . . .

He stopped crying and began asking me half-whispered questions: What would my life be like? What were the dangers? What were my chances of happiness? More than anything, he was concerned about me. If Mother had put him up to this, he had clearly abandoned her mission. The questions were his own. If they trembled with sorrow, it was the sorrow of his own heart.

The ultimate question, of course, was, "How can we tell Mother?" He asked it with his characteristic worried look—knotted brow and tightened lips. We toyed with a number of ideas, all of them unworkable, futile on the battlefield we both knew so well. But we had to find an answer. For a while it seemed we had reentered our old world as we struggled to find a solution. After a long period of silence during which we both sat thinking, he said in a low, almost plaintive, voice, "There's only one thing I can think of. We really don't have any choice. Would you consider . . ." He hesitated. "Would you be willing—just to make her feel better—to see a doctor . . . a psychiatrist?"

I'm sure he saw the disappointment in my eyes. So he was going to let me down, after all—side with her, after all, just like always. Yet I had to admit he was right. She was ill, she was in pain, she would never understand, she would never accept it.

Mother had always been uncomfortable with physical intimacy. Daughter of an abusive father who eventually deserted the family, she had zealously determined that her own house would squeak with cleanliness and order. Propriety was scrupulously observed, kisses a matter of pecks on the cheek. She rarely embraced me, except after a violent argument, when she'd burst into tears and need me to soothe her. As in everything else, Dad had gone along. When I reached adolescence, he had stopped kissing me altogether, explaining that grown men didn't do such things.

Yet as I reluctantly agreed to see a psychiatrist for Mother's sake, Dad suddenly leaned over and kissed me, then hugged me tightly. It was a little awkward for both of us, but I couldn't help feeling hopeful. Perhaps, after all, this was a beginning, not the end Earl had predicted.

Finally, Dad and I stood before Mother's bed, where she cushioned herself from the pain in her back. It was a little bit easier to utter the words, "I'm a homosexual." She cried, long and inconsolably. Though it was hard for me to watch her, I stood my ground, vaguely understanding that my confession was also a declaration of independence from her. I wanted her to know and accept me for who I really was. Only at the last minute, reminded by Dad's beseeching eyes, I added, with a mouthful of bitter gall, that I would see a psychiatrist.

They made an appointment for me with one of the top psychiatrists at the university. I did not look forward to seeing him. I had read enough to know that homosexuality was considered a pathology and that psychiatrists often tried to make you heterosexual—"normal." I had no intention of allowing that.

I had a real chip on my shoulder as I entered the doctor's office. But soon I was laughing—and so was he. I had met him at a party on campus during my freshman year. He, too, was a friend of Dorothy.

My parents were fighting when I walked in, on my next trip home a few weeks later, but not quite as fiercely as usual. Most of the day was consumed in pleasantries. Once, when we were alone, looking at some books that had belonged to her father, Mother began to talk about the "old days." "I had such a horrible childhood," she said. "I know my father loved me, but he never told me so. He was terribly severe, Mennonite, you know. He mortified me by making me wear long black stockings to school. I never forgave him for that. It was so humiliating. None of the other girls had to wear them." Her hand, pink with the ravages of years of cleaning, explored the deep embossing on one of the leather bindings, then came to rest reverently, as if on some sacred object. "Yet I wish I'd told him how much I loved him," she added softly. Tears came to her eyes, and I held her hand to comfort her. She made no effort to embrace me, but I felt she was indicating a new kind of respect for me, perhaps trying to let go a little, for the first time. In her own way, she was telling me she loved me.

The rest of the weekend was strangely subdued. Everyone went about their business as if nothing unusual had happened. The doctor was never mentioned. They seemed to want to forget the whole thing. But now there was an extra distance, a kid-gloves caution in every statement, every gesture. Even when we talked, I felt I was getting the silent treatment.

Finally, on Sunday night, after I turned out my light, Dad opened the door of my bedroom a crack.

"May I come in?"

I said yes. He tiptoed in and sat for a moment on the edge of the bed.

"How's it going?" he asked.

"All right," I replied.

"Good," he said. "You know I'm all for you."

Then he leaned down and kissed my brow and squeezed my arm.

"Good night."

ONCE, I EXPRESSED my frustration to my father about the "silent treatment." "We're trying," he explained. "Please give us time." He smiled, and I was reminded of an incident from my childhood, at about the age of six. He had taken me fishing. He hauled in one fish after the other, while I caught none. At the end of the day, I burst out crying. Kneeling beside me, he told me gently, "Don't be too sad. Remember, it takes a long time to get good at something. Be patient. Don't think of today as fishing, just think of it as 'fishing practice.'"

Years later, when I brought home my first long-term lover, my parents accepted him as part of the family. By then all our friends and other members of the family knew about me. (I had told them about Stonewall and the Gay Activists Alliance in New York. They had read about us in the newspapers and magazines.) Yet they were still reluctant to talk about it. Occasionally, Mother would ask how I was doing with "that problem," but she never waited for an answer. Maybe she would have with time; unfortunately, she died young, of breast cancer, and there was never the opportunity.

Dad's widowerhood and the breakup with my lover coincided. We comforted each other about our losses, exchanged feelings about learning to live alone again, and spoke of our longing for companionship. He began dating, over the objections of his scandalized neighbors. Increasingly isolated, he turned to me for advice. I told him that from my own experience I thought he would discover who his real friends were by simply continuing to do what he needed to do. He saw that I was right, and it brought us even closer together.

Then he met the woman who would become his second wife, and I met the man who would share my life for the next eighteen years. My new stepmother began our relationship by asking, "Is he just a friend, or is it more than that?" "He's my lover," I answered. "Good," she responded. "I wouldn't want to be your mother without knowing something as important as that." Since her arrival, our family has become much more expressive—showing our feelings for each other, demonstrating love and affection—and they've "come out" about their gay son to all their acquaintances. They've lost some friends in the process, and some family members have distanced themselves, but that's never deterred them. What we've gained as a family has been well worth the risks.

COMING OUT.
GOING BACK IN.
COMING OUT AGAIN.
ETC.

Brad Gooch

I CAME THROUGH a door into another room in myself when I was thirteen, in 1965. That's when I started doing it with—let's call him Dirk. His real name was much less sexy. Dirk, twelve, lived up the street.

I first met Dirk when I was five. We had just moved to a two-family house one Pennsylvania town away from where I'd been born. As I was idling about the giant wheels of the moving van, Dirk appeared on the opposite side of a tire. We went off to play in the sun as it baked the sidewalks. He guided me to the end of the street.

For many years our friendship was platonic. We played games. We dressed up as a priest and a minister. We shuddered when lightning preceded a storm that dumped needles of rain onto the glamorous (to me) lilac tree on my front lawn. Together we pressed colored leaves into wax. Together we lay on the grass feeling the earth turn as we made clouds into Rorschach tests. We watched soap operas on his mother's TV. We visited the brewery where his father worked. We discussed the comparative salaries, cars, and religious denominations of our parents.

Then things changed very quickly. It was a summer evening. We were on the second floor of my house playing Monopoly. As an only child, I had an entire room devoted to my games and toys, practically an entire floor. Like some sort of visitation from a Universal Archetype, an impulse made itself known to my brain to put my mouth on Dirk's sticky penis to create a wonderful warmth. I don't know where the idea came from exactly. Soon all the boys at school seemed to be discussing such activities with loud scorn and hilarity and obvious experience or interest. But this night was perhaps the summer before the fall when the boys began mouthing off on the subject. So its inception remains a mystery to me.

Well. Not entirely a mystery. During the previous winter and spring I had been exploding with strange notions. The first occurred when I rubbed up and down on my double bed, which formerly belonged to my grandmother, while gazing at the cover of the Christmas edition of *War Cry*, the Salvation Army magazine. The cover illustration showed a pirate in big boots he stuck out toward the face of the reader. I don't know what that mustachioed villain had to do with Christmas or the Salvation Army, but as a future reader of *Drummer* magazine, I caught on immediately. Then I began to replace him in the magic lantern of my mind with boys in my classes doing piratical things. I wound up filling my pants with a sweet-smelling cream. I think I naturally, and empathically, transferred those sensations to Dirk, or wanted him to feel them, too. We didn't go all the way that humid evening as the little plastic houses on Boardwalk and Park Place scattered, along with all the pastel-colored paper money, but it was the beginning of an affair that would last on and off for the next two years.

Dirk was lanky, olive-skinned, part Italian, part Irish. His straight hair fell over his skull like a fox's, or like Rimbaud's. Sometimes he seemed to me a young Abraham Lincoln because of his tall boniness. What were his passions? I can't remember exactly. I remember mine. I liked to lie on his bed while he watched *Get Smart*, smelling his socks on his oversized feet. I liked to wait for him while he confessed on Saturday afternoons at the Roman Catholic white clapboard church. I wondered if he confessed about me. I'm sure he didn't, or he wouldn't have walked out of there so jauntily. What did he wear? He wore chinos. He wore the kind of nylon socks old men wear. He wore the striped shirts moms buy for their kids. He liked to watch TV, as did I. He didn't get grades as high as mine. I believe he owned a lava lamp. He had an older sister who had already moved out, so he was virtually an only child, too. But much about him is a blank. Of course the blank is really in me. What made him tick? I didn't care that much, I suppose. I was a bit of a Maria Callas, waiting for my chance to go on stage. As are many misfit kids. I appreciated his laid-back quality. It didn't impinge on my high-strung melancholy.

I could catalog our tiny adventures. I think I will. But I've chosen our two-year affair mostly because it's somehow still an X ray of my life today.

My exploration of Dirk over the Monopoly board was driven by daring, curiosity, and sexual euphoria. I was magnetized. The trouble I was getting into was part of a phase. I was also in trouble for riding my girl cousin like a horse, for which I was driven out of the house by my aunt. And something was up between me and the older girl down the street who tutored me in math. My mother forbade me to have any more geometry lessons.

My affair with Dirk was characterized by strict roles we'd now define, or in the seventies would have defined, as "top" and "bottom." There was no penetration. That was a distant craggy horizon I don't even remember considering. But there were feet and there were penises, and of course there were power plays. There wasn't love. Certainly not in the sense Malcolm Muggeridge meant when he said that love is the extra bit you do for someone you don't feel like doing. (But then, is any teenage boy "in love" with any teenage girl? No.) Closer perhaps would be Dante overthinking his love for the nine-year-old Beatrice in *La Vita Nuova*, with all its implications of fear, desire, and control. I took care of Dirk in his closet. I took care of Dirk while he lounged on a beach chair in the garage. I even put whipped cream and a pineapple ring on his penis and ate the entire glop off as if it were an ice-cream sundae.

When Dirk and I were alone together, I was always (to use Auden's phrase) "the more loving one." But like boyfriends who cruise the bars together for a third, we shared an attraction to other boys. When Dirk wasn't the young master and I the young slave, we were two teenage girls on the prowl. Not that we ever actually scored. We were often attracted to the same guys.

First there was Matt. (Or was it Francis?) Dirk claimed that Matt had forced him down into one of the moats surrounding the high school, where he inflicted various humiliations upon him: spitting, name-calling, eliciting promises of favors. Sometimes Matt would call on the Princess phone while I was at Dirk's. There was talk of the three of us getting together. I pictured the moats when I rubbed up and down on the couch in my parents' living room. (I was partly getting back at them for not allowing my dog on the furniture in that sacrosanct parlor devoted to newspaper reading and television watching.) Dirk claimed to have participated in a circle jerk with Matt, beneath the ancient chestnut tree that had been the terminus of our walk to the corner on that first moving day.

Eddie the paperboy, with whom we both flirted, forced me to lick his dirty P. F. Flyers on Dirk's porch one summer afternoon. I was mortified to catch Dirk's father watching us through the living room curtains. He and his son obviously both had a touch of the voyeur.

Together Dirk and I lured and groped Richard, a curious introvert with black circles beneath the bright slits of his eyes who spent most of his time in his bedroom projecting eight-millimeter movies of Dracula, the Werewolf, and Lady Godiva. Richard's mother was a single parent who didn't mind her son's collection of *Playboy* magazines. Eventually Dirk became creeped out by Richard's musty old castle of a bedroom. I stayed behind to watch his creaky flicks over and over again.

One night on a dare to each other, Dirk and I crawled down the pavement of our street on our hands and knees to prove our kinkiness—competing, as a witty New York friend later put it, for the bottom—terrified the entire time that a parent or friend would drive by. At the chestnut tree we turned into bipeds again and walked the few blocks to the school yard.

My mother hated the school yard. That's where I learned the word *fuck*, which I proudly used at the dinner table, causing her to start crying. The asphalt school yard, at dusk, was the gathering field of hoods, older boys, and generally more independent types than Dirk and me. That night we ran into Marty, a basketball player and, later, captain of the golf team. Marty's voice had been one of the first in my class to change. His eyebrows had grown together across his forehead like a dash.

Dirk and I were both pleased that he was taking time for us. The encounter began with Marty forcing us into a backyard with a high hedge on the sidewalk side that came up to his chest. He spit on us and we tried to dodge the big globs as they came flying our way, giggling, tripping over our own feet. This trial was reminiscent of the time two hoods locked us in a basement and threw rocks through the casement windows while Dirk and I cowered behind an oil burner. The spitting spate ended quickly that evening, however. We then walked with Marty to the stone steps of the stately brick high school, across the street.

We sat down. Marty spit directly on the steps and swirled the goo around with his finger while efficiently filling us in on the facts of life: Boys screw girls to make babies. Even moms and dads? Yup. Nooooo! Sensing a window of opportunity, I pried for details about his liaisons with Patsy, a girl whose breasts I'd noticed developing about the same time as Marty's voice was deepening. He confirmed that the rumors were true: She did indeed swallow him. He bragged that he had black hairs around his penis. He pointedly invited me to verify those wiry hairs if I would step into the lav with him after gym class one day. I never took him up on his offer.

When Dirk and I returned to Dirk's front yard we were both reeling. Partly from the information about reproduction. Partly from the deep violet air tinged with fireflies. Mostly from being with Marty. From that night on the two of us constituted a fractured Natalie Wood from *Splendor in the Grass*. Marty was our Bud. Our idol.

What I lacked in coming out, I made up for in exhibitionism. When my parents took us for a drive in their burgundy Ford Galaxy, I would sit in the back seat mussing Dirk's hair, trying to kiss him, groping. They pretended not to see or hear any evil. One morning we dressed up in our mothers' clothes, I in a red dress, pearls, and white, waxy, wobbly heels. We stepped into the June air. Dirk held back. I made it all the way to the end of the driveway and out onto the street. Many a time I was caught by Dirk's mom with my hand down her son's pants. A large Italian lady with elaborate eyeglasses studded with fake jewels, she always forgave me, with a heaping plate of spaghetti covered in red sauce. Why not? We shared a passion for *As the World Turns*.

When I was fifteen, Dirk moved a few blocks away. Then an entire city away. To visit him required planning, transportation, logistics. Without the ease of impulsively and secretly slipping into his garage—one of our favorite spots—our affair gradually wound down. He was also becoming standoffish, like David toward his teenage amour in *Giovanni's Room*. All of a sudden, Dirk seemed to have qualms. The upside was that with age he had begun to emit a bunch of musty new smells I loved. Dirk briefly became my human lick-'n'-sniff card. Such were the pleasures of full-blown puberty. Eventually, though, we lost touch forever. I heard an unconfirmed rumor a decade later that he'd become a dancer. And then no more rumors. The phone went dead.

I went a bit dead, too. For a few years I reverted to sexual nothingness, a sort of android existence. It was the late sixties, so there was lots for an android to do: protest, smoke pot, buy records. When I was nineteen I arrived at Columbia College. I had never sweated my sexuality, though I can't say why I hadn't moved on from Dirk to a Matt or a Terry or a John. Maybe I just didn't meet the right teenage boy, or the right forty-five-year-old man. Within a day of arriving on campus, I visited the Gay Lounge in the basement of Furnald Hall. There I met the president of the campus gay group, Morty Manford. I told him how gay I was. He introduced me to the dean of housing, who was also gay, and pulled a string to get me a better dorm room. I met W. H. Auden when he came to the lounge, his face as lined as a catcher's mitt, his eyes quick and catching. I thought: This gay stuff is really a lot of fun.

I did feel ever so slightly guilty, as if I had maybe lied to Morty since I had never actually had sex with a man. I had never even discussed the matter with anyone before appearing full-blown on the doormat of the Gay Lounge. In my mind I held on to Dirk as my visa—but he was already so long ago and far away, and many have brushed off such adolescent crushes without claiming gay status. I felt uneasy. Like an illegal alien.

One weekend Morty took me to the International Stud, where I stared down at the floor the entire time. All I remember of that bar are a bunch of shoes and a first brush with the searchlight known as Last Call. The next weekend Morty took me to the Firehouse, a dance hall in SoHo run by the Gay Activists Alliance, where I finally met someone and revealed my character in action. Passport stamped!

What came out of me when I was thirteen was a whole galaxy of feeling that hasn't changed much since. Only the faces have changed. And the bodies. And the locales. I never did come out to my parents. They didn't ask, so I didn't tell. But I had a lover with whom I visited them on Thanksgivings and Christmases over eleven years. The last year, as he was dying of AIDS, we hired a driver, a nurse, and rolled him in a wheelchair. They were quite loving and accepting of the entire passion play. So I let them off the hook without the formal coming out, the saying of the words, or word.

I still don't feel inclined to disclose a particular word with pinpoint accuracy: *gay*. Yet I feel an inordinate need to confess, reveal, tell all. I find that men on men (to borrow another anthology's title) still constitute a pileup of friendship, doggy lust, domesticity, outsider thrills, and wrestling matches. When I meet someone, I know less and less whether I want to be friends, husband and husband, teammates, monks, or outlaws. Life grows more complicated, rather than simpler. And I have the odd, ever-present feeling that I'll be coming out again at least one more time before I die.

Now what could that mean?

MEMORIES OF HEIDELBERG

Andrew Holleran

PEOPLE ASKED TO explain male homosexual promiscuity in the seventies often came up with the theory of delayed gratification, which goes like this: Since most gay men struggling with their sexual orientation were celibate during adolescence—when heterosexual peers were not—gay men were simply making up for a long period of starvation.

And it's true that people fall into two categories when they tell their coming-out stories, it seemed to me years ago when every new friendship in gay life entailed an explanation of How I Got Here: those who knew they were gay when they were three years old, and those who kept the truth from themselves just as long as they could, horrified by the implications. For the latter, the remarkable part of their coming out was not the actual debut but what preceded it, I always thought: the long, glacial period of denial.

I was always skeptical of those who said they knew they were homosexual in the bassinet—how can one know such a thing then, much less remember it?—but I knew just what the others were talking about when they told me they were twenty-six before they admitted to themselves certain facts. (There are men, of course, who marry, father children, and wait until their sixties before coming out; but these seemed to me as rare as the people who claim they knew in their crib.) Most people, surely, fall somewhere in between. And their stories of coming out are always inextricably tied to the tale of what preceded it—the long, arduous, humiliating attempt to pretend that the door had not even opened to that forbidden room. Their coming-out tales really begin with the first moment they heard the hinges creak and realized they would have to go through life alone, rather than in the usual crowd that most adolescents like to travel in, no matter what they're doing.

That is at least where mine would begin—in sixth grade, when boys and girls finally started to mix socially at parties, and I experienced a brief golden age of popularity based on my ability to jitterbug (it was 1955) with several popular girls. The reason was simple: Sex suddenly lay beneath the surface of Society. Even that of twelve-year-olds. When asked by Sally McGrew into the dark bedroom of a party for a kiss in sixth grade—the girls got to make requests—I pretended to stub my toe, cracked my shin on the furniture the minute I closed the door behind me, and fell across the bed, like Jerry Lewis in a movie, rather than search for her in the suffocating darkness. A week after that profound embarrassment I stopped going out—and began spending Saturday nights at home with a peanut butter sandwich and a novel called *The Robe*. *The Robe* was succeeded by *The Silver Chalice*. When Garry S. walked home with Bonnie F., they stopped, Garry said, every three steps to kiss; when I walked home with Bonnie, I discussed Religion, God, and the Future of Mankind. No girl could linger long enough alone with me, in a dark bedroom, or on a path along the beach; no glance could be pregnant enough to interrupt my speculation on the Miracle of Fátima; I was not about to cross that space of terrifying air between our two young bodies. I remained a consecrated virgin.

The son of a minister who lived down the street was more fun to be alone with in an empty house, of course; but after a few such sessions, I realized I wanted to play the games we played much more than he, and the realization was the sound of a door opening I did not want to hear. Even at the age of twelve this was a lesson in unrequited desire, if not love; in being different from someone else of the same gender. Not good, I thought subconsciously; and I went back to *Quo Vadis*.

And that was how I addressed the issue of sexual awakening. I read my way through puberty, living in the ancient past while classmates went forward—in parked cars down at the pet cemetery, on beaches, at parties, at home afterward. Even in college, when a date offered me her face for a good-night kiss, I stood there politely discussing *The Divine Comedy* while the couples around us mashed their faces together during the last ten minutes before the women had to sign back into their dormitory. When I complained about this to a psychiatrist in Student Health, the suntanned father of five, smiling in a large framed picture on his desk, dismissed my fears about homosexuality by saying, "It's simple. Next time, kiss her."

There was no next time. I retreated even more deeply into the library. I spent the next several years with books, in college and graduate school. Not till I was drafted into the army in 1968 at the age of twenty-four did I find myself for the first time forced to deal with human beings in a nonacademic setting, and with their common preoccupations: Sex and Gender.

I took a paperback of *Myra Breckinridge* with me to basic training, like an antidote, and read it whenever I had a moment to myself; but mostly those few months were Life unmediated by Literature. I was back in a sort of all-boys' summer camp among males my age, all males, who went on marches, ran obstacle courses, shouted at sergeants in voices the sergeants claimed were not loud enough. One of the verses we shouted while running through the woods before breakfast contained the refrain "Jody's got your girl and gone," but while this thought (of the girlfriend you'd left behind to follow your country's call) may have actually bothered some of the other men in my platoon, I knew this lyric was inapplicable to my own case as I jogged through the dark pine trees. Jody could have my girl, I thought; I didn't have one. One evening, toward the end of basic training, a very handsome sergeant who looked like a mountie in *Rose Marie* (*Indian Love Call*) found me idly turning the pages of the only thing I could find to read in the barracks—an old *Playboy*—and said in a sympathetic, comradely voice, "Why don't you go downtown and get some? Don't read about it! Why not have the real thing?" *Because the real thing*, I remember thinking as I looked at his friendly face in the doorway, *would be you.*

Meanwhile I developed a crush on a friend Fate left behind with me after the rest of the platoon shipped out. A delay in checking our backgrounds (I'd been born abroad, his mother was German) had held up our records, and we lived, the two of us, in an otherwise empty barracks as the weather turned cool and acrid-smelling coal smoke from a dozen chimneys descended over the pine trees and white barracks in a sooty pall. We were lost, left behind, with only a pool table to while away the somnolent afternoons. At evening, in the little notebook we'd been advised to write in during basic training ("What is the spirit of the bayonet? To kill!"), I wrote poems about my friend—the sight of him aiming his cue beneath the conical overhanging light, his blond stubbled head in shadow, his forearm in the lamplight. Metaphors for pool halls, cues seemed obviously sexual here. But when a third friend, a young black man who was already the father of three children, asked me, one evening in the library when the three of us must have been discussing our personal lives, "Are you a virgin?" I froze in embarrassment, stammered something, and left the room. My friend shipped out to another base for advanced infantry training; I remained behind as a clerk-typist at company headquarters, where an older, big-boned, freckled boy from Atlanta who smelled something about me christened me Daisy Mae. The black woman who was the captain's civilian secretary asked me how I could let him do this; I forget my answer. I was not homosexual enough—I mean a seasoned, confident homosexual—to throw it back in his face, nor heterosexual enough to deny it; I simply ignored his taunts and typed faster.

And then I was told one day at lunch that my orders had arrived, and learned my destination was Germany. Not Germany, exactly; HQ USAREUR 7TH ARMY APO NY 09757—a pale squibble of letters devoid of any particularity until, after a plane trip across the Atlantic, they turned into some fir trees drenched in fog beside a highway filled with Germans in small cars, headlights on, driving into Frankfurt to begin their day, while the bus bearing us American soldiers took us to our processing center. Germany was exciting by the time I got to Heidelberg and saw the rose-red castle perched above the roofs of the Old Town on its forested hillside; and I decided to do my best to stay right where I was and go no farther.

Farther was more uncertainty—Baumholder, Weilflicken, Grafenwöhr—places, I suspected, where other GIs would ask me if I was a virgin because there'd be nothing else to talk about; places that the thin-lipped, trembling, tart clerk-typist who took my records at his desk in the personnel office told me were indescribable cesspools in which you passed your days polishing belt buckles and tanks in a sea of mud. So, when the clerk said he'd see what he could do about keeping me in Heidelberg, I expressed appreciation. Specialist Higgins, I learned, had a certain say in which recruits passing through head-quarters were plucked out for the office's use—the way clerks in any bureau-cracy do—and, though I never asked afterward if he had recognized immediately in me what the cruel clerk back at Fort Benning had noticed, like the kindest of fairy godmothers, he granted me my wish. By nightfall not only was I assigned to Heidelberg but also to an empty bunk in the same room at Campbell Barracks where Specialist Higgins (alias "the Clam" because of a perpetual film of perspiration which covered his face and made his palms clammy) lived. I was home, taken in, under the wing, I realized much later, of the man who was to bring me out—in homosexual parlance, my mother.

I'm not sure when I realized where the friendship was leading. "Now this is your bunk," the Clam said in that trembling voice that seemed to be holding back a great deal of tension, "and down the hall's the latrine and shower room," he said. "And over there's the EM Club," he added, pointing to a low building across a space of grass when we went outside, "where most of your roommates count the days till they're back in Texas, while all of Europe goes on around them, madly partying. And that's the mess hall, and that's the library, which I don't use, because I prefer to do my research downtown!" Not I. I retreated the next day back into books and Art.

Art was downtown in the churches and castle. Books were in the post library, at one of the desks beside tall windows overlooking the spigots at which GIs washed their cars. The Clam went off every evening to drink. I began reading Proust. (The army provided the perfect opportunity for that, since Proust re-quired lots of time.) The Clam did not read. He had already read enough, it seemed; a graduate of Columbia College, he was a walking encyclopedia those first few evenings when he took me downtown to the castle and gave me a detailed history of the war during which the troops of Louis XIV had burned it. On Wednesdays, we went together to the chamber music concerts given in the castle courtyard, and then I left him outside one of the many bars on the Hauptstrasse from which he returned in the early morning to catch only a few hours' sleep before hopping the bus to work.

One day at lunch I met some of the people with whom he partied down-town. I knew the moment I saw them, the moment I heard them—the sarcasm, the teasing (what I would later call camp)—that they were members of another species. There were two in particular he called the Terrible Twins—Tully and Terwillegar—short, blond, loud. "Well, look who's here," Tully said in a brassy voice as he came to our table the day I met him. "I thought you'd still be in the bushes, Clam. You were awfully busy last night!"

"I was awfully drunk," said the Clam in a tart tone. "I think you've confused the two activities. Being drunk and being busy. You were busy last night in the bushes, I was drunk!"

"Is that what they call it?" said Terwillegar. "You should get drunk more often. Unless my ears deceived me, you were talking fluent Turkish to that man with the black beard."

"That's because I am not, like you, an Ugly American," said the Clam as he cut his flounder. "I attempt to communicate with *gast-arbeiters** in their own tongue."

"You said it, not me," said Terwillegar, and the Terrible Twins emitted shrieks of self-congratulatory laughter; after which I asked Tully politely if he had been at the concert in the castle.

"What concert?" said Tully, holding up his bread. "What castle?"

"Tully doesn't do concerts," said the Clam. "Tully doesn't do culture."

"Bitch!" said Tully, flinging a spoonful of Irish stew at the Clam's immaculate uniform.

"The truth hurts! After the fifth strip mall, you forget how to read!" said the Clam, standing up and dumping the contents of his tray onto Tully's, and walking off so quickly I was barely able to make my excuses before following him. "Mary, don't ask," was all he muttered when we were outside again.

Nevertheless, the Clam asked me to tea at a friend's house in Kirchheim— a small village separated from Campbell Barracks by a cornfield—later that afternoon, but I refused when he told me Tully and Terwillegar would be going, too. The Terrible Twins were one thing in the hubbub of the mess hall; in the privacy of somebody's apartment, they would be another. When four-thirty arrived, ignoring the Clam's plea, I went off to the library and sat down at a desk beside a window not far from my true soulmate, an unmarried German librarian in her forties named Lily Schroeder with whom I had already spent a pleasant Sunday hiking through the Odenwald. Better Lily, a fellow celibate, than the anarchy of the Terrible Twins and all the other people I felt sure would have nicknames, too. She smiled across her desk at me; I smiled at her—confirming our solidarity—and opened my Proust to a famous passage in which the subject I was trying to avoid is discussed, head-on, in the most somber and minute detail: the first scene of *Cities of the Plain*, in which the narrator realizes, when he sees Charlus and Jupien stare at each other, that Charlus is homosexual.

For reasons I could not then admit, I could not keep myself from rereading the whole moving meditation on the peculiar fate which this sight stirs in the narrator. "Race upon which a curse weighs," it went, "which must live amid falsehood and perjury, because it knows the world to regard as a punishable and a scandalous, as an inadmissible thing, its desire . . . friends without friend-

*Guest-workers.

ships . . . lovers from whom is always precluded the possibility of that love the hope of which gives them the strength to endure so many risks and so much loneliness . . ." I read, while Lily tapped on the side of the aquarium, ". . . brought into the company of their own kind by the ostracism that strikes them . . . numbering its adherents everywhere, among the people, in the army, in the church, in the prison, on the throne . . ." I read, lifting my eyes at that moment from the melancholy page to look out the window—where, with a great sense of relief, I saw, over the top of the wall that surrounded Campbell Barracks, the Terrible Twins, with their dyed blond hair and acne scars, walking down the street toward Kirchheim, both talking at the same time, while (an unusual sight, so prodigal was his use of taxicabs) the Clam followed a few paces behind, his dark hair slicked back from his freckled forehead, a gold scarf tied around his neck an inch above the collar of a mauve silk shirt he had purchased in Saigon; all of them on their way to tea—a living illustration of the doom I had just read a description of.

Denial is always astonishing in retrospect, that one was able to compartmentalize oneself, to proceed with one part while putting another on ice. As long as I was only writing poems to Livingston in my notebook at Fort Benning, as long as I was only reading about the Cursed Race in Proust while the Clam and the Terrible Twins actually went to the tea party in Kirchheim (which consisted, I learned later, of a depressed clerk-typist from ODSCOMMEL who built harpsichords and was desperately hoping a New Face would show up that afternoon—i.e., me), I was still somehow part of the mainstream; I had not separated from the herd; I was still part of the *Volk*—I was not homosexual.

Of course I was not heterosexual, either. I was sitting in the bus the following week on the way to work behind a young lieutenant who turned to a lieutenant next to him and said, "I've decided to get married. I think, after a while, it's hard to live just for yourself."

Well, I thought, that makes sense to me, but I don't have a choice. I did not even have a girlfriend, much less a wife. The only friend, male or female, I had besides the Clam in Heidelberg was someone I'd gone to college with, a tall, dark-haired Virginian who'd surfaced one day on the bus to work as a general's secretary assigned to the building next to ours. We'd decided to play tennis together when we could. Sometimes on our way to the courts he would read aloud to me from the letter he'd just received from a woman who was coming over that spring to travel through Germany and France with him. Once, sitting on the tennis court, he lowered the letter to his lap, looked off into the distance with a misty expression on his face, and said, "I think the deepest, most mystical experience in life is the physical union between a man and a woman. Compared to that, nothing matters."

I was as dumbstruck as I'd been when asked "Are you a virgin?"

Her arrival in May was all my friend lived for, I could see—the way my roommate Keasler lay on his bunk counting the days till he was back home in Texas. I had no lover to visit Chartres with, or greet me on my return home; adrift between two categories, in a vacuum, I was either taking walks with Lily Schroeder, reading Proust, or listening to Bach in the castle courtyard Wednesday evenings with the Clam.

Sometimes after the concert I went with him to Tiffany's, a cheerful bar with a big window on the Kornmarkt popular with tourists, where everyone locked arms and sang at the top of their voices a song popular that summer—"Memories of Heidelberg (Mean Memories of You)"—when it got late enough. (The Clam managed to sing it in a manner that made it seem, when I turned and found his glittering eyes fixed on me, strangely sinister.) No matter how late, however, I always left the Clam on the street outside the bar and went back to get what was left of a decent night's sleep, while he went on with whatever it was he did when I was not with him.

The Clam drank somewhere every night of the week—sometimes at the EM Club with the Terrible Twins and sometimes off base; more than once I saw them all getting out of a taxi at seven in the morning in front of our barracks, in scarves and civilian clothes, as the rest of us were setting off to work. There was, I knew, a well-known string of bars that served GIs outside the gates of Campbell Barracks—one for whites, one for blacks, one for straights, and (I learned later) one for gays—called the Sewer Circuit. There was even a brothel between the barracks and the PX I shopped at every Saturday morning; a plain stucco building, beige-colored, unmarked, which the Clam pointed out to me the first day we walked by. GIs in street clothes were going in and out; "Memories of Heidelberg mean memories of you," the Clam began singing as we watched them.

Then, one morning on the bus, the Clam introduced me to a clerk in Accounting named Harvey, a pale, slender man with pewter-colored hair and small, wet, red lips, and a certain soft, rabbitlike alertness. The Clam told me after we'd left him that he lived off base with a prostitute so obsessed with him she paid his rent and walked to work so that he could use her car. One Saturday we went to visit Harvey—the Clam wished to pick up some marijuana—and when he opened the door of his apartment in another plain stucco building near the Odenwald at three-thirty in the afternoon, he was still in his underwear, and I realized Harvey had been lounging in bed.

He was very pale, with milk-white skin. He wore white underpants and a white T-shirt, and behind him the rumpled, used sheets were white, not to mention the walls of the room and, through the window, the very fog outside. As we walked inside, I felt I was entering the interior of a chambered nautilus—Build Thee more stately mansions, Oh my soul!—a milk-white chamber in which Harvey, this nervous, nondescript American army clerk from Nebraska, had been sequestered by a prostitute—a connoisseur of men—to lie in bed, smoking cigarettes, while she plied her trade (at the brothel near the PX) to get money to spend on him. This was what lay beneath the world, I thought, the long boring winter afternoons which I so often spent trudging through the firs toward the Königstuhl high above this little apartment house, or reading Proust back in the library at my desk by the tall window.

It wasn't Proust I thought of as I sat silently in a corner, however, while Harvey and the Clam negotiated, or Oliver Wendell Holmes; it was Henry

James, and the climactic scene in several of his novels in which the person to whom the story is happening suddenly realizes, beside a fire in Tuscany, or a river in the French countryside, that Other People are having sex with one another. When I entered the library that evening, and the librarian, looking up from the aquarium whose fish she was feeding while Viennese waltzes played softly on the radio behind her desk, said, "Ah! Florida boy!" I smiled, and went to my desk, and opened Proust; but I didn't read. I thought of Harvey. And thought and thought.

The day after New Year's I went to Vienna. The city was covered with snow. I could hear my shoes breaking through the ice crust as I walked to the fountains of Schönbrun. Inside one museum I stared at the car in which the Archduke Ferdinand had been assassinated, the bullet holes still visible; and then the feathered headdress which Montezuma had been wearing when he received Cortés. Inside the palace, the rooms lined with mirrors reflecting an icy silver light, small clouds of vapor at our lips, the guide extended his arm toward a Sévres urn on the mantelpiece and said, "These are the entrails of Franz Joseph. His heart, however, is in the Saint Sulplice in Paris." Ah, I thought, like me—Sex here, Ideals there. Homosexual lust in one urn, the urge to please my parents in another.

Outside the palace, still making lists, I got on a streetcar. It was dusk; skiers were returning from the surrounding hills, including a young man with rosy cheeks and golden hair in a blue parka, who, when the streetcar stopped and he descended the steps and walked off toward the crimson sunset at the end of the street, made me want to follow him home. Instead I went back to Heidelberg the next day and told the Clam about the museums I had visited, and he told me about the history of the objects in them and the ones I'd missed. My docent, my mentor, my Mum.

"Of course there's no reason to travel, Newbie, nowadays," he said when he came into the room that evening after one of his long showers in the shower room down the hall—an expedition for which he equipped himself with sticks of incense he lighted on the windowsill, soap of Castile, English shampoo, Swiss potions, and lotions for the imperial epidermis. "I used to think you had to go to London to see the Elgin marbles. Not anymore. All you have to do is take a shower down the hall. There's still time if you hurry. *Mach schnell, Newbie, mach schnell!*"

I hurried. After the loneliness of my solitary trip I was glad to enter the big room down the hall, with its low wooden bench along one wall and spigots on the other, and find a friend from Accounting named Roish, a colleague from my office named Waldrip, and, standing in the middle of the room, his pale, glistening torso enveloped in the clouds of steam created when all the showers were turned on at once, the Clam's favorite, a cook from Arkansas who used to stand in the serving line and ask us, when we reached the vegetables, "Peas, broccoli, or a piece of pussy?" Taking a place in one of the streams of hot water, it was bliss to hear their echoing voices, talking to one another, and see, in between the clouds of steam parting and re-forming, a thigh, an arm, a pair of dog tags, or a hand slowly soaping a glistening stomach. This was where I wanted to be—not Vienna. All I could think of as the cook stood beside me, moving a green bar of soap around the concave depression of his solar plexus, was not the feathered headdress Montezuma wore when he met Cortés, but a famous Mexican proverb in which a lover begs to be the cup that touches her beloved's lips; here, in the billowing shower, I wanted to be the bar of Palmolive being slowly spread over the flat white surface of the cook's veined groin.

"Why, Newbie, you're as wrinkled as Sergeant Prager!" said the Clam when I finally returned to the room after more than an hour in the shower room that evening. He looked at me with a mocking smile. I said nothing. There was no need to. There was no question I was dissolving, as it were, in the steam. An accumulation of impressions had resulted in a paradox: What most of us considered to be the expropriator of our freedom (the army) was proving to be my liberator. The green summer twilights, the MPs in their shiny helmets at the gate, the brothel near the PX, the visit to Harvey, the torso fragments in the shower room, the fact that the Clam clearly had another life I stopped at the edges of, the way Lily Schroeder had refused, on smelling the traffic fumes, to come any farther down the hillside when we parted after our hike, were, like individual drops of water, eroding the stone of my refusal to take tea months earlier.

It was another sort of gathering we had to attend that night, however, a going-away party at our sergeant's house for a fellow clerk who was returning to Maine to marry his fiancée. Everyone was drinking, including me; the forced camaraderie of an office party, the ribald jokes about Tyson's nuptials, the off-color stories, even the startling information that women in Vietnam had no pubic hair, made me drink more than I usually did, as my smile tightened on my face like the skin of someone dying. When finally I walked down the concrete path with the Clam to a waiting taxi, I was a patient prepared for an operation: The Clam pushed me in, gave the driver directions; I lay my head back, closed my eyes, and let the air rush over my face as the tires bounced crazily on the cobblestones and the Clam sang "Memories of Heidelberg mean memories of you" in an acid quaver. When I opened my eyes, we were on a street directly underneath the castle at a wooden door; the Clam drew it back and pushed me inside.

It was the Whiskey-a-Go-Go, a small, pleasant room with soft lighting, a wooden counter, and several tables opposite the bar. An hour later I found myself sitting with the Clam, a black American friend of his from another office, and two Germans. One was Central Casting's idea of a Teutonic knight: blond, square-jawed, chiseled features, blue eyes, a deep voice, and powerful handshake. The other was a pale, pudgy, pear-shaped programmer who hardly spoke. It was agreed we would all go home together. The car took us back to the modern gray concrete part of Heidelberg that had appeared since the war between the Old Town and the village of Kirchheim. Streetlights floated past. I knew I was going somewhere, but felt helpless to determine the destination; a vast passivity, a giving up, of all the years of denial, paralyzed my limbs.

At Campbell Barracks the Clam, to my surprise, got out, saying something about his imperial beauty sleep. I'd decided by now that, yes, I would probably permit Parsifal to have sex with me. We got out at a gray apartment building and went upstairs. And then, as if it had been planned all along (it had; the blond German, who became a friend, was obsessed with blacks), Wilhelm and Troy retired to a mattress in the corner, and the pale, pudgy programmer beached himself upon me on his bed. Shortly before dawn I awoke and insisted he drive me back to the barracks, where I went directly to the shower room and symbolically washed my mouth out with soap while absorbing an important lesson that would preoccupy the rest of my gay life: It is one thing to come out; it is quite another to get the person you really want.

Then I gathered up my things, went back to the room, found the Clam awakening, and heard him say, on catching sight of me, something I would hear many, many times over the next twenty years: "Well, my dear, *how was it?*"—a question he had been longing to ask, I learned later, after he said, "My God, you took a long time coming out, but there was nothing I could do!" Then he patted the bedspread next to him and said, "Come here, my dear, and tell Mother all about it."

I did. Then, saying I'd forgot to wash my hair, I went back to the shower room, in truth to wash my mouth out again and wait for somebody else to come in and take a shower; the two instincts (desire and remorse) that would characterize much of my homosexual life to come—a life, I would discover, that was, just as my teenage self had suspected when it retreated into books, easier to read about than live.

In fact, I never slept with another person that year in Heidelberg; and when I returned to America, I retreated into books again, this time at law school, for a whole year before realizing, one summer night in Philadelphia, that I had to come out all over again—so powerful is the wish in some people to deny their sexual orientation.

BEYOND WORDS

Philip Gambone

WHEN DID I start to feel things that let me know I was a homosexual? In my journal, which I began in July 1968 at the age of twenty, the words *gay* and *homosexual* do not appear for almost a year. What does that mean? That I simply resisted the words to describe myself until they felt safe, familiar? When does any coming out really begin?

One of my earliest memories is of a neighborhood playmate, a blond, blue-eyed boy named Erik with perpetually rosy cheeks and lips of a color that seemed far too intense to be natural. His parents spoke with a thick foreign accent different from the one I'd grown accustomed to hearing from my Italian grandmother. They were Norwegian, my mother explained, from a faraway country called Norway. Abstractions like "Norway" were interesting, the kind of facts I knew, even as a little boy, it pleased my mother that I learn.

But it was Erik's and my playmaking that better pleased me. I remember one toy, his painted wood jack-in-the-box, and how, when we turned the handle together, our little hands overlapping on the knob, we'd already be giggling in anticipation of the moment when the clown would pop up and send us into squeals of delight. I remember getting annoyed when Erik's little sister burst in on us, chattering away in an incomprehensible language of pursed vowels and alien consonants. When Erik answered her in kind, I felt abandoned. And I remember getting angry and bewildered the day my mother told me it was impolite to let myself into Erik's house uninvited, that I must always knock and wait to be admitted.

"But why?" I demanded. "He's my best friend."

"It doesn't matter."

This seemed silly and confusing, my first experience of parental wisdom gone amiss. My mother simply did not understand the nature of our friendship.

Toward the end of that year, Erik and his family moved from Massachusetts back to Norway and our contact abruptly ended. I was five years old and soon found other playmates.

At age seven, my brother and I rummaged through my mother's bureau drawers, trying on bras and girdles and petticoats, wriggling into her skirts and blouses and sweaters, clipping on earrings, rouging our cheeks, smearing our mouths with her lipstick, donning pearls and purses and perfume. What kind of information was I picking up then?

Or at age eight, walking along the beach near our summer cottage on Cape Cod, fascinated by the lifeguards slouched on their perches, lean and tan and naked except for their regulation orange boxer-type bathing suits, their navels showing just above the waistbands, their faces impassive and unreadable behind mirrored sunglasses, the zinc oxide on their small, pink American noses as white as war paint?

What was I feeling at age nine, that New Year's we went to visit relatives in New Rochelle and I shared a bed with a distant cousin, laughing and giggling and horsing around despite repeated admonitions from our parents?

Or at age ten, staying after school to play jump rope with my friends, all girls, realizing that the boys they pronounced cute were often the ones I liked, too?

What was I gleaning from these experiences? Was I beginning to see myself as a little different from the others? Yes and no. I still got crushes on girls, still wanted them to notice me. And yet, the year I went to see *Seven Brides for Seven Brothers* three times at the movies, for whom was I feeling those warm fuzzies, Jane Powell or Russ Tamblyn? Remarkably, no one ever called me names or made me feel badly about myself. There are times now when I almost envy people who were called "faggot" in school. At least they got a clear signal they couldn't ignore.

I entered Wakefield Junior High in early September 1960. I'd just turned twelve. On the first day of seventh grade, I was given a list of athletic equipment I needed for phys ed classes: gym shorts, T-shirt, white socks, sneakers, and something called an athletic supporter.

"What's that?" I asked my mother.

"It's something boys wear to protect their *pisciatelli*," she explained, reverting to Neapolitan, the vocabulary we used in matters too private or subtle for English. "Kind of like a bra, but for down there."

Straightforward and innocuous, nothing to worry about. Off we went that weekend to the store. The clerk efficiently retrieved the various items on our list. When he got to the final one, he looked first at my mother, then at me.

"What size?" he asked. "I'd guess a medium."

I nodded, the awkwardness of the situation dawning on me. He handed me a package about the size of a small box of chocolates, with a cellophane window through which I could make out a mesh fabric in a color that, even then, I probably knew as pale celadon.

"Don't you want to examine it?" my mother asked. "Take it out of the box."

I managed to say something about how I thought that wouldn't be necessary. By now, I couldn't look directly at her or the clerk. No other boy, I was sure, had brought his mother with him on this shopping excursion. No other boy had needed to buy an athletic supporter; a *real* boy simply came equipped with it.

The night before my first gym class, I lay awake, trying to imagine what the next day would be like. I'd never undressed in front of other boys. I was nervous at the impending embarrassment, afraid I would humiliate myself by not knowing how to wear the supporter. Everyone had gone to bed. The house was quiet. I got up, went to my bureau, and silently took out the box, tucking the supporter under my pajama top. I went to the bathroom (the only room with a lock on the door), removed my pajama bottoms, and, after a few seconds of confusion, managed to work my legs through the right straps in the glare of the fluorescent lights.

The effect was powerful, electric. Even before I looked at myself in the mirror, I felt strong, athletic, masculine, and, most of all—did I have this word yet?—sexual: things I'd never felt before. Until that moment, my body had been a source of discomfort, vulnerable, awkward, prone to sunburn and bee stings and measles, a giver of pain. My mother, my grandmother, my religion all spoke of the body as a shameful vessel. What were these new feelings, so far removed from shame?

As I stood admiring my girded loins in the mirror, the pouch of the jock strap began to bulge as my penis swelled, becoming longer and thicker, pressing against the elastic mesh like a sponge expanding in a glass of water. I pulled down the supporter and out sprang . . .

How could this be? In a matter of seconds, I had grown the genitalia of an adult, my first waking erection (another experience I didn't yet have words for). Quickly, I slipped off the jock and pulled on my pajama bottoms. The thin cotton cloth brushed the head of my penis, creating a rush of sensitivity, something between ticklishness and an exquisite burning. I hurried back to my room, doubled over to hide my state. Holding up the bedsheet, I stripped off my bottoms to stop the excruciating sensation of the tip of my dick's chaffing against the cloth. As the sheet gently descended on my cock, I exploded, a raw, ecstatic sensation, my whole body in spasm, lifted to a place beyond words.

With a little practice, I learned the best ways to stroke and rub, how to prolong the buildup, and, since my mother did the family laundry, how to catch the semen in a tissue before it stained the sheets. I tried thinking of girls when I jerked off, but it was images of boys—boys in my class, older brothers of boys in my class, boys from TV shows and movies, boys in a muscle magazine I stole from our local news store—only images of boys that could bring me to climax.

By the eighth grade, I had found a jerk-off buddy, a boy in my confirmation class who, after our weekly catechism lesson, would take me to his house to play Photographer and Model. Timmy had a darkroom and several expensive cameras. He would pose me on his bed, imitating the pictures in his photography magazines.

"Take off your clothes," he'd coach.

Off came my shirt.

"What did you say your name was, baby? Lolita? Yeah, that's good, Lolita," he'd say, looking through the lens of a make-believe camera. (We never used real equipment.) "Honey, now let's try some completely naked shots."

And off came my pants and underpants.

"Hey, what's *that!*" he'd say, pointing at my erect dick with feigned horror.

Coyly, dumb blond that I was supposed to be, I'd shake my head: Why, I had no idea how that got there.

"Well, we can't have it in the photo. Maybe if I rub it, it'll go away. What do you think, baby?"

After a few months, we abandoned this pretext and just jerked each other off. "Why don't you try blowing on it?" I suggested one day. (Somewhere I'd heard the term "blow job," a concept I was eager to experience but whose execution remained vague in my mind.) Timmy wouldn't hear of it. "Come on," I coaxed. "Just try it." But no, that's where he drew the line. Even then, I knew sanitary fastidiousness wasn't the issue, but the intimacy, the physical and emotional closeness the act would betray. Timmy's refusal to blow me and, not long afterward, to continue any sexual play with me, was yet one more piece of information. I came to understand that our get-togethers had meant very different things to each of us. It was horsing around for him, something far more powerful for me. But what?

During the summers of 1965 and 1966, my mother sent me for six weeks of "enrichment" classes at Phillips Academy in Andover. To a bookish, introspective kid like me, Andover was paradise, a place where I could let down the guard I'd developed after my rejection by Timmy. And though here as well heterosexuality was the norm, Andover provided me with the first forum in which the topic of homosexuality could be addressed. (My second summer there we read Mann's *Death in Venice*.) It was at Andover, too, that I first fell in love with another boy.

Barry was a dark-eyed, sweet-faced sixteen-year-old from Queens—smart, funny, musical, and cute. I took to him from the day we met. Soon we were hanging out together all the time, spending our free periods talking about literature and music and life. I envied Barry's New York sophistication, loved listening to him talk about the city and its arts scene. On Saturdays during the winter, he would go to the Metropolitan and Guggenheim museums. He'd heard Rubinstein play at Carnegie Hall. He traveled alone into Manhattan to buy records at a place with the extraordinary name of Sam Goody's. Even the sound of his voice captivated me: mildly nasal skewed vowels, a softened version of the grating New York accents of my New Rochelle relatives. When he laughed, his voice twisted around a giggle that was almost feminine. I began to notice his beautiful long eyelashes, the adorable way his chin was adorned with two or three acne blemishes. I have a photograph of us, taken that second summer, wearing identical outfits: penny loafers, light-colored chinos, white shirts open at the neck to reveal T-shirts, sleeves rolled up to exactly the same place on our arms.

Andover's parietal rules were liberal enough to grant us weekend passes. I suggested to Barry that we borrow a car and go off to Tanglewood some weekend to hear the Boston Symphony. He agreed; we made plans for early August. When the day arrived, I picked up the car from my parents and off we drove to hear Van Cliburn in the Berkshires. Driving west along the Massachusetts Turnpike that morning, the windows down, my friend at my side, the prospect of wonderful music played by a great Romantic musician and listened to with Barry, I felt exquisitely happy. What more could life hand me?

We stayed with a former music teacher from my high school, a woman in her late twenties whose summer place was a short distance from Tanglewood. When we arrived in the late afternoon, she greeted us warmly and suggested we might want to freshen up before dinner and the concert. Overnight bags in hand, we followed her through her backyard to the guest cottage. "It's small," she said, "but you'll have your privacy." She turned the handle and pushed the door forward, revealing a room all knotty pine and soft lamplight. "You don't mind sharing a bed, I hope." My heart pounding, I said as nonchalantly as I could that sharing a bed was no problem at all.

It was late by the time Barry and I returned from the concert. We tiptoed through the darkened house and across the lawn toward the guest cottage. "Look at the stars," Barry said, stopping midway. "You can even see the Milky Way. We don't get that in New York." We stood silently side by side, craning our necks, close enough that I might have put my arm around his shoulder.

In the cottage, I tried not to look at Barry undressing. I went to the bathroom to brush my teeth. When I returned, he was already in bed, scrunched up on one side, his back to the other. I got in and turned off the lamp. "It was a great concert, wasn't it?" I asked, my voice soft and friendly. By now I had a full-blown erection. We talked for a while about the music and Van Cliburn and plans for the fall. He'd be a senior in high school; I was about to begin freshman year at college. "I really hope you apply to Harvard this year," I told him. "It would be great to be classmates. You can stay with me when you come for the interview."

I turned toward Barry. Less than a foot now separated us. We talked a while longer, then Barry said he was tired and thought we should get to sleep. We wished each other good night. I listened to the sound of his breathing, not daring to stir, trying to gauge his little shifting motions. A few minutes passed. Was he waiting for me to make the first move?

Barry nodded drowsily in my direction. "You're getting awfully close, aren't you?" he mumbled, then turned away.

I didn't sleep that night. I lay on my stomach, as far over to my side of the bed as possible, trying to ignore my erection, desperately hoping that Barry would wake up, roll across that vast chasm, and fall into my arms.

THE PROSPECT OF having to join a fraternity terrified me. Like other all-male institutions—the army, the YMCA, the Boy Scouts—a fraternity loomed in my imagination as a place that would reveal me for what I truly was: a young man inept in the ways of normal young men. Indifferent to sports, increasingly uninterested in romancing women, secretly pining after guys, I was sure that in a fraternity I would, at last, be found out. Fortunately, there was Harvard. Though still largely all male when I applied in 1966, the university's house system, modeled on Britain's Oxbridgian colleges, made fraternities unnecessary. More to the point, Harvard was large enough, diverse enough, and, I hoped, *refined* enough that I would not be pressured into participating in activities—mixers, dating, petting, intercourse—I wasn't ready for.

Is that what I told myself, that I wasn't "ready" for women yet? More likely, I simply avoided thinking about the issue, ignoring what my behavior and my fantasies were trying to tell me. Choosing Harvard meant that I could enjoy, in my own timid, unexamined way, the company of hundreds of beautiful young men and at the same time remain relatively inconspicuous.

Well, almost. One night in the spring of my freshman year came a knock on my door. It was Jimmy, a young African American, the Glee Club's star baritone soloist. Jimmy's deep, mellifluous voice belied his delicate, almost feminine features. Small, thin, and wispy, he'd laugh with a high-pitched, crowing cackle like the sound of certain comic movie starlets of the thirties. Remarkably, I never heard anyone utter a whisper, malicious or otherwise, about Jimmy's sexuality. His race and his artistic prowess must have been enough to keep him beyond criticism at polite, WASPy Harvard. I was surprised to see him. Though we were both in the Glee Club, we had not become particular friends. I was fascinated by him, but wary that too close an association would cast suspicion on me. Nevertheless, sometimes after rehearsals, as I walked back to my dormitory, I'd suddenly find Jimmy at my side, striking up conversations I anxiously kept steering in the direction of the weather or the way the rehearsal had gone. Now Jimmy came into my room, looking distraught.

"What's the matter?" I asked.

It was "this person," Jimmy began, someone he was in love with. He was tormented—by his feelings, by the apparent indifference of the other person, by whether he should declare himself. The conversation must have lasted a half hour, but Jimmy never volunteered the gender of his beloved and I never asked. He sat on my bed in an opera of high emotions and theatrical gestures, now weeping, now laughing his signature laugh, recounting the unbearable events of the last few weeks. I must have offered advice, sympathy, consolation; the details remain foggy, for other thoughts were crowding my mind: Who was this unnamed person? Why had Jimmy chosen to tell me? In silent panic, I assumed I was the person with whom he was smitten, but as he supplied more details, I figured out it was someone else. In fact, I knew him, a guy I also found strikingly good-looking. I'd seen them hanging out together, walking to class or sitting over coffee in one of the many cafés in Harvard Square. Hearing Jimmy's confession allowed me to admit I had a crush on the guy, too. Now I knew why Jimmy had come to me. He suspected—no, he knew—that I was a kindred spirit.

Still, I said nothing, acknowledged nothing, disclosed nothing. Jimmy left. We never discussed love issues again, nor was he ever as friendly to me. Today the alumni office lists him as "address unknown."

As that spring semester drew to a close, a deep sense of sadness overtook me. I felt isolated, friendless, anonymous. I'd thought to find at Harvard a milieu that would challenge my intellect while leaving me in peace as far as sexual matters were concerned, but that rarefied society, if it ever existed, had long since died. Sex—heterosexual sex—was everywhere, in the music that blared from dorm windows on any given weekend, in the stories guys brought back of dates at Radcliffe and Wellesley and Smith, in the trashy popular books that circulated like contraband. (*Candy* was especially popular my freshman year, 1967.) Worse still, my hormones were raging and I could not stop thinking about boys.

As lonely as I was, the prospect of returning home for the summer filled me with even more dread. I was eighteen. After a year away from my parents, I couldn't bear the thought of living under the same roof with them again; whatever tiny gains I'd made toward erotic self-knowledge would be smothered by another family summer in suburbia. I signed up to take Italian at summer school, telling my parents I needed an additional foreign language to fulfill Harvard's graduation requirements.

"But why should you live in the dorms?" my mother asked. "Your father and I haven't seen you all year. Your brothers miss you. Harvard's twelve miles away. Live at home for the summer and commute."

I capitulated; at least I'd be away for the better part of the day.

The class met for an hour each morning, followed by language lab and a lunch break, with another hour in the afternoon. There were about fifteen of us, mostly women, liberal arts types majoring in subjects like French or English or art history who needed some Italian for their research. One of the only other males was a guy about my age named John, who quickly adopted the Italian equivalent, Giovanni, which our professor called him. Giovanni had a high forehead, a small, deliciously sloped nose, hazel eyes, and a ruddy complexion that made him look like he was always blushing. Handsome, lively, and clownish, he was a big hit with the young women in the class.

Our professor encouraged us to form *gruppi di conversazione* in order to get in more practice. Giovanni, two or three of the young co-eds, and I would gather between the morning and afternoon sessions at a café in Harvard Square, drinking cappuccinos and talking, sometimes in Italian, sometimes in English, bunched together elbow to elbow because the tables were small. Whenever possible, I made sure to sit next to Giovanni. On one such break, I became aware of someone's knee pressing against my leg, rather more deliberate than accidental. Or was I imagining this? I let the knee stay there, pretending I hadn't noticed, then, out of curiosity, moved my leg away.

The conversation continued, Giovanni as always taking the lead, regaling us with stories and jokes the women laughed at indiscriminately. In the middle of one of his tales, the mysterious knee touched mine again, rested there. I was sure it was Giovanni, but when I looked at him, his attention was directed toward the women. His face seemed even ruddier—was I imagining that, too? Otherwise, there were no clues that he was the one touching me. As if by accident, I dropped my napkin onto the floor. Stooping to retrieve it, I glanced quickly under the table in time to see Giovanni's knee pull away from mine.

On the way back to class, I tried striking up a conversation with him—Was the sandwich he'd ordered good? Had he understood those new uses of the subjunctive? Where was he living this summer?—anything to get him into a one-on-one situation. His answers were friendly but brief. He seemed more intent on entertaining the ladies. The next day, I made sure to sit next to him again.

As usual, the group talked and joked and made fun of the ridiculous dialogues in our textbook. There was no knee against mine. I might have rectified this, but the idea of taking the lead terrified me. Besides, I wasn't sure anymore that Giovanni's knee resting against mine hadn't been an accident. I watched him play the *cavaliere* with the girls. Yes, it was clear he was a ladies' man.

The following day, just when I'd forgotten all about it, the knee was back, pressing into my thigh. I didn't move, for fear of calling Giovanni's attention to what he was doing and thereby losing the exquisite feel of his body against mine. I tried to concentrate on holding up my end of the conversation. I laughed at his jokes, sprinkled my sentences with the latest words from our Italian vocabulary. His knee never strayed from my leg.

"Oopsie," one of the girls exclaimed, checking her watch, "we're going to be late for the two o'clock session."

I picked up the bill and began figuring out what everyone owed. "*Filippo il Finanziere,*" the girl said with teasing affection. We all laughed, and Giovanni pressed his knee more firmly into my leg, as if he were patting me on the back for a job well done. If he had leaned over and kissed me, he could not have given me more pleasure.

Our group continued to meet daily, and always it was the same. At night I'd go home to Wakefield, eat dinner with my parents, and perfunctorily answer their questions about what I'd learned that day. After dinner, I'd throw myself onto my bed, trying to memorize the next day's lesson. But the only thing in my head was Giovanni—his looks, his laugh, the feel of his knee against mine. Emotionally exhausted, I'd drift off to sleep, my book face down on the pillow.

The final week came. One of the girls announced a potluck party at her house, a little end-of-course gathering. I put together a plan. I'd borrow the family car, go to the party in Cambridge, then, at an hour late enough that my parents' resistance would be lowered, I'd call home to say the party was running late, maybe it would be best if I stayed overnight at a friend's (Giovanni's, of course). Naturally, this depended on Giovanni, but I assumed that his desire to do more than just rub knees with me was as strong as mine. All I needed was the right signal and I would do anything to make sure we could be together that night.

The party was a bohemian affair: people sitting on pillows on the floor, candles stuck into Chianti bottles, the wax dripping down, India-print throws on the one or two pieces of furniture. A wood door had been laid across two sawhorses as a buffet table, with gallon jugs of wine nearby. Giovanni held forth to a couple of captivated young women who had not been part of our conversation group. I walked over and sat down on the floor.

"What did you bring?" I asked Giovanni when he finally paused in his monologue, an uninspired conversation opener, but I was hoping to pick up information. Bread would tell me what? That he was earthy, romantic, poetic? A lasagna for luxury? A salad for creativity? Wine for passion? But what would tell me that he was a homosexual, that he wanted me?

Giovanni seemed slightly drunk, his ruddy face aglow in the candlelight. "Beer," he said. "Help yourself. They're in the fridge." He looked at the girls and smiled.

"Yeah, that sounds good," I said feebly, then got up and made my way to the kitchen.

Giovanni was embroiled in conversation again, so I circulated the room. Our professor reclined on a futon, drinking wine and chatting amiably with some students. He raised his glass to me—"Ciao, Filippo"—and I sat down beside him, sipping my beer and trying to follow the conversation. All around me were festivity and merriment. Whenever I looked across the room, there was Giovanni, holding forth. Would he ever tear himself away long enough to pay attention to me? In this public arena, had he become scared? Self-conscious? Closeted? (Another word I hadn't yet learned.) Eventually, I fell into the jovial atmosphere, enjoying the beer and the good food, although I kept a lookout for Giovanni, where he wandered and whom he talked to. Finally he joined our group, but did not sit near me. Then the telephone rang.

Our hostess came into the room. "It's for you, Filippo."

I knew who it would be.

"Your father thinks it's getting late," my mother said.

"Ma, it's not even eleven."

"By the time you get home, it'll be close to midnight. Your father has to get up for work tomorrow."

"So, go to bed," I snapped.

"Angel, you know we won't fall asleep until you get home."

"Ma!" I bleated.

"Come on, you have to get up early, too, you know. You've got your final day of class tomorrow."

"For Pete's sake."

"Philip, enough's enough. Please, now. Come home."

I slammed down the phone and glanced at Giovanni. He was no older than I, but he had something, the ability to get what he wanted, that seemed light-years away for me.

I said my good-byes and was seen to the door—not by Giovanni. I paused on the stoop. Voices and laughter spilled out the open windows of the apartment above me. The night was warm and dark and strangely soothing. I walked down the street to my parents' car, the click of my footsteps echoing on the ancient brick sidewalk. "Next summer," I vowed, "so help me, it will be different." I didn't know how I'd get away or what I would do, but next summer would be different.

THAT WINTER, I got a call from Hal, who worked for the Boston Symphony Orchestra and, in his spare time, oversaw the financial affairs of the Harvard Glee Club, a largely student-run organization. In addition to being a second tenor in the group, I was being groomed to take over as manager during my junior year. Hal thought it would be good for me to get some firsthand experience before I assumed the helm. Would I consider working as his assistant at Tanglewood that summer? I'd be a kind of factotum, a philharmonic Figaro, helping out with the day-to-day Tanglewood activities, which included not only the orchestra's concerts but a program for would-be professional musicians.

I was stunned—a lowly sophomore being given a chance to work with the BSO, one of my cultural idols? I would have scrubbed floors.

That spring, I described my upcoming job to a woman friend also acquainted with Hal.

"Just watch out for him," she told me. "You know about Hal, don't you?"

I shook my head, bewildered.

I cannot remember how she conveyed to me that Hal was homosexual. In that year before Stonewall, how did a nice, liberal, straight person in Cambridge warn an unsuspecting lad to be on guard? Well, enough said, she must have concluded, trusting that the mere suggestion of Hal's queerness would suffice to keep me, a Ganymede in the court of Zeus, alert and wary.

This was the first time anyone had ever pointed out to me, discreetly or otherwise, that another man was gay: a chilling, terrifying, exciting moment.

ON A WARM Sunday in late June 1968, my parents drove me across the state, a three-hour trip that felt more like the quintessential leavetaking than the drive two years before to my freshman dorm in Harvard Yard. At last, I was making a clean break.

When we arrived at Tanglewood, the grounds were open but, apart from a few wandering tourists, the place was deserted. The concert season wouldn't start for another week. A message from Hal at the main gate told me I was to move into a dorm about a mile down the road. Hal would meet me in the morning for our first day of work.

The dorm, too, was deserted. As we hauled my bags from the family Ford, my mother kept asking, "Are you sure this is where you're supposed to be?

Don't you think your father and I should stay until you make sure this is the right place?"

"No," I snapped. "And don't show up tomorrow with my rubbers!"

My mother laughed nervously. It was a family joke. Four years earlier, after dropping me off at summer music camp, she'd actually returned the next day with a pair of rubbers, explaining, "I thought, in case of rain, you'd better have them." The reference worked. She announced that maybe it was time for them to go.

As I followed them to the car, a white Volkswagen pulled up to the dorm. I immediately recognized the driver.

"Andrew!" I called. I turned to my parents. "I know that guy from college." Andrew was three years older than me. My mother looked as pleased as if I'd said the baby-sitter had arrived.

Andrew had been assistant conductor of the Glee Club my first year, then left to do graduate work at Princeton. We'd not known each other well; indeed, I'd shied away from him. There was something almost Apollo-like about him: his blond hair, dazzlingly white when it caught the sun, his lanky good looks, his aristocratic manner. He played the piano, the organ, the harpsichord, composed and conducted, organized impromptu musical soirees, and had cooked elaborate dishes from Julia Child on a sterno stove in his rooms at Eliot House. He sprinkled his conversation with German, French, and Italian words and phrases. It was rumored he was distantly related to Shakespeare.

"We're sharing rooms," he said. "I just saw Hal and he told me he thought it might be a good idea."

"Oh, isn't that nice," my mother gushed, "you two Harvard boys together."

I shot her a nasty look.

"Come on, Nancy," my father intervened. "It's time to go."

As the car drove past us, my mother leaned out the window.

"Call me tomorrow, honey."

I helped Andrew carry his things into the dorm. He'd filled every inch of the VW except the driver's seat with boxes and bags of clothes (including a tuxedo and a set of tails), stereo equipment, cocktail glasses, orchestral scores, record albums, manuscript paper, and, most miraculous of all, a small harmonium. Inside our rooms, I watched him set up his music system—turntable, amplifier, speakers, with a network of wires as complex as the lines in a Bach fugue.

"Let's test it out," he suggested after he'd made the final connection. He rummaged through his record albums. "Ah, this should do."

I looked at the cover. He'd selected a Mozart opera, *The Abduction from the Seraglio*. He leafed through the boxed set until he came to the disk he wanted. "Listen to this, Gambone." He placed the needle down. "Konstanze's big aria, '*Martern aller Arten.*'"

I was enthralled by this passionate martial music, which seemed like a small concerto for soprano: the florid runs and trills, the dips and swoops, the vocal line soaring, floating, bouncing along on the swift currents of the full orchestra. Andrew ferreted a score and baton out of his pile of stuff and began to conduct, now caressing, now insisting, shaping the line. During the lyric parts, his eyes closed and his head fell back in gentle ecstasy. When, almost a quarter hour later, the aria reached its rousing finale, Andrew's blond hair was disheveled and wet with sweat.

I applauded.

The next day, our summer jobs began. I was basically a glorified office boy. I typed program notes, ran errands, negotiated with the phone company to install more WATS lines. One day I might drive a truck to New York to pick up a celesta for a performance of the *Nutcracker* Suite, the next organize a cocktail party for Erich Leinsdorf, the symphony's conductor. Andrew was assistant to the choral conductor, a more creative position. In the evening, over supper, we'd discuss the music being rehearsed, the composers, their styles, the *Zeitgeist* of their era. (German was creeping into my sentences, too.) Andrew seemed to know a lot about music, architecture, food, wine, languages, literature.

"Did you know that the German word *selig*—'blessed'—is directly related to the English word *silly*?" he asked during one of our conversations. "Blessedness means divine silliness."

My days at Tanglewood began to take on the glow of such blessedness. Divine silliness seemed to pervade everything: the music, the pastoral setting of the Berkshires, my feelings for Andrew. I was tipsy with happiness, like a peasant in a Schubert song bowled over that the mill girl is his. *Mein, mein, mein!* That this man, so beautiful and knowledgeable and adept—so sexy (yes, I'd begun to notice)—should befriend me, should like me!

The office staff included a woman named Marilyn, a Radcliffe graduate who had landed a full-time job with the symphony. Sometimes she would join Andrew and me for dinner, after which the three of us would sing madrigals far into the night. Marilyn was obviously fond of Andrew, laughing (as I did) at his jokes, agreeing with him (as I did) in his pronouncements about music, complimenting him (as I did, as I did!) on his mixing of after-dinner drinks. I started to wonder if they might become lovers. I felt like a little brother trying to keep up with two worldly sophisticates—or a rival for Andrew's attention.

Andrew and Marilyn loved playing Higgledy-Piggledy, an elaborate word game in which the participants compose eight-line poems in double dactyls. (A dactyl is a metrical "foot" of three syllables, the first stressed, followed by two unstressed; "higgledy-piggledy" is a double dactyl, and hence the name.) The fourth and eighth lines were four syllables and had to rhyme; the second line had to incorporate a person's name ("Ludwig van Beethoven" is a double dactyl; "William Shakespeare," trochaic dimeter, is not); the sixth line had to be a single word, which resulted in some wonderfully contrived adverbs (*dodecaphonically, anal-retentively, photoreceptively*). Soon the three of us were sending one another higgledy-piggledy interoffice memos. It would take me hours to work one out. Andrew tossed them off.

For my twentieth birthday, the twenty-first of July, a higgledy-piggledy appeared on my desk, the style unmistakably Andrew's:

PHILIP GAMBONE

Higgledy-piggledy
Philip A. Gambone
All of a sudden his
Teenhood did lose

Leaving for Ewig the
Antepenultimate
Year when illegal are
Voting and booze.

Though indeed illegal for me, booze had become a regular part of our Tanglewood social life. Gimlets were our favorite drink and had to be made, Andrew insisted, with Tanqueray and Rose's lime juice. We drank them copiously, in the dorm, picnicking on the great lawn listening to concerts, and especially at the postconcert parties for staff and musical celebrities at Hal's lakeside cottage. I began to notice that males far outnumbered females at these ostensibly co-ed affairs. An effete Englishman who worked for a record company. A beautiful rising star in the conducting world. An office manager and his younger, opera-loving roommate. A prissy sound engineer. I remembered what my friend in Cambridge had told me about Hal. But could all these men be . . .

"Do you want another gimlet?" Marilyn drawled, the words sloshing through the sluice of her wide, goofy grin. As we concocted them at the bar, Hal came up. He'd removed his tortoiseshell glasses, a sign, Andrew and I had learned, that he'd had a lot to drink.

"If you want to go for a swim, there are plenty of towels stacked up in the bathroom," he informed us.

"That sounds like fun," I said, "but I didn't bring my bathing suit."

Hal put a hand on my shoulder, shook his head, and chuckled.

"Gambone."

And so I watched Andrew swimming, his trim, pale body and blond hair luminous in the moonlight. We horsed around a bit, splashing water and trying to push each other over. Whenever he touched me, I felt a quiver of pleasure, sharper even than the sparks I'd gotten from Giovanni's knee under the table.

We drove tipsily back to the dorm. The road was dark and winding, but Andrew handled his VW with aplomb. Woozy, I rolled down the window. The mild night air rushed in. As the car pitched this way and that, the breeze cleared our heads. We began to talk.

In September, Andrew would start a graduate degree in theology at the Episcopal Theological School in Cambridge. For the past two weeks, I'd been grilling him about the differences between Catholicism, the religion I'd grown up with, and Episcopalianism, which Andrew maintained was a branch of Catholicism, a position, like so many of his that summer, I found both incorrigible and utterly sophisticated. Andrew took delight in gently ridiculing my rather uptight interpretation of Catholicism, a kind of Sunday school version preoccupied with sinful acts which came in two flavors, mortal and venial. He'd begun to teach me about situation ethics, which, he said, emphasized the intention behind an act rather than the act itself. As an example he offered—purely academically, I was sure—homosexuality: "A sin," he assured me, "only in those instances where love is not involved." Now the subject somehow resurfaced.

As Andrew talked, rehearsing for me once again these wild, thrilling, danger-ous notions of men loving men and its being okay, I wanted to reach over, cup his hand with mine on the stick shift, and tell him, Yes, yes, I love you in exactly that way. It's not lust I'm feeling, there's a spiritual bond between us, a bond that I want to . . . What was the word? *Consummate? Consecrate?*

It was late when we arrived back at the dorm. I opened the door to our room and flicked on the light.

"Jesus, Gambone, turn it off! It's too bright."

We undressed in darkness. I stripped to my T-shirt and the boxer shorts my mother still bought for me. My head was spinning—with alcohol and with the implications of our latest conversation. I got into my bed, a prep school single with a soft mattress and squeaky springs. I heard Andrew settling into his, no more than five feet away.

Silence engulfed the room. I imagined Andrew drifting off to untroubled sleep. I grabbed my pillow and hugged it close, trying to contain my elation and stifle the pain of not really possessing it, knowing it was slipping away with each passing moment. I must have giggled or moaned or started talking into my pillow, because Andrew spoke.

"What's the matter?"

My heart raced.

"I was just thinking about what you said in the car."

"About?"

"About this business of two men loving each other."

"What about it?"

Was he being coy? Or did he want me to commit myself, as clearly and competently and unambiguously as he had about so many things, by stating exactly what I wanted?

"Do you really think that if two men love each other, then it's okay for them to . . ."

"To what, Phil?"

"To, you know, express that love physically?"

"Yes, I do."

Silence again. I squeezed the pillow tighter.

"Andrew?" I whispered.

"Yes?"

"Can I crawl into bed with you?"

"Sure."

My heart was pumping like a volcano. I pulled back my sheet and stood up, glad that the dim light filtering through the windows couldn't expose the erection tenting my shorts. I was not yet comfortable with the idea that my desire could be returned. I remembered an illustration from a junior high school mythology book: Psyche, lamp in hand, leaning over the sleeping Cupid—the closest those old school texts had ever come to showing me what it would be like for two people to make love.

Andrew lifted his sheet in welcome. He took me in his arms and kissed me.

"Andy," I murmured.

My arms cradled him. I caressed his back, his thighs, his hair, his hands. There was so much to explore, so much that was *body*—his body, my body. He kissed my chin, my Adam's apple, my sternum, my chest. His tongue lapped at my nipples. Suddenly, I didn't know what to do with my hands, whether to touch him, guide him, or just lie there letting him explore me. What had Psyche done when Cupid made love to her?

Andrew rested his lips on my navel, pushed his face deeper into my stomach. When he raised his head, saliva drooled from his mouth. He bent again and drank it up, licking and sucking at my belly. He moved his lips lower still, kissing my pubic area. My erection brushed against his face. And then his mouth was on the head of my penis.

"No!" I whimpered, stopping him.

"Why not?"

"I don't know."

I took his head in my hands, his hair sweaty now, and pulled him back up to me, face to face.

"Not yet."

I wanted to do everything for him, give him everything, surrender totally, the way the saints had surrendered to God. I wanted our bodies to merge mystically, not through the specifics of this undeniably carnal act. Getting down to it, the nitty-gritty of genital sex, somehow felt wrong, not in any moral sense—*those* scruples I had more or less worked out in our conversations over the past two weeks—but wrong physically. The only words I knew for the act Andrew was about to perform—*blow job, cocksucking*—seemed crude and vulgar. They had nothing to do with the sublime fusion I envisioned.

"Just hold me for a while," I said quietly.

We lay cradling each other, our lips brushing, his breath on my face, hot, sweet, foreign, and intimate. Then his tongue slipped between my lips, seeking to penetrate. I clenched up.

"Please, let me," he urged softly.

My lips parted. His tongue filled my mouth, played lambently, burrowed deeper. He began sucking, as if he wanted to eat me—eat all of me. And then I was eating him, licking his tongue, biting his lips, sucking on his nose, small and sloping and slightly flared at the nostrils. It was a delicious nose, an exquisite nose, a nose, I realized, I'd been fixated on for weeks. And lovely, most of all, because it was not mine, but his.

"Your heart is pounding so fast," he said.

"I'm sorry."

"Relax."

He held me closer. I took slow, deep breaths, trying to calm myself. I wanted to say something, to find a sentence that would encompass everything

I was feeling, that would, like some ritual pronouncement, declare and bless this stupendous coming together of everything holy in the universe.

Selig.

Andrew began kissing me again. We lay side by side, our pelvises grinding tightly against each other. His hand cupped my ass, moved under the waistband of my shorts. I squirmed.

"Please," he said. He kept fondling my buttocks.

Then my hands were on him, thrilling to the feel of the soft combed cotton of his Jockey shorts, a material I'd never touched before. For a second, I thought of someone I'd watched in the locker room in high school. He'd worn Jockeys, too. I felt a double erotic charge, as if that boy had come into bed with us. Shocked, I immediately dismissed him from my mind.

Andrew began to slip off my shorts and again I resisted. Things were moving too fast. Every time I started to get my mind around what was going on, something new happened.

"Let me," he pleaded.

Soon we were naked, his belly, his hipbone, his thigh, his *erection* against mine. I wanted to hold it. My mind hovered, not quite ready to give the okay to my body. I couldn't bring myself to do it. The idea of touching his penis felt—to use a word I would learn twenty-five years later—*transgressive.*

Andrew gently pinned me down, bent over, and took my penis in his mouth, far back into his throat, despite my writhing. He was the able one, the competent one. Of all crazy things, he felt like a Boy Scout making use of skills— and a manly boldness—I couldn't imagine in myself. When at last I tried reciprocating, my teeth scraped his cock.

"Ouch!"

"Sorry."

"It's all right, darling. Just watch your teeth."

That's what I wanted—to be his darling. Wasn't that enough?

When I came, Andrew exclaimed "Wow!"—a verbal ejaculation that seemed almost pornographic. "Jesus," he laughed, "you shot so far, you got me in the eye."

I was panting, my heart thumping. I laughed. Was this what truly excited him? What about me? Didn't he love me?

I let these doubts slip away as I embraced him and we kissed again. He squiggled, slathering my semen on his chest. Then he directed my head toward his erection.

"My turn," he said.

This time I remembered my teeth, but I still couldn't quite get the hang of it, and Andrew pulled away more than once in pain. He pressed me farther down; I gagged. It seemed unfair that so much should depend on technique. Wasn't love supposed to just happen, a spontaneous communion of like-minded souls?

I was exhausted, my mouth dry from too much booze. I worked on him for what seemed like ages. Finally, Andrew gently lifted me off. Grabbing his cock, he masturbated to orgasm. I listened to the frenzy of his stroking and breathing, feeling that I'd failed him. The best I could do was embrace him tightly, like a mother comforting a child who's lost something precious.

Much to my surprise, it was Andrew's first time as well. Over the next five years, at his place in Harvard Square (it was impossible to take him to my dorm room) or later in our apartment in the Midwest, our foreplay often involved repeating, almost verbatim, words we'd said that night. By then we were both more adept at the mechanics of sex.

"Andrew?" I'd whisper.

"Yes?" he'd whisper back, recapturing his first note of encouragement.

"Can I crawl into bed with you?"

"Sure."

And we'd fall into each other's arms again.

SIREN SONG

Dr. Charles Silverstein

THE YEAR WAS 1968. Hippies were smoking weed, dropping acid, and eating magic mushrooms, and flower children handed daisies to the police. Left-wing politics decreed that organizational decisions be made by consensus, not by leaders, who were perceived as bourgeois elitists and, as such, enemies of the people. The Black Liberation movement was already well under way and women were joining consciousness-raising groups to free themselves from their dependence on men. The Gay Rights movement was about to emerge from the shadows. I identified with all these groups, perhaps because the turmoil in society paralleled the turmoil within me.

I was thirty-three years old and in the process of completing my degree in psychology at City College in New York. Prior to that, I'd taught elementary school in Westchester for six years. I was an eager student, reading attentively in personality theory and psychopathology. But the books about homosexuality only discussed competing theories of the etiology and cure of an "inappropriate object choice," nothing about how gay people lived or the sub-rosa society gays had built everywhere. No one at school knew I harbored homosexual desires; I sat mute through frequent lectures about the psychopathology of homosexuality, fearful that any word from me would be a sign that I was also infected. A child of my generation, I swallowed the propaganda that turned me against myself.

At the orders of my analyst, I dated women and made every attempt to convince them—and myself—that I was passionately attracted to them, that I thought of nothing but touching and fucking their naked bodies, even though my sexual fantasies were all about men. Unfortunately, the women believed me. I had sex with a number of them, trying to please them romantically and physically—and trying to please my analyst by making him feel as if he were curing my homosexuality. It was all a sham, a conspiracy between my analyst and me to use women and their positive regard for men to treat my "affliction." Since the women I dated were bright and sensitive, they always sensed my anxiety and tried to comfort me, not realizing that the only comfort I sought was to put on my clothes and flee. It was a bitter stew, an indigestible diet of life which seemed impossible to change. As a result, I was wretched. I felt lonely even in the company of friends and fellow students.

One day in the Psychology Center, a bunch of us were talking about the upcoming comprehensive exams and what we wanted to do after they were over. When my turn came, I announced that I'd like to fuck someone all night long—a safe if adolescent response, like throwing pepper into the nostrils of bloodhounds who might otherwise sniff out my real desires.

"You can fuck me all night," said Judy. We had been friendly in the past, but I hadn't a clue that she was interested in me sexually.

I was trapped; the Kinsey 6 had convinced his colleagues he was a Kinsey 1, and now I had to go through with it. I also knew that, the day after exams, my fellow students would be buzzing around me to find out what had happened.

I told them Judy and I had had a great time. We hadn't. It was one of the worst experiences of my life. I didn't want to be there. I didn't want to kiss her, to fondle her breasts, to play with her vagina. And I wanted her to keep her hands off my cock, not put it in her mouth—and to stop asking me to "put it in her cunt." I was unable to get it up; I felt no sensation at all. Judy was wonderful, sensitive, and caring. She left the next morning and we never talked about it, a gift of kindness on her part. Later, I would envy how relaxed she'd been, in contrast to the basket case beside her.

It seems so stupid today, but this happened one year before the Stonewall Riots. My closeted condition was the norm in those days. I didn't know any homosexuals, and would have run in the opposite direction if one had tried to come out to me. Self-hatred built a wall around me which filtered out any positive information about homosexuality. I didn't even know the word *gay*.

Not that I didn't try. Years earlier, I'd spent many lunch hours in the library across the street from my high school reading books on homosexuality, all of which concluded that fags were destined to suffer depression and probably commit suicide. Of course, the books didn't say that the reason gays were depressed was because the police arrested them, gangs of kids beat them up, parents threw them out, employers fired them. At the end of those lunch hours, I'd walk back to school, past a storefront church with a large clock in the window. Above the clock a sign read IT IS TIME TO SEEK THE LORD. That clock could be seen from the windows of many of my classes. It felt as if Big Brother were watching me. I hated it.

Most people don't understand the difference between guilt and shame. The distinction is central in the lives of gay men, particularly those over thirty. I often masturbated in my adolescent years and felt guilty about it. Guilt means one has done something wrong, which could have been avoided. It's a matter of will; I could have chosen not to jerk off. In reality, it made no difference whether I masturbated or not: The toxin was within me. What I was, not what I did, resulted in my deep sense of humiliation: My homosexuality was the shame built into me, and embarrassment over my condition created self-hate. It made no difference that I bedded women. *I* knew the truth. That's what shame is about, and I learned it well.

The next summer, in Boy Scout camp, I fell in love for the first time. It was 1951. I was sixteen years old and a junior counselor. Steve was fifteen and a camper. He was tall and slender, with dirty blond hair, a magnetic smile, bright blue eyes, and a charming personality. I loved him more than anyone else in the world. I often saw him nude, when he and the other boys changed before and after swimming, and I wanted to touch him. One night, after taps, while the boys in the cabin were talking, I slid my hand under Steve's blanket and touched his penis; then, with supersonic speed, withdrew my hand. Steve just went on chatting, cheerful as ever.

I often wonder how different my life might have been if I had left my hand on the taboo object, softly rubbing his dick and as much of the rest of his body as I could reach. Thoroughly inhibited, trained to substitute shame for desire, terrified of exposure, I lost my chance with Steve.

Not that I didn't have others. After camp we became best friends. Every Saturday, we went to the movies, talked for hours, ate together, complained about our parents, and attended Scout meetings. For years, we took overnight hikes, or slept at his house or mine in only our underwear. That was the most painful: pretending that the occasional contact of my body against his in bed was an accident, keeping up our teenage repartee when I wanted to look into his eyes, feigning sleep when Morpheus himself couldn't temper my excitement. I sometimes sneaked out of my house in the early-morning darkness, long after everyone in my middle-class Brooklyn neighborhood had gone to bed, walked to Steve's apartment house, up one flight of stairs, down a long, very wide hallway, the white octagonal tiles magnifying the sound of my footsteps, and sank to the floor next to Steve's door—where I sat in the blue, ugly fluorescent light for hours, accompanied only by my memories and fantasies. There were about six or eight apartments on the floor, and I knew from experience that no door would open until daylight.

What did I do there? I dreamed:

I was walking through Steve's front door, down the long hallway that led to his living room, turning left, into his bedroom. There he was, in T-shirt and shorts, as I had seen him so often in camp, lying on his bed, arms raised around his head, smiling at me.

"Hi, Charlie."

"Hi, Steve. You know I love you."

He opens his arms, his eyes saying everything. I sit on his bed, like I did in Scout camp, and softly touch his chest, then slowly (perhaps not so slowly) move to his genitals, his dick already like steel. And all the while, Steve is smiling at me—lovingly, warmly. Then he sits up, puts his arms around me, making me feel safe and protected. We kiss tenderly, falling together in a heap on the bed, an endless embrace, folded into each other's arms, and sleep.

Sitting in that cold hallway, I embraced myself, imagining Steve was with me, that I was holding him. At home later, I would embrace my pillow (something I still do).

Steve never knew how often I spent the night outside his door. Our friendship ended when I left for college. Furious at me for abandoning him, Steve refused to speak to me again. What an absurd situation: Two young men, each feeling the stab of abandonment, each crying over the end of an intimate relationship, each blaming the other for the rejection. I'd hear this scenario many times as a therapist, from couples struggling for love. The wound has never completely healed in me, though forty years have passed.

Thirteen years after I said good-bye to Steve, I was interning in psychology. It was winter 1968, and I bought a new pair of skis. I'd started on the slopes the year before, and quickly found that I was no more incompetent than lots of other would-be skiers. The trails seemed large enough to hold the speedy, competitive teenagers, the bunnies in their new, fashionable outfits, and people like me, who merely wanted to enjoy the outdoors and improve our skiing skills, but not too much. I took the lift to the top of a modest slope and began my descent. As it turned out, my flashy blue metal skis were in a peppy mood: They began to slide considerably faster than I did. In my attempt to bring them under control, the skis caught an edge, getting stuck in the snow while I lunged forward. The *crack* produced by the breaking of my left tibia could be heard by my cousin Marilyn, skiing nearby.

The cast began just above my toes and ended at the top of my thigh, just below the hip; I underwent two operations before the fracture healed well enough to remove the lump of plaster. By then nine months had passed; my leg, from lack of exercise, had shriveled, but with the aid of a physical therapist knowledgeable in the tortures of his profession, I nursed the weakened muscles back to normal.

During this period, broken leg or not, I had to fulfill my obligations, which then included working full-time at Lincoln Hospital Mental Health Center in the Bronx and teaching part-time in the psychology department at City College. I was obsessed with surviving on the streets of New York, trying not to fall down stairs or slip on the ice, hobbling fast enough to please impatient cabdrivers. Shopping for food on crutches and carrying it home, hopping up stairs and taking down the garbage, were major hazards. The cast was so intrusive, so heavy, I had to sleep on my back when I wanted to sleep on my side. Unable to get my hand comfortably around my cock, I was forced to stop masturbating until one night six months after the accident.

I had been invited to dinner by a colleague who lived nearby, whose journalist husband was writing an article about sex ads in newspapers. He had an enormous collection of periodicals such as *Screw* and the *East Village Other*, and after we ate I started reading them. Page after page of come-ons made my head swim as the testosterone-producing cells in my body, quiescent since the first days of the fracture, came back to life and chugged out male juice. While I sat and read all the delicious things men wanted to do with each other, I actually experienced hot flashes in my face. My good leg tapped the floor so hard that it joggled the paper in my lap, making it difficult to read.

For six months my sex drive had been corked tightly under plaster. Now the cork came popping out, as if from a bottle of champagne, and I bubbled up—giddy, intoxicated, filled with sexual energy, overcome by lust. I excused myself hastily and ran (so to speak) home, determined to do something about it that very night.

Taking a shower, I began to cry, grateful that the falling water masked the sound, as if I could hide my sadness and fear from myself. I was terrified of what I was about to do. I told myself, If I do this thing, this sex with another man, there will be no turning back, I will be one of *them*, a homosexual. Carefully stepping out of the shower, I realized how successfully I had kept myself ignorant: I didn't know where to find other homosexual men. Even if I found them, what would I do, how should I act, how should I dress—how did one homosexual attract another? Question after question came to mind. But the flow of testosterone would not be stilled. I dressed and drove down to Greenwich Village, which was described by the newspapers I had just read as a "gay meeting ground."

"Now what?" I wondered aloud, leaning on my crutches on a Greenwich Avenue corner. I barely realized what a sight I must have made. Then I noticed a waiter behind the counter of a coffee shop. He was so effeminate, even I could tell he was gay. I walked inside, sat at the counter, and ordered something to eat.

"How'd you break your leg?" he asked.

Great, I have his attention, get the information, I thought.

"Skiing. By the way," I asked, quickly as possible, lest others overhear, "I'm from out of town and I'm looking for a gay bar. Any around here?"

"Where you from?"

His simple question caught me in my lie: I had to provide an excuse for my ignorance.

"New Jersey."

(Even then I was snobbish enough to be biased against the "bridge-and-tunnel crowd." I believed you could blame anything on New Jersey. Besides, I had relatives in New Jersey. They *weren't* like New Yorkers.)

"Oh! That's not really out of town. Just go to Julius's, around the corner," the undiscriminating waiter suggested.

I gave him my thanks and a big tip, lurched out of the coffee shop, and hobbled around the corner to meet my fate.

I made a display of myself entering one of New York's oldest gay drinking establishments. First I stood to the side of the door. Leaning forward on my crutches, I grabbed the doorknob and pulled it, quickly using one crutch as a doorstop. I placed the other crutch inside the door saddle and pushed the door open all the way with my body, turning toward the entrance and bringing the first crutch parallel, then leaning on both crutches and scooting my way through. Luckily, I didn't trip in the process and land on the floor, or on top of a customer. I stood for a few seconds, my left trouser leg ripped almost to the waist to accommodate the cast—and noticed all eyes beamed in my direction. Then, as if by some prearranged signal, everyone turned away and continued talking among themselves.

I stood in shock. There were so many of them.

A number of people engaged me in discussion at the bar. My absurd appearance was a conversation piece. I was grateful to the men who chatted me up, though I was too confused to respond except in the most superficial way. Finally, a pleasant-looking guy about my age came over and introduced himself. Don was an elementary school teacher (in New Jersey!), as I had been before I'd entered graduate school. We spoke for about an hour. He seemed to enjoy talking to me. He was so disarming that the fear I'd experienced in the shower evaporated. I trusted this man I'd only just met. I racked my brain for a way of enticing him home, still finding it hard to believe he might want to go with me.

"I have some really terrific pot," I said, having decided that a bribe was my best chance. "It's great shit. Why don't you come home with me and have a smoke?"

He said yes.

Don and I drove in our separate cars from Greenwich Village to the Upper West Side, where I felt like a fool as Don helped me up the flight of stairs that led to my apartment. My whole body was tingling with excitement and anticipation. I unlocked the door and we walked down the long corridor leading to my living room.

"What a charming place," Don lied outrageously.

Then, standing in the center of the room, with a great flourish I tossed aside my crutches and attacked him, frantically pulling off his shirt, unbuckling his belt, yanking down his pants.

"I guess you haven't had it for a long time," Don responded good-naturedly.

"You have no idea."

I pushed him onto the couch, simultaneously propping my plaster cast across his legs to prevent any retreat and tucking my hand under the waistband of his briefs. Don slowed me down, gently reminding me of my promise of "great shit." A few minutes later, the marijuana smoked, our bodies relaxed, he removed his pants and sat in his underwear. I looked long and hard at his body, because I could, it was allowed. I thought of Steve and all the times I'd seen him like this but pretended not to notice.

There are a limited number of sex acts that can be performed with someone in a large cast. Don showed me all the spots on the body one can kiss, and

I, the dutiful student, followed his lead. We touched everywhere my forty pounds of plaster allowed. I placed my hand between his legs and was startled when he spread them to accommodate me and my stroking of his dick. When I stroked too hard, Don sweetly cupped my hand in his and showed me how. With his other hand, he massaged my cock. We touched for a long time, masturbated each other, kissed as we ejaculated. He wanted to spend the night, which pleased me. We cuddled and talked until he rolled over and went to sleep—something I couldn't do.

I lay awake for hours, touching his body from time to time—no place in particular, just spots here and there—lingering wherever I wanted in the joy of knowing that it was permissible. After sex, I'd held his penis in my hand, examining it as if it were some newly discovered artifact from Mars. Now, looking down at Don as he slept, I held his genitals in my hand, kissed them, then his lips, touched his chest, then sat up and continued to look.

What a needy person I was that night, and for a thousand nights yet to come. Don forced me to hold a mirror to myself, demanding that I look at the image before me and question how I had been spending my life. He did it simply by being himself, a tender lover. By night's end, I felt like a man scarred. *What have I done?* I screamed inside my head. All the years I'd condemned my homosexuality and curtailed my passions appeared before me like a nightmare. Gazing upon sweet Don sleeping comfortably beside me, I remembered the hundreds of hours I'd spent with Steve, censuring my every action, never once divulging my love. I remembered, too, any number of boys and young men who had wanted to get it on with me, toward whom I'd responded with coldness, only to masturbate later to fantasies about them.

No one should have to live in shadows, I told myself. From an early age I had been taught that discrimination was wrong. Yet here I was, a homosexual man, discriminating against myself, as if I were the agent of my society. I had been a slave to the superego of my mind and now had to revolt against the taskmaster who censured my passions. That night, watching Don, I decided to become a catalyst for change, for the acceptance of homosexuality in society, so that other gay people could be spared the pains of my generation. And more: I decided I would no longer allow *myself* to be a passive victim of discrimination. I could choose how to respond to the hatred society expresses toward homosexuals, and my choice was to fight discrimination openly, to no longer acquiesce to demands for self-censorship and depression. I had no idea how to go about it, how to join the struggle with other gays. That would take me another three years to learn. But somewhere inside me, I knew I would find a way to heal myself and dedicate my professional life to healing others.

I started that night, by asking myself why I was so prejudiced against homosexuals—in today's jargon, the root cause of my homophobia. Stock answers wouldn't suffice. I was too good a psychologist to believe them. Society condemned homosexuality. Religion said we're sinners. Police wanted to lock us up. Psychiatrists said we're mentally ill. Fuck that. I was too rebellious to believe that any of these reasons could explain how successfully I had blotted out my true sexual desires. I cared nothing about disappointing society, or religious leaders, and certainly not the police, psychiatrists, and psychologists, whom I judged to be police and clergy in disguise. Who, then. was I afraid to disappoint? The answer, once sought, seemed clear.

I saw a vision of myself:

I am a child of seven, returning home from a classmate's birthday party. I enter my parents' apartment and hold out my hand to my mother, revealing a cup of sweets with colored crepe paper around it and a colored pipe cleaner handle. "It's for you, Mommy," I say—proving, yet again, that I am a good boy, ready to deprive myself to make her happy. In the cup are a variety of candies, nuts, and raisins, all for her; there's nothing for me, no homosexuality in the cup, only a son's love for his mother, who has declared him her personal property, which he, in his innocence, has accepted as how it should be.

This was the model of how I deprived myself of passion, of love, how I vowed never to give in to my dreams. Now the grown man realized what a terrible bargain he'd made, how devoid of love he was, how desperately alone he felt. Now he envied, once again, all the bad boys of his youth who had lived their lives oblivious to the wishes of their parents and society.

My parents stood at the root of my homophobia. I feared disappointing them, to pain them by my perversity. My homophobia protected my parents, particularly my mother, from disappointment. It sprang from my family ties, my wish to be accepted and loved by my parents, their wish that I marry a woman and give them grandchildren. The more I tried to please them, the more I had to hate my homosexuality. Good boys weren't queer. Good boys didn't want to suck cock, or eat out a man's asshole, or fuck other boys—or any of the things I longed to do. The self-hatred I'd felt for so many years had to be a reflection of what I believed my parents felt about homosexuality, being queer, being a fag. It was intimately tied up with my being a man; my failure on that score was, therefore, all the more humiliating to me—and, I perceived, to them.

As I look back on that night with Don, I see the steps of my dance, and I wish they could have been different. I should have told him, "Don, you have beautiful eyes, and your lips are as enticing as the song of the Sirens. I want to make love to you." Mature in years but sexually retarded, I could hardly have said such words. They may seem corny, but I'm a corny kind of guy. I was about to have my first homosexual experience, but it would be years before I learned to love the homosexuality in myself and in other gay men.

In the morning, I told Don about watching him sleep, about touching his body and kissing him everywhere I could reach. He was a bit embarrassed, and asked why I didn't wake him up if I wanted more sex. I said it wasn't sex I craved, I just wanted to feel the connection between our bodies, for our skins to unite. I tried to explain that the intersection between my fingers and his flesh was like a switch that turned on the love in me.

I don't think he understood. Why should he? I barely understood myself. But I did have the good sense to tell him that our night together had changed my life. I took his phone number, knowing I'd never call him. Dumb bastard. I was not yet the liberated man I aspired to be. We said our good-byes over breakfast, and I let him walk out of my life.

So let me say it now:

Thank you, Don.

1955

BEING ALIVE

Keith McDermott

IN MY FRESHMAN year of college, I lived with a woman. It was 1968; I was eighteen. We slept on a sagging couch in a room I rented off campus. We had sex every night, not so much out of passion but because it gave us a reason to be together. Jean refused to eat in front of me. I would fix something on the hot plate and she would claim not to be hungry, and busy herself in a book while I ate. I found it difficult to sleep with her. Of course, the couch made a narrow bed (it wasn't a convertible), but physical sensations would keep me awake: her hair against my neck or face, a too-warm thigh, a touch so tentative it irritated.

Jean and I were better in public. We were both acting majors at Ohio University. Our affair was common knowledge in the theater department. At a cast party, a professor drunkenly said he would trade his tenure to sleep with either one of us. By the end of the year I think we were both eager to separate. Jean was going off to be an apprentice in summer stock. I had lacked confidence, or been too lazy, to audition for any theater work. But I dreaded spending the summer at home with my parents and took a low-paying job as a camp counselor in the hills of Pennsylvania.

For ten weeks I lived and slept outdoors with groups of eight- and nine-year-olds from inner-city Pittsburgh, eating three starchy meals each day in a communal mess hall. I gained twenty pounds. I had smoked cigarettes since I was fifteen, but now the fresh air with its wooded scents of pine and earthy moisture seemed to open my lungs, expand my chest. Even my voice became fuller, more direct—perhaps from the practice of herding young campers. I realized how much I had changed when I returned home. My mother referred to my improved complexion as ruddy, claiming me to her Welsh side of the family. My friends from the theater department eyed me almost suspiciously before giving their raucous greetings.

When Jean saw me, she looked at me warily and said, "Scary. What happened to you?" She told me she had taken a room in a private dormitory with a woman she knew slightly, a dance major. I was relieved. I couldn't imagine sharing my couch for another year. Besides, I was looking forward to experimenting with my new looks. The camp crew cut was growing out; now, instead of the tangle I'd worn pushed behind my ears, I used a blow dryer to straighten and style my hair. Always disdainful of sports, I had fulfilled my phys ed requirement with two semesters of bowling. That fall I ventured into the campus gymnasium for the first time and signed up for gymnastics. I even let my mother replace the oversized thrift-shop clothes I'd been wearing with jeans and shirts which actually fit.

In the second week back, I had sex with my scene partner, the prettiest actress in the class. I was also sleeping with an Israeli potter, but she wouldn't do it on my couch, so we only got together the weekends her roommate was away. I seemed to get more attention in the department, too. I was the only underclassman cast in *Murder in the Cathedral*, the first play we did that year. My role as the messenger wasn't large, but I had a funny, down-to-earth little speech which came as a relief after the reams of verse that preceded it.

The obese graduate student who played Sir Thomas More seemed to take an interest in my work. He showed me an exercise to correct my "i-for-e" substitution (I'd say "pin" instead of "pen") and had me run around the theater before my entrance so that I really would be out of breath. After the show one evening he invited me to a party in honor of an alumnus visiting from New York. We went to a loft-style apartment above a bar. Heavy velour curtains blocked the light from the street. A bedroom area had been created in one corner, with a partially opened tent of parachute silk. The room was lit by candles.

It was a small party, ten or twelve people at most—oddly, all men. I knew the host slightly. He had begun teaching first-year speech that semester; though he was still a graduate student, his dark beard and basso voice made him seem older. I was led into the silk tent to meet the guest of honor, who lounged, pashalike, on a mattress covered with a patterned Indian cloth.

He had thinning red hair and an enormous nose which would have been ugly except that he held his head at an extravagant tilt, as if his face were a platter on which to display the grand object. The angle also gave the impression that he was looking down his nose at me, although I was standing above him. He reached up to shake my hand by the fingertips, and said, "Lovely"—implying, I thought, "Lovely to meet you"; but then he turned to a fellow who reclined alongside him and added, "Isn't he?"

A mysterious underground feeling about the gathering thrilled and repelled me. I sensed something secretive, almost illegal, in the heavily curtained room, in silences that fell between chatter. Looks were exchanged. From a cushion on the floor a raised eyebrow telegraphed through the opening in the wall of translucent silk and was answered with a nod. I sat on the floor in front of a stereo speaker, "getting into" the music (a common practice at the college parties I usually attended), but I had trouble concentrating on the mournful tunes sung by an unfamiliar female vocalist—and the lyrics were in French. I was grateful when the guest of honor came over to sit by me, even though he seemed to bring with him the attention of the room.

He'd seen the play that evening and told me I was the only *real* thing on the stage. He was an actor, too, but was working temporarily at a shop that sold stage makeup. I said that I planned to be in New York during the Christmas break. He suggested I give him a call, and handed me a card which read "William Lidel, Actor & Make-up Artist."

My parents wouldn't let me go. My father had been transferred to Dayton and my mother insisted that she needed my help to "get things out of boxes." By the time I arrived at our new house, however, she had joined a bridge club and a tennis group and was taking art classes; the boxes remained sealed in the basement.

I didn't know anyone in this town, had no friends to make plans with. I joined the YMCA and began using the weight room. I became workout buddies with a muscular guy about my age who was a floor manager at Walgreen's. He came to the gym every day on his lunch hour. He'd encourage me by shouting, "Come on. One more. Ya got one more." He said we should get together some evening, maybe drive to Cincinnati. I gave him my number. It was Christmas and the gym was closed. Shortly before I returned to school, my mother said, "Oh, someone with bad grammar called for you." I thought he had forgotten.

Back at school, the Israeli potter was no longer in my life, but Lonnie, the pretty actress, had become a regular. The great thing was, she never wanted to spend the night; we saw each other only during the day, after scene class. She had been a sorority type before switching to theater, and I think she might still have had a boyfriend from her other life. We'd get stoned in the afternoons and "play around." We never thought of what we did as actually fucking, because we were just friends—and I always pulled out.

In the middle of the spring semester students protesting the Vietnam War rampaged through the tiny college town of Athens, breaking windows and looting stores. My house was two miles away, but the acrid smell of tear gas reached me while I was reading *Uncle Vanya* on my front steps. Lonnie, eyes red and watery, stopped by to tell me the news: The dean was closing the campus—and her period was two weeks late.

Just as I could never picture myself being drafted and sent to Vietnam, it was impossible for me to imagine becoming a father. The premature end of the school year left me little time to think about either eventuality. I was going to New York. I already had eight-by-ten pictures of myself with my high school and college credits printed on the back. I could start auditioning, get jobs. I wasn't sure I'd come back to school at all.

My father gave me money for bus fare, which I kept. I hitchhiked east. My last ride, into New York, was with a man from New Jersey who was spending the night in the city on his way to Florida. He talked a lot about his marital problems, about how his wife was always mad at him. He wanted me to have a drink with him after he checked into a hotel, but I said I needed to meet friends. He insisted on waiting while I called the few phone numbers I had of people who might put me up. When I got no answers, he asked again.

"Come on," he said, "let's have a drink. I got the blues."

At his Forty-second Street hotel, he insisted on ironing the dirty clothes I had in my knapsack while I took a shower. Afterward, we went to Child's bar and drank Manhattans to try to shake his blues. He got into an argument about politics with a young Spanish guy at the bar. I sided with the guy and showed him the picture of Che Guevara I kept in my wallet. The bartender, sensing trouble, asked us to leave. On our way out, the young guy told me to get rid of my "hick friend" and come back.

I still couldn't reach anyone, so when the man suggested I stay the night at his hotel ("Hey, pal, it's got twin beds"), I agreed. We got into separate beds in our underwear and pretty soon I heard him snoring. I had been worried how I might handle an advance from him, and now I was surprised, even disappointed, that he hadn't tried anything; maybe he did just want company. I awoke in the middle of the night to find him kneeling beside my bed. I feigned sleep, watching through half-closed eyes as he gingerly pulled down the elastic band of my shorts, pressed his nose to my crotch, and, whimpering softly, inhaled deeply while he jerked himself to orgasm. He was quick, furtive. I didn't move. I felt as if I had caught him going through my wallet.

The next morning, he asked me to wait in the room while he went to his car; he had something he wanted to give me, but said we shouldn't walk out together. I told him he didn't need to give me anything, but I did what he said. When I got to the parking lot, of course, he was gone. It was pouring; one of my sandals fell apart. I discarded the other one and walked barefoot in the rain. A man in a Greek coffee shop told me that if I came back at three, he'd give me a pair of shoes. I said okay, but never returned. I took a card from my wallet and called William Lidel.

William's Spring Street studio was tiny, but between his daytime job at the Make-up Center and part-time work as a waiter, he was rarely home. He said I could stay until I found a place. I tried to be a good guest. I kept the apartment tidy and bought fruit or inexpensive flowers. I walked his dog, Luv Pug, at least twice a day. We shared a fold-out bed. A couple of times, William pushed me to have sex with him; I told him I wasn't really into guys, that I had a girlfriend at school. He said it didn't matter, that sex was something he could take or leave. However, he always made me buzz from the street before I came up, in case he was "having cocktails."

One day while William was out walking Luv Pug, a woman called saying she was his sister. She asked me to tell William that she was coming into town and would be staying with him. When I gave him the message, he made a show of being furious ("Oh, she always does this to me!"), but I had recognized his "sister's" voice as belonging to a girl he worked with at the Make-up Center.

He must have enlisted her to help get rid of me. I said it was okay, that I had run into some school friends who'd invited me to stay with them. I took my stuff and went to a youth hostel all the way uptown where you could get a cot in a dorm-style room cheaply.

That afternoon, walking down Eighth Avenue in the theater district, I saw an unusual and elegant breed of dog that looked like the jackal on an ancient Greek vase. I stopped to admire her. The dog's owner, a darkly handsome man dressed in jeans and T-shirt, told me her name was Dido and that she was an Ibizan hound. He was very friendly and seemed interested in me. He guessed that I was new to the city and asked why I had come. He said his name was Larry, that he was also an actor, and that he was appearing in a musical on Broadway. He asked if I'd like to see the show that night and offered to leave a ticket for me at the box office. Before I left, he squeezed my biceps and said, "Be good."

I didn't expect to be impressed. I had seen touring productions of *The Sound of Music* and *Oliver!* at school and found them corny and old-fashioned; I thought musicals weren't serious theater. But this show was up-to-date and sophisticated, and Larry was the star. In one scene he sang a duet in a bed with his shirt off. I knew that under the sheets he was probably wearing trousers, but he looked naked. I recognized the details of his body from pictures collected in my head since adolescence, images so clear I could have had a scrapbook in my lap. His athletic build belonged to the man in the bathing suit ad at the back of *Esquire* magazine; the light pattern of hair fanning across the chest, fading briefly at the abdomen and starting anew above the navel, was Clint Walker as Cheyenne Bodie. He was the figure model in the *Drawing from Life* book I had found in the library; the swimmer squatting front row, second from the left, in the team snapshot from my father's college yearbook. I covertly adjusted my erection and forced my attention back to the show.

During the bow, Larry winked at me. I was flattered, but wondered if the gesture was a little unprofessional. I went backstage. Larry looked just as he had on the street, dressed in jeans and T-shirt. He asked me over to his place, which was nearby, for a drink.

I had an idea of what his apartment would look like: wall-to-wall carpet, dimmed lights, a stereo-bar unit. I worried about what drink I should request. Not Manhattans; they made me queasy. My parents drank whiskey sours or Rob Roys, but that might be too much trouble.

I didn't need to worry. There was no bar, no stereo; the only furniture was two folding chairs and a card table scattered with mail, menus from Chinese restaurants, and pot-smoking paraphernalia (papers, screen, a plastic bag of pot, a saucer full of seeds). Larry offered me diet cola from a big bottle and asked if I knew how to roll a joint. I did; as I ran my tongue along the sticky line of the paper, I looked up and saw him staring at me.

"You really are something," he said.

While we were smoking, Larry put the lit end of the joint in his mouth and leaned toward me to blow the marijuana smoke directly through my lips holding the other end. I shut my eyes in concentration so I wouldn't cough, feeling his face close to mine. He was still there when I opened them. As I began to release my breath, Larry drew the pale smoke back into his mouth, then put down the joint.

He kissed me. The roughness of stubble against my lips felt otherworldly, shocking. I became self-conscious and pulled away.

"I smoke like that with a friend of mine at school," I said, thinking of Lonnie.

We finished the joint. Larry said he needed to walk Dido. He asked me to wait in his apartment.

Alone, I fantasized about stealing the TV and leaving. The idea seemed funny; I thought I would tell Larry when he got back. Then I wondered if he even had a TV. I went into his bedroom and saw a mattress on the floor, with a TV beside it, covered with one of those plastic sheets that diffuse light into psychedelic patterns. Next to the mattress, a big mirror was propped against the wall, reflecting a stranger: a young man with shoulders broadened by a year of gymnastics and long blond hair parted high and pushed behind the ears, framing a face so boyish no one could imagine he was about to have sex with a Broadway star.

This is not conjecture; I can describe the young man I was twenty-five years ago, or look at photos to check my memory. What I can't say with any assurance is what I was feeling. We make more of a situation in retrospect by labeling it. I knew I was going to have reciprocal sex with a man for the first time. Was this "coming out"? Or did I imagine I was just stoned again and ready for an adventure? I had little idea about what men did in bed. When I masturbated, I approached my real desires circuitously, through a heterosexual route: one (or two) extraordinarily virile men demanding pleasure from a compliant, nondescript female. Wasn't that what all straight men fantasized? I desperately wanted to make love with a man, but I needed the scene to be played in slow motion, with lots of prelude.

Sex with Larry was brief. He was all expedience while I was all restraint. I wouldn't let him touch my ass, sucking made me gag, I struggled against any position that put me under him, and when he went down on me I became inert. When we finally found a rhythm, me on top, his penis between my thighs, he snapped something between his fingers and put it under my nose. I had tried amyl nitrate once at a party and it made me dizzy. It made Larry passionate and aggressive. I felt as if I were in some far-off place, watching myself undulate.

After we finished, Larry told me that I had to leave because men were coming to lay carpet early in the morning. I was still feeling stoned, so I suggested he set an alarm and I would get up before they came. He said he didn't think I'd be able to sleep with the noise from the midtown traffic. I started to explain that I was used to noise, then realized that he just wanted me out.

Back on Eighth Avenue, still reeling from the grass and poppers, I decided to walk downtown to Greenwich Village, some forty blocks, to Riker's, an all-night coffee shop I knew about. I didn't want to go back to the communal situation of the hostel. At Sheridan Square, I passed two drag queens, full of amphetamine bravado, shouting and posturing as if they owned the place. The sky was beginning to lighten. A team of sanitation men stared ominously at the queens.

Two days later, I waited outside the theater for Larry to emerge. I didn't know what I was going to say to him. Maybe nothing. Quite a few fans milled around; I wondered if Larry would feel nervous, seeing me. Too bad.

He spotted me right away when he stepped out the stage door. He kept looking at me while he signed programs, giving me his "You really are something" smile. Then he came over and asked if I'd like to have dinner with him. We went to a theater restaurant, where people kept stopping by our table. Larry would introduce me and tell them that I was an actor. He seemed proud to be with me.

That night, and almost every night for the rest of the summer, I slept on his mattress. A chorus boy I met through Larry warned me, "If you get fucked once, you won't be able to stop." As a result, I never let Larry fuck me, although our sexual repertoire broadened. I could have made love every night. Larry wasn't always in the mood. He said I was sex-crazed, that I made him claustrophobic. Lying in bed, I'd try not to touch him, but I couldn't go to sleep unless I had an arm across his body or my cheek against his back.

After several nights together, he would start clearing his throat and hum up and down the scales, a worried look on his face. This meant his voice was giving him trouble. I figured it was because he stayed up late, smoked too much dope, and did too many poppers. But he held me responsible for his vocal cords; the throat clearing and scales were a warning. I learned when to stay away, returning to the hostel. Larry always called me within a few days, asking if I wanted to come and see the play again (I saw it about forty times) or drive with him to the beach on his day off.

He introduced me to people who might help me with my career. I got a job with a photographer friend of his, modeling a suede suit with a fringed jacket for a popular entertainment magazine. I used the photo as my résumé picture. I started to get auditions, too, and thought I really might not go back to school.

By the end of summer, Larry was having constant vocal problems. I stayed away for a week—which was difficult, not only because I liked him so much but because I had little money and depended on him for at least one full meal each day. When we got together again, I noticed a tube of lubricant he'd just bought was nearly empty, and I found a bottle of shampoo for blonds (not mine) in the shower. I decided to return to school, half expecting him to ask me to stay. Instead, he gave me the money for a bus ticket back to Dayton.

One evening before I left for the university, my mother and I were sitting on our screened porch. I was telling her about some of the people Larry had introduced me to, people whose names she knew. She looked directly at me and asked if I was a homosexual. "No," I said. "I like girls, too."

When I ran into Lonnie back at school, she told me, "Everything's okay; it was a false alarm."

"What was?" I asked. I'd forgotten completely.

Later in the year, Jean and I went on a double date. She took Lisa, the dance major who had moved in with her, and I took Bill, also a dance major, who lived at the Sigma Chi fraternity house but was spending most of his nights with me. The four of us went to a concert, where we sat boy, girl, boy, girl. Afterward, we went to Jean and Lisa's room and they kissed on the bed while Bill and I slow danced.

I had told most of my friends about my summer in New York. When the picture of me came out in *After Dark*, I showed it around the theater department. An acting teacher called me into his office and warned me that I was beginning to get a "chorus boy" mentality. I didn't give it much thought. I had made a group of gay friends. On Fridays, we'd hitch sixty miles to Columbus, a larger city with a gay bar. We called these treks "desperation nights," because we all *had* to meet someone or risk trying to hitchhike home at three in the morning, when the bar closed.

After I graduated, I continued my studies at a drama school in England. While I was there, Larry's show opened in London. We began to see each other again, sometimes romantically, more often not. We became friends and remained so for over twenty years, until Larry died from AIDS complications in 1991. During that long friendship we had many occasions to go over our first night together. "The men will be here to lay the carpet in the morning" entered our personal mythology, as well as the idea that Larry had "brought me out."

But had he?

Let me look at myself once more in the mirror beside his bed. I am twenty years old, high from a joint, and I have just been kissed by the handsome star of a Broadway show. I slowly unbutton my shirt. Perhaps I want to make certain the pale, skinny teenager is no longer there. Defying my inhibitions, I pull off my boots, my jeans, the rest of my clothes, and lie back on the bed, staring happily at the psychedelic pattern on the television set. I worry about nothing. I'm not exactly sure what will happen, but I feel safe, suspended in the grace of knowing that right now I *want* it to happen. More than a part in a play or a place on the dean's list. More than anything.

With Dido

SLOW LEARNERS

Christopher Bram

I.

I WENT TO college in a quaint, damp, green Virginia town, where I spent four years falling in love with men and going to bed with women. There were many men—usually a new one each semester—and only a few women.

I already suspected I was homosexual, but in a detached, oblivious sort of way. Falling in love with anyone was such a relief for a boy who feared he was cold and heartless that the skew of my affection didn't panic me. I told nobody and worried only over what to do with my nervous elation. Sex seemed a good idea, except I was physically attracted only to men I fell in love with, and love made me too respectful to propose anything so rude. There was no terror of being odd, no hunger for normalcy, no conscious guilt—nothing worse than a fear of scaring off the other person. Yet that was enough to freeze me solid.

I fell hard my freshman year for a classmate named Hal who had a boyish face and grown-up swagger, a love of motorcycles and philosophy, and an inexplicable grin for me. My infatuation drew me into his circle—Scott, Lyle, and Rowland—but abruptly ended when he disappeared one night during exams. His parents came to collect his things and reported that Hal had joined the army. Heartbroken, I shifted my private excitement to a cute if insipid counselor at the Boy Scout camp where I had worked.

First semester sophomore year, I bought a fifth of bourbon with a fake ID and the intention of seducing an ambiguous freshman who ate with us. When

I announced at dinner that I had booze, the freshman passed on my invitation; but our friend Marsha accepted. We went back to my dorm and, while *Boris Godunov* highlights played over and over on my portable stereo, I lost my virginity to a woman. Marsha was amused to be my first, the one satisfaction she could take from the evening. I came instantly, three different times. The novelty of another naked body was so strong that the gender seemed a minor disappointment.

This was 1971 and we were still waiting for the sixties to reach Virginia. We were all good sons and daughters, although many of us pretended otherwise. Men did not cry, and never touched or embraced each other. Women were expected to be charming. I came from a lower-middle/middle-class family full of Protestant work ethic and Swiss-German chromosomes, the eldest of four kids who were all bound for college despite the expense. I went to school on an ROTC scholarship, a quirk my bookish and bohemian friends politely overlooked. I barely noticed it myself. Coming upon an antiwar protest outside the Campus Center one afternoon, the sidewalk lined with students holding placards, I stopped and chatted with a girl from one of my classes, Ellen, a petite tomboy with long lank hair and enormous glasses. Neither of us mentioned my combat boots and army fatigues.

Compared to fiction, real life has more characters and incident than necessary. My coming out was a prolonged narrative with a surprising continuity of people. I suspect I write novels instead of short stories because my past is full of such long, tangled strands.

Ellen and her suite mates, Donna and Carolyn, all of them juniors, invited me, Scott, and Lyle, all sophomores, over to their dorm one night for screwdrivers. The women joked about an orgy. In the end, Lyle and Donna passed out on the floor, Scott and Carolyn demurely held hands in a corner, and, on her bed, Ellen and I drunkenly necked and undid clothes and kept going. Afterward, I modestly covered her nudity with mine and we sang "Farewell" with Judy Collins on the radio into each other's ear. "At least you turned off the light," Scott grumbled when we left.

Lessening my embarrassment over balling with a friend among friends was the feeling that I'd proved something: not that I was straight but that I wasn't a disembodied brain after all. I later wondered if Ellen had needed to declare something herself. She was awfully attentive to Donna, who was beautiful. I easily attributed my platonic sexuality to others.

The next time Ellen and I had sex, at the next party, we were sober and withdrew to another room. I confessed, after we finished, that I felt bad because I didn't love her.

"Nothing wrong with good friends having sex now and then," she said.

That seemed reasonable enough. Ellen's flippancy and hiccuplike laugh only half hid a melancholy solitude at her core, but I didn't press the issue, and neither did she.

We went to summer school that year and saw each other regularly, with Scott and Carolyn and Rowland and others, but we were just part of the gang again. The following semester, however, her senior year, Ellen had her own room and we resumed having sex. Our friendship remained on a separate, parallel plane—for me, at least. I remember intimate talks about family in the local deli, but only wary postcoital chats when Ellen lay slim and white on her black velveteen bedspread and I sat naked on her cold floor, both of us in glasses. I liked sex almost as much as I liked being in love, yet was guilty that the two activities did not involve the same person. (Ironically, I can't remember what boy I was in love with that season.) I never spent the night with Ellen, and returned to my dorm feeling oddly sinful, loitered in the lobby, and watched guys who didn't date shoot pool, envying their uncomplicated lives.

There were three or four openly gay men on campus, but they didn't interest me. More important, I didn't interest them. I knew I gave off the wrong signals, but I refused to remake myself. I wanted to invent my own homosexuality. I wrote a gay short story that year, a chaste account of a high school kid's crush on a college student, more about love and fear than sex. I read it aloud in my writing class, showed it to friends, even published it in our literary magazine. I recognize now what a brash declaration that was, though delivered in a whisper. But nobody heard—not Ellen or that season's infatuatee, only an English professor who didn't mention it until much later, when he said, "I couldn't tell if you were very brave or very stupid."

Ellen and I signed up for a comparative literature seminar with a charismatic teacher notorious for challenging his students' beliefs. In the class were a freckled blur named Sam—I developed a migraine while watching him and found it a most romantic headache—and a transfer student from a Catholic women's college in Wisconsin, a young Italian American named Anna. The teacher enjoyed baiting Anna for being so earnest, but she held her own with him and everyone else.

Ellen and I took a solemn walk in the woods with Scott and Carolyn that spring, on the eve of Ellen's graduation. She was angry with me for talking about new movies when she wanted to talk about . . . she couldn't make clear what she wanted to discuss. I became angry with her anger. We sat against a tree away from the others and looked out on an overcast pond full of stumps and algae.

I went off to ROTC boot camp at Fort Bragg, only to receive a medical discharge from the army for my migraines.

Without the excuse of military service to justify my inaction, I returned to school knowing I should do something about my sexuality. But with whom? I was embedded in straight friends and stamped with the habit of silence. I briefly courted one of my roommates, more in thought than in deed. (One night I desperately lay beside Doug and asked if I could sleep, just sleep, with him. "You're just lonely and drunk," he dismissed me nervously.) I buried myself in editing the literary magazine, running the film society, working as a projectionist at the college library, and writing a short novel as an honor's thesis. I lost my temper constantly that year, blind eruptions of anger which had me punching walls and refrigerators and once knocking a plate glass window from a door.

The one bright spot was my new friendship with Anna. I got to know her better when she briefly dated Doug, then on her own. Friends warned her against becoming involved with my circle. We were too moody, they said, too serious, always arguing and hurting each other's feelings, which only intrigued Anna. She had enormous emotional energy—"The girl would wear out a mood ring in a day," someone said—and reported the most startling dreams, such as one where her affectionate father, a veterinarian, took her out to their driveway to put her to sleep with an injection. She was short, bosomy, and very female, but with a wild swing to her arms when she walked. I enjoyed her lack of self-consciousness. She kicked off her shoes to sit on sock feet at the movies. She washed her long black hair with dog shampoo. And I admired her sincerity, the earnestness which some people mistook for innocence but was in fact a fearless desire to address the true and real. She was becoming an ex-Catholic, like Ellen. I decided not to confuse this friendship with sex, and Anna's seriousness guaranteed that wouldn't happen.

I began experimenting with my secret self, telling an acquaintance that I had once been in love with a guy, then telling a friend back home that I'd been in love with *him*. I always spoke in the past tense, as if sharing an amusing anomaly, until one night, over beers, I bluntly told Rowland, "I am gay." A squat, stocky, down-to-earth fellow who constantly pined over women (including my sister), Rowl nodded sympathetically, then asked if it were real or did I just need a new subject for my writing.

II.

I finished school with no commitments, no notion of what to do next. I stayed on as a projectionist at the college and moved in with Ted, a brainy, competitive extrovert with big teeth, in a complex of old brick apartment buildings outside town. Stuck on Ted, I soon learned that he saw me as solely a live-in ear who could help with the rent. Living downstairs, however, was Hal from freshman year, now back from the army.

I was hurt Hal hadn't searched me out when he returned, but three years was too long to sustain a crush; I'd been in love with an idea before, not an individual. This time I discovered the individual, then slipped him back into the old idea.

The army had changed Hal, although not as much as he thought. It hadn't undone his boyishness. Ted and others called him the Kid. He had been stationed in Germany for two years and so avoided Vietnam. He still had a hard-rubber bounce to his walk and stance, an openness in his spring-loaded smile. With finely turned nose and cheekbones, hair thick and disheveled after years in a GI crew cut, he was carelessly, unconsciously gorgeous. His one flaw, eyes pinched in a permanent squint, only made him seem more human and accessible. I always saw his body whole, never in parts. Dropping by his apartment late one afternoon, I caught a flash of him against a bright window, crossing from the shower to his bedroom, a clean silhouette of shoulders, narrow waist, and squared haunches.

We were often together that summer, sometimes with others, frequently alone. When we didn't talk about books or people, we could be companionably silent. Hal strongly identified with Prince Andre from *War and Peace*, a disillusioned stoic, so I became the bumbling, bespectacled Pierre Bezuhov. He clearly enjoyed my company, which seemed promising. And he made no mention of girlfriends or women, which promised more. I anxiously showed him my gay short story. He read it, said he liked its technique, but insisted that the high school kid wasn't gay or even in love, only lonely.

Bored and restless one night, Hal wanted to go to a city and drink. We drove to Norfolk and ended up in a backstreet bar full of Filipino navy stewards who flirted with a brassy, middle-aged Southern belle on crutches. Hal shared his Winstons with me and talked about his stupidity in joining the army, his wasted months in Germany, his inability to decide what to do with his life. He blamed his current misery on his happy childhood. He loved his family very much.

We went out on Granby Street to walk off the beers. Under the empty marquee of a dead movie theater, a man in a gaudy vest asked if we wanted to buy grass. Hal asked if he had any smack. The man said yes, but we had to come back to his place for it. "No, it'll be just me," said Hal.

I was stunned, horrified that Hal could do heroin. And yet, I wanted to go with them and watch Hal shoot up, even do it myself if necessary, for the profane intimacy. He brushed me off as a baby and left with the dealer. Hurt and angry, I waited for him in the grim, half-deserted Greyhound station, worried about how fucked up he'd be when he returned—if he returned.

An hour later, Hal walked in and irritably nodded at me to follow him. There'd been no heroin at the dealer's, only a pal with a knife who told Hal to hand over his money. Hal cursed himself for being suckered. Driving home, he talked about doing smack in the barracks a half-dozen times out of raw boredom. I finally let go with how angry I was, at him for wanting to do that to his body, and myself for wanting to be part of it.

"If you're so damn bored, there's better kicks than heroin."

"Like what?" he said. "Tell me."

But I couldn't. Not yet. Instead I proposed we do something natural and outdoors.

So a week later, Hal and I rented a canoe and went up the Chickahominy River. And it was beautiful: wisps of morning fog curling off the water, crows cawing over the green cornfields, the smooth, glassy river narrowing and widening, chambered like a cow's stomach. Hal's shoulder blades shuttled under his T-shirt while he paddled in the bow and I steered from the stern. We went up a side creek where the trees closed overhead, beached the canoe, sat with our feet in the water, and ate peanut butter and jelly sandwiches. I was sunburned, exhausted, and satisfied, even though we didn't take off our shorts when we went swimming.

Summer ended and I could not move on. I now see that I waited for my buried life to catch up with my college degree. All I really wanted to do was write fiction, but I suffered a failure of confidence, a fear that I didn't know enough to be a writer. Instead I read history, book after book of it, generally about class and revolution. I decided to apply to graduate school in history and remain in Virginia for another year while I supported myself as a night clerk at the local Ramada Inn.

Returning for her senior year at school, Anna was pleased to find me still in town. She and Hal promptly took to each other. Hal had enjoyed our day on the Chickahominy so much that he and his younger sister Ruthie rented a house out there, a half hour from town, a summer cottage with a glassed-in porch, weeping willows, and a pier. He invited me to move in with them. I leaped at the offer, grateful, excited, eternally hopeful.

I lived with Hal and Ruthie that fall and winter, riding into town every day with them (we had only Hal's car and motorcycle) and seeing Anna every night at the library. Free from school, my mind sparked with new ideas and discoveries which I eagerly shared with Anna: Marxism, *Middlemarch*, French New Wave cinema, *The Golden Notebook*. Anna and I were both so intellectually excited that we couldn't always find words for what we wanted to say. We helped each other finish thoughts and sentences, a habit that annoyed our friends when we did it to them.

The Golden Notebook had been recommended by Ellen, who was now in graduate school in Charlottesville. I visited her and we went to bed once more, but on my next trip she said my hot-and-cold attentions confused her and we shouldn't do it again. I sheepishly accepted her terms; the sex confused me, too.

I still couldn't talk about love with Hal. We never talked about sex, either. Despite his fondness for alcohol, drugs, and reckless driving, Hal was oddly squeamish, even puritanical, about sex. He preferred classical music. A Eugene Fodor concert excited him into taking up the violin. We drove back to Norfolk with Anna and Ruthie, not to drink but to see *La Bohème*.

My deep longing was diffused and silenced by daily contact with Hal. Frustration slipped out only in odd notes, such as my difficulty in passing a lie detector test required by the motel to work with money, or the party at the house that winter where I got insanely drunk and announced that I wanted to stand naked on our pier in the freezing fire of the stars. Which I did, joined by my friend Bill and a gnomelike philosophy major named Allen. Everyone came out to watch; Ruthie snapped a flash picture. Later at the same party, Anna and I hoisted a very drunk Hal into his bunk and climbed up with him, while other guests wandered in and took turns trying to play his violin.

III.

Life seemed good, until the rainy night I drove Hal's car into a ditch and the insurance company declared it totaled. Nobody blamed me, but, our transportation gone, we had to move back to town. Hal found a basement room near campus. I returned to my old apartment, where Rowland now lived.

Only then, when we were apart and Hal was no longer a seamless piece of my life, did love kick in as raw, painful need. I felt I had to see Hal at least once a day. I strained to make our time together count. I was working nights, sleeping days. I saw Anna every evening. Often we ate dinner with Hal, who began to do yard work for a retired colonel. I constantly offered to work with him.

I was no longer quietly, unobtrusively present, but actively hunting Hal down.

Suddenly there was tension in the air. Nobody mentioned it, but the mood infected our dreams—and we continued to report dreams to each other. Anna had one where Hal skipped town to reenlist and I was in tears because he didn't say good-bye. Hal dreamed that we three were in a car stopped by a gang of drug dealers and Anna saved us by pulling out a gun we didn't know she had. I dreamed that we galloped in a dangerously small field on three muscular, nearsighted horses without reins. Even Deborah, Anna's roommate, had a nightmare, in which Hal and two other men, neither of them me, beat up Anna and robbed her.

One afternoon at the library, Anna said she needed to talk to me, alone. We went outside. It was beginning to rain, so we went down into the sunken terrace and took shelter under the bridge of the library's entrance. Anna burst into tears and buried her face in my chest. She continued to sob, unable to say anything except "I'm sorry, I'm sorry." The rain fell harder and Anna confessed she couldn't function around people anymore. She didn't know who she was. She didn't feel like a woman when she was with women, she hated the smirkiness of men who treated her as a girl. She enjoyed being with me and Hal, except we made her feel like an intellectual neuter. She could sense affection from us, she said, but nothing physical.

I wanted to explain my sexual indifference, but couldn't. Instead I said that I was bad for her, cold and fucked up. We sank to the pavement while we talked, Anna's hot eyes against my shoulder. She described spending the night with a painter friend, trying this and that with him, without intercourse, and how detached she'd felt. When the rain stopped, Anna got up to leave, saying, "For a cold person you can be very sympathetic."

That night at work, after I balanced the day's accounts, I wrote Hal a letter. I said that I was gay and in love with him and knew it made me demanding, but could he bear with me until it passed. The last clause was not fully sincere. I put the letter in a stamped envelope, but didn't seal it, was not yet ready to send it.

The next afternoon, I found Anna and Hal laughing together in the Campus Center, thoroughly enjoying each other without me.

The day after that, alone with me in the center's cafeteria, Anna talked about how attractive Hal was. "He's so compact. Not just hunky. That, too, but his personality has no loose ends, no frazzles." Then she observed that, whenever Hal and I were together, sparks were thrown off.

"From both of us?" I still couldn't tell.

"Mostly you. Or is that just my imagination?"

I was very excited, very frightened. I reached into my pack, took out the letter, and handed it to her. I knew she was not just a bystander, but involved, in one of two ways.

She read the letter slowly, took a deep breath, and said, "Wow. You're gay? I could feel what you felt about Hal but thought that was only him."

I explained that I'd felt the same about other men, but never women, and never as strongly about anyone as Hal.

Years later, Anna told me that this moment toppled what was left of her Catholicism. "But the Church says homosexuality is immoral," she'd thought. "Except this is Chris and Chris is not immoral, so the Church must be wrong." What she said then was, "I could feel what you felt about Hal. Because I feel the same way myself. About you."

My joy over finally telling the truth to someone who understood became terribly complicated. I was not surprised. It was what I'd feared, although I'd also thought that if Anna loved Hal, things might work out for us all. She could have him if he were straight, I could have him if he were gay, and he'd remain in the family.

"What're we going to do?" I asked.

"I'll go back to Wisconsin. Maybe you'll break through."

We discussed the triangle without anger or alarm, so awed and relieved to be talking that we were not yet distressed by an impossible situation. Despite her own stake, Anna did not dismiss Hal as a lost cause for me. She was as mystified as I was by the bend of his heart.

Then Hal strolled into the cafeteria, grinning and shining after an afternoon of yard work. With his army fatigue pants, pink tie-dyed T-shirt, and the cockeyed stance that turned his entire body into a friendly smirk, he was both less and more real than the figure Anna and I had discussed. He seemed pleased to see us together. We went to a nearby diner for dinner, where we were joined by Allen, the philosophy gnome.

I hated being around Allen. At the end of the month, after exams, Hal was driving a family car cross-country to leave it with his older brother in California. He'd told me he needed to take the trip alone, but Allen had invited himself along as far as Denver. I wasn't jealous. Allen was a clown, socially awkward and nuttily abstract. Hal clearly pitied him. I feared that he had only pity for me as well.

Over the next days I kept forgetting and remembering to show Anna the consideration I hoped Hal would show me. Early one evening, the three of us went for a walk in the woods around the campus lake. We came to a rope swing and Hal had to give it a try, gracefully sailing over the pollen-speckled water and back. Trying to follow his example, I slipped and fell in. We all ended up in the cold lake, laughing and splashing in our clothes. Hal went to his nearby basement to change. My apartment was on the other side of town, so I accepted Anna's suggestion that I use the dryer in her dorm.

I sat in her room, wrapped in a bedspread like a chenille toga, chatting with

Anna and Deborah about a book by George Steiner while we waited for my clothes to dry. With an unexpectedly nasty smile, Anna dared me to give them a show. I accepted the dare, but found that the thought of nudity gave me an erection. Not wanting her to misunderstand, I exposed myself only in sections. Then Anna asked her roommate to leave, there was something she needed to tell me.

She was still depressed, she said. She talked about the men she'd loved and how emotional she became in their presence, wondering *at* them so much it hurt. She began to cry. I sat beside her in my bedspread, her hood of black hair against my bare shoulder. And despite everything I knew, I kissed her. I hoped she would refuse my body, knowing where I was coming from. Instead, she asked me to turn off the light and undressed slowly, worriedly.

I told myself this wasn't real sex—we used only our hands and my mouth— but I couldn't pretend we were just friends fooling around. Our two naked bodies seemed only large and awkward to me without undivided lust to draw them taut. My mind was split from my body, full of fear and responsibility. And yes, there was the stupid hope that if I were kind to Anna then Hal would be kind to me. As if the categorical imperative works in sex, as if sex were going to solve this—although with superficial love, sometimes an orgasm is all that's needed.

When we finished, I asked Anna if it'd helped or been irrelevant, as if her depression weren't about me. She said it had helped some, but she didn't want me to feel obligated to do it again.

Strangely enough, it did seem to help. Anna went out a few nights later with her painter. I went off with Hal, Allen, and Rowland to share several pitchers of beer at the deli and cheerfully argue about the nonexistence of God and the human need for transcendence. "But when you're dead you're dead," said Rowland. We rode home together in his car, dropping off Allen, then Hal. Bold and tipsy, and challenged by my night with Anna, I reached into my pack and gave Hal the letter I still carried. "I wanted you to see this. Good night."

Back home, Rowland heated a can of spaghetti and discussed his chances with my sister while I worried that Hal would never speak to me again. Someone knocked at our door. Hal. He looked serious. He said he couldn't sleep and had gone for a walk—three miles to our apartment. He asked if I'd like to join him.

We marched up the long, dark highway toward Frank's Truck Stop without speaking, cicadas chattering in the kudzu along the shoulders, my nerves strung between terror and hope.

Hal launched into the story of a girl from four years ago, now married, who had been his real reason for joining the army. He'd chosen flight over responsibility, he said. He talked about his history with women, how he'd had sex twice, in brothels in Germany. "Because of this feeling about women," he said, as if he'd made that feeling clear, "all my close relations are with men. I consider you one of my closest friends."

Then he chastised himself for lying, always lying, although the lies he cited were trivial, such as his tale of losing a hundred dollars in a crap game. This led to an existential turn, talk about the lie of meaning, the lie of God. "Prince Andre is a lie," he sneered. "All is a lie over a void of despair." He respected Allen yet scorned his belief that greater meaning existed if only he could find it. Hal believed the universe was meaningless. He wished Allen weren't coming on his drive west; he wanted to be alone and authentic.

I tried to insert myself into this metaphysical murk by saying that I didn't care about greater meaning, only the tick-tock of my own emotions. "Which I guess makes me a lesser person than you or Allen," I bitterly added.

"Or greater," said Hal, without conviction. "Maybe greater."

We were at the Truck Stop now, eating eggs and grits. Impatiently waiting for him to get to *us*, I suddenly wondered if he'd misread my letter and missed the part about my being in love with him. So I followed his airy monologue with a detailed story of my infatuation, from freshman year through our months on the Chickahominy River. I ended by saying that, of the men I'd loved, he was the only one who deserved admiration.

He listened without comment, only discomfort, then skated off into fresh abstractions.

On the hike back, I claimed to have a low threshold of need. All I required to requite my love was his friendship.

"That you have," he said. "That you have."

When we reached my building, I invited him in, but he insisted he needed to walk some more and forget the stupid things he had said. We embraced— me with both arms, Hal with one. I stood alone and watched him wane in and out of streetlight halos until he was gone. I was thoroughly baffled, touched by his coming to talk, disappointed by how little he'd had to say. He seemed to have said no, but so abstractly that I wasn't sure what to think. Neither of us had mentioned sex.

When I told Anna about it the next day, she sympathized with Hal: Learning a friend was gay must be a shock for someone who knew homosexuality only by hearsay, a complete rupture of meaning, which was why he'd turned existential. I could not believe Hal was so ignorant; I wondered if his philosophical smoke hid something else.

Exams began, adding to the stress. I waited for Hal to continue our conversation, but he didn't. He remained himself when we were with others, but avoided being alone with me. One evening among a pack of friends, he grumbled that "a queer" had tried to pick him up the night before. I was stung but said nothing. That weekend the pack went on a picnic and Hal offered to put suntan lotion on my back. I sat very still while his large, callused hands rubbed my skin. I glanced over at Anna, who was as surprised by the gesture as I was.

Anna and I were thrown closer together. Because Hal wouldn't discuss it, she became my partner for talk of my love, just as I was her only confidant for her love of me.

Alone at the Ramada one night, sitting behind the front desk at four o'clock, the hour of the wolf, I fell into a cold, deep rage. I imagined using a shotgun on anyone who'd ever caused me grief—first an old roommate whose journal

I'd once read, then a teacher who'd snubbed me, then Hal, and finally Anna. I wanted to horrify myself, but the images had an oddly soothing effect.

A week remained before Hal would leave for the summer and Anna forever. She was starting graduate school in Wisconsin. The three of us spent an evening together, walking around town, Anna saying good-bye to people. Hal seemed at ease with me again. I was working with him for the colonel the next day. Anna appeared cheerful, until she abruptly drew me aside and whispered, "I can't spend tonight alone. Please." I promised to come to her room later, after I walked out to my apartment and got my bike, which I needed to ride to the colonel's in the morning. Hal and I told her good night and resumed walking.

"Odd how reluctant everyone is to part tonight," he said wistfully.

"Yeah, well," I muttered. "I'm the apex of a crazy triangle." I hadn't said a word to him about Anna and me.

"Yeah. I know." He smiled. "Except there's no geometry in life. Only in mathematics."

"Do I make you uncomfortable?"

"No! What makes you say a stupid thing like that? I feel more comfortable around you than with anyone. Outside my family."

That pleased me. Yet after we said good night, I felt cowardly for not pressing harder. I wanted Hal to be as agitated and confused as I was.

Bicycling back to town on my way to Anna's dorm, I stopped by Hal's basement. His light was off. I assumed he was still out walking. Intending to wait up for him, I went into his room (we never locked our doors) and turned on the light.

He was on the bed, startled awake after falling asleep, his fatigue pants still buttoned. As if afraid I might drop by. I apologized for waking him. He invited me to stay a while, got up, and put water on for tea.

"What're you doing here?" he finally asked. "Weren't you going to go to—?" He couldn't finish, did not want to admit he'd overheard Anna and me set our rendezvous. I read disapproval in his silence. He did not want me to spend the night with Anna?

"Where am I sleeping tonight?" I said. "You tell me. I have two choices, don't I?"

He made a face and looked away.

"I'd go to bed with you at the drop of a hat, Hal. But it has to be your hat."

I wanted him to drop his hat, out of affection or jealousy or even to protect Anna. But once I made clear that my love of him was sexual, my insistence softened, my sympathy with his unease returned. I asked if he knew his brother's address in California, so I could write.

"No!"

He didn't want another letter. While we drank our tea, he took up a book of stories by Albert Camus and read aloud about a man who has his tongue cut out. I thought he was asking me to shut up. I finished my tea and said I'd see him the next day.

Not until a week later, after Hal left town, did I wonder if he'd read me the Camus to confess that he couldn't give tongue to something he wanted to say. Silent myself for so long, I thought I understood. I know now, years after the fact, that what Hal wanted to tell me was not what I wanted to hear. Anna's guess was closer to the truth: Hal was more old-fashioned than I'd ever imagined. He found homosexuality not just alien but unnatural, even evil. I was his first gay man, just as I was Anna's, inept though I was. I spoiled his moral certainty, yet Hal liked and respected me and remained loyal, despite his confusion.

I arrived at Anna's dorm at three in the morning. She apologized, said it wasn't fair when the beloved was also the confidant. She was angry with herself for needing me, angry with me for giving in. My mood was as foul as hers. We spent the night together, just sleeping, both of us in underpants. Her muscles formed a deep cup in the small of her back.

The next day Hal and I went out to the colonel's and worked together, lugging flagstones for a walkway, as though nothing dangerous had been touched on the previous night.

Anna's family came to town for her graduation, and she was no longer free for late-night confidences.

They departed within hours of each other. Hal left in the afternoon, taking me and Anna out to the Truck Stop to say good-bye to us together. Anna and I wasted our last night by riding to Newport News with Rowland and friends to see *Mandingo*, stopping off afterward at an all-night supermarket with a restaurant for coffee. Needing to be alone, Anna and I went for one last walk, not in the woods or on a dark street this time, but in the produce section of the Giant Open Air Market. She asked for an update of my last days with Hal. I had nothing to report. "If only he were interested in women," I said. "Then I'd have no reason to hope." I confessed how, seeing her with Hal, I wanted them to become a couple and set me free. Anna said she'd had a dream where she and Hal made love while I watched in disgust, and another dream where she made love to a woman and I was nowhere around. We rode back to town holding hands. Anna spent that night with her parents at their motel before she left with them the next morning. We promised each other we'd write.

I woke up the next day bereft yet relieved that both legs of my triangle were gone, much as Jules feels at the end of *Jules and Jim*, when his wife and his best friend are dead.

IV.

This was merely the end of the beginning, just as coming out is only a beginning. Doors were unlocked; none had been opened. We were like a piece of chamber music where a single theme is tried by one instrument, then another and the next, in every key and variation until all is resolved in a completed phrase or silence.

I saw Ellen again shortly after that day of good-byes in 1975, visiting her in Washington before she left for Europe to see Scott and Carolyn, now married and living in Edinburgh. I'd written her about Hal. She wrote back, "Now I get it. I never understood what you wanted from me, but you needed a disguise."

The letter infuriated me. Going with her when she picked up her passport and tickets, I argued with her letter. Yes, I'd been mute and selfish, I admitted, but had never pretended we were more in public than what we'd been in private. And I never lied about my lack of feeling, quoting back her line, "What's wrong with friends having sex now and then?" She admitted her own careless indecision over me, and more recent problems with love and sex, men and women. She criticized me, however, for confusing someone like Anna. I pleaded guilty.

Six months later, still in the same Virginia town but with my own apartment, I finally got one male, then another, into bed. It was easier than I'd imagined, although both were only curious, timid, and drunk. (One of them threw up before sex, the other threw up after.) Getting to Europe myself that fall, I was set to spend the night in the train station in Amsterdam when a passing Dutchman who looked like a truck driver said I could sleep at his place. I followed him home, still unsure what this laconic Good Samaritan had in mind when we casually undressed on either side of his only bed. He idly slipped off his peach-colored briefs just as he turned out the light, so I shed my skivvies and climbed in, wondering if the Dutch simply slept in the nude. We instantly seized each other, and I found that sex with any man who wanted me as frankly as I wanted him, even a stranger, engaged my body to its depths in ways that sex with women never had.

When I returned to Virginia, Hal asked me to move in with him again. It suggested a promising change of attitude, but while I was gone, Hal's search for meaning had ended in a leap of religious faith. Anna had been in town for the disturbing privilege of seeing him jump into beliefs that she'd jumped out of. Hal's Christianity was not fundamentalist or narrow, but tentative, open, even existential. It did not stop me from falling in love with him again. It did not turn Hal against me when I told him how I still felt. He asked only that I respect his wishes. I sighed as lover but obeyed as a friend, and occasionally spent the night with an acquaintance who was in love with *his* straight room- mate, a six-foot-six exterminator.

Not until Hal finally began to date women, a year later, did I abandon all hope of love. He was quite straight, yet as slow in coming to terms with his desires as I'd been with mine. Heterosexuality is not always as easy as it looks. I do not presume to understand, but it was as if Hal needed to shore up the uncertainty of self with something larger—religion, meaning, God—before he could expose it in love and intimacy.

Anna and I remained in touch, writing and visiting each other in different cities. Distance kept the resentment and guilt of unrequited love out of all that was good in our bond, usually.

Hal started med school. I moved to New York, ostensibly for the urban experience I needed as a writer. I found more basic, physical and emotional, experience instead. Anna came to the city to take a graduate course at Columbia that summer, then stayed on. I was overjoyed to be with her again. Very slowly, however, it resumed, our schizophrenia of angry love and necessary friendship, and it was worse than before. We were not so timid about what we craved and required. If either of us had been more sensible, or more cowardly, we would've broken off completely. I still cannot think about one period without feeling ill over the pain we inflicted on each other.

The fights did not end until Anna left for Buffalo to resume graduate school. Ellen had transferred there and reported tons of ready fellowship money. She needed a roommate. She and Anna knew each other more by reputation than time spent together, but they assumed they could get along.

That was in August 1979. Two months later in a bar, I met a book jacket designer from Tennessee who loved movies as much as I did. We saw each other every other night for weeks, then months, without running out of talk or shared interests or warmth. Requited love was a new world for me, a strange, baffling peace. The morning of my twenty-seventh birthday, Draper asked me to move in with him.

Anna and I remained in touch. Again, distance helped. She telephoned one night that spring, sounding oddly content, even tickled. She quickly told me why.

"I'm in love."

"Who is he?"

"It's she," said Anna in a very small voice. "It's Ellen. And she loves me."

I was thrown by the symmetry—fiction could never get away with anything so neat—and said, "But you're so different."

She laughed. "I'm afraid we're too much alike."

I was also thinking: Of course. They belong together.

I later came up with the image of Ellen as rock and Anna as fire, which does justice to neither but suggests how they complete each other. When Draper and I visited Buffalo that fall, I saw that they were goofily in love, but also that Anna brought Ellen out of her solitude and melancholy, while Ellen smoothed and anchored Anna's wild swings of mood. They had far more in common than their detour through me. (Anna recently confessed how, in the seminar where we first met, she'd been equally struck by me and Ellen, attracted physically and mentally to us both yet certain neither of us would ever notice her existence.)

Perhaps we were only symptoms of one another's homosexuality, but the three of us seem to have shared something more valuable than error. I like to think it was a belief that the conflicting jumbles of emotion, intellect, sex, and—there's no other phrase for it—moral life actually do connect and can be experienced most fully by two bodies speaking to and through each other. This reckless ideal appealed to us all, even Hal, but Anna pursued it furthest, without fear or compromise. In her friendship with me, she found herself in a house with too many sealed rooms. Then she met Ellen, whose rooms were all open to her.

That July, Hal married Becky, a smart, attractive, subtly tough woman who later became a pediatrician. Anna was unable to go south for the wedding, but I attended and gave her a detailed report the next time we spoke. Hal and Becky spent the following summer in Honduras as rural medics.

They have three kids now, but are no longer in Virginia, so I don't see them as often as I'd like. Hal remains full of passionate beliefs, some I agree with, some I don't. His Catholicism is more doctrinaire than his wife's, but my loyalty to him has made me more open-minded about religion than is natural to my skepticism. Hal might be described as liberal-leftist in his politics and ultraconservative in his moral attitudes, with one glaring exception.

Not long before they moved, I went down for a visit. Hal and I were exiled to the porch one evening so I could smoke (Hal had quit). We discussed a mutual friend, a so-called confirmed bachelor who actually lives the life of a confirmed bachelor. I'd never shared my suspicions about Mitch. Suddenly, without prompting from me, Hal snapped in exasperation, "Why can't Mitch wake up and accept that he's gay? He needs to go out and meet guys. It's the one way he's ever going to be happy."

We continue to confuse each other into more complicated, less easy, truer understandings.

LET THE LIVING CREATURE LIE

David Bergman

I HAD TO be the ugliest boy who ever lived. My mother often told me—and anyone else who cared to listen—that I had been a hideous newborn, even then covered with coarse dark hair, my neck scarred by a twisted umbilical cord that wrapped around it like a noose. When I was five or six my mother became obsessed with how large my ears had grown. At odd moments she would push them back and muse aloud that I ought to have them surgically pinned. Then I broke my nose—my large Jewish nose—and her response was that now I could have plastic surgery without anyone saying it was from vanity. When I developed the most minor of spinal curvatures in the fifth grade, she had my clothes meticulously altered to hide what she called my "deformity." For twenty years I was taught how I failed physically. I was brought up believing that, like Lady Bracknell, I was a monster without being a myth. A Caliban without an island. And everything that happened to me seemed designed to prove just how ugly I was.

For example, during one summer break from Kenyon College in Ohio, I visited a friend every weekend at his dingy walk-up in the gayest part of Greenwich Village. It was 1971, two years after Stonewall. I loitered along the New York streets, dressed in the tightest clothes I was allowed to wear out of the house. No man passed without my giving him a searching look. There was much talk even then of the predatory nature of homosexuals, how they feasted on young flesh like lions and jackals. I was offering myself up to be caught, yet no one, not a single person, even turned around to look at me.

Back at school that autumn, I picked up the most effeminate boy on campus, a rail-thin art major who wore long lavender silk scarves which billowed behind him as he sashayed down the paths between classes. I was at a party given by some friends who lived off campus, a household of writers, artists, and one very cute classicist. I got very drunk on low beer whose alcoholic content was in inverse proportion to its ability to nauseate. When I got sick, Mark offered to walk me back to my dormitory room. He held me close, to keep me from falling. Once inside, he gave me a wild and passionate kiss, placing his tongue in my mouth. When I kissed him back, he pulled away.

"I wanted to see if you would," he said, laughing.

"I would and I have," I replied. I stepped forward and tried to take him in my arms.

"But you're not my type at all—not at all." He opened the door to let himself out, stopping only to add, "But now I'm sure you're queer."

And he went skipping down the hall.

I was afraid—not that he would blab my secret to everyone but that he would keep it to himself. Mark had many friends who, if not quite as flamboyant as he, were clearly as gay, and I was willing to let any one of them take my virginity. I felt shame, not at being gay but at still being a virgin at twenty.

People recognize the direction of their erotic interests at different times in their lives. I've met men who say they didn't know they were gay until their fifties, and while that seems a long time to remain in the dark, I have no reason to doubt their honesty. I, however, have always known I was gay. When I was five or six, I simply understood this as being different from other boys. But soon this grew into a desire for closeness to other males—more than friendship; a closeness with a forbidden romantic quality. I matured before all the other boys in my class (yet another example of my freakishness) and would rifle through my parents' copy of *Psychopathia Sexualis*. By the fifth grade I could put a name to my desires: I was a homosexual. Having come so early to this understanding, by the time I was in college I was all the more horrified by how long it was taking me to act upon that knowledge. I was writing my senior thesis on W. H. Auden—itself an act of sublimation and liberation—and his remark that virginity was the only perversity echoed in my head. I saw myself as twisted, my innocence an illness only carnal knowledge of another man's body could cure.

A decade earlier or a decade later, my anguish might have been less intense. I might have fitted into the late fifties era of sexual repression, or joined one of those religious groups of the eighties whose participants wear virginity on their sleeves as a badge of spiritual enlightenment. Or I might have used AIDS to explain my isolation. But I was a college student in the late sixties and early seventies, when sexual liberation was the credo. I was the only virgin I knew. I felt as if I wore a white *V* on my chest. I would gladly have traded it for the pink triangles that became so popular a few years later.

BECAUSE I WAS a senior and an honors student, I was assigned a private room at the top of Leonard Hall, a great gray pile of neo-Gothic stone. It was known as the Owl's Nest and was the only single on the fourth floor; all the other spaces there were lounges. I had a bathroom to myself and a piano on which I'd play out my miserable heart. From my window in the Owl's Nest I could look across the campus, through the woodland, and far out into the river valley. The owl is a solitary bird and a carnivore. I was alone and I wanted meat.

It was a Wednesday night in February. I was to be graduated in June. Time, as always, was running out. I sat in my room reading Lytton Strachey's *Eminent Victorians*, the section devoted to "Chinese" Gordon, for a seminar in nineteenth-century British cultural history. I looked up to see a note had been shoved beneath my door:

> *Mr. Bergman:*
> "In my arms till break of day
> Let the living creature lie,
> Mortal, guilty, but to me
> The entirely beautiful."
> *Meet you in the coffee shop*
> *Midnight   Friday*
>
>   *Tom*

Was it a love note? I wasn't even sure; I had no experience with the genre. Were it not addressed to the rather formal "Mr. Bergman," I would have assumed it had been slipped under the wrong door. I figured it was some kind of misguided attempt at sophistication—most likely a trick, some ruse of Mark's to humiliate me. Well, I was fully prepared to be humiliated if that was what it took.

I knew very few Toms, as it happens. The one I was closest to had lived next door to me in my freshman year. He was a sweet fellow from one of the WASP enclaves of Pittsburgh, with blond hair that flopped in his face and little wire-rimmed glasses. When I first met him, I said, "I bet your house is white, with dark green shutters, and there's an oak growing on your front lawn." He answered, surprised, "The shutters are brown." He once came to me, upset. "David, you know something about psychology. For the last three nights I've had a dream of being locked in a closet with my little sister, and I'm holding her very tight and she begins to cry. What do you think it means?" This Tom knew about my senior thesis; he was capable of copying those lines of Auden's "Lullaby" from the *Norton Anthology* without understanding their implications. He even had a reason to write to me. Tom was the producer of a play on which I had worked as translator, a student production scheduled to open in two days—on Friday. The note could have been an overheated invitation to a cast party.

The next day I saw him coming from class.

"Did you leave a message under my door?" I asked him.

"No," he answered. "Was I supposed to?"

"No. It's just that someone named Tom left me a note and I don't know who wrote it."

"Well, it wasn't me."

Another Tom, a freshman I had met at a frat party, I found in his dorm room. No, he hadn't sent me the note. I was acquainted with only one more Tom, a swimmer who shared a statistics course with me. I thought it unlikely he would even know who Auden was, but I went to see him anyway. He, too, had not sent the note.

I was at a dead end. I tried to put the note out of my mind all Thursday, but it would not be ignored. Friday came, and with it the opening of the play. I went backstage and congratulated the cast at eleven o'clock, then returned to my room. I took another shower. I brushed my teeth again. I gargled, rinsed, and gargled once more. I was not going to be saddled with virginity because of poor hygiene.

A little before midnight, I went to the coffee shop. The early seventies was a time when clutter constituted a statement. The coffee shop had been newly redecorated to look like a country antiques store: weathered barn siding walls dotted with hubcaps and chewing-tobacco signs, with birdcages, elk horns, moose heads, and daguerreotypes hanging down, jutting out, and dangling in studied nonchalance. The place was packed. (It was the only late-night eatery on campus.)

I met some friends, none of them named Tom. We talked for a while. I saw some cast members from the play and went over and congratulated them again. They looked like miniature stars, their faces cleaned of makeup, shiny with the kind of excitement opening night can give amateurs. This should be my opening night, I thought. But I couldn't imagine how the curtain would be raised, or if I would receive even polite applause.

Someone offered me a cigarette. I didn't smoke, but I was feeling nervous, and I wanted to appear sophisticated, and I was afraid of what I would do with my hands if I didn't have something to hold on to, so I accepted. I pushed out the smoke too quickly. I felt light-headed.

"What time is it?" I asked the person next to me.

"Twelve-thirty," she answered.

"I'd better go."

She shrugged. "Suit yourself."

The coffee shop was in the basement of the dining hall. It had two entrances, one directly off the loading area (the more popular entrance at night), the other through the dining hall, down a flight of steps, and beyond a corridor lined with heating ducts. I decided to take the long way back, through the dining hall. I opened the big metal fire door and heard it latch behind me. The loud babble of voices suddenly sounded far away. I was shut out of that happy world of people who had sex. Adam and Eve had been banished from Eden because they had eaten of the tree of knowledge; I had been cast out for not having taken a bite. I didn't blame Tom—whoever he was—for standing me up. I was, after all, the ugliest boy in the world. I just wished that he hadn't lifted my hopes, hadn't driven so forcefully home my hapless situation.

I walked down the empty corridor inert, hardly able to push my legs along. Lightbulbs burned against the white walls. I could smell the sickeningly sweet odor of rotting food. Then the fire door opened and I heard footsteps approaching. An artificially low voice, imitating my own deep bass, called out:

"Mr. Bergman."

I stopped. *I don't care what he looks like*, I thought. *I can't be choosy. This is the man who will take away my curse. I will do whatever he wants.* And then I turned.

It was someone I had never seen before on campus, although clearly a student. He was shorter than I was (good, he wouldn't be able to overpower me) and soft-looking. He had curly hair and a reddish nose (maybe he had been drinking to work up his courage). His eyes twinkled and he had the most inviting grin—devilish, delighted, mildly drunk. And I knew at once—how do we know these things? how could *I* know such things?—that it would be all right, that I was the cooler one, I was in charge.

"Want to go back to my room?" I asked, without any introduction.

He walked up to me and, rising on his toes, kissed me on the lips.

"Sure," he answered.

And we went out into the night.

HE HAD BEEN following me for months, preparing a dossier on my comings and goings, my likes and dislikes. He had heard me speak at a peace rally, a memorial service for those who had died at Kent State, and developed a crush. Mark, the queen bee of the campus, kept a list of all the queers at college, and when my name appeared on it Tom took courage. After sending me his note, he employed a small army of friends to keep tabs on me. A betting pool had been formed between those who said I would keep the date and those who said I wouldn't. His roommate had sat behind me at the play and watched me nervously flip through the program, then went back to Tom and told him I was definitely *on*.

Now that I was finally to lose my virginity, I remembered my body—that ugly, monstrous deformity. Long before this evening I had decided that I probably would be impotent. In a popular TV ad of the sixties, a man and his stomach consulted a psychiatrist about how they mistreated each other. The psychiatrist recommended Alka-Seltzer and the man and his stomach were blissfully united. I had been hospitalized for bleeding ulcers, and despite all the medications I had taken, the best the doctors had worked out was a truce: Alternatively, my mind or my stomach would be blocked with tranquilizers or antacids. And then there was my bladder. During the night my kidneys developed amnesia, and in the morning, it was as if my body had to learn all over again how to urinate. Even alone I found it hard to pee. If anyone was around, my body would panic and be paralyzed for hours. From my virginal perspective it seemed only logical that once again my body would fail me. Desire, no matter how strong, could never overcome the intransigence of my prostate. The spirit was willing, but the body was a dumb and stubborn coward.

I can only suggest my surprise when I felt those familiar sensations that lead to orgasm. Sure enough, my toes were curling, my back was arching slightly. Then I felt that tingling which culminated in a release into Tom's eager mouth (he had come in mine minutes before). It seemed so easy finally to be a sexual being, so deliciously simple, that I let out a strangled laugh of pleasure and self-affirmation, a comic eureka. *Look*, I wanted to tell my body, *Look how well we have come through!* Freud says there are always at least four people in bed when we have sex, but at that moment there were only two—me and my body —and for a second we loved each other. Tom, poor Tom, had become irrelevant, the mere occasion for our reconciliation. It was a long time before I stopped laughing, and although I told Tom I was not laughing at him but at myself, I don't think he ever felt comforted by my explanations.

Tom stayed the night. At some point I heard him doze off, but I didn't sleep at all. Not that this was unusual. I often suffered (and still do) from insomnia; if my body could forget how to pee, it could also forget how to sleep. Early in the morning, I got him up and we went for breakfast. Then he went to his room to sleep some more, while I went to the library to slog through Lytton Strachey. If it seems odd that I could go back to my studies so quickly, that I didn't revel in this long-awaited change in my life, I can only say I do not know how to celebrate myself. I had been taught that one's job is to go on with one's life as if nothing remarkable has happened, and I did.

At three o'clock I returned to the Owl's Nest, slowly ascending the four flights of stairs, which seemed even longer and steeper that afternoon, since I'd gotten no sleep the night before. I pushed open my door, which I kept unlocked (there being nothing to steal), and stood in the doorway.

My room had been filled to the brim with flowers. In the window was a large spray of gladioli, long red stalks in a large plastic basket. A vase was crammed with daisies and baby's breath, encircled by lacy ferns which looked like a swirl of green snowflakes. A great horseshoe made of mums, like something you might hang around the neck of the winner of the Kentucky Derby, was propped against the back of my one easy chair, and lying across the bed were a dozen roses, tangled together in an orgy of red. Mafia bosses have been buried with less. Tom had emptied out the town's only florist shop, in the first of his drunken displays of prodigality I was soon to get used to.

Instead of entering my room, I closed the door and turned to one of the lounges that filled my floor. In a window seat in the oak-lined Campbell-Meeker Room sat my good friend Denton, with a yellow pad on one knee, a history book on the other. He was slightly older than all of us, having dropped out in the middle of his college career to enter analysis. There was a rumor he'd had an affair with an older woman during his year-long sabbatical. Like Tom, he was a doctor's son and took a clinical view of life.

"Denton, I need to show you something."

My voice must have contained a certain urgency, because he immediately said "All right," put down his book, and followed me back to my room. With a push, I flung open the door to reveal Tom's floral tribute. Denton gasped, then reached up his hand and squeezed my shoulder.

"David," he said, "I'm so happy for you."

"You are?"

"Of course. Who is he?"

The last word lingered in the air, and we both burst out laughing.

"Tom," I said. "His name is Tom." And I cleared the roses off my bed.

Photograph by Tom Epps

BOYS LIKE US

Michael Nava

FROM THE TIME I was a child I had planned to get as far away from Sacramento as I could and never return. The only means available to a brainy, unathletic kid from a poor family were academics. So, while my classmates adopted the postures and attitudes of the sixties, I studied hard and accumulated the kind of achievements that looked good on college applications: debate team captain, class president, honor student. I was college bound, a first in my family—none of whom encouraged me in this ambition. For that I relied on teachers, among them Jack and Lauren Hart, who had come from backgrounds similar to mine.

Jack taught speech and coached the debate team. A pale, slender, freckled, redheaded Irishman with a droopy mustache, he was not much older than his students. Lauren was pink-skinned and fleshy. The slight asymmetry of her features, combined with her clear, grave eyes, gave her the look of one of the saints in the stained-glass windows of St. Joseph's, our parish church. The Harts were small-town bohemians. He was cynical and political, she was senti-mental and artistic. Contemptuous of the suburbs, they lived in downtown Sacramento, behind a white picket fence in a little house decorated with framed Picasso prints, beanbag chairs, ceramic planters filled with lush ferns, and book-shelves crammed with Lauren's art books and Jack's collection of the subver-sive texts of the time, from *Why Are We in Vietnam?* to *The Whole Earth Catalogue*. They listened to jazz and brewed oily cups of espresso in a stain-less steel pot purchased in San Francisco—and befriended a group of preco-cious misfits, like me. Their house was a haven from the stifling atmosphere of the overgrown cow town in the central valley of California none of us could wait to leave.

A few days before I turned seventeen, the Harts threw a reunion for members of the debate teams Jack had coached over the years. It was the end of summer, 1971. I was about to begin my senior year at high school. It was still light out when I arrived. The oaks that lined their street were touched with bronze. A faint breeze blew in from the nearby American River; the air smelled of tomatoes, from the Del Monte cannery a few streets over. I was drenched with sweat from pedaling through the August heat. I leaned my bike against the side of the house and followed the sound of voices around to the backyard.

My bejeaned, beaded, long-haired classmates were sitting in circles eating fried chicken and drinking beer. Jack interrupted his tirade against the war to toss me a can. Lauren, at the center of her own circle, said, "There's plenty of food in the house, Michael. Eat something."

Inside, a group of kids was standing around the kitchen table, filling paper plates with chicken and potato salad. I picked up a plate and got in line. Jack came in and took a six-pack from the refrigerator. On his way out, he stopped and said, "I want you to meet this transfer kid from Hayes [a school across town]. He debated for them last year. I'm thinking of partnering you."

My debate partner had graduated the previous year and there was no other senior to pair me with.

"Is he any good?" I asked.

"His coach says so. Check him out."

I loaded my plate and went into the living room to eat.

A few minutes later, a thin boy in shorts and a tank top, wearing a string of blue beads around his neck, sat down on the floor beside me. A shock of mahogany hair fell across his forehead. He pushed it off his face with a bony finger, revealing a patch of acne. His face combined Anglo and Latino features: high cheekbones, a narrow mouth, slightly slanted hazel eyes. His nose looked like it had been broken. He smiled at me.

"Michael," he said, "I'm Joey Spencer. Jack said I should talk to you. He thinks we should be partners."

Joey and I talked about the writers we loved, the subjects we did best in at school and the ones that caused us trouble, the colleges we planned to apply to, what we hoped to major in, who we hoped to become. He told me how his nose got broken. Despite his Anglo last name, he was half Mexican, which made him a target for both Anglo and Chicano gangs at Hayes. The previous spring, he'd been attacked at school by some white boys, who broke his nose in the process. His mother got him transferred, for which he said he was glad. Hayes was the worst high school in the city academically, and Joey had his sights set on Berkeley. He needed the advanced placement classes available at my school to compete for a slot at the university. He was a boy like me, from a poor family, ambitious but diffident, hungry for encouragement but fearful of being mocked. Beneath our conversation flowed another one, in which we sought and found assurance that the things to which we aspired were not ridiculous or out of reach, though his father was a machinist at the local air force base who barely supported his seven children and my stepfather laid pipes and drank too much and beat his wife.

When the last guests had been reluctantly hustled out the door, Joey and I were still sitting on the floor and talking. Jack came into the room and said, "It's late, you guys."

Joey sprang to his feet and pulled me up.

"So," Jack continued, "are you going to be partners?"

Joey looked at me. We hadn't even discussed it.

I said, "Sure."

"Great," Jack responded.

We said good-bye to Lauren and left. Joey asked if I wanted a ride home. I pointed to my bike.

"So," I said, "I guess I'll see you when school starts."

"That's not for two weeks," he said. "Maybe we could do something before. Go to a movie or something?"

"Saturday?" I asked quickly.

He smiled. "Give me your number. I'll call you."

He didn't have anything to write it down with, so he made me repeat the number until he'd memorized it.

THE BLUE TV light flickered across the faces of my mother and stepfather as I stood in the darkness outside our house and watched through the window. I did this out of habit, to try to determine how drunk my stepfather was before I went in. He lifted a tall can of beer to his mouth, drank, set it down, picked up a cigarette, inhaled, exhaled, and reached for the beer again. My mother fanned his smoke from her face. My younger siblings sat at her feet.

I let myself in through the back door and went to my room. The TV blared through the thin wall on which I had tacked up a map of the world. I locked my door with the chain I'd installed myself, the only lock in the house. I put on a record, undressed, and got into bed. A little while later, there was a tap at the door. My mother.

"Mikey?"

"I'm in bed," I growled.

After a moment, she said, "Good night, *mi'jo*," and shuffled away.

JOEY STIRRED SOMETHING in me besides excitement at finding a new friend: the queasy sweetness of attraction, the thrum of sexual longing for his long-limbed dark smoothness, his musk, the light in his pale eyes. I was a queer, something I'd known since I was twelve and had never told anyone. Because I didn't play sports or date girls, I should've been the target of jibes from my classmates, but I lived by my wits, employing a fierce, preemptive sarcasm to protect me from open taunting. I was a sissy with fangs, and people kept their distance. I was extremely defensive around boys, especially the ones toward whom I felt attracted. But I trusted openness in others. Joey seemed to lack that internal gauge against which other teenagers measured their manliness. Whatever he was feeling flickered across his face or inflected in his voice. It was clear that he liked me, so I let myself like him back.

On Saturday, I biked across town to Joey's. He lived in a working-class neighborhood of small, prim houses which projected an anxious tidiness. Sprinklers sprayed jets of water across green squares of yard, and rosebushes lined walkways to spotless porches. Lace curtains fluttered in windows; as I pedaled past, I was aware of silent watchers.

Joey's was the last house on a dead-end street. In contrast to its neighbors, it was unkempt and ramshackle. A big deodar tree shaded the scraggly grass littered with children's toys. I leaned my bike against the sagging porch railing and went up to the screen door. Sly & the Family Stone sang "Everyday People" above TV sounds. I smelled the familiar odor of beans cooking on the stove. A woman yelled.

"Joey, turn that damned music down!"

I knocked at the door frame. A little girl of five or six came and studied me through a gash in the screen. "Can I talk to Joey?" I asked her. She shuffled away.

A moment later, Joey appeared, wearing only cutoff jeans. He led me through the living room, where the girl who'd answered the door sat on a rust-colored sofa watching TV while a toddler slept in a playpen on the floor. The air smelled of baby shit. We went down the hall past the kitchen, where a tall, thin, dark-skinned woman was rolling tortillas on the counter.

"Who's your friend?" she asked without looking up.

Joey introduced me to his mother. She interrogated me about my family, continuing to make tortillas. I sensed Joey's embarrassment, but he said nothing. It turned out she'd gone to high school with one of my uncles. Once that quasi-family bond was established, she became friendlier and sent us off munching *tacos de mantiquilla* (hot rolled tortillas smeared with butter).

"So, your mom went to school with my uncle," I said to Joey as I followed him down a hall lined with family photographs. "Does that make us like cousins or something?"

He grinned at me. "I've got too many damned cousins as it is," he said. "Don't mind my mom. She's a snoop." He opened a door and said, "This is where I hide from her."

His room was a narrow, whitewashed rectangle which looked out on a backyard as cluttered as the front. A single bed was pushed against one wall, a wooden desk against the other, with scarcely enough room left to walk between them. Clothes lay scattered on the floor, along with piles of books, a tennis racket, and a battered hi-fi next to an orange crate crammed with records. Posters advertising rock concerts at Fillmore West, Bill Graham's concert hall in San Francisco, covered the walls: Grateful Dead, Big Brother & the Holding Co., Santana. Joey collapsed, cross-legged, on the bed. I sat down opposite him.

"This is cool," I said.

He laughed. "There's hardly enough room to fart. When I have my own house someday, this will be the size of my closet."

"There's a palace in Vienna that has a thousand rooms," I told him.

He named it. "Do you get high?"

"You have some pot?"

He reached over to his desk, opened a drawer, and took out a small plastic bag and some rolling papers. "You roll it," he said.

I picked up an album from the floor to use as a surface. Joey opened the windows and closed the door, stuffing a towel at its base, then turned on a desk fan and put on a record. He came back to the bed and sat shoulder-to-shoulder next to me. I handed him the joint.

"That's good and tight," he said admiringly, and lit it. We passed the joint back and forth.

"Where'd you get the grass?" I asked.

"My brother Carl," he said. "Try to exhale toward the window."

"It's hot in here," I said. I pulled my T-shirt over my head, inhaling my own odors, and stopped. I was stoned.

"You need help?" Joey asked, giggling.

"Yeah. I'm stuck."

He grabbed my shirt and pulled it off my head, laughing. He waved it around and tossed it to the floor, hitting the record player. The needle skittered across the vinyl.

"Ooh," he said. "Shit."

He sprang from the bed, kneeling in front of the record player. I studied his dark back, the knobby spine, the splay of his ribs, the smooth flesh packed between them tight as feathers. The pot made his presence more intense. I felt the ache of sexual loneliness. When he stood up and turned to me, I could make out the bunched-up dangle of his dick and balls beneath the faded denim of his cutoffs. It was all I could do not to touch him.

THAT NIGHT, LYING in bed, I slipped off my underwear and quickly masturbated. I imagined Joey in his room, naked and touching himself. I came with a grunt, feeling guilty and alone.

Later, the noise of my stepfather lumbering drunkenly through the house awakened me. I lay quietly, fearfully, until all was still again. There would be no screaming, no fighting tonight, nor would he rouse me from my bed to listen to another drunken monologue about how unappreciated he was. It was September; in a year I would be gone for good and safe at last. Then I remembered sitting on Joey's bed, watching the muscles in his back move, and I realized that my sexual nature was the one secret I could not escape by going away to college. There was no escape from it—and no safety anywhere.

SCHOOL BEGAN A few days later. I walked down the crowded halls to my first class. The five-minute bell rang. A cloud of girls drifted by, in their wake the scent of perfume, cigarettes, and chewing gum. Friends shrieked greetings to each other, teachers hurried into classrooms. A group of boys from the swim team were finishing practice. I stood at a distance from the pool and watched them out of the corner of my eye, pretending to look elsewhere. Their hard bodies, brown from the summer, made me feel soft and useless in my own skin.

Someone tapped my shoulder. I jumped.

"Did I scare you?" Joey asked. I turned my back to the swimmers.

"I was waiting for someone."

He smiled. "Me?"

"Yeah," I said. "Do we have any classes together?"

We compared schedules. Our only shared class was Jack's, at the end of the day, but we had the same lunch period.

"Where should we meet for lunch?" he asked. I liked that he assumed we would.

"At the tree out front."

"What tree?"

"There's only one," I said.

The last bell rang and we hurried off to class.

THE HIGH SCHOOL had opened only a few years earlier. Its architectural style was California motel, with long open walkways, an A-frame cafeteria, and rows of classrooms like the cars on a freight train, all painted pus green. The class of 1968 had planted a tree in a patch of grass at the front of the building which had become the gathering place of the same misfits who hung out at Jack's on weekends. Not much more than a sapling, the tree's skinny branches cast a meager shade, and we were quietly but intensely selective about who we allowed to share it. Interlopers were politely ignored, until they got the hint and left. When Joey came out, I introduced him around. My friends took a look at his unkempt hair and striped overalls and made room for him.

We leaned against the tree while half a dozen conversations floated on the warm, silty air, talk of books, movies, classes, colleges, weekend plans, student council business, the school newspaper, who had pot, whose older brother could be counted on to buy beer. Joey plucked a long stalk of grass and tickled my face with it. I searched his face for a clue as to what the gesture meant, but he simply smiled and brushed the grass across my cheek until I smiled back.

We became inseparable. We ate lunch with our friends beneath the tree. After school, we practiced debating, in preparation for the weekend speech tournaments, or went to the local state college library to research. Joey was as single-minded as I was, and we worked well together. On weekend nights we got high and went to the movies or to Jack and Lauren's house. If Joey could borrow his father's car, we drove around looking for parties and ended up at two in the morning at the local McDonald's with everyone else, watching the class drunk stagger between cars and piss on his shoes.

In mid-October, the long valley summer ended abruptly. I woke one morning to find frost on the lawn. The nights got shorter and the air was sharp. When the winter rains began, my stepfather's construction jobs dried up and he sat in his boxer shorts drinking beer, watching TV, and simmering. My mother went off to work at a local hospital and came back bleary-eyed and exhausted. I spent less and less time at home, often sleeping in the spare room at my grandparents' house or on the couch at Jack and Lauren's (they were the only grown-ups in whom I had confided the details of my stepfather's drinking).

Joey was always ready to take me in, too, without any questions. By then, he'd spent enough time around my stepfather to figure out why I sometimes appeared at his house asking if I could stay over. His parents didn't seem to mind the addition of one more kid to their brood. His mother treated me with the same weary sarcasm with which she addressed her own children, especially Joey, whom she called "Mr. Know-it-all." I recognized in her scorn the peculiar mixture of embarrassment and pride that my own mother sometimes meekly expressed toward me. Unlike my stepfather, Mr. Spencer was a friendly drunk, a jovial, red-faced man who slapped me on the back and talked football, about which I knew nothing.

Joey treated his parents with friendly contempt, but I could tell that his mother's mockery hurt him, as did the sight of his father snoring in an armchair in front of the TV night after night. The only person in his family Joey looked up to was his older brother, Carl. Carl managed a restaurant, had his own apartment, and studied part-time at the state college. Joey was proud of him for what I thought, snobbishly, were pretty modest accomplishments. I was polite to Carl, but secretly jealous of his relationship with Joey. He didn't seem to like me much, either, and when I overhead him describe me to Joey as "your girlfriend," I stopped going to his apartment. Joey never mentioned it.

One morning, I was sitting at the kitchen table at my grandparents' house, eating breakfast. My dour Indian grandfather sat across from me, reading the *Sacramento Bee*. Suddenly, he looked up and grunted.

"What's wrong with you?"

"Nothing," I said, instantly on edge.

"You were singing," he told me. Then, rattling his paper, he muttered, "You must be in love."

I bolted the rest of my meal and fled.

HE WAS RIGHT: I was in love, with Joey. It had crept up on me, a feeling different than I'd ever had for any boy. A kind of contentment, and a kind of restlessness. I couldn't wait to see him, but at the same time I dreaded it, because the one thing I wanted most to tell him, I never could. In the past, I had lusted after half my male classmates, but the impossibility of realizing those fantasies kept me from feeling anything save self-loathing. It seemed possible that Joey might return my love. One night we got hold of a bottle of wine and went down to the river. We sat at the water's edge, passing the bottle back and forth until we'd finished it. The air smelled of rotting fish and decaying earth. Stars burned in the black sky. Drunk and filled with yearning,

I recklessly laid my hand on his. For a moment, neither of us moved; then Joey turned his hand over, lacing his fingers with mine. "You're the best friend I ever had," he told me, rubbing his thumb across the surface of my skin. Just before Christmas, he appeared at my house with a present, a pair of sterling silver cuff links in the shape of peace signs, with a card signed "Peace and love in '72. Joey."

It was all truly exhilarating—and truly terrifying.

I STOOD AT the window in Jack's classroom one winter afternoon, my back to him. Jack was at his desk grading papers, scratching his usual sarcastic comments in the margins with a red pen. The scratching stopped.

"What's got you down, kid?" he asked.

"Nothing," I lied, still peering through the window. Joey was out with the flu and I was lonely for him.

"Something going on at home?"

"No."

"Well, I'm closing up," he said, clearly disbelieving me. "Come on."

We drove to his house, discussing our chances at the state qualifying debate tournament in San Francisco later that month. Joey and I were among the five top-seeded teams in the Sacramento Valley and we thought we had a shot.

Lauren was in the kitchen, making dinner. "Hey, honey," Jack shouted, "I brought home a stray." She came out, saw me, and smiled. They settled me in Jack's easy chair with a glass of wine and Joan Baez on the record player singing "Where Have All the Flowers Gone" in German, while they talked quietly together in the kitchen. A few minutes later, they rejoined me.

"Michael," Lauren said, "if something's going on at home, you know you can tell us about it. We want to help you."

Looking at their concerned faces, I felt as if I was about to explode with my unexpressed longing for Joey.

"It's not that," I said. "It's something else."

"What?" Jack asked.

"I think I'm in love."

In a perfectly natural voice, Lauren asked, "Who is he, Michael?"

I looked at her, then at Jack. Their faces showed only kindness. I burst into tears.

I told them it was Joey. They exchanged a glance, but all Jack said was, "Joey's a great kid. He really looks up to you."

"Should I tell him?" I asked them.

"If you want to know where you stand," Lauren said, her logic unassailable.

"But what if . . ." I began, then stopped myself. What if *what*? He got angry? He turned against me? What if he didn't? What if he felt the same way? I didn't finish the sentence.

Years later, I asked Lauren, "How did you know?"

"Every other boy your age was trying to get laid," she said. "You never had a girlfriend. You didn't even date."

"Was it that obvious?"

"If you'd been a different kind of boy, maybe not," she said. "But you had such passion. It had to be going somewhere."

IN SAN FRANCISCO, Jack found us lodgings at a run-down hotel off Union Square. The lobby was papered in whorehouse red flocking and the reception desk was topped with marble, but the stairs up to the rooms were uncarpeted and the windows were fogged with grime. Joey and I shared a room. After dinner, we went back to the hotel and worked until midnight, then smoked a joint and got ready for bed. There was only one, a sagging queen-size thing covered with a threadbare chenille spread. The wooden head- and footboards were plain as a pauper's coffin, painted shiny black. I'd shared a bed with Joey many times, but not since I'd decided to tell him how I felt.

"What's wrong, Michael?"

"I'm nervous about tomorrow."

He stripped to his underwear, threw a towel over his shoulder. "We'll do great," he said. "I'm going to wash up."

I pulled the cover back on the bed and asked, "What side do you want?"

"It doesn't matter," he said, indicating the sagging mattress. "We're going to end up in the middle anyway."

While Joey was in the bathroom, I went down the hall to Jack's room. He came to the door in his T-shirt and suit pants.

"Hey, sport, you ready for tomorrow?"

"I'm too nervous to sleep."

He wagged me into the room and produced a pint of brandy from his suitcase. He poured some into a water glass.

"Just a swallow, okay?"

The liquor blazed in my chest. I blurted out, "Jack, I want to tell Joey how I feel about him."

After a moment, Jack said, "When? Not tonight?"

"I feel like I'm going to explode."

"I know," he said. "But you're both under a lot of pressure right now. Maybe you should wait until after the tournament."

"I'm not going to be able to sleep at all tonight."

"Here," he said, pouring, "have another drink."

The light was off when I returned to Joey. I went into the bathroom and brushed my teeth, then picked my way through the darkness until I ran into the bed.

"Hey," Joey said, "keep it down."

I crawled into the bed and muttered, "Good night."

Joey sniffed the air. "You been drinking."

"A nightcap with Jack, to help me sleep."

"Trying to sleep in this bed is like trying to sleep on a bag of marshmallows," he said.

"Just go with gravity," I suggested.

Joey giggled and rolled toward me. We sank into the sag of the mattress. The brandy had made me tipsy, and I felt as if I were falling. I reached out to steady myself—and laid my hand on his crotch. I felt his long, thin cock beneath the smooth surface of his BVDs. I knew I had to remove my hand, but it was as if my strength had deserted me. I couldn't. I felt him harden beneath my fingers and waited for him to say something. The only sound in the room was the rasp of our breathing. A spot of wetness stained his shorts. I slipped my fingers through the fold and touched the tip of his cock.

He murmured, "Michael," then leaned above me in the darkness and kissed me.

SEX WITH JOEY was so different than I had imagined in my solitary fantasies, like going from black and white to color, from silence to sound. It astonished me, how easy it was to do these forbidden things. Once and for all, I knew that I wasn't a late bloomer or waiting for the right girl, or any of those other phrases with which my family and friends kept open for me the door into the world of men and women. I would never pass through that door. I was a queer. And after making love with Joey, there was no terror in it. I was too dizzy with excitement to sleep, even after Joey finally dropped off. I touched his back. He shivered. I felt his eyes open.

"I love you," I told him.

"Ssh, go to sleep."

"Are you sure?"

I touched him. We went at it again.

THE NEXT MORNING, when I came back from showering, I found Joey dressed, frantically tearing through the unmade bed.

"What are you doing?" I asked.

"I can't find my shorts," he snapped.

"You can look for them when we get back," I said, not understanding his anxiety.

"Didn't you hear the maid?" he said. "She wanted to come in and clean. What if she finds them?"

He pulled back the bottom sheet to reveal the stained cloth covering the lumpy mattress. The air was thick with his shame. I looked at the bed: What we had done on it seemed as dirty as the gray ticking. It was as if he had taken back all the tenderness that had passed between us. I saw a bit of white cloth sticking out from just beneath the bed and retrieved it: his underwear. I tossed the shorts at him.

"Here," I said, furious. "Burn the fucking things."

He crammed them into his suitcase. "Why are you pissed off?"

"What do you care what the maid thinks?"

More subdued, he said, "I just don't want everyone to know."

"Are you sorry we did it?"

"Aren't you?"

"No," I said. "I'm not sorry at all."

Jack banged at the door. "Come on, boys, or we'll be late."

"You better get dressed," Joey said, and left the room.

WE BOMBED AT the tournament, losing in the qualification rounds; there was no reason to spend another night in the city. On the drive back to Sacramento, Joey and I sat as far apart as possible in Jack's VW bug. If Jack sensed any tension, he must've chalked it up to our disappointment at doing so poorly. I was relieved that he let me off first, because I dreaded being alone with him. When I got to my room, I locked the door, put on Neil Young's *Harvest* album to cover the sound, and sat on my bed, sobbing.

The next week was terrible. The bond I'd shared with Joey was unique. We were both struggling, against long odds, to create ourselves, connected by a belief in our own potential, which we sustained without much encouragement from our families, and which our middle-class peers, who assumed their own secure futures, could not have understood. Our self-doubt and loneliness were constant. Joey had relieved my loneliness and encouraged my belief in myself. Now I felt rejected by him, isolated again. As if by agreement, we avoided being alone together. My grief was tremendous. Worse, I couldn't tell anyone, not even Jack and Lauren. The wound was too fresh, the hurt too deep. I had to pretend that nothing had happened.

One night, my mother knocked on my door.

"What?" I snarled sullenly.

In a timid voice, she answered, "Your friend is here."

I opened the door. Joey stood behind my mother.

"Hi, Michael," he said. "Can I talk to you?"

I let him in and locked the door. He sat down on the edge of my bed.

"Are you mad at me?"

Having anticipated every reaction but this one, I didn't know what to say.

"Because if I did anything wrong, I'm sorry."

"No," I said. "I'm not mad at you. I thought you were mad at me."

He shook his head and said, emphatically, "You're my best friend."

"What about what happened in San Francisco?"

He stared at his hands. "Michael," he said, "I'm not queer."

It shocked me to hear the word from him. I hadn't thought of what we'd done as queer. Queer was guilty jerk-off sessions and trying not to be caught looking at other boys in the showers. Queer was the loathing I felt toward my treasonous body, the loneliness that engulfed me when I thought of the future. Queer had nothing to do with Joey and me.

"I didn't think you were," I said.

With a puzzled expression, he said, "What are you talking about? You know what we did."

"I didn't think of it like that," I said feebly.

"How did you think of it?"

"I didn't put a name on it."

"But it has a name, Michael. There's a name for guys who do that with each other. And I'm not one of them," he said decisively. "Are you?"

I wanted to say no, for things to be as they had been between us, but I couldn't lie to him, not even to keep his friendship.

"Yes," I said. "I'm a queer, Joey."

"Shit," he said, like he was about to cry.

"I'm sorry," I told him. "I love you, Joey."

"I love you, too, Michael," he said. "But not that way."

"Then why did you sleep with me?"

"Because I wasn't sure. I wondered about myself sometimes, but if I hadn't met you, I wouldn't have done anything about it."

"And now you know you're not."

"Yes."

I couldn't think of anything else to say.

"I know I'm not," he said in that stubborn voice I recognized was his last word on the subject.

"Okay," I said.

After a moment, he asked, "Can we still be friends?"

"If you want to be."

"I do," he said. "Really."

I KNOW HE meant it, but it was impossible to go back. However briefly, I had known what it was to have my desire returned, and it spoiled me for mere friendship. I wanted more, and I wanted it from Joey. But he had made up his mind. He was never unkind about it, but he made it clear that the experiment would not be repeated.

The fabric of our friendship began to unravel, and this led to awkwardness, misunderstandings, tension, silence. It became easier for us to see each other less often, then not to see each other outside of school. This was tremendously painful for me (and, I think now, for him, too). At first, I talked to Jack and Lauren. They were consoling, but it wasn't enough. I stopped talking about it. The hurt became more fuel to propel me out of Sacramento and into a different life. In September, Joey went off to Berkeley and I began college in Colorado. It was years before I stopped missing him.

I saw him for the last time in Los Angeles, in 1986. He called me out of the blue one day. He was in the city for a conference, had learned from mutual friends that I was living there, and invited me to lunch. We exchanged statistics: Joey was a pediatrician, married, the father of two small sons; I was practicing law and about to have my first book published. There didn't seem much else to say. We finished our meal, paid the check, and stood outside the restaurant. Good-bye was forming on his face.

"I'm really happy for you, Joey," I said.

He looked puzzled.

"Why?"

"Everything turned out right for you."

"For you, too," he said.

"Yes," I said. "For me, too."

He shook my hand.

"Good-bye, Michael."

"Good-bye," I said.

The light closed around him as he moved into the ghostly glare of the summer afternoon.

HOMO SEX STORY

Matthew Stadler

MY PARENTS BOUGHT sex books and left them in the basement for the children. It was 1969. We lived in a big house by a woods north of Seattle. I was ten years old when the first book appeared—*Everything You Always Wanted to Know About Sex* by David Reuben. It was cold all the time, and clouds covered the woods where I played alone by a stream; on gray days, wet from rain and mud, I built stone dams. My dog sat in salal, his fur beaded with mist. No one else played there, and I walked home. The basement of our house was warm. I stripped my muddy clothes off by the washing machine, toweled my damp skin dry, then lay down in the clean laundry.

One day I took Dr. Reuben's book with me to the laundry pile, to find out about homosexuality. Could I be homosexual? I had no idea really, just a puzzled curiosity about myself, and the laundry, and my solitude. I looked to the book for instruction. Dr. Reuben described the many objects homosexuals routinely shove up one another's assholes. As a doctor, he often found himself called to the emergency room to extract lightbulbs, small animals, and flashlights from the rectums of men for whom sex was a festival of dangerous insertions. It made no sense to me. The story Dr. Reuben told was so clinical and distasteful, I had no desire to read it. I put it back by the TV.

The next to arrive was *The Sex Book*, a Scandinavian "encyclopedia" with photos. My parents bought it when I was eleven. The picture illustrating homosexuality was of two boys, one blond, one black-haired, standing nude, kissing. They were very slim and attractive, and it was clear they enjoyed what they

167

were doing. I have forgotten the text completely. More startling to me, the photo beside "masturbation" was of a boy's flat belly and thighs with his hand wrapped around a shapely, arching erection of such size and, well, nobility, I guess, as I had never before seen. The image made me dizzy and religious.

I stared at that boy every day. I mimicked him, though my little dick and soft belly were no match for his. I wanted to meet him. I imagined a pilgrimage, or an appointment in Stockholm. I decided my older brother must be like that boy—I mean, that his dick must be like that boy's dick—and I resolved to find ways to see it. This was not a moment of revelation or "coming out." The force of my resolution dwelt only in my belly and hands. It never reached my head, or gave rise to a story.

COMING OUT IS telling a story. The declaration is a lie, the way a good story is a lie, and it's useful like a story. The lie lets you hold on to some things, but you risk losing anything that won't fit inside it. Sometimes you need to tell lies just to go on living. I hadn't reached that point yet. My body was still arranging itself around the laundry, and a kind of buzzing, diffused sensuality that felt like an internalization of the pervasive clouds of rain we lived in. Things had no edges for me. Desire floated over this blurred wet world like fog.

MY BROTHER WAS thirteen, and he made a room for himself in the basement. He had a stereo from J. C. Penney, copious hanging cloths surrounding the bed, and a bong we built together using clay and an aluminum lantern. He was blond and I was dark-haired. Every morning I'd rush to the basement to wake him up for school. My brother didn't get out of bed when I roused him, but always I would see his bare shoulders and chest and inspect the outline his body made beneath the blankets. I feigned sleepiness, acting casual, and I lingered by his tie-dyed curtain while he struggled under the covers. It was humiliating to loiter every morning for such meager rewards. I spent more time by myself, observing my own dick in the mirror, remembering that it was cousin to the elusive dicks that haunted me.

About this time my brother and I began calling each other "fillies," which we believed was the word for homosexual seagulls. I imagined fussy, dumpy seagulls with bitchy attitudes, the sort that steal a perch from the more elegant birds and then hold on to it by squawking. Maybe this was my early, internalized homophobia; I'm not really sure. (Where *does* a child find his ideas about homosexual seagulls?) The birds' sexuality was a style, an attitude really, and not a set of practices or desires.

"Fillies" satisfied some need in me, a need to locate and debunk mysteries. Cowed by the face of God—that dick I saw in *The Sex Book*—I wove our conjectures about gulls into a heavy cloth, a shroud to mask the mysteries and make them plain. Seagulls might not sound plain to an outsider, but in the Pacific Northwest they were as common as pigeons. My sexuality lurched forward, drawn by these two competing beacons: the sacred mystery of the mute dick and the reassuring plainness of gulls. This, I guess, is where my story begins.

ONE DAY WHEN I was twelve I sat in the bathroom naked, manipulating myself and striking poses. I was very happy. I was thinking about my friend Jeremy. His haircut resembled the head of my dick. It had the same rakish tilt, fullness, and inward curve at its bottom edge. The equation made me giggle as I worked my hand up and down him, tickling the fleshy haircut. I want him, I thought, rubbing my little friend raw. I want to touch him.

"I am a filly." Identity settled like pudding, or a grid in my head, framing scenarios, style, and an aggravating uncertainty. What was expected of me? I knew rumors of love ... it involved courting and kissing. And I knew what Dr. Rueben had said.

The implications of this new declaration flooded my body. A buzzing erotic hum drifted from my palm, traveled through me, and burst in my head. The explosion, an idea, swallowed everything. My hand and dick became mere players in a theater of my mind. This crisp, new declaration gave me a neat bundle of stories. Standing there, naked in the bathroom with my dick in my hand, I tried out scripted lines, playacting, and elaborate plots that dissolved the white tile walls and transported me to a Scandinavian future with my mop-top friend Jeremy. We would be best friends, gull-like partners in a business exporting books. We would be bedmates in a blond wood frame, under soft eiderdown, somewhere in the swankier districts of Stockholm. The scenario alone gave me a hard-on.

I ASKED JEREMY to sleep over at my house and told him it was a party. I invited no one else. It was late winter and I had just turned thirteen.

THE STORY I told myself (the one that began "I am a filly") was a happy story, kind of like James Bond. There was a great deal of secrecy and adventure, events moved swiftly and interestingly toward happiness (a triumph of the good), and the hero had lots of love and sex along the way. There was only one story line, Jeremy, and no sequels were planned. I spent all my time inside this tale, and my dick became a mere appendage to it, something to hold on to during the ride. The boy in *The Sex Book* lost his power. Subordinate to my new story, he became less an altar and more an illustration. This is what Jeremy will look like, I thought, gazing at God.

JEREMY BROUGHT HIS own glass and flatware because he feared catching strep throat. His sleeping bag was rolled neatly, with the pillow crushed inside like filling. White cotton burst from the ends like cream.

"No one else is coming," I told him. He smoothed the unrolled bag and put the pillow at its head.

"Why not?" he asked.

"I don't know." I paused, unbearably, and improvised. "Doug Luft said I was a filly."

"Doug Luft said that?"

"Un-huhn." My head was full of lies. Plots blossomed and collapsed like flames. The floor looked filthy, littered with socks and books, a thousand feet down from the immense, towering bed. "We both have to sleep in the bed."

"Why?"

I stared at the crushed socks on the floor. "My mom gets mad if we use the floor."

"This floor?" He pointed his toothbrush case.

"Uh-huhn."

"But it's not healthy."

"No. It's a very dirty floor."

"I mean sharing the bed isn't healthy."

"Well, we don't have to, you know, *do* anything."

"You'll get germs on the pillow. Unless we sleep head to toe."

"Uhmm . . ."

Jeremy laid his bag out on the bed, its zippered end shut by my pillow, his pillow against the footboard. He unpacked pajamas from the sleeping bag and took them with his toothbrush case to the bathroom. I stripped to my underpants and lay down on the bed. He turned the light off as he came in, and I lay in the dark hearing his "Good night," the pull of the zipper down, and then a faster pull, tight, back up again. I was silent. I climbed under my covers.

All night I rocked my knee against his back, believing the erotic charge in my body could pass through sheets and blankets, his thick down bag and clean pajamas, to burst inside him, at the base of his spine, washing over his skin and waking him. Jeremy snored and shifted in his sack. I fell asleep. When I woke, the bag and pillow were rolled back up and Jeremy was downstairs making tea.

LIFE WAS EPISODIC. Moments abutted one another like photographs in an album. I leapt to catch a soccer ball on a muddy field at school, desperate to stop its flight, and collided with Tony. We fell together in the mud. For a moment he lay still, his head resting on my thigh. He closed his eyes. This was both erotic and terrifying. I thought he looked dead, in that beautiful, arousing way TV soldiers look dead once they're shot. It was afternoon. I cradled him, and I yelled, "Sergeant, Sergeant, he's been hit!" I felt the weight of his head and got a hard-on, which nudged my jeans against his bare wrist. Tony laughed and pushed me into the mud.

It was eighth grade and Tony became my best friend. I never told Jeremy what I really wanted. He drifted away into fussiness and lint traps, Tupperware, creased trousers, volunteerism, and junior achievements. Nothing ended. I kept forgetting to scheme or worry. I didn't notice what he wore. I rushed past him in the hall, failing to hear the last, weak belch of my sunken desire, a pathetic stunted burble spit up as if from a sewer, a drain swallowing the last after-dreck of a dead storm. Is it ending *enough* for us now? In retrospect I can make it end—by turning it into a story, and I do that, and I lie when I do. Jeremy simply blurred and drifted. He never ended. All that was left that ended was a story. But a life will drift away like old, bad weather if we don't make a box to put it in, a bordered story that ends.

NOW HERE IS a story that really ended:

Tony's nipples were soft and flat as rose petals. I saw them each day in gym when we stripped down to take showers. His belly button was shallow and perfect, a jewel of boyhood set amid skin of such smoothness and luminescence I often thought he would glow, pale as the moon, if I could lift the veil of his bedding at night to see him. His skin stretched taut over ribs, a medial indention of his torso (creating perfect symmetry), and the twin hollows of his collarbones, to rounded shoulders which fit my hands exactly. He was taller than me, and angular. Tony liked to make trouble. We were fourteen.

The gym was a box of mysteries, a monolithic stone casket masked by tin painted blue and gold, scarred by rocks and torches. Two kids drove a Chevy through its side in a suicide/love pact based on a reading of *Jonathan Livingston Seagull*. They had "Free Bird" playing on the car stereo. Mr. Voyuvich, my counselor, said they wanted to join the seagulls in some misty, coastal heaven where Lynyrd Skynyrd played eternally. Mr. Voyuvich wore thick glasses and called me a thespian. In his office he mocked the other students. He said the suicide pair was pathetic, then he mimicked the stoned grip on the steering wheel, the rocker's bobbing head, the crash. There was no grief counseling. The hole they made in the gym was patched up with cinder block.

Naked boys filled the gym's steamy lower reaches. Sadistic, tight-trousered men surveyed us from a glass booth, tilting back in rolling chairs, slapping clipboards against their thighs. Tony's shoulder blades were elegant and pronounced. Undressed, amid the wreckage of adolescence, he projected an off-handed civility and grace. I wanted to run my fingers along the twin blossoms of his nipples, and Tony could see that I did. Proximity raised desire to a pitch where it became obvious. Mr. Buzzard glared out at me through the glass, rubbing his polyester thigh. I hid inside diesel towels, taking three to cover my body, and slid toward the shower. The tile floor was clammy, unclean, like snails.

TONY'S DAD WAS divorced. He had a Camaro, mag wheels, and a woman he dated named Jeannie, whose poodle threw up in the front of the car whenever we went driving. We drove a lot. Denny owned a trailer on an island north of Seattle, and one weekend we went there.

It was winter still. Our breath froze and hung in the air before our faces. It rained until late afternoon, and then it sleeted. Denny and Jeannie drank, and we spun doughnuts in the Turkey House lot. I tried coffee, which spilled as the Camaro spun wide circles in the leaf-mucked gravel. Tony got to drive on the state roads. The island was tiny, a forested hump of rock at the mouth of Deception Pass. Mist, luminous and uniform, blanketed the flat gray bay. We took a powerboat from a dock on the Whidbey side and motored into the clouds. The bridge over Deception Pass, two hundred feet up, was lost in it. There was no sound, only echoes of sound.

The trailer was planted on cinder blocks with aluminum flashing that made it look like a house. It sat on a stripped half acre of mud by the dock. Curtains kept the light out, turning the carpeted rooms dim and orange. Everything inside was small, except the television and the beds. The beds were king-size, like in hotels, and Tony and I shared one. In the drizzle Denny fumbled with the key. Tony kicked a dead mole off the pile of feed where it had been poisoned and Jeannie looked at me. "Fish sticks," she said, smiling.

I ran with Tony to the top of the island. It was just a rise, covered with moss and curtained by fir trees on all sides. A ditch led to the far shore, fifty yards through the trees. We discussed the dead mole, its feelings, its anatomy, as we walked in the ditch through the trees. There was light in the gray air above the water, visible ahead, but where we stood was almost dark.

"If you were Della I'd kiss you," Tony said. Della was Tony's girlfriend. He made fun of her all the time. He described kissing on sink tops and beneath counters. I liked hearing about Della. It was like hearing him talk about masturbation. She was nothing.

"I'm not Della," I whispered. He stared at me and said, "I know." We walked to where the trees opened up and you could see the water moving through the pass.

Tony and I were muddy from the woods, and we washed and changed together in our room. His skin was flushed from running. I was speechless and clumsy. I stole glances from behind my plush towel. We put on extra socks and went in to dinner. Denny and Jeannie liked to watch TV while they ate. Denny set four trays in a line by the couch, facing the TV. Jeannie's poodle sat in her lap and ate from a fork. All the food was pale—potatoes and fish sticks, wax beans—and it billowed steam. The couch kept me pressed against Tony. He called me "Stir," I'm not sure why. "Salt for your potatoes, Stir?" he asked. I shook my head no. The television had sports scores. Denny watched and Jeannie let the dog lap water from her glass. Denny told us to play in the toolshed after dinner.

"Why, Stir?" Tony asked him.

"Don't be a smartass."

"To play with our tools," I said. "For retooling."

"Work on that boat motor."

"Do you mean 'we' or me and Matt?" Tony kept needling. "I mean, is this a kind of dad-and-son thing?"

"Just play in the goddamn shed."

Denny dragged the TV to their bedroom and watched a dirty movie with Jeannie while Tony and I stood outside watching their shadows flicker on the curtain. Tony threw rocks at the aluminum flashing and barked like a dog. We couldn't make out the pictures, or see Denny and Jeannie on the bed. We ran to the top of the island and mocked them, guessing wildly at the contents of the unseen movie, mimicking postures rumored to be sexual. It was dark and I could only see his face.

"I can't see you," I complained while Tony humped the wet moss.

"I can only see your face," he said. "And your hands when they're showing." He rolled toward me and put his dirty hands near my eyes.

"Yeah." His hands were cold, and so were mine. He lay on his back in the moss. Ghostly swaths of skin appeared and disappeared where his shirt got pulled up. The lightless hollow swallowed all information, like half sleep, but I was wide awake.

ONCE I STAYED awake all night watching him sleep in a cot beside me. My vigil was religious, like fasting. It was summer and we put the cot in my room by the door. Tony went to bed before me. It was hot and he slept with the bag unzipped and open down to his belly. I watched TV, I think it was *King Kong*, then went upstairs to sleep. Light from the hall fell across his body and I could see his ribs move when he breathed. He slept on his back with his arms crossed behind his head. The lip of his belly button cast a slip of shadow across the taut round of its center, and I let my finger hover there. He had smooth, hollow armpits. My hand was a dry open wound. I moved it over his contours without touching him. I knelt by the cot all night, sometimes resting my head on its canvas-and-metal edge. Thoughts are so volatile and elastic. That moment by his bed, my hand almost touching him, expanded like a burst star and swallowed the rest of my life. It blossomed, uncontained, because I never spoke a word to him. But that cold night on the island, I would speak and draw a boundary, mark an ending to contain him.

SO MUCH OF what is interesting was only in my head.

We ran through the ditch to the shore, then raced back to the trailer, circuiting the island over rocks and gravel beaches. Tony got there first and the trailer was dark. The trailer was a box, already crowded with sex. Our bed was a destination, a marked spot in my geography. No matter what else I was thinking, I knew the distance and direction of the bed. Tony slipped through this matrix of calculations like a particle through charged space. He tossed his clothes on the floor and took a shower. I followed him, and then came back to the bedroom wrapped in just a towel.

Tony was in bed with the lights off. I let the towel drop and got in beside him. We said nothing. The warm cotton touched me everywhere. My skin was electrical and clean. He was on his back in the far half of the bed, and I slid toward him, willing myself into an irresponsible half consciousness. Who could be accountable in sleep? He rolled over and his hand touched my hip, at a point where my underpants should have been. The real details are so tawdry and mundane. I had hoped this retelling would elevate us to some purer realm, like a photograph, all shadow and light: Tony asleep on his back, the elegance of his flat belly, his noble thighs.

Tony propped himself up on an elbow and turned toward me. "Stir?" he said. "Are you obscene?" I couldn't speak, but turned my body some to move his hand closer to my belly. He let his palm rest there and pried a little at my navel with the tip of his finger. My dick was hard, and the head touched the edge of his hand. Tony drew his arm away, but slid closer and pushed the blankets down. The dog was in the kitchen, scratching at the cabinet where its dry food was kept.

"What do you want . . . ?" he started to ask, whispering. "I mean, to do?" What I wanted had been mute—had been mute forever—but he asked me, and I looked toward the outline of him and said, "I want to touch you. I mean, in some places." I'm not sure where I found this formulation. Maybe it came from Dr. Reuben. Regardless, it emerged, parched and half swallowed, from my mouth, and now it floated in the room with all our thoughts and the heat of our bodies. Tony drew himself up onto his knees. He pulled the elastic of his underpants down and took my hand and wrapped it around his dick. He was pale and ghostly, except where my hand held on, and there he was dark, with soft black hair. He reached over and held on to me in return, and then we moved our hands a little. Despite a great deal of practice (uncountable, endless hours of practice), our motions were hesitant and inexpert. Tony stopped, flipped my dick back and forth a little, then pushed my hand away.

"I don't want to do this," he said. Then he turned over and went to sleep. The end, I know now. At last the end.

WE SLEPT TOGETHER always and never touched each other's dicks again. We played in the woods on the island and made enormous painted advertisements for imaginary funeral homes, for concrete plants and flatware consultants, which we nailed to trees on the bay side where the stream of passing boat pilots could read them. We talked about birds, and skewered one dead gull with a stick up its butt, to mount as a talisman or warning on the beach. I thought of Piggy and the carnival of mad, devouring boys in *Lord of the Flies*. Sand fleas peppered the dead, sagging gull. We retreated behind logs and tried to hit it with stones. We took the powerboat and drove the bird into the strait and gave it a decent burial at sea. Tony lowered it slowly on a noose of twine and let go. The bloated, dirty bird disappeared into the water, then the rings of its disappearance were gone, too, and then there was nothing.

THE *OTHER* INVISIBLE MAN

Essex Hemphill

for George Hart

I MET GEORGE by chance in the shy spring of 1975, during my senior year of high school. Had I not been preparing an article for the school news magazine, George and I would never have connected.

Our intimacy began innocently enough. My journalism instructor assigned me to interview the reverend of a local Episcopal church. Under his pastorship, volunteers from the congregation were providing daily meals for the poor and homeless. I phoned the church later that afternoon to schedule an appointment. George answered my call.

His thick baritone voice overwhelmed me. I stammered through my introduction, my purpose for ringing the line. As I explained myself, his breathing sounded as inviting as his supple, leathery voice. I had not felt desire like this even when I was messing around, a few years earlier, with a grocery clerk who was also named George, an older, white homosexual who lived and worked in my neighborhood in Washington, D.C. As this new, brown-like-me George breathed in and out of the telephone, there was nothing for me to clutch, nothing to grasp, no way to resist him. I didn't really want to resist.

When at last I finished my rambling, George politely said, "The reverend isn't in at the moment." I paused. I was becoming increasingly aroused by his soothing baritone. His mellifluous voice lingered long after he ceased speaking. The phone sweated in my hand as I regained the focus of the conversation, which was loping away from me every time he spoke.

I asked could I leave a message and George replied, "Yes, you can." The notes resonated, in my loins and in my imagination. I was called to answer those startling, enticing blue notes. I was called to receive them, to claim them, to own them proudly. I would later discover that this music between men can be sacred, worth fighting and dying for, but at that moment my mind and reasoning weren't in control—my hormones were. I was enchanted and curious. I allowed the liberal hand of pleasure to rule.

After giving George all the necessary information to pass on to the reverend, we lapsed into a momentary silence. Sensing the imminent good-bye, George lowered his saxophone voice a half octave and brashly asked, "Why don't you come on up here and meet *me?*"

I feigned protest, but he pursued me anyway, neutralizing the little resistance I halfheartedly pretended. I wanted very much to meet the man possessing such a voice—a voice offering possibilities I had not yet dreamed of or considered. But I wasn't completely sure. I wasn't convinced of his motives—or my own.

"My name is George—George Hart," he continued, just as I said, "I don't even know your name."

"Well, now you know it. I'm George," he offered again. "Where are you calling from? Home?"

"No, I'm at my part-time job, downtown."

"Where at?" he insisted.

"I work on Seventeenth Street."

"Near Seventeenth and K?" he asked.

"Yes," I replied.

"You're not too far from the church. You can take the S2 or the S4 uptown and get off at Newton. The bus stop is on Sixteenth Street, a block east of where you are. What time do you get off?" he asked.

"I get off at five-thirty."

"Where do you live?"

"I live in Southeast, off Martin Luther King Avenue."

"Anacostia?"

"No, I live a couple of blocks from Ballou. That's where I attend high school."

I wanted to stop the information from flowing, but I couldn't. Everything he asked me, I answered. Every breath he released, each syllable, every enunciation, beckoned me.

I would be leaving the office in another hour. I considered the possibility of meeting him and getting home by eight. I figured I could call and tell one of my sisters my magazine assignment would delay me. I could then scoot up Sixteenth Street, meet George, race back down Sixteenth, cross the Eleventh Street Bridge, the Anacostia River, and walk in the front door around eight, and not create unnecessary suspicion. That wouldn't be too hard to pull off, I reasoned; all the factors suggested that I could.

"So, Mr. Essex, what's your decision?"

He was purring again, coaxing and calling me out. I can hear his breathing even now, as I remember him effortlessly. I considered the risk variables and concluded that the odds were in my favor that I would be relatively safe with him. The possibility of danger could be minimized by agreeing to meet him at the church instead of his apartment.

I was about to meet a black man with a sexy voice, in a church, in a city famous for its churches *and* the black men who reside in the city. Was I excited? Yes! Yes! Yes! Was I overwhelmed? No. *I* was deciding to take this chance on meeting him, and the thought of being able to do so thrilled me. As much as I was intrigued by George and drawn to him, *I* made the decision to see him. The devil didn't make me do shit, it can't be blamed on my mother's single-parent love, and no gun was placed to my watermelon head to force me into George's bed.

My dick went bone as I sat behind my desk in an office with six black women, who were like aunts or mothers or older sisters to me, advising me and loving me, teaching me some of the ways to be friends with women. They had no idea that at that moment I was getting my life on the office phone. And if they had known, it is likely they would have snatched the phone out of the wall and whipped my tail blue with the cord. They cared for me that way, and they wanted to see me succeed in the world. To have discovered me on the phone listening to a man luring me into his arms was not their idea of "success," nor were they any more ready than my own mother to accept an announcement that "I am a homosexual." Had I announced my sexuality then—or, more important, had I possessed the confidence to announce this truth to any of these women—all hell would have broken loose. So, on that fateful afternoon, I began playing more earnestly with masks, adopting new practices of deception that I would eventually, thankfully, discard.

When I later left for college, the women I worked with gave me an ample supply of multicolored condoms as a going-away gift. It tickled them more than it tickled me. I recall their acting so silly and giddy over this particular gift. It implied certain presumptions about my sexuality, and it also conveyed their concern that I be responsible. They fully expected me to use those condoms heterosexually. I recall putting one of those latex socks on and masturbating into it, but I also remember thinking it a rather dull and boring experience.

Now I think how prophetic and wise it was of them to give me protection against risk and infection. I dismissed their gift as simply inappropriate for the person I was becoming—a black male erotically attracted to other males. To my mind, condoms were for preventing pregnancy. They were for males to use with females, and for that reason, the gift was eventually thrown away, not out of ingratitude, but because the condoms weren't useful at the time.

I was then a part-time file clerk at a civil service outpost and a part-time senior high school student with only morning classes to attend. The afternoons belonged to me—or, more specifically, they belonged to Uncle Sam, which allowed me to *earn* money honestly and not flood my neighborhood with drugs and terrorize it with gunfire. In a few months, I would graduate from high school and attend the University of Maryland for a year. But at that moment, I was seventeen—*seventeen*—a clumsy waif of a boy, in possession of raging hormones and an embarrassing erection, listening to the husky breathing of a man named George, a man I imagined I could love, just from the sound of his voice. If my supervisor had needed my attention while I was getting turned on over the telephone, if she had summoned me at that moment from the spell of my sexual enchantment, I would have been unable to rise to her call without exhibiting a complete lack of composure and self-control.

"I will come to visit you—I mean, I will come visit the church," I corrected myself. "Maybe the reverend will have arrived by the time I get there."

"Very good," George enthused. "I look forward to meeting you, Mr. Essex. I anticipate us having a pleasurable meeting."

"Good-bye," I croaked, my mouth and throat cotton dry. I rang off the line and sat hidden behind my desk. I needed to calm down and call home. Yes, I was going to the church. Yes, I wanted to meet George, to see what size and shape of a man he was. I expected him to be tall and broad, upright, older.

And he was. He was all that. He was more than I could have imagined.

I ARRIVED AT the church shortly after leaving the office at the end of the day. The bus ride took about twenty minutes. He was right: The church was sitting on the same side of the street as the bus stop when I disembarked at Newton. I entered the church from Sixteenth Street, stepping into a quiet, but noticeably busy, sanctuary. I asked for Mr. Hart. I was politely shown down a dimly lit hallway to a small office, where a nutmeg-brown, broad-shouldered man sat crowded behind a fragile desk. He simply overwhelmed it: His hands, his face, his body swelled up over that desk and soon shadowed it, when he rose to shake my hand as the person who'd delivered me to his office departed, leaving the door open.

George stared at me for the longest time. Thick brows waved above his brown eyes. I stared back as intensely, as candidly, taking in his salt-and-pepper mustache and his full crown of salt-and-pepper hair. He was wearing dark trousers, a white shirt open at the collar, and a light gray sports jacket. He was significantly taller than me, and I imagined he weighed at least two hundred pounds. I believe George was cruising into his late forties when we met, although he never told me his exact age.

I could see that his body retained some of its tautness and definition from his youth. I could also see his stomach easing over his waistband to peek down at the tops of his shoes. His jacket constrained obvious arm muscles and an expansive chest. His hands and fingers were thick and strong, capable of beating and punching; but I would never know his hands for those reasons. I would know them only for tenderness, caresses, touching. I would know them as teachers of pleasure; I would watch his hands, so capable of violence, turn the pages of books he would sometimes read to me.

In front of his desk was a chair, which he offered. "Please, have a seat," he suggested, his sound filling the room, changing that small space into a concert hall featuring his voice, which triggered arousal in me at every sibilant octave and every husky pitch.

"Thank you," I replied as I sat appreciatively. Sexual desire crackled through the room, popping and snapping like queens, but I was not frightened. There was no danger. I sensed there would be no harm.

I studied George. Standing before me was a powerful black man. A man clearly interested in me. His round, moonlike face glistened under a sheer veil of nervous sweat. His solid, thick-boned body seemed so overwhelming, so completely mysterious. I was in awe. I could have been standing in Memphis, and before my eyes flowed the sensuous, secretive Nile, undulating and hypnotic.

George slowly proceeded to tell me about the services the church offered to the surrounding community. This ten-minute explanation allowed him to use his voice to great effect. Masked beneath his intricate, intimate detail was a subtext of desire, encoded in his mellow tones and body language.

"Now, let me take you down to the community dining room," he said. "Any person who comes to our door seeking food is fed. We turn no one away. We find a plate, or a bowl, or a cup of something to serve. We feed nearly two hundred people a week. Many single-parent families and elderly people come to us, as well as the homeless. The food is donated and prepared by volunteers from the congregation. For six years—that's how long we've been doing this—and still it's not enough."

"How long have you been working here?" I asked as we rose to leave. Just then an awesome growl let loose loudly from my stomach, rudely interrupting our conversation.

"Are you hungry?" George quickly asked, then smiled with just a bit of slyness. "I can have a plate prepared for you when we get to the dining room."

"No, thank you," I said. "I'll be going home to dinner when I leave. Please, finish telling me about how you came to this church."

"I joined this church eight years ago," he proudly continued. "I immediately volunteered to work in one of the community programs. Prior to this I was a boxer, prancing and pounding my way around the ring. I'd been stepping to fellas since I was sixteen, up and down the East Coast; I did some Southern gigs, too. I made a bit of a name for myself. The promoters told me I had promise. I was quick with my hands and my feet, swift with my fists, and graceful. But an automobile accident forced me to give it up. My leg was permanently damaged in that accident. My left leg is mostly made of pins and luck," he said, as he dislodged himself from behind his desk.

I walked out of the office ahead of him, then turned back to watch him catch up to me after he locked the door. He did favor his left leg, with a slight limp that you barely noticed. He smelled of English Leather or Brut— it was difficult to determine the aftershave. He was pleasant in his manner as he showed me around the church, introducing me to some of the volunteers and diners. When we completed our tour, we returned to his office.

"How would you like to see the reverend's office?" he asked.

"Do you think he's in?" I questioned as we left George's office again.

"We can find out right now," he replied.

I followed him a short distance down the hall to an arched doorway with a heavy wooden door filling out the frame. It was a simple door: functional, no unnecessary adornments. It suggested privacy and strength. George took a ring of keys from his jacket pocket, located one from what appeared to be a dozen, and unlocked the door. It creaked open, yawning quietude as we stepped inside.

This room was filled with tall standing cases lined with books. There were a few comfortable-looking chairs, and floor lamps for reading. George ambled the short distance across the room and unlocked and opened a second door. We stepped inside a smaller room, the reverend's private office, and shut the door behind us.

The walls here sagged with religious paintings depicting the Last Supper, Jesus on the cross, the Resurrection. Crucifixes and palm fronds were in evidence. White candles stood on wrought iron holders, like unlit streetlights. Several Bibles of different sizes and colors lay open on top of the desk, like Pandora's boxes. This was the quietest, the most soundproof room in the church. No noise, other than our breathing and our heartbeats, could be heard. The cacophonous eating utensils of the hungry could not be discerned. Only our hunger was now apparent, already the most naked thing between us, louder than gnashing teeth and clashing silver.

"Take down your pants," George suddenly instructed me.

I was startled.

"What?"

"Take down your pants," he repeated. He watched me patiently. I could feel my erection growing again.

"I'm not taking my pants down in here!" I said incredulously.

"I want to suck your dick," he said. "Have you ever had your dick sucked?" He went behind the reverend's huge desk, sat in the creaky chair, then called me to join him.

"I can't do this here," I protested. "What if someone comes? What if the reverend returns?"

"The reverend won't be returning tonight," he interrupted. "Come here," he called to me. "Come here, let me look at you. Come on."

I finally walked over to him, carefully measuring my eager steps. I stood on one side of the reverend's crowded desk and stared across at George, suggestively rubbing his hand in his lap. I could see his crotch bulging and straining like my own.

"Come on," he urged. "This is why you came up here. I could tell you would check me out when I talked to you this afternoon. You know what's going on. You have nothing to fear from me. Come on. Come on over here."

And he was right. I was feeling fearless. I *definitely* knew what was going on.

I walked around the desk and stood in front of him, arms akimbo, legs apart. He rubbed his hands inside my thighs and over my crotch. He rubbed his hands up and down my chest, pinching at my tender nipples, pulling at my tight flesh. I was soon trembling, soon out of control. He unbuckled my pants and pulled them down, along with my undershorts. My dick sprang out in front of us, striking about in the air until he lowered his mouth over it like a net over a panther cub. A sigh escaped my chest and resonated throughout the room like an organ note.

I couldn't believe that only a few hours earlier we had met on the telephone, and now, in the belly of this church, we were fervidly making out, driven on to orgasm and high-spirited ecstasy, driven by the force of different thirsts and different hungers. Behind a locked door in this sanctuary, I was drunk with passion as his hands had their way with me, then I had my way with him.

After we spent ourselves like lottery money, we tidied up in the reverend's private bathroom. George then walked me to a nearby bus stop, but not before writing down his phone number.

"I don't live far from here, but at the moment I share an apartment with my sister. I do have guests over occasionally. Perhaps you'll pay me a visit—soon," he urged, as he handed me the hastily folded slip of paper.

We stepped from the church into a mild, lavender-hued April evening. As we approached the bus stop, he turned to me and asked, "Can I call *you?*"

"I can't give you my phone number at home," I quickly replied. "My mother might suspect something. She doesn't know—"

"She doesn't know *what?*" he interjected.

"She doesn't know I . . . I . . . I like men."

"You mean she doesn't know you're *homosexual,*" he corrected me with slight amusement. "My sister doesn't know I chase around after brothers, either," he revealed, "although I sometimes believe she suspects that I do. I haven't found it necessary to tell her. I don't know if she'd understand."

"I may tell my parents," I blurted out. "In time, I might tell them. I've given it some thought, but I have to be sure."

"Think about it carefully before you do," he warned me. "Sometimes families can react very strangely when a son tells them he's homosexual. Not everyone can handle that. They may act like you're supposed to cut that part of yourself off and hide it away. You'll see what I mean. The life will show you many things."

We stepped to the bus stop in silence after these remarks, oblivious to pedestrian and automobile traffic. George's warning would be echoed in subsequent conversations about "the life." I was too inexperienced to understand then that the warnings he uttered were meant for us both, not simply stated to eradicate my naïveté.

"Well, Mr. Essex, I won't pressure you for your phone number. You just be sure to call me. Come back and visit me when you're sure you want to see me."

"I will," I assured him as I boarded the bus headed south into the unfolding twilight.

IT DIDN'T MATTER that I had lied in order to make this evening a reality. The only issue that mattered was that the meeting had been consummated. When I paid my first visit to George's home, it was clear that the household was struggling to stay afloat—mostly on the income of his sister, I would learn. His residence in the apartment they shared was really an act of sibling kindness.

George wasn't ever going to move out on his own, unless he could earn the money to do so on a regular basis. For reasons still unknown to me, George's primary employment seemed to consist of working administration for the church. God was his employer and, materially speaking, meager was his reward.

My involvement with George lasted nearly two years. During that time I learned more than sexual practices from him. By late spring, our time together became planned and frequent. By late spring, I was borrowing my mother's royal blue Dodge sedan to drive uptown from far Southeast to spend a few hours with George. I borrowed the car under pretenses such as needing to go to the library to study.

I *was* studying, but I couldn't explain my subject as clearly then as I now can. From this reflective place in my present life, this place of measured solitudes, I am able to look back and count my many blessings, not to determine how many I have, or how many there have been, but to acknowledge my thankfulness to George, in this instance, for being as interested in my mind and its workings as he was in my then-sweet, coltish body. He demanded pleasure from my intellect with the same intensity I used to demand pleasure from his body. I was hungry to know his mystery, his power. He was also hungry, hungry to know what existed between my ears other than my face and its expressions.

George discussed Shakespeare's plays and Plato's philosophy, Langston Hughes's poetry and Dr. King's dream. We argued local and national political issues. He read some of my early poems and encouraged me to write more. He never offered me money for my body. He didn't offer me drugs and alcohol. He gave me pleasure at times when I was too selfish to return the same. He gave me pleasure in ways that at times had nothing to do with my body. Eventually, I learned that he ranked training the mind to think and reason over training the body in sexual practices. This didn't disappoint me; it expanded the quality of our interactions.

George loved to read and debate. He loved to discuss the meaning of life in terms particular to his experience but common to every soul faced with the struggle to live and maintain dignity. He was the most well-read adult black male I knew at the time, other than my schoolteachers. His mind was a beautiful, stimulating place to visit. His mind had not died the common zombie death that plagues ghettos. His mental faculties were lean and well muscled, as alert and as inquisitive as my own. He nurtured his intelligence in utter contrast to the evidence of poverty that surrounded him.

I told no one of George until after we ended our relationship. In some ways I knew, and he knew, too, that the thirty-odd years between us posed a tremendous barrier, an obstacle our passion could not diminish.

I was fortunate to have met George and to have learned some *real* truth about caring for a man horizontally *and* vertically. Driven by my hormones and my imagination, my horniness was easily exploitable, but George wasn't interested in playing games. I could have been corrupted, but instead, George treated me like a student, an apprentice, a man ultimately responsible for his actions. When he entered my then homo-secret world like a gust of forceful wind, George diverted me from making foolish choices just so my life could be defined as typically black and typically male. He blew all that shit away. He pointed me toward the only acceptance that matters: acceptance of myself. He intervened, not to interrupt my destiny but to take his place in it. His kisses upset the predetermined path that seemed to await me, had I adopted the rigid identities a black male is supposed to embrace. I didn't want to strike cool poses on the corner and father numerous children to prove my manhood. I didn't want my anger to disfigure me with various kinds of self-abuse and self-hating behavior. I could not use exaggerated bravado and butch drag to smother my homo yearnings.

George didn't make me feel like a sissy or a punk because I enjoyed reading. He didn't think I was "acting white" because I enunciated clearly and conjugated my verbs. These were defining signs of manhood and intelligence, and George respected both qualities, and to the extent that he could, he nurtured these qualities in me while expanding my sexual knowledge. George understood my curiosities and my fears. He pointed out a different way to me, hinting at others who had gone before us, suggesting a tradition, a history, ways of being.

I WAS TWENTY-FIVE years old when I read of George's death, over breakfast one morning. My first live-in relationship was breaking down after three years. My partner and I would make attempts to mend the damage, the wear and tear, but that only temporarily forestalled the inevitable. I can say we were fortunate men: We lived together openly and flagrantly, our families and friends fully aware that we were a gay couple.

I was stunned by the unexpected death notice in the paper, flooded with sudden memories as George gazed at me from the obituary page. He was pictured in a dark suit which made him appear successful, a winner; he looked like a champion, the victor of all his fights. It was clearly an early photo of him; his face was not as weathered as I remembered. I hadn't thought about George in quite a while, consumed as I was with my boyfriend, a military man with a lifetime commitment to the navy but not to me.

George's obituary made me pause and consider heart attacks. Even now, I ask, *What does that mean?* I want to know what exactly attacked his heart and caused him to die. The obituary didn't mention the loneliness for a man's love as a possible accomplice in George's death. The commentary about his life didn't mention the blue note longing for a companion. It didn't say the factors of his death were complicated not only because he was black and male, but complicated because he was also homosexual, which I would later understand to mean he had managed multiple identities, oftentimes contentious and contradictory. Each identity was capable of causing him profound pain and profound invisibility. Each mask he wore could put him at risk, even as it served to protect him. He carefully used masks to avoid danger, accusation, discovery. But each false identity was a chosen denial, and the same masks could bring sorrow to his heart without warning. His boxing was the ultimate cover he used, to discount any speculation about his manhood and his sexuality.

George Hart—another black male, another native son, the *other* one, *the* funny one, the *truly* invisible one—dead in America before sixty-five. Whatever really killed him, I knew, was much more complicated, much more insidious, much more deadly, than a mere heart attack.

Courtesy of Lois A. Holmes, sister of the author

L E T ' S   S A Y

Stephen McCauley

I.

LET'S SAY YOU'RE nineteen years old, a sophomore in college, a not especially bright, attractive, or motivated young man. You haven't figured out what to do with your life or how to support yourself once you get off the parental dole. For atmosphere, let's pretend it's 1975 and everyone you know, give or take a few premed students and a brother with CIA aspirations, is more or less in the same floundering boat. Up to this point, your student career has been a series of pot and drinking binges interrupted by sporadic attendance at a variety of introductory-level courses on subjects ranging from music appreciation to geology. Let's say college life isn't going as you'd hoped. You'd like to drop out of school altogether, but the paperwork involved is just too daunting.

Imagine that the second semester of your sophomore year, you hear about a professor with long blond hair who's making a name for himself around campus with his provocative teaching style, his wardrobe of vests and army fatigues, and his outspoken views on Gay Liberation. You sign up for one of his courses. The professor is thirty-three but is often mistaken for an undergraduate. We won't bother mentioning that he's intelligent, amusing, and handsome, because in this kind of scenario that goes without saying. Besides, this college is in a rural part of New England where, frankly, looks and brains are not what matter most. The professor is a vegetarian hippie. That matters. He claims, on the first day of class, that Henry James was probably a homosexual. Within a week, you look up his address in the phone book and start to wander through his neighborhood, hoping he'll walk out his front door just as you pass by his house.

Let's say you've known you were gay since you were sixteen. You were on a Florida-bound airplane which, due to a bomb scare, aborted takeoff at the end of the runway. As you were exiting toward the narrow emergency door at the rear, a steward groped you and you popped a boner. Before you stepped onto the tarmac in the cold March rain, you'd put two and two together and come up with a queer number.

Pretend it didn't shock or worry you. In fact, let's pretend the realization was a relief. For a good while you'd been wondering why you didn't want to fuck your girlfriend, didn't want to go to the prom, actually liked gym class (or at least the locker room part of it). Now you had the answers to these and other questions, all in one tidy three-letter word.

Keep in mind that this airplane epiphany would have taken place in the early seventies, when everyone you saw in the papers and on the TV news seemed to have a cause, a rebellion, a chosen form of dissent. People not much older than you were rioting in Chicago, robbing banks in Boston, dancing naked in Woodstock. Mia Farrow and the Beatles were dropping acid in India. You, on the other hand, were stuck in the suburbs; your mother drove a station wagon with fake wood siding; your father was in the navy and was bald; your brother was hoping to get a job with the CIA and was bald. Let's say you were forced to be bald, too. Let's say this bomb scare boner business made sense of the whole roiling mess of your adolescent angst. It gave you a private rebellion, a hidden cause, a secret direction.

You started to buy the *Village Voice*, listen to a gay talk show on an alternative radio station, watch Lance Loud traipse around Andy Warhol's New York on *An American Family*. You borrowed books from the library by Truman Capote and Gore Vidal, Gordon Merrick and Gertrude Stein. You had faith that somewhere out there a world existed into which you might, eventually, fit. In the meantime, you had the good sense to keep your private rebellion private. Every day after school, you rode your bicycle around the suburbs and into nearby Boston and Cambridge with maniacal determination, thirty or more miles, even in the rain. You discovered a leafy spot along a busy parkway where men in windbreakers and Perma-Press pants congregated and smoked cigarettes and gave each other blow jobs. Not the world you'd longed for or imagined, but let's say you spent more than a few afternoons there in guilty contentment anyway. You gave up the girlfriend, you didn't go to the prom, you stopped writing for the school newspaper. You waited for the day you'd leave for college—the day, you imagined, your real life would begin.

But let's say you made a tactical error in selecting a school. You chose scenery over sex and ended up miserable and lonely in a dorm room with a terrific view. You longed to drop out, not because you were unmotivated and intellectually insecure, but because you were disillusioned. Perhaps, you thought, all your earlier, silent enthusiasm for Gay Liberation and your own sexual leanings was misplaced. Perhaps the world you imagined fitting into existed only in the pages of the *Village Voice* or on the airwaves of alternative radio stations or in books which, come to think of it, usually ended unhappily. You began sending letters to your old girlfriend.

Let's say this was your frame of mind when you signed up for the course given by the longhaired professor. The truth is, you secretly pinned a lot of hopes on him before you'd even met him.

As winter wearies on and spring hesitantly approaches, your fantasies run wild. He writes complimentary comments on your papers, agrees with much of what you manage to say in class, suggests you sign up for his course the following year. All that must count for something.

Let's say it does. Let's say the professor invites you out for coffee at the end of the semester and even though you don't drink coffee, you go. You end up at his apartment. He offers you vegetable juice. He disconnects the phone. He puts on a Joan Baez record.

You have a summer job lined up back in the suburbs, but you call your boss and tell him you'll be a few days late. It's early May and the trees are beginning to bud, although there's still snow in the mountains. You stay with the professor for close to a week and then reluctantly pack up your things and leave. True, your future is as uncertain as ever, your career options as limited, your academic prospects as unpromising. But something has happened. The ground has shifted beneath your feet, a door has opened. Let's say you've fallen in love.

II.

So far, so good. But here's where things begin to get sticky, where you have to make some decisions, where you could, possibly, make some serious miscalculations.

Let's say your job is clerking the front desk of a cheap motel back in the sweltering suburbs. You work the night shift with a couple of ancient men who bring in thermoses full of "coffee" and pass out watching television. This leaves you hours to read magazines and the books you were too depressed to finish during the semester, and write long letters to the professor.

Fine.

But at least have the good sense to tell the professor not to send his almost daily letters to your parents' address, even if you want nothing more than to read his romantic, sex-drenched missives. If you don't, your mother, who monitors the mail, might get suspicious. She might ask you, "Who is sending you All Those Letters?" A friend, you might tell her. (As if that will satisfy her curiosity.) She might read one of the letters before it gets to you. She might pull you aside one morning, sit you down, look you in the eyes, and say, "I have a feeling this friend of yours—the one sending you All Those Letters— is really your lover."

If she does, for Christ's sake stop and think before you respond. Think about the last time she asked you a direct question ("Is this a marijuana cigarette I found in your pocket?") and you answered honestly. Try to remember that your mother is Italian, steeped in Catholicism and the emotional histrionics of bel canto opera and papal worship. Remind yourself that she's probably never heard of Gay Liberation or the *Village Voice* or listened to much of anything on the radio outside of weather reports. That the professor with the vests-and-army-fatigue wardrobe isn't really your lover just because you spent a couple of days in bed together and are carrying on an overwrought correspondence.

If you're so big on honesty you can't stop yourself from saying, optimistically and boastfully, "Yes, he is my lover," here is what you might reasonably expect:

Your mother, who's never raised her voice in anger, might slap you in the face, call you fag, fruit, homo, say you can't be trusted to sleep in the same room with your brother who wants to get a job with the CIA. She might tell you she always suspected the homo-fag-fruit stuff because you read too much as a child, listened to too many records, spent too much time at the movies. "You do yoga!" she might finally cry.

Eventually she might calm down and implore you not to tell the rest of the family about your perversion—then tell them herself. On your next day off, your father, a tall, stern, unforgiving naval officer steeped in the icy pessimism and bullying impulsiveness of the Irish, might come home in the middle of a hot afternoon, enter your bedroom, and lock the door behind him. He might shout at you for five, six, seven hours, a frequently incoherent rant combining insult and accusation with pleading, desperation, and love—fueled by rage and frustration.

Maybe I screwed up, you might think as your father goes on raving. You have no prospects for the future, you're still financially dependent on your parents, and, for the next few weeks, you're still a teenager. Now that it's too late to do anything about it, it might occur to you that maybe you should have lied back there when Mom asked about All Those Letters. Maybe lying would have been simpler, saner—and probably what your mother was hoping for.

After hours of shouting in your small, suffocating bedroom, your father might pull you to him and kiss you on the lips, thrust his tongue into your mouth, punch you in the stomach, all in one swift movement. Crumpled up on your side, confused and in pain, you might think, Maybe I should get out of here.

"Maybe you should get out of here," your father might say.

"Maybe you should get out of here," your brother, who hasn't spoken to you in days, might concur.

You could find a cheap apartment in Boston, keep your job at the cheap motel, save some money. Or you might call up the professor.

Let's say you call the professor. Let's say he listens sympathetically while you tell him the situation. Let's say he offers you a few rent-free months in an extra room he currently uses for storage.

III.

There are two ways this living arrangement could go.

You could feel as if you've fallen into a sweet, hazy dream. You could find that you have an amazing ability to forget your family's ugly words spoken in anger, your fleeting physical pain. You could spend an embarrassingly blissful summer with the professor, driving through the countryside, swimming in mountain pools, playing out every sexual fantasy you've ever had. You could, with the professor's help, discover literary worlds which could stay with you for the rest of your life. You could start lifting weights, running, hiking, exploring a physical side of yourself you didn't know existed, start paying attention to the clothes you wear and the pictures you hang on your walls and even the plates off which you eat. You could come to the conclusion that before now you never really saw the world around you.

You could join a fledgling Gay Liberation group and commence acting on the political theories you've read about for years. Your doubts could fall away and the happy, productive life you imagined for yourself begin.

Or:

You might discover that you're not quite as strong-willed and independent as you at one time believed. In the void left by the sudden disappearance of your family—a comforting, dependable irritant, as it turns out—you might find yourself leaning more heavily on the professor, passing along to him bigger pieces of yourself, letting him dictate your friends and your reading, your food and your conversation. You might find that he's molding you in his own image, a bit like a science project. After it's too late, you might discover that he doesn't even like himself that much, that what he originally liked about you was that you were so different from him. That he was hoping you'd force him to change, not comply with his wishes and adjust to the demands of his quirks.

As summer fades and the initial rush of romance and lust gives way to the dull realities of daily routine, you might feel a disjunction between the person you were for your first nineteen years and the person you are now. What happened to that family of yours, those assumptions about yourself? Where did they all go? As winter—a long, unforgiving season in this part of the country—approaches again, you might find a chill entering your bones, making it difficult for you to concentrate, to read, to watch movies or do yoga. To sleep. You might lose your enthusiasm for music and food and the people you once considered friends. The angry words might come back to haunt you. You might begin to believe some of them. You might feel as if you've been turned inside out, all your nerves exposed to the cold.

At two A.M. one subzero morning, you might sit up in bed in the room in the professor's house once used for storage, the walls and the floor and the sheets on your bed blue in the winter moonlight. You might look down and find that your skin, too, is blue, milky blue, with thick and throbbing darker blue veins visible just under the surface. Where am I? you might wonder.

You might run to the professor, but he keeps his door closed and you've never dared to disturb his privacy. You might call someone, but you can't remember who still counts as a friend.

You might think, Somewhere along the way here, I really fell off the track. Maybe I should get out of here.

And maybe you do, even if it takes years.

IV.

Let's say it's twenty years later. You're pushing forty. A lot of water has flowed under the bridge.

You've lost contact with your first lover—a professor, wasn't that what we said? A few years ago, you came across All Those Letters he sent you all those years ago and wept with laughter at the thought that you were ever so young as to find them believable, let alone romantic and sexy. Let's say rereading them at age thirty-seven, you realized for the first time how young the professor was himself. Let's say you weren't melodramatic enough to burn the letters, but you were practical enough to throw them away. The last you heard, the professor had given up academia and moved to Texas, a steamy town in the Panhandle where he'd opened an air-conditioning business.

The once-bald brother is bald again, although not, this time, by choice. He never did get that job with the CIA. He has a wife and children, one of whom bursts into tears whenever he sees you. You're hardly friends, but you're cordial to each other on holidays and at the occasional family funeral, and that seems to be enough for both of you.

Let's say your father died a few years back. Let's say his last words to you, uttered mere days before his death, were: "Get a haircut." There are many ways to interpret these words. Let's say, after much consideration you've decided to interpret them as meaning "I'm sorry, I love you, I'm proud of you, good-bye." Let's say your last words to him, in response to his haircut comment, were: "Forget it!" And what you meant, you've decided, was "I'm sorry, I love you, I'm proud of you, good-bye."

You and your mother are on good terms. You talk on the phone regularly and occasionally have a meal out together. Let's say she's changed over the years, almost as much as you. Let's say she has a neighbor whose name used to be Tom and is now Tonya. Let's say that when you ask about this person, she answers, "She's a transsexual. It's not such a big deal. Honestly, I wish I had her wardrobe. What are you having for dinner tonight?"

Now:

Let's say you've been asked to write about coming out, things that happened twenty years ago, things you choose not to think about too often. Try to be honest. Tell it more or less exactly as it was, not tidy it up too much. Try to resist the temptation to distance yourself, push the experience away somehow, hold it off—which is, after all, pretty much the same as falling into the trap of regret.

Let's say it's easiest to believe that you did the best you could at the time, and so did everyone else. It's a blessing even to be alive, an accomplishment, a privilege. Let's leave it at that.

MY FOUNTAIN PEN

J . D . McClatchy

I HESITATE BEFORE starting with this particular detail. I want to begin with what for me was a simple fact but what to others may seem a tiresome metaphor. The psychiatrists didn't invent this metaphor, but I suppose they helped popularize and thereby trivialize it. Psychiatrists have never done me any good, so I'll hold my present hesitation against them as well. As I said, for me it was simply a fact: At about the same time I discovered my penis, I started writing with a fountain pen. It was the most sensual thing I had ever held or used. Just to touch it excited me. It was an Esterbrook.

The casing was of a raven's-wing purple, with flat-top ends and a budded clip. On the side was the silvered lever my fingernail would catch behind and slowly pull to draw the ink upward. I loved dipping it into the little glass mezzanine of ink inside the Scrip bottle, listening to the faint guttural sucking, and then gently wiping off the sad excess with a tissue. Why did the whole ritual make the ink seem like blood—blue blood, at least? I would sometimes imagine the squattish ink bottle to be a disgraced but noble Roman senator in his tub. And the nib! Once filled, the capillaries of its ribbed, bee's-body underbelly ached beneath the pewtery fleur-de-lis. The airhole was a moist miniature of the ink bottle itself, the pen's own private well, in love with the long slit at the nib's bulbed tip. Down that slit, out from that tip, poured the permanent black and blue of my early lessons.

I didn't admire this pen as much as my mother's Sheaffer, and I used often to take hers from her desk to rub my hand over it. Along with her schoolgirl tooth marks, there was the white mole and tooled clip on its cap, and a gold band around its lacquered barrel, itself an iridescent length of striations all black and eelgrass green, like the shadowy reeds among which a baby in a basket might be found. The nib was two tiers of fogged copper and iridium, the airhole was a tiny heart, and the point was sharper. My Esterbrook was what you would call a "starter" pen: blunt, cheap, dispensable. It cracked. It spattered. It leaked. It left an archipelago of small blots on my thumb and middle finger: the faraway islands of desire. If there was little to admire about it, there was everything to love.

Long before I was given that fountain pen, of course, I had learned to hide things. Childhood's true polymorphous perversity, its constant source of both pleasure and power, is lying. But that pen helped me to discover something better than the lie. Almost as soon as it was given to me, I learned to hide inside the pen. Or rather, the pen allowed me to learn the difference between *hiding* something and *disguising* something—that is to say, making it difficult but not impossible to see. Even when I knew the difference, I couldn't always keep myself from confusing them.

Once, for instance—this would have been about 1956 and I was eleven—I was hopelessly in love with my counselor at summer camp. His name was Red. It was Red I saw first each morning, shaking me awake, and Red's drawled fireside stories to which I fell asleep each night. But it was nap time I liked best. Through the eye I pretended was shut I gazed—like some chubby, crew-cut, pimpled Psyche—on Red sleeping: his stubble, his sweatband, the nipple pressing through his T-shirt, the dream-drool on his chin. On a shelf over his bunk he had taped a snapshot of his girlfriend, who stared down at him with a vacant smile that had none of my cunning, my ardor. When I asked for his address at summer's end, I gave him a shot of myself. I didn't suppose he'd replace hers with mine, but perhaps I, too, hoped to keep an eye on him, from inside a foot locker, say, or from between the pages of a psychology textbook.

He was on his way that August to enroll as a freshman at the University of Virginia. I returned to my parents' house at the Jersey shore for the last few weeks before more grade school. I spent the time with my old friend the fountain pen, writing letters to Red that transfigured the dull gossip about the camp cook or the impetigo scare at the beach into what I felt were witty, knowing parables of my own superiority and devotion. I never mentioned my family, that I even had a family, or anyone I wouldn't cast aside for Red's amusement. I waited for the reply that kept not coming. The thought of him reading my letters stoked my pretensions; his very silence only confirmed my sense of the power of words. It was then, too, I decided that, when I grew up and started publishing novels, my ugly Scottish name—so common, smelling of peat fires and wet sheep fleece—wouldn't serve on the spine. I would adopt a pen name. I borrowed "Christopher Renquist" from the mailbox of a dentist down the street: It seemed a name with leather-bound editions in its bookcase and a pipe in its mouth. With my title page now readied, I was about to start on the novel itself when—after how long?—two letters arrived for me on the same day.

One was from the Ukrainian cook at camp, full of the same warm misspelled gush she'd served up all summer. A fat, plain, back-country girl whom I loved to spend time with, she was so easy to impress, to confide in, to tease. I had never thought that my imagined charms would outrun my ability to control their effect. Casually picking up the letter I had deliberately left on the hall table for them to read, my parents smiled at their son's precocious effect on women. I myself was of two minds, alternately flattered and saddened by my own talent to deceive.

The other letter was from Red. The silken writing paper had three strange blazer-blue symbols embossed on top—his fraternity letters. It was brief, but it was *typed*. I postponed reading it as long as possible, no doubt to prolong a thrill as textured as the paper, as enigmatic as the Greek. Finally, I began. "Hi kid! Gee, it was sure great to hear from you, and all those funny stories. Hey, college life is really swell. You'll see. Well, I've got to get back to the grind. So long for now." I pored over it as years later I might a paragraph of Proust. I wanted to be alert to every nuance, every implication. Nothing would be lost on me. Before long, I had it by heart. Here were lines to be read between, sentiments suffused with feeling.

Still, my first impulse was to hide it. Hide it *from* my parents, yes, but also hide it *for* myself. I ran with the letter to the beach and, carefully calculating an imaginary line from my bedroom window to the gable of the lifeguard shack and beyond to a deserted stretch of sand, I buried it. As if to prove it truly a treasure I had laid up in my heart, I let a day go by before I snuck back to dig it up and read it again. The mental *X* that marked my spot was suddenly confused by new maps of seaweed and broken shell pointers. Was it three feet this way? Or two steps to the right? Had I forgotten about the night's high tide? Let's just leave me there, furiously digging, my eyes blind with tears.

THOUGH I'D MEMORIZED what he'd written, I wanted the beloved's *writing*. I had put my trust in fetishes, in secrets. I had hidden something—my feelings—that I ought only to have disguised. A little later, I had learned the lesson better. The hole I had dug in the sand—the sand itself having run through the hourglass of several years—was not as dark as the confessional's velvet gloom. If I felt at home there, it was because I was both reluctant believer and artful dodger. That is to say, I didn't want to "sin," but only to enjoy myself. A great part of the enjoyment was confessing the forbidden pleasures, because a great part of the pleasure lay in the subsequent fall from grace. This required that I find the dimmest priest. I got to know the sound of his particular mumble—or perhaps there was a slightly longer line in front of his box. But to pull the heavy curtain behind me and wait until his wooden slat slid open . . . that was the moment I most enjoyed. It was for that moment I had rehearsed my disguise.

The point was to confess my sin without actually naming it; to let the priest know enough to forgive me, but not enough to picture what I had actually been up to. "I have been impure in action twelve times." That formula seemed sufficient: both bland and correct, evasive yet official. Sometimes it prompted the priest's prying follow-up: "With yourself or with others?" But more often than not there was the unseen knowing nod, the sorry words of sympathetic disapproval, the routine vows and penances, the smug walk to the altar rail to kneel and ask forgiveness from a statue of some muscled martyr ecstatic with arrows. It was only when I had finally begun to sin in ways I couldn't think how to disguise that I lost my faith in both religion and language.

Of course, language had been my religion all along, and my faith in its powers of salvation was only temporarily shaken. In the end, it was merely the heavy burden of the Church's authority that I had once and for all to shrug off. That was the easy part. So was Christopher Renquist's work-in-progress. Language and a literary ambition come with their own dead weight attached: the pressure every buoyant syllable of English puts on the tongue, the gravity with which every past achievement charges the imagination. But there was something more immediate, more intimate, and much heavier.

I cannot remember a moment of my life when I didn't know I was gay. My homosexuality was never a tendency, a phase, a discovery, a conversion, or a choice. Every instinct, every desire, had from the start been directed that way. Like a drop of ink let fall into a glass of water, it was a small part of the whole but imbued everything, was everywhere apparent. Still, at a certain time in your life, you become conscious of what you know. At about the same time I left the Church, I started being self-conscious about being gay. Can I make this generalization—that a gay person is always more aware of his sexuality, and therefore may encounter it as a kind of *fate*, something apart from himself that also *is* himself? This in turn may lead him to hate or resent his sexuality, this possessive god within. For me, though, it was simply a fact, not a fate. It was a fact—like being a writer—that both signaled my difference from others and linked me to a secret band of brothers. And being conscious of this fact was less a problem than a challenge: how to act on it without being caught, how to live with it without being Known As Such. It's no wonder my first short story dealt with a single man who wrote stories under another name—not a pseudonym but an allonym, the borrowed name of an actual person. It was my age of disguising.

There comes a time, however, when you have to tell. Admitting things to oneself is often difficult, but that sort of understanding—however tortured with tea and sympathy it was in the old novels—is usually reached privately and undramatically. Telling one's friends can be awkward, and occasionally frightens off one or two of them for good, but is rarely painful. The hardest disclosure—well, it was for me—is to one's parents. More than sibling or confidant, priest or teacher, they represent both authority and security. Their hold on one derives its force from history and myth: We have spent more time with them—emotional, physical time—than with anyone else, and in our minds we have made them over into figures larger, more loving, and more threatening than any mere human could be. And if there is a thorny hedge of denial around any topic between parent and child, it is sex. Neither can imagine that the other even *has* a sex life, for instance—it is an unbridgeable embarrassment.

For years I kept my secret to myself. Even if I could figure out how to put it, I dreaded hurting them and was afraid to defy them. In one scenario, it was fire and brimstone; in another, tears and cold shoulders. It took me the longest time to face up to it. In fact, not until I had settled into a happy relationship with another man—I was in my late twenties—did I have the courage to tell them the truth. Half of it was Dutch courage. I was home on a visit. My youngest sister was still living at home, and she and my parents and I had all downed a couple of stiff drinks before dinner. By dessert time, there was an odd and entirely uncharacteristic soul-baring atmosphere around the table. Each of us had decided to tell the others something we'd never told before. My sister disclosed I no longer remember what, but at that moment it seemed an intimate, probably racy, secret. When she was finished, I took another long slug of red wine and pushed back my chair.

"Okay, my turn now. I think it's time I told you something about myself, something I've wanted to tell you for a long time, something very important to me."

I reached for my wineglass again. Over its rim I could see my mother's eyes narrowing.

"Don't bother," she said crisply. "I know what you're going to say."

Of course she knew. What else could she have concluded, years ago, from all those afternoons I'd spent listening to Brahms in my room while my father took my sister to the football game, from my wanting to play house with the neighborhood girls when I was young and later insisting on late-night pool parties with the classmates in my all-boys prep school, from my acting out Eve Arden roles in our living room, from the too-glamorous dates I found for the proms—oh, from hundreds of things done and not done, felt and not felt. My parents could see as well as I the texture of my life, like a cobweb on the lawn that if touched anywhere trembles all over, so tender that it feels everything. But what was more important even than my "orientation" was that it not be spoken about. That is what my mother's interruption meant: *Whatever you do, don't put it into words.*

In one sense, we were collaborators. Both sides had a stake in maintaining the ruse. They preferred silence. I preferred a manner-of-speaking. One hid the truth, the other disguised it. But wasn't my sudden insistence on coming out meant to subvert all that? And wasn't I making something more than a declaration? Wasn't I saying that from now on I would be in charge of my own life? It seems a basic desire, but how rarely granted to anyone! I meant to take control of a situation whose hypocrisy had been festering too long. Even more, I meant to change the way all of us "knew" what was what.

Keeping a secret is one way of sustaining the illusion of control; spilling that secret is the desire to manipulate what another knows and feels. We were a family, not of secrets exactly, but of a fearful incuriosity. Neither of my parents knew the names of their great-grandparents, or had any interest in finding them out. Here I was, nearly thirty years old, and I had no idea what all my father's business interests were or his income or his war record, what my mother's major in college was or if she'd ever been in love with anyone else. It's not just that we never discussed such things, we never even asked about them.

I was going to change all that with one simple sentence, as easily as unscrewing the cap from a pen. Not only was I going to force them to *know* about me, I was going to force them to talk about it. Not-speaking-about meant not-dealing-with. By putting it all into words, I would move the matter to a higher plane than mere "knowing." From my sleeve of disguise, now turned inside out, I would pull the words that revealed and redeemed rather than belied and protected.

I swallowed the wine. I paused for dramatic effect. I looked at each in turn, and said in a flat tone that combined soulful resignation and matter-of-fact pride, "I'm gay." Let's just leave me there at the table, tears of relief in my eyes, tears of a different sort in my parents' eyes as I went on confessing my history, forcing them to listen, determined to reshape the facts of my life into a myth that would change them as well.

IT WASN'T UNTIL a year or so later that I discovered the truth. Or rather, a larger truth than the one I'd told that night. It was during a casual telephone conversation with my father. He asked what I was working on. In fact, I was writing a poem and needed a detail. I asked him if he remembered Dr. Schreiber. He did, and it was then he told me *his* secret.

Years before—I was a young graduate student at Yale then—I'd found myself curled up on the floor of the dining room in the little house I rented, wedged into a corner, sobbing, staring at the telephone beside me, waiting for it to ring, waiting for I didn't know who to call. A friend had happened by, easily sized up the situation, and suggested I check in with one of the psychiatrists at the University Health Service. Bursting out in tears, I'd picked up the phone and made an appointment.

In those days, a student was allowed ten free sessions with a staff psychiatrist, after which you were either cured or referred elsewhere. I was assigned a young resident, and everything about him both prompted and confused my reason for being there. It was clear even to me that my motive in coming was to find some way of living with the fact that I was gay. Being gay was not itself the problem. Everything *else* was the problem—the pressures, the opprobrium, the future, the double life. I could manage being gay, but not the added burden of disguising it. And as soon as I walked into the consulting room I knew there would be a new problem. My doctor was young, blond, handsome. His name was Will. He was, as it turned out, the older and better-looking brother of a movie actor who was starring as the heartthrob in that season's blockbuster. I fell for him at once.

"What do you think the problem is?" It was the second time he'd asked that question, and it finally stirred me from my daydream. Since I couldn't tell him that *he* was suddenly the problem, or stood in for what had always been the problem, I shrugged. I looked up his name in the faculty directory (his wife's name in parentheses beside his) and the address of his apartment complex in the suburbs. I took to driving out there, parking in the lot, and gazing up at his balcony—or at the baby bucket in the back seat of his car. I was obsessed. By the tenth session, I was in tears again, begging him to keep me. He consulted his supervisors, agreed to continue seeing me, and started smoking a pipe.

Week after week, I came clean with him or lied—whatever I thought would deepen our intimacy. The purpose of the sessions was lost in this feverish new business of disguising my feelings. He came home from work later and later. I knew because I was already parked, with the visor down, in a far corner of his lot. I once saw him arguing with his wife on their balcony. Another time, I spent the night: My car had stalled. The sessions, too, seemed stalled. Getting the story out of him was hard, but at last he opened up. He began to tell me about his domineering father, his jealousy of his brother, all the time a new baby takes. By now I was smoking the pipe. I almost hated myself for what I was doing, but I was fascinated by the curl his story, like pipe smoke, was taking around the currents of my sympathy. I asked if we could talk about it all outside the office. Perhaps dinner? He'd phone next week. The transference was complete.

By which I mean—the call came soon—I was transferred to another doctor. Poor Will, having confessed, was yanked off the case, and it was suggested by his superior that I see someone named Dr. Schreiber. Of course, I was crushed. But also intrigued by the fuss I had caused—and by the graybeard sitting like a pasha under a canopy of diplomas, as "distinguished," indeed as *admirable*, as my mother's classy fountain pen. *Schreiber*: His very name, the German word for "writer," betokened my ambition. We talked about "arrangements to be made," his fee and my life, and agreed on a schedule for both. Then, for nearly a year, we plunged back into my past, back to . . . well, to a happy childhood. That is to say, my memories were largely happy ones.

Oh, but how I hate to disappoint. I would zero in on anything I thought might accuse my young self of betraying its desires. I would renounce anyone— my parents, Red, Will—in order to make a new conquest, this time not someone to love but someone to emulate. Our weekly hour seemed so fluent and worldly wise, as poised as any poet's stanza. The doctor's increasing silence only brightened my chatter. Perhaps he knew what he was doing. The more I carried on and tried to please, the more I grew convinced that my sexuality wasn't a choice—like pleasing—but a given, a fact, a discovery to be made of a treasure buried there from the start.

But even that wasn't right, exactly. What it lacked was a body. So I began to alternate the shrink with the disco, the therapy of someone's Rush, the umpteenth round of "Smarty Pants," the floor full of cavaliers in designer jeans, each partnered by the trance he'd turned himself on to, by the glamour of a type he'd turned himself into: dropout honcho, wasted dopehead, guardsman with advanced degrees. Let's just leave me there, in the middle of the flickering dance floor, head thrown back to the singer's wailing promise of "what you've been waiting for . . ."

THE WAITING SEEMED interminable. We'd been talking in circles for months. (It would take, by the way, another few years before I met the man whom I decided to spend the rest of my life with—a man now long since gone—and who soon gave me the courage to speak to my parents about being gay.) All that small talk while a fantasy undressed was getting me nowhere. I told him so. He didn't seem offended. "Rejection especially tells us what we want, now doesn't it?" What did he mean? I was rejecting Schreiber, not the other way around. I walked out of his office for the last time late one stifling August afternoon. The night before, the disco's license had been revoked.

What I didn't know then, didn't know until that phone call to my father, is that, after my first meeting with Dr. Schreiber, *he* had telephoned my father. The deal had been that Yale would pay half his fee for our sessions and that I would pay the other half. I couldn't afford it, and had called my father to ask if he'd cover me. I told him I needed to see a therapist. He didn't ask why, and agreed at once to help. I told Schreiber to send his bill to me and my father would pay. That was that. Behind my back, to insure that his fee would be fully taken care of, the doctor called my father to verify the payment plan and told him why I had sought professional help in the first place. He told him about Will. He told him what I had been disguising all those years.

In the years that passed between those two phone calls to my father—first Schreiber's and, later, mine—he had never said a word, had borne his own disappointment or confusion in silence, had never confronted or accused or advised me. Only gradually did I realize how much I owed to my father's loving forbearance. But what first struck me, when I found out about that doctor's weaselly call, was what a farce his betrayal now made of my brave, overrehearsed coming-out scene.

Whose secret, after all, had been revealed that night? What is the effect of telling someone a "secret" he already knows? And who precisely had been keeping the real secret all along? It seems to me now, so many years later (years even after my dear father's death), that I had been both right and wrong that night. Right, I guess, to bring things to the surface, though all it really occasioned was months of the kind of tense confrontations that Family Discussions so often become. Emboldened by my own bravado, I overdid everything. I insisted that they not only know but accept, even applaud. They refused— silently; and the silence *after* a spoken revelation is even more maddening. I climbed onto one political hobbyhorse after another and charged the vanes of their resistance. And that, too, is how I went wrong: by my insistence on being *right*.

I look back on it ruefully. One's life comes to seem less and less individual, and the crises and battles of the past, the anguish and assertiveness, tend to blur. I'm no longer young, and not yet old. I'm not attractive, not ill, not hip, not angry, not hopeful. I don't dance. I don't march. And I don't have any secrets left. They are what I miss most. By making things impossible to overlook, coming out is the opposite of *hiding*. What I wanted, for the longest time after I forced the issue, was the opposite of *disguising*— which is, of course, nothing but another sort of disguise, something more subtle, more hesitant, more wistful, something with more soul and less willfulness.

It is while in such a mood that one takes up again an old school text. Late at night, in bed, with a book or my pen, I could trace other men's secrets. I'd look there for echoes of my own secrets, so long vanished into the thin air of honesty. The great poet Horace, for instance, gave me one cue. At the height of his career he was the most elegant and admired poet in Rome, and the emperor, Augustus Caesar, commissioned from him a fourth collection of odes. The first poem in that book is addressed to Venus, the goddess of love, imploring her to leave him alone, to pay attention to the devotions of younger men. Horace was fifty—my own age as I write this—and he felt his erotic and romantic life was over. Yet the poem itself finds tears still left in the poet, like a buried secret, a hidden fountain. They were the same tears I suddenly found in my own eyes as I read the Latin—and I set about making a contemporary version of the old poem. I called it

LATE NIGHT ODE

It's over, love. Look at me pushing fifty now,
  Hair like grave-grass growing in both ears,
The piles and boggy prostate, the crooked penis,
  The sour taste of each day's first lie,

And that recurrent dream of years ago pulling
  A swaying bead chain of moonlight,
Of slipping between the cool sheets of dark
  Along a body like my own, but blameless.

What good's my cut-glass conversation now,
  Now I'm so effortlessly vulgar and sad?
You get from life what you can shake from it?
  For me it's g.-and-t.s all day and CNN.

Try the blond boychick lawyer, entry level
  At eighty grand, who pouts about the overtime,

Keeps Evian and a beeper in his locker at the gym,
And hash in tin foil under the office fern.

There's your hound from heaven, with buccaneer
Curls and perfumed war paint on his nipples.
His answering machine always has room for one more
Slurred, embarrassed call from you-know-who.

Some nights I've laughed so hard the tears
Won't stop. Look at me now. Why now?
I long ago gave up pretending to believe
Anyone's memory will give as good as it gets.

So why these stubborn tears? And why do I dream
Almost every night of holding you again,
Or at least of diving after you, my long-gone,
Through the bruised, unbalanced waves?

    I think back now to all my long-gones. I think back to Red. And to poor Will. I think back on the men I've had secret crushes on and couldn't say anything to. And I remember those I could tell, or sort of tell. And I dream about the three men whom I have loved most, love still, the men whom at the start I kept secret from others because they had so changed my life. Each of these men I have disguised in—or, really, transformed into—poems, in order to keep hold of them. Like some minor god in an old myth, I've changed them back into secrets. A poem needs disguises. It needs secrets. It thrives on the tension between what is said and not said; it prefers the oblique, the implied, the ironic, the suggestive; when it speaks, it wants you to lean forward a little to overhear; it wants you to understand things only years later.

I'VE JUST NOTICED a stain, here on the underside of the spread (I'm writing this in bed), that must be ink. It looks like a birthmark or puckered galaxy. I shouldn't be using my fountain pen in bed at all. It's old-fashioned, and messy to boot. How many times now have I fallen asleep still holding the thing and by morning found it had spilled its secrets all over? Yes, its secrets. That's what my fountain pen holds. It has drunk up all the slow-dripping sadness, engorged itself with rapture and the grief that comes to. My pen is filled with a heady elixir compounded of salt water and sweet fire, of hearts-blood and aftermath, of furtive arousals and a mirroring solitude, all blended to the tincture of time, a cloudless midnight blue. When I hold the nib to my nose, I can smell it. It's the smell as well on my fingers and inside the genie bottle of ink on my nightstand. The smell of fresh bandages, wet leaves, quicksilver. It might as well be the smell of memory itself. What may have begun as a hidden guilt eventually surfaces as merely a memory, and we want to keep a few of them secret because, in the end, memories seem to be our true, our only, innocence.

Photograph by Christopher Cox

H O W   T O
G R O W   F R U I T

T i m   M i l l e r

PBS MADE ME gay. Yes, here we have every right-wing nut's three A.M. nightmare come true. They broadcast that homo beam right into my family's suburban living room in the mid-seventies and saved my life. It was that *Theater in America* production about Oscar Wilde. Thank you, KCET! From you, Public Television, I received my first dose of queer images and a sense of historical place and lineage. (I got a mug and a tote bag, too, but that's another story.) Well, maybe I can't give PBS *all* the credit. It could also have been the Los Angeles Civic Light Opera. Its revival of *A Funny Thing Happened on the Way to the Forum*, perhaps? That hopeful utopian downbeat of the tuba in "Comedy Tonight" may have been that certain magic wand to make me queer. That showstopper, mixed with the cute chorus boy queens in their tunics, of course. Or, while we're indulging a Greco-Roman mood, maybe it was those delicious Mary Renault novels with all the buffed Athenian ephebes going for Truth and Beauty? A little dab'll do ya! No, wait, I know. It had to have been George Frideric Handel. His music helped tell me who I was and sent me zooming out of the closet accompanied by those tacky sparklers he wrote music about. Yes, there is absolutely no question: Handel's *Messiah* made me into a faggot!

Allow me to explain.

It was 1976. Ah, 1976! Let me sniff the crotch of my maroon corduroy bell-bottoms and remember 1976. The capacious toothy grin of soon-to-be-president Jimmy Carter spreads like a shovel full of smooth peanut butter over the land.

Let me take a whiff of Jif and sniff that tremulous year. Let me rub those bell-bottoms through my ass crack. Let me reach inside the pockets of those pants, past the pocket-size tube of Clearasil acne ointment, and grab my dripping teenage weenie.

I was seventeen going on eighteen and I was desperate for love and dick. I searched everywhere for it. I hung around the Whittier Public Library, leaning suggestively against the stacks in the psychology section, waiting to be picked up by some graduate student. I leaned too far, once, and almost knocked over an entire row of bookshelves. This scared off a man in a trench coat reading Havelock Ellis. I left the library, went into town, and walked down Hollywood Boulevard. I lingered outside the Gold Cup Coffee Shop at Las Palmas, where all the teenage boy prostitutes perched. I wanted the courage they displayed in their open-for-business bodies. This was *the* Boy Scout troop I wanted to be part of. Maybe something would rub off on me from these saucy young men. I, too, could get a merit badge in cocksucking. I just needed somebody to grab me and show me the way.

There had been a few kisses already, of course. First there was my girlfriend Janet Mauldin in the eighth grade. We kissed on the Journey to Inner Space ride at Disneyland. Feeling her Marcia Brady hair, I reached my arm around her waist and held her close. We climbed into the royal blue automated car that would carry us into the microscope where we would be shrunk and injected into a water molecule. I kissed her pool-tanned neck as we journeyed through the snowflake field. We put our lips together as oxygen and hydrogen atoms swirled around us. I stuck my tongue into her mouth as we approached the pulsing red nucleus. The atom got bigger and bigger, this huge throbbing nucleus hanging in front of us as our wet, wet, wet tongues danced around each other. We walked through Tomorrowland with our arms entwined for the rest of that June day. I felt the full hot cradling breath of nascent heterosexual privilege wash over me. It floated me up as an offering to the gaping mouth of Walt Disney's hidden queerness, *his* closet the size of Frontierland. I was thirteen and I had a cute girlfriend and she would sing a song to me at eighth-grade graduation. The world was fine as I walked arm in arm with Janet Mauldin down Main Street, U.S.A. Everything was good ... except that very soon (once I got my first pubic hair the next year) I was going to become a big fag.

Disneyland would again loom large three and a half years later, at a white-trashy trailer park in Anaheim on New Year's Eve, 1976. The Magic Kingdom's fireworks exploded and Tinker Bell twirled with a frozen frightened smile, dancing on her tightrope descent through the fiery bursts from the Matterhorn while Robert and I kissed and groped in a dark bedroom a few blocks away. Robert was my first boyfriend. At the last moment, he wouldn't put out. We greeted the New Year drinking cold marijuana tea on opposite sides of the bed.

I arrived at California State University, Fullerton, a reluctant virgin and a proto-punk-rock wanna-be. I slipped into my tights and Patti Smith T-shirt and entered the studio for Modern Dance 101A. I was about to start my warm-up when my eyes were pulled out of my head by the sight of a sleek, dark-haired fellow doing some deep pliés in the corner by the barre. His arm windmilled over his leg, which seemed effortlessly to circle his ear. The room began to tilt in his direction, and I began to slip and slide toward his embrace. Then another dancer boy, with an obvious perm and perfect butt, touched him on the arm and said, "Hi, David."

His name was David! That means "king," I thought. Or, if it doesn't, it fucking well should.

He was totally beautiful. He looked like . . . *David Bowie*. (I'm talking about the *Station to Station* Bowie, not *Diamond Dogs*, okay?) The dancer David, like his namesake, had long legs and fine black-brown hair—maybe a henna high-light rinse. Who knows? He boasted a tight hard body, skinny and thickly sinewy at the same time. In those days there was more than one possible body type, unlike today's monolithic coke-provoked fantasy ideal sold to us by clos-eted fashion designers. David's arms were as long as a giraffe's opera glove, his face set off by a delicate strand of puka shells around his neck. He, without question, represented one version of the homo physical ideal of 1976, at least as far as my seventeen-going-on-eighteen eyes could see.

David was the best dancer in class and the big queen dance teacher obviously favored him. David dove into each arabesque, devouring the space as he flung himself through the dance combination, scraping the acoustic tile ceiling every time he leapt. I was in the last group, and I tried to match his power as I danced only for his eyes.

Who was he? Who was this man who would be so much to me? The fuel he gave me still fires lots of kisses. The taste of the food we ate together is somewhere on the plate at every table I sit with a man by my side. The touch David taught me is at the tip of my fingers, on the skin of the many men my hands have danced over ever since. The back of David's neck is suddenly there on another man in a bed fifteen years later, in a blue house in Minneapolis. To this day, I still strive to nuzzle that neck, to sniff my way back to that moment that seems a long time ago. Of course, I didn't know how he'd change my life and memories then. I just wanted to hold this man with the black-brown hair very close to me.

And who was I at that moment? With the blitzkrieg of puberty, I had come to occupy a world of romantic-cum-homoerotic forces that were a strange cocktail of *Crime and Punishment* and *The Front Runner*. Some dream life where I was the star of the gay romance Fyodor Dostoyevsky never wrote. A place where Raskolnikov would get enlightenment and a locker room blow job. Maybe I was looking for this imaginary scenario instead of keeping my eyes peeled for the messy real life that just might present itself. I was too smart for my own good and yet not smart enough to know my heart's highways. I finished the combination and caught a glimpse of myself in the thick aviator glasses which often made people mistake me for a lesbian separatist from Ann Arbor.

What did I really look like then? Well, my boychild cuteness had done the usual teenage weedlike thing. Hair, bones, and ego had all grown in the most unlikely directions. My cheeks and nose often sported several zits, sometimes in patterns as recognizable as certain constellations (Cassiopeia one week, Ursa

Major the next). Nothing that would show up in a dermatological textbook, but enough to cause me panic.

I stood near David at one end of the studio and I got incredibly anxious. I began fiddling with my fingers in the new, "natural" Afro hairstyle that my barber, Big Al Stumpo, had given me. (Big Al Stumpo had tried for years to tame my relentless curls. All during high school, he had forced me to brush through my bristles and comb all those curls to one side. They'd pile up like an electrocuted poodle over my left ear, then, one by one, spring back with an audible *twang*. In 1976, Big Al Stumpo finally gave up. He threw his enormous nicotine-stained hands in the air and said, "*Basta!* Have it your own way. A curl's gotta do what a curl's gotta do!") Forcing my fingers to leave my hair, I danced my way a little clumsily through the next part of the teacher's combination, a really hard turn and jump, watching David the whole time, the dance belt under my tights straining to its polyester limits. Somehow, I managed to get through every contraction and release without popping a noticeable bone.

LET US NOW praise famous dance belts. Oh, dance belt! Dainty of the penis realm! Delicate armor for the dancer hero! I get down on my knees and thank my Lowell High School drama and dance teacher, Mr. Bucalstein. He was not queer, but knew us queer boys when he saw us. Starting in eleventh grade, he made us all take dance class—and, thus, helped us escape from phys ed. My life really began once I stopped getting hit in the head with various soft and hard balls and started learning how to move my body. One Saturday, Mr. Bucalstein piled the gay boys in a school van and drove us to the nearest Danskin shop, in Santa Ana, to buy that special item for our dick and balls. No mere coarse jockstrap (though I would come to appreciate them and today love a good chew on one). A dance belt. A mysterious and resilient article of clothing that holds you close to home. This was the clearest acknowledgment I ever received of my gay boy's body: my teacher taking his queer male students to buy their dance belts.

NOW, WATCHING DAVID demonstrate the final set of movements, that dance belt was smashing my hard-on against my belly as a head full of frizzy curls pulled me toward that dancing man in that studio. I wanted time to stop, to walk up to David and begin our pas de deux then and there. I had that scared, excited feeling I had only read about in big books by nineteenth-century writers: Everything in my life was about to change.

At the end of class, my eyes connected with David's for one wide-screen moment in the mirror of the rehearsal studio. My dance belt had crawled up my asshole; there was a big wet spot on the front of my tights. I turned quickly away, trembling. Out of the corner of my eye, I saw David walk with clipped dignity toward the door. At the last moment, he crisply knelt down by my backpack and slipped a folded piece of orange paper inside. He shot me a nervous look, then quickly left.

I took a breath, counted to three, then raced over to my bag. There it was, right next to my Carter-Mondale campaign literature: a flyer for the lesbian and gay student group, on which he had written, "Call me later. I'll be home around 9:30. David."

I looked at my watch every three seconds for the next seven hours. Why do I have to wait so long to call him? I wondered. I sat in a litter-strewn McDonald's, writing desperate poetry in my journal. Finally, my heart playing the bongos, I called David.

No answer. I waited a few minutes and called again. He picked up.

I didn't know what to say. "I got your note," I stammered.

"Good."

I could hear a tiny creak in David's voice, too. I listened to his anxious breath flow in and out against my sweaty ear at the receiver.

"Umm. Thanks for the note."

"Do you want to come over?" David asked.

"Sure."

I sped to David's sprawling stucco apartment complex off Yorba Linda Boulevard, just spitting distance from the little house where Richard Nixon was born (and buried). I parked on a side street by David's building. I walked past the hot tub, overflowing with the usual fraternity-style soap suds. I sniffed the tart *whoosh* of the swooning marigolds in the hot breath of the September Santa Ana breeze: sharp chlorine, Mr. Bubble, and the desert wind. I climbed up three flights of stairs, found David's unit, and knocked softly.

David opened the door slowly, glowing in his fifties red rayon bowling shirt. The smell of herb tea and something baking drifted through behind him.

"Come in." David opened the door wide.

I had never before visited a friend who had his own place. He showed me around. Even today, I can draw the floor plan accurately as any architect. The deep shag living room. Piles of books and musical scores. Pictures of scantily clad men on horses, over the piano in the corner. The military organization of the kitchen. The red-lightbulb bedroom with the auto repair shop sign over the bed which read ALL DELIVERIES MADE IN THE REAR. The bamboo balcony overlooking the Mervyn's Store parking lot. This was David's house; it reflected his independence and his point of view.

We sat down on the small couch in the living room and began to talk. I was awed by the "adultness" of this situation. I kept using big words in absurd sentences:

"You know, David, I think postmodern dance creates an existential situation for self-awareness. And, for me, the artist must be a kind of *Ubermensch* amid stultifying normative bourgeois patterns."

David smiled mysteriously and changed the subject. He told me about his family. I began to glean that he must be at least twenty-four, and I was shocked. I had never hung out with anyone quite so old before.

David had been much hurt by this weird life we've landed in. He told me about being queer-bashed in front of a gay bar in nearby Garden Grove. The attackers had stabbed him many times with an ice pick. He showed me the denim shirt he'd been wearing, still bloody, with thin tear lines on the fabric where the ice pick skated until the sharp point found its way into his neck. I still have that shirt. I keep it safe in what's left of my closet.

These last bits of information were a bit *too* adult and scary. I finally shut up.

At last, we got to the main subject. David said, "I am a musician." In addition to his dance studies, he was taking classes in music and conducting.

"What kind of music do you like?" he asked me.

"I like bel canto opera and classical vocal music mostly," I lied, omitting Patti Smith and show tunes.

He lit up at this and jumped to his feet. He told me that in his conducting class they were working on Debussy's *La Mer* and the "Amen" from Handel's *Messiah*. He walked to his Radio Shack combo record-player/eight-track deck, his butt shifting lazily beneath his thrift-shop tuxedo pants with each step. He put a record on the stereo. The needle found its scratchy groove and clicked into the end of *Messiah*. David listened and then slowly began to talk about the music, as stately voices vaulted through the cheap speakers.

"Tim, listen," he said. "I love this. How simple it begins. The voices make a community. People gathering. Did you ever see *How the Grinch Stole Christmas?* Well, it's like all the Whos down in Whoville or something. Everybody holding hands. Greeting each of the voices. Blessings. Honor. Glory. Power."

David moved slowly nearer and nearer to me on the couch as he spoke. I smelled the steeping peppermint on his skin. I put down my tea and turned my body toward him, my center of gravity slowly shifting into his orbit.

"Handel does something great here!" he exclaimed. "It's like the tenors are chatting up the altos. Baritones flirting with the soprani. They find a way of understanding this weird world. A way of understanding who *we* are."

David moved his leg up and down against mine as he slowly rocked with the music. I pantomimed a yawn and maneuvered my arm to rest behind his head on the couch. He grabbed my knee, hard.

"And right when it seems it can't get more intense," he continued, letting his hand fall to the inside of my thigh, "at that moment all the voices come together and zap it up one more notch. Tim, they remind us to listen to ourselves. To know ourselves. Loving our bodies. Trusting each other. This is how we should be."

David gently pulled my hand into his. I worried that my palms were too sweaty.

"It's like they're building a doorway for us," he whispered with the music. "The string continuo kicks in and joins the celebration. It's a way out of a place we have been trapped inside of for so long and never knew it. Finally, we walk outside together."

The energy of the chorus built. David stopped talking. He put his arms around me and looked into my eyes. His lips moved slowly closer. I felt his breath on my face. Very gently his lips touched mine and then—so softly, softly, softly—my new friend David, who looked like Bowie, kissed me.

For an instant, I thought my brain would explode. I saw shooting lights and every picture in my photo album race in front of my eyes, a crazily shuffled deck. Then, David broke away and noisily removed the needle from the record.

"I think we've had enough Handel for one evening," he said, hiding a little panic.

David made a beeline to the kitchen and boiled some water. He shifted us

to soothing chamomile tea. Then we held hands some more, listened to the
Bach *Mass in B-minor,* and called it a night.

As I drove down La Habra Boulevard past Richard Nixon's first law office,
I felt David's tongue on my lips, his taste as fresh as a bite of an apple that's
so shiny you can see your face in it. I pulled my 1965 blue Volkswagen bug
in front of the plaque by Nixon's office and remembered my fourth-grade crush
on Nixon's second cousin Scott Milhouse, who'd once walked me home.

I had always subscribed to the slash-and-burn school of relations with my
parents: fits of outrage, extreme ideological transformations, a knee-jerk willingness to pass judgment on their lives. The usual. I wore a Chairman Mao button
on my sleeve to family reunions, just to provoke my folks and to keep their
parental reflexes up. This scorched-earth policy would now cut to the chase.
It seemed like a perfectly good time to come out to them.

This is a big moment for most gay people, the moment so many of us carry
close to our skin. Our own personal epic poem we each get to write, direct,
and star in: Coming Out to Our Parents. This is the moment we speak the
truth to ourselves *and* to these strange people we find ourselves related to.

It was late, really late, when I got back home. My parents were still up. I
walked into their bedroom and Bettie and George looked at me, my dad over
his *Time* magazine, my mom over her book, a cleavage-festooned romance
novel. My mom had her nightly mud pack on her face; the Noxema had
started to harden around the edges and turn a graham-cracker-crust brown.

"I think we need to talk," I said. "I know you've been wondering about me
ever since I first did that summer theater intensive before eighth grade. And I
just have to tell you something very important. I'm gay."

The pause lasted at least a millennium. My dad rolled his eyes. My mom's
book fell onto her nightgown.

"I just hope you're not going to blame me," she said. "I know they always
try to blame the mother."

"I want you to be careful," my dad offered. "Don't wear dresses and you
won't get beat up."

My mom asked, "Do you have a boyfriend?"

I answered, "Yes, his name is David. He looks like David Bowie. He lives
by Cal State Fullerton. He teaches piano lessons and works on the weekends
in Hollywood. If I'm not home at night, you'll know where I am. I'll bring him
over so you can meet him."

"Don't forget to put out the trash," my dad reminded me.

They went back to their reading. At that moment, like Peggy Lee, I had to
wonder: Is that all there is? I slipped into the kitchen and called David.

"Hi, David? It's Tim."

"Hi, hon."

Hon! He called me "hon." Have any two people ever been more intimate?
We whispered to each other as I twirled the lazy Susan on the kitchen table
around and around. I laid the side of my head on the Formica and watched
the tray circle. The salt began to blur with the A.1., which got mixed up with
the ketchup. This swirling and twirling of our lives, as lazy as that Susan.

I told him about the conversation with my parents and their lackadaisical response. David laughed. Then I said, "I need you to meet them sometime soon."

"I want to see you tomorrow," David said. "I want us to make love."

"!"

"I want it to be special."

"Oh."

"Meet me in the second-floor dance studio at Cal State at nine P.M. I have the key. I'll be waiting for you."

"I'll see you there, David. Umm, should I bring anything?"

"Well, don't bring any Noxema, whatever you do!" David said, cracking up. "Why don't you get a large-size bottle of Vaseline Intensive Care lotion and bring that?"

"Okay. I'll see you tomorrow night."

THE NEXT DAY was my eighteenth birthday. After shopping for the Intensive Care Lotion at the SavOn Drugstore (I told the checkout girl it was a birthday present), I vigorously wrote a long time in my journal. I walked up to my special place in the hills of La Habra. I reread the sexy bits from Mary Renault's *The Persian Boy* for the zillionth time.

As the night arrived, I bathed and then drove to the frigid modernist architecture box collection of the California State University at Fullerton. I parked my car by the gymnasium and went into the performing arts building. I paused at the door, inhaling the night's blooming jasmine. Up to that point, my life had felt like it had been written by somebody else in a big weird dusty book on a top shelf, just out of reach. That was about to change. I stepped up the stairs into the building as if I were going to accept an Academy Award.

I climbed to the second floor and slowly opened the heavy metal door. The dance studio was dark, except for a single white candle. I tried to see where David was.

A LOUD CLICK: "Amen" from Handel's *Messiah* begins to play on the cassette tape. I close my eyes and fall into the music.

David's arms enfold me and we begin to kiss, the kiss I have been waiting for my whole life. Our lips hunger for each other, make a dance together. David bites the corner of my upper lip gently. This is the touch I have been trying to find ever since I learned to tie my shoes—this son this brother this friend this father in my arms as the sun rises inside me at last. He bites my neck. Yes. Oh. Fuck. Yes.

David's hands roam over my body, each rolling feeling letting me know myself even as my hands slide down his back, feeling his chest, his heart beating within, how much I want this man. I want to climb into his mouth and swim around inside him, find every hidden wet place, which I know belongs to me now. Coming out inside of his body, even as he teaches me the turn of each bone and muscle.

His hair slips through my fingers. I reach under his shirt and feel his skin, stroking the scars where the bashers' ice pick almost killed him. He peels my clothes from me, uncovering a new life underneath.

Handel's voices waver around each other in great waves like all the angels in heaven around Dante in the Doré engraving, or the June Taylor Dancers on *Jackie Gleason*. A swirling kaleidoscope of kicking legs in high heels. This is what God wants me to do. What's right for me.

David reaches down and grabs my dick; the touch blows my brain to some scattered galaxy I forgot I knew. My eyes look to the back of my brain: Stars shoot inside me, through me, his hand moving on me. His lips surround me. Comets whiz by my eyes. A shower of meteors inside my heart.

David and I spin around each other to the music, leaning far back in each other's arms as we twirl. He falls to his knees and my cock is in his mouth. WOW. All the voices in my head get really loud. Now. Here. Finally. To find *this* place inside *myself* with another man. I am eighteen fucking years old. I know the touch I want on my skin. We jump through each other, blessing each other with our touch. Blessing our lives as we live them. One big fucking AMEN to guide us through them. The trumpets pull us higher. All the voices reach a peak. In that moment of complete and absolute rest, you can see everything you ever hoped you'd be. Everything is right and makes perfect sense.

The music climaxes.

And so do we.

Amen.

EIGHTEEN YEARS LATER, I stood in front of that dance studio at Cal State Fullerton. My fingers traced the chipped corners of that beat-up metal door. What does that eighteen-year-old boy I once was have to say to me now? Could he have known the good and terrible places he and David were gonna go together? The short time they would love each other? Could he have imagined the other friends and boyfriends his life would offer him? If he knew how many were going to die in just a few years, what would he have written in his journal at that fast-food joint in Fullerton? Just five Septembers later, that eighteen-year-old would be at Bellevue Hospital in New York, visiting his ex-boyfriend John, one of the very first to become sick. What really happened to him behind that door? Who the fuck was that teenage boy?

And what do I know now, anyway? What do I think I could even tell him?

I know now that life is harder and better than he can possibly yet imagine. That the pleasures that hang on the Christmas tree get sweeter and sharper every autumn. That the year-by-year of life goes by faster than the opening credits on *Johnny Quest*. I know I've discovered one or two things about love that feel true. I wish I could whisper them softly into his ear, as he lies on that hardwood floor kissing David, their come like a Milky Way smeared across their chests. I know I've lost one or two good things that that teenager had. I envy his fearlessness. What open-eyed wisdom might that young man teach me? Do I still wish I could date Raskolnikov? I think, maybe, I already did. What can he tell me, that boy who is now half my life away?

As I stood that night in the place where I'd first made love, I remembered how, eighteen years before on my eighteenth birthday, I left that dance studio and wrote these words in my journal. I drove home and snuck into the house where I had been a child, hoping my parents wouldn't wake. I wrote these words. I felt David's come, dry and hard on my belly and neck, and I wrote these words. I lay myself down on my bed, in my room with the fluorescent green walls and the life-size poster of Oscar Wilde over my bed, and I wrote these words:

> September 22, 1976. I am eighteen. I love. I don't want this ever to stop. Round and round. The great circle. We die too soon. Lying and hiding chews on us. Must learn to reach out. What else can we do? All wandering in the dark. Nothing to fear. Nothing to lose. I must remember that. Not fearing has brought me the most wonderful man. We will all be dead in a hundred years. All we can do is to touch all the sunlight. All the experience. Eyes meet and a bit of death has been conquered. Everyone wants to be touched. We all want it. We often fear it. Downturned eyes on the sidewalk as someone walks by. Not hugging your mom when her father has died. Not telling someone you love them. All are terrible victories for death. I have grown an entire lifetime since I first wrote in this book. I am only beginning. Everything is before me now. It's late. The sun is sleeping. I have hardly begun to see. I am eighteen. I am happy. I love David. I love life.

The youngness *and* the truth of that boy's words still call me, challenge me. The skin that wraps around me carries lots more loves and lots more losses. The death he so fearlessly wrote about has hit the gas and driven its eight-cylinder El Camino right through the plate glass window and knocked the record off its turntable. The coming-out story that he began, I have tried to continue every day since.

Eighteen years later, I leave that dance studio at Cal State Fullerton and walk away. Humming a nice bit of Handel. The click of my shoes echoing in the deserted hallway.

HELL'S KITCHEN

Douglas Sadownick

I.

IT WAS A cold Bronx day in December 1978 when my father told me about the theaters in Manhattan where men danced naked for other men. The scene was uncanny. He was frying a flounder he had caught on Long Island a few months back. He pointed to an ad in the *New York Post*, to show me "what the goddamn world was coming to," and opened my eyes.

I looked at him—his hairy forearms, his lanky frame, his bumpy nose. My father appeared to me as unreal, a half-assed Old Man in the Sea, the kind who whacks down your door at night, informing you that you are experiencing an initiation. No wonder my brother and I awoke many a night screaming. (No wonder my father did, too.) It occurred to me, turning my face from his angry eyes to the image of Toby Ross silhouetted in the ad, that I might like to know Toby.

Open sesame.

THE ADONIS THEATER became my home away from home; within a few days, I saw the dirty blond Toby Ross up on the screen. But it was Jack Wrangler who captivated me. He was the kind of guy I could bring home to my father. I got brave on occasion and let men touch me in the dark, though not much more than that.

Actually, they were mostly nineteen-year-olds like me, Italian and Puerto

Rican kids with hard stomachs and skin so pliant it giggled. Ribs protruded from their sides like piano keys; you'd poke them and songs would burst forth, annunciations: gamelanlike bells on the skinny boys; on the more powerfully built, hosannas. I wasn't a Catholic—*not no dago or spic neither*, as these guys sometimes introduced themselves—but I knew something about Gregorian chants and a thing or two about the Virgin Birth. In the heat of their cigarette breath and their wet wool smell, I was sure these dungaree-jacketed high school seniors were incarnated flesh, the Holy Spirit's experiment at trying to wake us closet cases up. A boy who called himself Angelo knew this. He dribbled some of his spittle on my tongue, saying, "You like holy water, doncha?"

These escapades, innocent as they were, would have blown my fuses and turned me into a pagan were it not for my Jewish heritage. I had no heart to turn my back on my family. My father would be snoozing on his La-Z-Boy and an eerie voice, sounding vaguely like Edward G. Robinson in *Soylent Green*, would mutter, "Be fruitful and multiply." I thought God was speaking through my dad's snores.

My grandmother, with her tumors and amulets, dismissed my theophany. "When a vision comes," she'd say, "it doesn't speak through morons." She liked my father well enough but did not think him worthy of prophetic vision. She believed God to be a personality in the body. When she wasn't asking me about my dreams she was telling me stories about the Angel of Death. "We die in our hearts every day," she'd say, burping up my mother's potato salad.

My mother, lighting a Salem, rubbed a knuckle across her own flat chest as she watched her husband steal drinks from a flask he'd hidden under a cushion in his chair. "You've been running off these days," she mentioned to me one night, heating up a cold plate of roasted chicken for me. "Your father misses you."

My father had just retired from his job as a mailman and had a lot of time on his hands, which threw him into a depression.

THE WORDS ABOVE the entrance glittered: *GAIETY MALE BURLESK.* I paced the sidewalk at Forty-sixth and Broadway, stamping my feet on the slush near this peep show or that massage parlor, to keep warm. I worried that I'd bump into an uncle or aunt who worked in the garment district. A hailstorm forced me to return home. I got on the uptown-bound IND subway line. But by the time I reached Harlem, even the warmth under my metal seat couldn't extinguish the hunger in my bones. I headed back downtown.

Night had descended on Broadway. I kept telling myself, "You don't have to do anything you don't want to do." I was back at square one.

Red carpet lined the stairs from the street outside. I stormed into the place; I don't remember paying to enter. Men crushed near the door. Someone asked, "Are you of age?" I elbowed my way inside.

The air hummed with wisecracks: "What's Carter and the Long Island Railroad got in common?" "They both pull out of Roslyn at seven A.M."; or "You got other fish—or should I say *chicken?*—to fry." I looked for men with familiar features: hooked noses, olive skin. The Las Vegas–style music was full of false starts. A muscle boy with "USMC" tattoos danced on a runway jutting into the audience. Sweat sprouted from his pinkish thighs. Another dancer, more Latino and angular, had Caribbean, acutely oval eyes glazed over with oblivion. A man in a red bow tie tried to paw him; he skirted away so quickly that several men booed.

I despaired. But the boy came out again, this time around the back, to avoid everyone's eyes, wearing a touch more clothing and a lot of hair spray—unrecognizable to anyone but me. He lit a half-smoked cigarette. His hair reached in oily, coal-black strands to his shoulders and blew about in the breeze created by a rusty rotating fan. He wore light blue jeans and a dark blue pea coat, with very little underneath, maybe a skintight white T-shirt. I thought I saw him nod to me, but couldn't be sure. I was about to nod back when I felt a crick in my neck. The dancer kicked open the swinging door with his right sneakered foot and scurried down the stairs to the street.

You will never see this person again, I thought. I pushed through the throng and found myself outside, gasping in the cold, stabbing air. I looked to the right and left, and spotted him crossing the street.

"Yo!" I cried out.

He stopped.

"Leaving?" I asked.

He laughed, took a drag off his cigarette, and began to walk toward me. In a moment, we stood face-to-face.

"I have to get up in the morning," he said, shivering. "It's late."

"Nah," I protested, finding it in myself to make a twisted-up face with my lips. He made the same face. "Sez who?" he asked.

HE WAS NINETEEN, like me. His name was David. He said he was a hustler.

"You 'shamed?" he asked.

I shrugged. "I can't see why I should be," I said.

To me, to be a hustler was a good thing. My mother equated it with godliness. Now that my father had retired, she'd say to him, "Willie, Shirley's husband, he *knows* how to work. You should see him selling shoes right and left in Macy's. Such a hustler!" I told David this and he laughed.

"No," he said. "I sell my body for a living."

I took a deep breath, cauterizing my lungs with cold air.

"I knew that," I said.

"You wanna come over my house?" he asked, throwing his neck back so that it looked as if it might crack off by the veiny coils near his Adam's apple.

"Where you live?"

"Hell's Kitchen."

DAVID HAD TO call his pimp, to make sure he was free for the night. He referred to him mockingly as Dad. ("My real *papito*, he was such a shit," he said.) As David waited for the line to pick up, I clapped my gloved hands to keep them warm. He looked me in the eye.

"I never had the clap," he said. "I'm clean, you know?"

I wasn't concerned about it, although I voiced my appreciation.

I don't think I had ever been to Tenth Avenue before, or, for that matter, to a stranger's home. I had never stayed out late in Manhattan, never stared without a certain self-effacing fear at the back of a guy's head, where his hairline meets the array of pimples by his neck, as he walked west to the Hudson River.

The door to David's tenement, painted in black-and-white graffiti, opened the moment he clicked his silver key in the lock. The hallway stairs, steep and narrow like the stairs to the Gaiety, were lined in a red material which resembled the velvet coverlets of Torah scrolls.

The first thing I noticed in David's one-room studio apartment was the portable TV, which had been left on and was playing the *Mary Tyler Moore Show* theme song. There was also a black metal milk crate, an antique rocking chair, and a mattress on the floor, with a chipped brown night table next to it. A Chinese paper lantern encased a red bulb dangling from the ceiling. The place had a just-scrubbed quality, except for a half-drunk cup of takeout black coffee, an opened can of Lemon Pledge, and an unemptied ashtray. I looked at David as if to signal approval, but he turned away.

"Don't you gotta use the bathroom or something?" he asked, his voice shy and effeminate. Then, as if composing himself, he added, "Help yourself to a beer."

He pointed to a refrigerator the size of a file cabinet.

After peeing, I followed in the footsteps of my mother, who always rifled through a person's bathroom to find out a thing or two that person didn't care for anyone to know. David's medicine chest revealed two rows of neatly arranged makeup: compacts and lipsticks and pancake, several types of eyeliner, some rouge. I noticed as well some lip gloss and a pair of beige falsies.

The rusty chest shut with a click. I thought for a moment about going home.

IF ONLY I had known that my father picked on me because he was so plagued by my mother. It was hard to be a husband and a father who was also a mailman, especially in public. Sometimes the humiliation got to him.

Once, during a co-worker's barbecue in Great Neck, he blurted out over his cards and cigar smoke, "I can't make enough dough for that bitch!" My mother called a taxi. "One for the road," he groused to a pal, adding, "That's what she gets for nagging the shit out of me." I told him not to talk about his wife like that.

He started swinging at me. His friends tried to calm him down, but by then he had knocked over the card table, and the bar holding the liquor and tonic. "C'mon, you goddamn party poopers, we're going home!" he barked. I shoved a Mets mug of black coffee his way. He threw it so hard against the Dodge Dart that it shattered into a hundred pieces.

My mother and I paid for our insolence with what we afterward referred to as the "Hell Ride." My brother, my mother, and I huddled in the back seat while my father weaved from Queens to the Bronx at eighty miles an hour, screaming about how he "busted his butt" and needed to have a little fun now and then. My mother nodded agreement. He spent as much time turning his bug-eyed head toward us as he spent looking through the windshield, spitting out things like "Nagging sonuva*bitch.*" My mother tried to smile, but he wasn't going for it. He settled on a word he liked: "Bitch."

The needle stuck in the groove the whole time we sped down the Long Island Expressway. At one point, my father pointed at me and yelled, "You're gonna grow up and be just like your mother—a ball breaker." An isolated personality, usually in the wings, had taken center stage. Like a tough kid stuck in a crying jag, a starved man sitting down to a rare steak, or a cop beating a hooker, my father couldn't stop himself. I had hardly ever seen my mother cry, but now she begged him, "Please forgive us." He only screamed more. My brother, who was two years younger than me and not a hand holder, gripped my left pinkie so hard I could barely concentrate on anything but pain.

"YOU DROWN IN there or what?" David called out.

I took up his offer to sit on his bed, a foam mattress set flat on the creaky pine floor, covered in a red, blue, and white old lady's quilt. He assumed the less comfortable position, in the rocking chair, which didn't rock. Strands of long black hair had become glued to his eyes. He was exceedingly polite about it, like he didn't want me to think he was fussing with his split ends because he was bored. He kept admiring my Frye boots and wondered if they were a Christmas present. I said something about Hanukkah. He shook his shoulders, as if he were wearing an invisible shawl, and said, "Same thing."

We chatted for an hour. He tapped two fingers at a time on the chair's wobbly armrest. In a bolt of anxiety, he got up to pee.

He returned from the bathroom and took a seat on the bed next to me. He smiled humbly. His thin brown-red lips revealed the next day's stubble, poking through a pore here and there. Suddenly he made a muscle with his left arm.

"See," he said, rolling his sleeve down and flashing what he called a "Colgate" smile. "I never had no one up here who I knew," he told me.

The statement mystified me, but I said nothing. His lips caught my attention.

I had never kissed a man whose face I could see before. I was about to tell him, but at that moment we connected: short, cool, delicate pecks which both revealed and concealed a burning truth—that satinlike brushes of skin can devour. The hunger that rose in me was vaguely inhuman.

Then we were pulled apart, away from each other, like two prizefighters who suddenly felt the same death wish. He lifted his gangly arms, slipping his white T-shirt off, looking banal in the moonlight, like a heroin addict. His slim chest was hairless, except for a pencil-thin line that snaked up from his belly button, with a busy, latticelike layering underneath his skin, as if he had done one too many handstands for a skinny person. With an arrogant nod of his head, he invited me to remove my shirt.

I could see that I felt good to him, too, by the way he regarded his hand as it made to touch mine. We kissed again while trying to wiggle off our pants. Then the kiss lost its rigor and became openmouthed. We lay entwined, sucking each other's tongues, our pants half off. His spit, a clear, watery translucence, tasted vaguely sweet. I could not help but moan, which made him laugh. He moaned, too. Then—and this has never happened since—we whimpered like babies, until the lament got so loud a neighbor banged on the wall.

At that moment, I understood how sex can make you remember everything in a terrible seizure. You drop down about one hundred stories and feel scared, in part because it occurs to you that you have been cultivated for this fall for many years, by your own psyche; it's been waiting on the sidelines for you, like a jilted lover. Or an alien. When your own moaning gets so loud that it seems like a baby's and an adult's both, you know once and for all that you are *not* what you thought you were.

Our clothes off, David hit the lights. If you screwed your eyes real tight and peered through the soot-stained windows of the tenement in front of his, David's room offered a view of the Hudson in the darkness. I felt a piece of cracked plaster near the flat of his back. At some point, we allowed the inherent softness of our clinging to become more of a rough grinding in. An exaggerated humping shook the air out of my lungs. I warned him I was getting close.

"Don't," he said.

We held our breath, let out a cackle. Then I felt another person in the room: pristine, invisible, sublimely fast-moving. I sat up in fright.

David gently set me down again.

"Hush, hush," he said, as if he knew what it meant to fear your father walking into the room just as you were about to lose your mind in come.

MY FAMILY NEVER forgave my father for putting our lives at risk during the Hell Ride. My mother and I cut out articles on drunk driving and placed them near his favorite haunts (the toilet, the bed, the liquor cabinet). For a time, he softened—screaming fits drain a great deal of energy from a person—but he was unable to apologize, or even refer to the event.

At times I swore that dark and light twins resided in my father. It wasn't what you'd call a split personality, but normal neurosis. He just needed someone to break the news to him: He acted the tyrant because he could not admit to being a failure. But he'd never have listened. It was easier for us to hold a grudge.

We stopped going places with him. He'd suggest something about the planetarium or the movies or a trout-fishing expedition and we'd beg off, citing prior engagements. He had few friends, so the isolation wore on him.

That was too bad, because we could have helped one another. He could have been Jack London, but life or fear, which for many are the same thing, had trapped him. He wasn't meant to be common. Yes, he read the *Post*, but on Sundays it was always the *Times*, along with bialys and brave attempts to eat as much lox, tomatoes, herring, and cream cheese as possible. "Last one to the toilet's a rotten egg," he'd say. "That means you, too, Pearly May" (his nickname for my mother). He wore his blue collar like a priest of the projects and tolerated blacks as he did the concrete: *mensa mensa*. The Bronx was the ground he stood on.

There were occasions when we did experiment. Saturday mornings (before the Hell Ride), he'd wake us up at the crack of dawn and drive us out to a lake to fish for trout, or to a beach for bass. My brother and I learned how to fly fish. There are pictures of all of us holding saltwater and freshwater creatures by their mouths. I remember some of the captions from these Kodak moments: "8 lb. Blue Fish, 1969, Jones Beach, Douglie-Do-Right and Dan-the-Man with Pearly May"; "11 lb. Flounder, 1974, Far Rockaway, Just Me and the Boys"; "5 lb. Trout, Lake Manhassett, 1972, Doug Pulled This Beaut In." There are photos of us later on, feasting on fried fish sandwiches or grilled filets— Dad's favorite food. I'd look at those images and wonder how a person could be so sweet one day and so mean another.

My father was a cook; in another life he could have been a galloping gourmet. He had few greater pleasures than making paper-thin pancakes or stirring up a quick soup with potatoes, leeks, and God knows what else. "Hey, Hammerhead," he'd call to me, "how about a Spanish omelette?" After the Hell Ride, my mother and I went on diets and strong-armed my brother into eating cottage cheese in coffee shops with us. The house never smelled more like oregano and pepper. Homemade cupcakes steamed on the kitchen table, untouched. Hot plates of chicken cacciatore and eggplant parmigiana got tossed into the incinerator. My mother threatened to bring in a foster daughter, to keep herself occupied. We bought cheap black-and-white TVs at Crazy Eddie's and placed them in the kitchen and two bedrooms, thus breaking up the one event we'd all done together.

Jocasta and I won, all right.

My brother, who like me would grow up with our father's rage and nicotine in his bloodstream, was the one who found the suicide note. It was written with my mother's maroon lipstick on the medicine cabinet mirror. I will not repeat the message because I never saw it. A sober and ethical man, my brother wiped it off with Kleenex before the message could unhinge the rest of us, whom he presumed were still sleeping (my mother was already calling the ambulance).

He needn't have been so protective of me. I could not have seen the medicine cabinet. I was not at home.

"YOU DROWN IN there or what?"

David and I had come maybe for the third time. We lay in a pool of sweat and spit and talked about getting together again. His voice cracked; he didn't believe a word of it.

"The Bronx is nice," he said. "You got the Botanical Gardens."

I told him it wasn't as far away as he thought. "You got the train," I insisted.

He tried not to think ahead. He expressed shock that a boy he knew knew how to skid fingernails along his back so as to cause wave after wave of goose bumps. I voiced amazement that another person's teeth could gnaw at flesh with deliberate pleasure that could make you scream and hold your breath at the same time. We had both discovered that if a person grabbed your testicles really hard your semen could hit your face. I traced the little upraised mole near his lower left lip, where some of his come had dried in milky patches.

A few hours passed. I had already missed the express bus; now I'd have to take the train. David was asleep. I whispered that I had to go. "I bet my mother's called 911," I said.

Naked, David wrote down his number as though he were tying a shoelace, or pulling down a blind, or dialing numbers on the telephone: no affect, just a little scratching of balls here and there. He made me promise to call him. I promised many times, but he wouldn't believe me. So I gave him my number.

"How can I be sure that this is it?" he asked.

"What?"

"What if you're shitting me?"

I dialed 411 and asked for my own number. By the time I put the phone to his ear, David acted as if he no longer required proof.

On my way home, I thought about what we had just done. Things about David made an impression. The way he skimmed his *National Geographic* while humming Donna Summer songs. The way he took a piss, sitting down. The way he talked on the phone, going, "Yeah, yeah," like he hated being bothered. The way he ate a leftover tuna sandwich, spreading mustard with a knife at each bite. I fantasized about meeting his mother and father, who lived in Jersey City. I thought about maybe visiting him at work. I envisioned myself making him Kraft macaroni and cheese in the middle of the night, when he had gone out to earn some dough and come back smelling of snow, Aramis, and exhaust fumes. It would be hard to introduce him to my mother and father. He was so brown-skinned. My father would ask if someone in his family were black. I resolved that problem in my mind—but I can't remember how.

WHEN DAVID CALLED, two days later, I was at the Veterans' Administration Hospital in the Bronx, visiting my father. My brother took the message. My brother, who made a copy of every phone message he took for me and kept a regular tab on people I did not call back—this time my brother lost track, blaming his sudden disinterest in the details of my life on our father's having hit the deep end. (My brother never forgot the blood. "It *is* thicker than water," he'd say, over and over again.)

Almost overnight, memories of David got clouded by memories of visits to the padlocked asylum. I'd think of David's hard body slow-dancing on top of mine in silence, as if some new life-form were being born. It occurred to me how, for a year, my father and I had not spoken to each other in the narrow hallway that connected our four-room apartment, acting as if neither of us had been born. I'd feel David's tongue on my neck, flicking the knob where the shoulder tensed into a sore muscle, and my father's dry mouth, dotted with a flick of tobacco, would materialize before me, prematurely old and sad, and very sore. I'd recall David gulping a beer (he liked Rheingold), and I'd remember my father's manner of wiping beer foam away from his lips with a paper towel and a burp. I'd think back to the way David had rifled through my textbooks (Nietzsche and Freud) when I told him I could not sleep over, and recall my father turning toward me, dropping his newspaper to the floor, his brown eyes wet with crusty fear, unable to blink or see or say anything when the doctors told us he could not come home for several weeks.

When my father did come home, he needed a lot of company. And when David didn't call back, I searched in a drawer for his number, only to remember I'd stuck it in the jeans my mother had just laundered. I felt a funny breaking down at that moment, like I was crushed by my inheritance. My father sat slumped in his La-Z-Boy in a blue wool Post Office cardigan. He asked me what was wrong. I turned away from his eyes, saying nothing.

II.

The story doesn't end here—that is, if this is indeed a coming-out story. Because over and above the little Bronx myth I call my autobiography, which theoretically takes place in the past, is an event that would take place in the future, namely my encounter with gay-centered psychological thinking in Los Angeles, which introduced me to the role of the "father" in everyday life. Now, to use the word *father* in a depth-psychological way is to refer to more than just the aging fellow we make small talk with on Thanksgiving. I'm speaking instead about an inner symbol, something alive—almost too alive—a reality whose dark truth most of us are defended against feeling, a psychic principle not unlike a just-lit stick of dynamite. This elusive symbol has much to do with how a person—in particular, a gay male person—might get initiated into the deep masculine of his own heart.

For me, psychological thinking and experience have begun to offer their own kind of radical coming out, beyond the social or political sort, in part because of the gay-centered nature of the archetypes I have learned to sense as part of the living psyche. ("Gay-centered" means nothing less than seeing psychic health and illness as coming from an immutable center which has as its source being gay.) This "inner view" of being gay is antithetical to the idea that our identities are "socially constructed." The myth of social construction insures that our social fathers—our families and the authorities—exert a certain ultimate control over us. The myth of "gay individuation" I am putting forward suggests that we have a queer inner father waiting in the shadows of the psyche. I'm not talking about Grandpa Walton, either, but a red-hot numen, more personal and yet collective—and therefore always frightening.

I went into analysis because it occurred to me, in a psychically implacable way, that I was a tad more than a construction; moreover, that I had a psyche, or rather that it had me. It seemed incumbent upon me to wrest myself from politically correct literalism and the me-first extroversion on which the gay community prides itself (never mind the nightmares I continued to have of my father driving my family home on the Long Island Expressway). Psyche speaks to a person of its own alien nature—a nature that exists apart from and independent of culture but is indeed the mother of the culture, too—through dreams and symptoms. I knew from the way I suffered that the conscious mind was not the *total mind*. I screamed at the people I said I loved the way my father had ranted at his. I began to sense that I had become a gay *Titanic;* in my heart lay ice and I was sinking. And still I could not see the iceberg.

I couldn't, however, help but notice a funny coincidence between my dreams of murder at the hands of my father and the weeping of many of my friends as they came close to death. It was as if the final crushing moments of "Hell's Kitchen" occurred nightly, an injury I could not bear facing but which had nevertheless pinned me—and not only me—into a corner. We often call this corner "AIDS" as a kind of political shorthand, but that shows a superficial understanding of our suffering, to say nothing of its Oedipal and pre-Oedipal root causes. Just because a person does not recall a rotten feeling does not mean it is nowhere to be found. A wound from early childhood that remains ignored will find ways to manifest in the present.

When the psyche, which has become exiled by the culture, comes home to roost, it is often felt as a horrible reunion. Symptoms of the absent inner father plagued me. With every psychic inflation came a deflation. A visit to a sex club during which I felt triumphantly handsome in a ten-person suckfest resulted in my contracting a sexually transmitted disease. An overdue dinner with my boyfriend, sweetened by Chianti, ended up in a dish-crashing fight. A plum assignment from an editor became a nightmare in which I could not keep my focus or meet my deadline. I lacked what depth psychologists call the "transcendent function," the ability to find the union between two terrible opposites, one conscious, one not. Fate had fucked me—as it had my dad.

I found out that I was murderously angry at my father, a silly thought which hadn't really crossed my mind because he was so out of his. By "father," I refer not only to the oaf who tried to parent me, but to an *affect*, a kind of feeling that comes up which you could almost dismiss, but to which I have learned to attribute a personality. To be sure, the inward fellow ("father imago") and the outward one ("Mr. Sadownick") are tangled up by memories of family life and hopes for redemption. This dynamic duo can, however, be teased apart. The radiant material around the "father" symbol is too fine to be wasted on the chain-smoking bully, who is often weighted down by his failure to live up to the archetypal projections, anyway. (By "inward" I refer to what shrinks call the "archetypal masculine": patrimony, phallus, self-regulation, and a room with a view. All this potential exists in a given psyche even before little Douglie-Do-Right begins projecting them onto his dad.)

But, as some psychologists teach us, we don't experience the archetypes in their pure state. We know them through our complexes—the associations, images, and feelings that cluster around an archetype and which, at times, exert (relatively independent) control over us. A strong complex, says C. G. Jung, possesses all the characteristics of a separate personality. It is something of a secondary mind, a revolting vassal of a psychic empire, which deliberately drives at certain intentions contrary to the conscious needs and wishes of the individual. Another way to understand these "other" personalities, especially if they remain unconscious, is via the more all-encompassing term "shadow." The shadow is a mythological name for all that is within us which we don't yet know. "Developing a healthy relationship to shadow" means accepting that there are at least two centers of psychic awareness: the rational ego and the unconscious. To accept something we loathe about ourselves may take an act of courage. But if we don't do it, the shadow functions anyway, behind our backs.

It's easy to see, especially for a gay man, how a shoddy relationship with the flesh-and-blood parent makes anything associated with "father" feel shadowlike. Hence our inner fathers are exiled to the backwaters of the mind. Out of touch, they're reduced to infantile fun and games; the more the conscious ego slights them, the more the archetypes remain as backstabbing kids. This exiling, of which we are unaware, can be seen as the source of our oppression: Our own soul and its transpersonal gay energies are exiled, too.

I MUST PAUSE here to address a question lurking in my mind—and perhaps that of others—about the role of commentary in making art. There seems to be no place for it. We are taught, as artists, not to get in the way of the deeds and words of our characters, who must speak for themselves. And although postmodernism has sought to advocate on behalf of the psyche's anarchy by intervening on the primacy of "narrative line," those ploys have, on the one hand, been assimilated and undermined by commerce (MTV, etc.), resulting in a jaded public, and, on the other, have become so commonplace that serious consumers remain unaffected. These days, I think, there is no way to expose hidden agendas except to call them by their real names.

A complex demands identification from the ego with its own sorry state. Sometimes we tell each other fables, not just to keep ourselves alive, but to enable our problems to stay alive, too. What seems like the integrity of a story, given our primitive awareness of our own psyches, is actually the integrity of our blind spots. These stories keep our complexes unconscious, yet intact as "subpersonalities," seen through the yummy gauze of feeling but not yet *seen through*. So much energy is wasted this way: Our shadows steal "energy food," sex and time, right and left. To name a complex (inferiority, mother) is to break unconscious identification with it. To fail to do this is to remain in a kind of closet.

To say this is to utter a kind of blasphemy. We gay people see our coming-out stories as being like scripture, and for good reason. Coming out signifies a great personal and collective triumph, a release from the familial clichés of the world around us into a new realm, for which we reward ourselves as heroes.

To be sure, coming out compelled me to leave the Bronx and find the where-withal to love a new society of men. But it did not offer me a way to do so psychologically. Desperation, however cloaked, hardly ever leads to much gain. I transferred my desperate need for approval, my need to be seen and held, which my mother and father could never satisfy, to lovers, and then, profession-ally, to editors and readers.

By rewarding ourselves for coming out we think we finally *have* come out. But we have not yet brought the psyche out. Undeveloped (closeted) arche-typal forces and complexes crave cultivation. Anyone who has lost himself—in rage, in a drunken orgy, in suicidal depression—must agree that the uncon-scious deserves no small credit for our darker moods. Our nightmares are symptoms of our inherent life force. But we don't give them the time of day, and we pay for this stifling literally, with our lives. Considered this way, our true history has not yet begun—nor our coming out.

Instead of the integrity of the artwork, I am interested in "integrating" the work it took to make the art—to my mind a greater integrity. Complexes must be *seen through* to be seen for what they are, a process we fight tooth and nail, by feeling "offended." When I told my father, who had already been offended by my mother's implication that he was too drunk to drive us home, not to curse my mother in public, he only cursed louder. He could not simply acknowledge that, like everyone else, he had failed here and there, he had inferiorities; so he punished the offending parties by subjecting us to the Hell Ride. Being offended is a signal that something has not yet been integrated. It's the best, perhaps the only, way to start to change. "The shadow is the block which separates us most effectively from the divine voice," writes Jung. But who can bear feeling his shadow consciously, especially if he has already been so of-fended by his father that he has become wooden, more apt to numb his feelings than flesh them out?

To complete my coming-out story, I'd like to put a difficult feeling together with a difficult idea. For without the idea that there is such a thing as an unconscious, or a shadow, we can see (or feel) neither.

SO LITTLE ATTENTION in gay life is given to the role of the father as a psychic principle, in part because so many gay men are mother-dominated, even the ones who pump up at the gym and go out in chaps. The "mother" here isn't the literal mother but the relating principle of Eros, as well as our attachment to creature comforts. Mostly this symbolic mother in the psyche represents the love of home and the fear of change. The gratification gained through some transcendence-seeking sex can be a symbolic return to wholeness represented by the inward mother which, because it's unconscious, can manifest as fierce and destructive—what some call compulsive behavior. This mother can seem nurturing, but since she has no masculine dude to balance her, she can become devouring. The ego overidentifies with her, in much the same way many of us got close to our moms. This may explain why gay men adore feminine heroes—Bette Midler, Barbra Streisand, Madonna—women who seem butch but who have not subordinated success to feeling. It is hard to recognize the psychic damage these inner ice queens do. The more we are drawn to the astral light of our female stars, the more out of reach the "archetypal father" becomes.

Gay psychologists suggest that a gay man's relationship to his father material is a special case, different from heterosexual men, hypothesizing that a guy born gay falls in love with the first man (rather than woman) he meets on the scene. (The theory here is that the libido, with its inner godly programming, teases the ego complex out from the Self through the first great romance.) The literal father, if he is a kind man, will deflect the nuclear projection of libido, which is devastating enough; if he's an asshole, he will repudiate the gay boy. All this takes place unconsciously, of course, yet it is often the filter through which the light of gay love shines, giving "love/hate" new meaning.

This early romance with the father is a hard notion to stomach, which is why it gets repressed. It stands to reason that, for a gay man, "father energy" can easily become a "father complex"; the home that forms around the foundational archetype is a pathology, a series of symptoms that cry out for amplification, storytelling, and archaeology. But a complex is more than a problem. It also can be seen as a personality, with its own hopeful attitudes and vengeful agendas. How unfairly he subverts the will of the ego, as in the case of the man who flies into a rage or is late for appointments or cannot find the drive to work. But the sabotage occurs only if we refuse to deal with this subpersonality. In fact, the neurotic who becomes conscious of this subpersonality (or "daimon") and develops an affinity to it, has ultimate access to the divine energy of the inner queer father, in a way that a normal but unconscious person does not.

I am speaking theoretically here, and perhaps I have no right. My own father complex is a bit of a dominator, in cahoots with a few other complexes (mother and inferiority), and often runs my show in the most covert of manners. This is what is meant by being shadow-dominated. My shadow often speaks in highfalutin' ways. He feels most alive, most with it, when he is talking in psychological language which is, truth be told, really a bit over his head. As you know from "Hell's Kitchen," he did not grow up in a happy home. His true state is one of almost bone-crushing inferiority. He overcompensates by trying to sound smarter and more grandiose than he is.

AN EXAMPLE OF how one gets caught in one's "father complex" from one generation to the next was demonstrated in a 1994 movie, *Nobody's Fool*. The star, Paul Newman, tries to redeem his failure as a "bad dad" by taking his grandson to work with him at a demolition site, an abandoned building soon to be sold to the bank. This dump—surprise!—is actually Newman's long-dead father's house. Frozen in a revenging thought about his own bad dad, Newman makes a terrible mistake: He keeps his little grandson (futurity, redemption) waiting in the cold. The kid grows hurt and seeks to punish Newman by ignoring him back.

A gay man "enters his father's house" when he is about to fall in love. And, like Newman, we become crushed by the condemned property while at the same time feeling enamored with the promise of renovation. Rarely does a person enter this house of his own free will. Our complexes can have an obsessive-compulsive quality, which is why they're so tied up with the elixir of romance and sex—and why sex can feel so very good and lead to so much ill. Sex is one of the closest things we have to immediate wholeness—flooding our resistances, transcending the pain of our complexes, at least for a time. Psychic wholeness, however, includes a great deal of shadow. We often encounter our shadows as projections: A partner seems suddenly evil or clingy; we feel a need to merge, a fear of closeness, or both. If consciously owned, it might be felt as a self-regulating low following the high of lust or romance.

That's the scary part. Given our self-hatred as queers, wholeness is not an easy thing to handle, even though it can feel great. We have to work hard to earn the axis point between heaven and hell. The little boy waiting out in the cold at the demolition site has grown godlike in power and hideous in demeanor. This orphan has not been consciously adopted and that pisses him off. His appearance in our lives can seem revenging, even if he augurs well; so much repressed vileness covers up any potential gold that to begin to meet the unconscious on its own terms requires no small amount of courage.

Where to start? Most begin on the outside. If the masculine energy that helps a gay man lead his life is felt primarily as a complex—a tangle of rage, neediness, and emptiness—then we search the social world for the symbolic father we inwardly lack, trying to get the recognition we never got from Daddio from another suitable source (ideally, a boyfriend). When we don't get the huggies exactly as we think we need them—and how can we?—we become angry or sad. This is why love can be so goddamn hard. (It has often thrown me back on my hidden hurt and smallness.) It is interesting to note that, in "Hell's Kitchen," the devastated condition of the father (outer and inner) keeps the protagonist from new life and new love. The moral of the story is a tough one: No love can be had unless someone refuses to pass on the soul injury. This "refusal" cannot take place through a sheer act of will. It seems clear that this so-called soul injury is its own subpersonality. The ego cannot boss this injured kid around any more than the physical father was able to do so; he must be seen and felt on his own pitiful terms.

How will we teach younger gay men to enter their haunted houses if we have not made a visit to our own? How hard it is to wrestle, Jacob-like, with the rascals inside the psyche. They may be angels, but through neglect they've become ghastly. It's no wonder few people bother with their darkest feelings. To adapt in today's world, it behooves us to bash down our own inferiorities, or to pin them on convenient scapegoats. Some people make lists; others say affirmations. It's all the same: coming at life from the ego's perspective.

But denial of the psyche can last only so long. Without empathy for one's secret personalities, one gets pulled unconsciously into their orbits. They are more commanding than the ego; they crave relationship as we crave sex. Then it all gets ugly. One's boyfriend has to deal with a litany of sore feelings

("Why didn't you call?" "You never hold me enough." "Why is it so hard to give me what I ask for?"). The injured kid and the ego are not the same, but we feel as if they are during most of our difficulties, our inner boundaries are so weak.

It's hard to argue this point; it has to be felt at a core level to be "gotten." That's a lot to ask of already oppressed people. To feel the agony of our moral inferiorities sounds like just one more burden to bear. Frankly, we can't see the profit in it. The incentive grows if we understand that the injured kid, who is neither rational nor cooperative, has a will of his own. He gets us into inconvenient situations to force us to cope with his condition.

Consider how many men fall in love with men who can never love them back. Consider the way AIDS brings out people's vulnerabilities, stealing every last defense they have against their pain until they're utterly raw and exposed. The inferiority complex, the injured kid—whatever you want to call him— wishes to be held by the only father he can have, which in this case is the "conscious ego."

An ego who adopts a humble and conscious alliance with his own complexes begins a partnership with the personalities of the soul which can give him more than a little energy back. He brings out his "inner family" as queer. This is why I think coming-out stories matter. It's not just because homosexuals have been oppressed for millennia, although that fact alone is reason enough to tell a story. There's another reason.

According to some, there is the archetype of the double in the unconscious of gay men, an inner presence more sinewy and sincere than any human, the secret intelligence behind the homosexual libido. He can be understood as the "double" of the conscious personality, maybe even its creator. The erotic inner romance between a person and his "unconscious twin," it is suggested, is what is really being provoked when a gay person falls in love. Mostly, we do not recognize this "double"; a series of complexes (inferiority, mother, father) stand like shadows between his true form and our consciousness. He is experienced instead as a projection: A lover will, for a time, wear his idealized disguise. To become more mindful of such disguises—to become aware that romantic love is, for most people, most of the time, a projection coming from one's own unconscious psyche—is part of what is meant by "coming out inside."

I understand that this theory is almost too esoteric to be applied at this point, given the crude state most of us are at in terms of meeting our shadows halfway. For with every projection of the double comes a projection of the shadow. One cannot even begin to greet the archetypes before addressing a great deal of unfinished personal family business—at least as far as psychologists are concerned. What's additionally interesting here is how powerfully the ar- chetypes of homosexual libido demonstrate their own autonomous volition. Isn't this what is meant by coming out—that one is brought out by something beyond one's control? A gay person's first great love will be sufficiently superhu- man for him to turn everything he had previously thought about his life on its head. For a time, a man gets to span the gulf between the godlike and the quotidian. What's more, he does so in a gay political context, which gives his new sense of becoming an extra bang for its buck.

And yet, it is hard to move past this initial stage, for new consciousness must be taught. It's harder still to get mentoring from our own people—gay people—because we're all pretty destroyed in the same way. The gay leaders or gay father surrogates who might teach us how to thaw our frozen hearts around the archetypal father lack the capacity to think symbolically. Or they lack simple trustworthiness—or empathy. If they are wounded gay men themselves, sometimes they want the younger man to take care of them, to love them in the way they were never loved. Few gay men have learned how to parent their own psychic kids consciously, so that no one else has to work overtime, abandoning his own sense of self to serve another. This deep and life-giving relationship to one's own shadow must be achieved by a person for himself, by himself.

Ultimately, it is a service to humanity. In a funny way, the ego becomes a kind of dad to the father archetype by "raising it up from unconsciousness." In turn, the Self, the ordering and unifying element of the psyche, gives back quite a bit of grace to the personality—and thus becomes a dad to the ego. One then gets a real father and becomes one to the world. This can be understood as the next step toward true coming out.

But this next step is very hard to take and filled with its own share of heartache and failure. When a part of the mind has been so repressed that it is presumed not to exist, its return to our lives may not be pretty. Anyone having the gall to refer to the possibility of this return is usually maligned. In this way, we are all trapped. Indeed, there would be no incentive to trust other people's word that the psyche is a force of nature, that there is more than one father in our lives, if our condition were not as barren and absent of masculine guidance as it currently is. Some have no place to turn but to the inner world of homosexual libido. In a way, our no-way-out situation is a kind of weird blessing in disguise.

CHEMISTRY

Ed   Sikov

THINGS REACHED THE breaking point when I walked in on my best friend, Jeff, fucking someone named Liz.

This was during my senior year at Haverford College, outside Philadelphia, in the mid-1970s. Jeff was not only my friend and roommate, he was my soulmate. We'd secured our souls' status earlier that year by dropping acid together, but even before that we'd watched Howard Hawks movies and adopted his ethos: Choose your friends carefully and say only what matters. Cary Grant in *Only Angels Have Wings*, John Wayne in *Rio Bravo*, Montgomery Clift in *Red River*—they knew how. With Jeff and me the talk was often about movies—Hawks, Hitchcock, Ford, Wilder. We also discussed drugs, philosophy, food, the Rolling Stones; knew things other people couldn't fathom; laughed at jokes we alone found funny. We opened our hearts and minds to each other, and to no one else. We talked about our futures. He was heading to Princeton in chemistry. I confirmed at last, to myself as well as to Jeff, that I was going to film school, not law school. I told Jeff everything I cared about. Sort of.

I didn't tell Jeff that LSD had pried open a particular passageway in my brain, one I had painstakingly nailed shut as a child. The moment was suitably bizarre. Several hours after doing some blotter, amazed at how a tiny stain on a slip of paper could produce such a wild effect in our heads, Jeff and I sat watching John Huston's *The Bible* on a substandard black-and-white TV. The image was only mildly enhanced by the acid, but the story took on broad, transcendental overtones. In one central scene, the Israelites celebrate Isaac's

230

growth with a primitive weaning feast. George C. Scott makes a better-than-Sunday-school Abraham, a psychological patriarch with ancient stature and modern nerves. But Abraham was not the cause of my anxiety. It was Ishmael, Abraham's chestnut-shaded prepubescent bastard, lurking on the periphery, causing trouble for the Jews—especially me.

Huston's symbolism is anything but subtle. The centerpiece of the festival is a phallic statuette, which Ishmael steals in a playful attempt to reclaim his birthright—a successful act of male aggression and authority at baby Isaac's expense. Flying on acid, I was back in my local theater in a jolt, nine years old again, watching *The Bible* with my parents, wanting the statuette but terrified of it, seeing myself as Isaac, robbed and wronged. And wanting Ishmael. Transfixed in a child's lust and horror, I shoved the whole dreadful matter into a mental storage cubicle; twelve years later, thanks to LSD, the door broke open.

It was a dramatic moment of high mental comedy. For the first time in my conscious adult life I half acknowledged myself sexually, and good God, it was all about penises. LSD also taught me a simple lesson that reverberated throughout that night with Jeff and well into the following weeks and months. There were no magical acid visions, no brain-frying colors, only a slapping recognition that I was my life's own author and so far I had been writing someone else's story.

This observation may seem foolish to people who have enjoyed their lives. But since I hadn't (an understatement so vast that it requires reinforcement), it was a revelation as clear and profound as any I have ever experienced. While tripping, I saw what might be meant by the term "well-being": It was what I didn't have. Some other boy had taken it. And it had something to do with sex. I'd spent my life running away from anything physical, grown used to feeling robbed, desexed, detached from my own body. Idiotic as it may seem, watching *The Bible* on a lousy TV during an acid trip with my best friend reconnected me. Beginning that night, I started to put my own pieces back together in a new and (I realized even then) healthier fashion. It was the first step in coming out.

Until I reencountered the scriptures on television, sexual longing had inspired a kind of unending fugue, a sad ecstasy in which hope and despair flowed in and out of each other until they blended in what ought to have been the final movement, but instead returned once again to the delicate, seductive opening phrases that pulled me to my doom. Infatuations with slim, overly smart boys had been needling me for years. Jeff was the most recent. I knew he slept with women. I'd even cried over it, wishing I was one of them. My desire for Jeff—as with all of my small-waisted, brainy, sublimely unrequited loves—was exquisite torture, and the sense of absolute personal ruin was becoming obscene in its appeal.

But now, having seen that I could creatively expand my sexual imagination on one trip, I went so far as to lose my virginity on another. Jeff was out of town, and I had something to prove, so I proved it with Sarah. Sex on LSD wasn't a complete physical success, but it was certainly a life-affirming mental awakening. Sarah had tripped and had sex since she was fourteen; at twenty-one she was an old hand. Taking me in her arms, she laughed, we played, and finally we went to bed to enjoy something on the order of physical love. One of the participants, of course, was caught up in a trippy, melty, out-of-body experience as a confused heterosexual, but it was fun anyway, an early effort at self-authorship which led me, however little I understood it at the time, to confirm my honest lust for men.

And then I walked in on Jeff in bed with Liz. It was around ten o'clock in the morning when I pushed Jeff's door open slightly and heard his too-heavy breathing for a sharp second before he barked at me to stay out. I froze, trying to hear more. Though I couldn't see in, the key visuals were all too easy for me to supply on my own: Jeff was dark and sleek like a young racehorse. He was a soccer player—not a very good one, but he moved as if he cared—and I remembered every inch of his body by heart. Standing at his door, I knew that Jeff didn't have his clothes on but that I was the one who was naked. The closed bedroom door added a cruelly literal touch, and the sweet, musky smell of its symbolism only served to push me off the edge of stability.

As if somebody had stuck a tube in my ear and pumped a tank of gas into my brain and under my skin, I was instantly sickened, poisoned by a mix of helium and sulfur dioxide. The helium yanked me off my feet, the sulfur dioxide made me want to puke. Still, I knew in an equally nauseating flash that the provocative agent wasn't chemical. No, it was intrinsic to me; that was the epiphany. It was in my blood, in my fat cells, muscle fibers, and valves, and it would never leave my system. This was who I was.

My own blundering stupidity had exposed, with heartless immediacy, the crumminess of my life as a closet case. A profile in denial and fear, I was an honors student at a top college. My grades were great, my professors encouraged me. I was going to be a film writer, not a lawyer, and the cinder block wall of self-hatred was beginning to crack under the weight of mind-bending drugs and my own creative growth. In fact, I'd been actively chipping away at the wall quite methodically until the moment when Jeff shattered it completely by ordering me out of his room. The sensation was that of a lifer granted sudden parole: The weight of freedom was suffocating. A failed heterosexual when I walked into Jeff's bedroom, I was a repressed cocksucker when I walked out.

I went crazy—manic, hysterical crazy—and I couldn't come down. I needed a Valium.

The nurses at Haverford were used to students showing up at the infirmary begging for drugs. Speed, not Valium, was the drug of choice. Nurse Broadhead, who ran the place, had gone through the sixties; her mid-seventies theory was that a controlled dose of pharmaceutical-quality amphetamines, available to everyone, was preferable to the street drugs certain students would otherwise buy and pop on their own. Still, she'd only dose you once a semester. This was fine for me. Rarely at a loss for nervous energy, I'd only needed the stuff once, when too many Great Books were due the same week. It was a fiasco. Although I certainly earned my uppers with *Ulysses*, *Moby Dick*, and *The Possessed*, I should have allowed myself the luxury of feigning illness and cutting classes.

Instead, I popped a pill, went flying, read a few paragraphs from each book, threw each book against the wall in a tantrum, and played furious solitaire until dawn.

From then on, I'd donated my semester's allotment to panicking friends in need. Everyone on campus knew that all you had to do was rub your eyes, quicken your pulse, plunge through the infirmary doors with a nervous air, and do an extemporaneous song and dance about some phantom philosophy paper, and they'd hand over the drugs. Still, only a few of us had the nerve to do it. The role of the reliable campus drug-runner was a good one for me, an upper-middle-class desperado. This time, however, I didn't have to fake anything at the infirmary, since I was legitimately berserk by noon. My pulse was racing, my eyes were red and teary, and I couldn't keep my hands from shaking (or even staying put on my lap). Nurse Broadhead gave me precisely five Valium, in a tiny manila envelope, and sent me on my way.

Waiting for the drug to kick in was hell, but soon I was resting in a comfortable cushioned box high in a familiar theater, the fuzz of a double Valium lending a muted pastel quality to the otherwise cheap student-apartment setting in which the action of this personal drama took place. Through beautiful soft-focus opera glasses, I watched in sick amusement as the "me" character went out of his mind on the wooden stage below. But now, the ironic distance on which I prided myself only sharpened the realization that although this tawdry little spectacle was immensely entertaining—the most exciting thing that had ever happened to me by far—I was nonetheless experiencing a walking nervous breakdown. In a muffled way, I was terrified.

In the opinion of this critic, the show wasn't terribly well written but was performed with dead-eye accuracy by a cast of experts. In one of the most disturbing scenes, the "me" character explained to his various acquaintances, one by one, exactly why he had been driven insane by having interrupted his best friend fucking a girl: It was all about feeling lonely and out of place in a hostile world. In a series of excruciating but curiously tender dialogues, the "me" character told everyone he knew that he was just a sensitive person who couldn't stand to feel stupid in front of people he liked, and it was this sense of having made a fool of himself more than anything else that caused the sudden rush of anxiety and madness. At least he didn't blame his parents.

Awful and predictable, the play would have been truly intolerable even through the pale gauze of Valium, if not for a hint, delivered offhandedly in the third act, that it really didn't matter what was going on in the script because the "me" character was graduating in a week and the curtain would fall.

After that, I moved to New York.

COLUMBIA'S FILM DEPARTMENT, chronically short on funds, had only one classroom large enough for a CinemaScope screen. It hung uneasily, afterthought that it was, at the very top of the room's front wall, a blank silver banner stretched tight by loops of black twine. Anything could be projected onto it, from scratchy sixteen-millimeter films run through standard educational projectors to elaborate thirty-five-millimeter Panavision films run past a set of brilliant xenon lamps. Thick, dusty drapes shut out the light and noise from upper Broadway. The chairs were functional, the sound system not so great. The room was a refuge as well as a frontier.

On one expanse of wall between two of the windows, a spectacular Magic Marker mural depicted the Road Runner disappearing in a cloud of dust on a mountain trail, racing triumphantly away from a characteristically thwarted Wile E. Coyote. Drawn spontaneously (and signed "with Acme love") by Chuck Jones himself during a lecture on Warner Bros. cartoons several years earlier, the mural had been spared (barely) from the latest institutional cover-all paint job and was now the visible if private symbol of my own glorious escape from other people's expectations. I could have been sitting in a law school classroom across campus; I wasn't. I might have been looking at static portraits of famous dead jurists; I wasn't. Instead, I was watching films, writing screenplays, playing with Arriflexes and Nagras and Steenbecks, bee-beeping a hostile and stupid world. I was learning, tentatively and with Acme love, to rewrite myself.

By the end of the first week of school, a smart-aleck second-year grad student with broad, muscular shoulders, small hips, and a taste for semiotic theory and Lou Reed entered my awareness. Howard didn't seem to care what other people thought of him—not his arcane opinions (with which I almost always agreed), not his slightly undersized "Kinsey 7" T-shirt. There were other gay students in the department, but they were no more than what I'd expected: gentle, nerdy, physically unprepossessing—a lot like me. They made no impression (except for the two second-year students I'd seen licking the same ice-cream cone at a Bleecker Street Cinema screening of *Pierrot le Fou*, an intensely erotic, almost pornographic sight, even though I found neither of the boys the slightest bit attractive). Howard was different. We got friendly over film theory, *The Rules of the Game*, marijuana, and the Stones, and though I was aware of being intensely curious about what he looked like in swim trunks or underwear, I made no effort to find out. I'd furtively try to catch glimpses of his lean stomach when his tight T-shirts pulled away from his jeans, but the image of myself I continued to project—to him, to everyone—was one of cerebral, above-the-fray asexuality.

One night in late September of 1979, Howard invited me to a party in a warehouse/loft neighborhood somewhere in Brooklyn. We were wandering through the beer-drenched, toked-up crowd with Howard's friend Davina when a particularly uptight fellow made some sort of strangled, distraught remark I can no longer remember. Later, Davina said to Howard, "I just can't understand how people who are wound up so tight can ever have sex."

It's easy, I thought: We don't. It was time to change that.

Jeff and I were still friendly; guilt was a great facilitator. Humiliated by my breakdown and the airspace it had opened into my cryptic sexuality, I was at pains to redeem myself in Jeff's eyes. For his part, he was embarrassed by his fling with Liz and, lucky for me, felt bad about having thrown it in my face. I disagreed with his assessment, but it was in my best interests to keep this opinion to myself. Months had gone by, and he was still trying to make it up to me.

Throughout September, Jeff would come up from Princeton on weekends and sleep on the sofa bed in my living room. One weekend in October, my parents were also in New York for a few days. They got the sofa bed; Jeff had to sleep in my room.

When gay people come out, we join the straight world in being able to radiate sexual energy outward. We're all accustomed to generating it within, but after coming out we're suddenly able to beam it electrically through our skin toward a particular person, a group of people, or just to the earth and sky. College parties, straight singles bars, gay gyms, lesbian twelve-step pro-grams—in terms of radiant sexual energy they're all the same, and the wave of desire emanating from people who are comfortable with themselves is so intense that you can practically smell it. At certain late-night gay clubs in New York and San Francisco, you actually *can* smell it. It's much better this way; I'm glad I'm out. It is immensely satisfying to finally be human.

But there is one thing I miss about being closeted: Energy that now flows outward used to stay completely inside. It would pump around in my veins and lungs, fill me up, bounce against the insides of my fingertips, circle back around my belly, go to my head, and make me high—dizzy, floaty, humming. The way I felt when I climbed into bed with Jeff.

The apartment was on the fifth floor of what had originally been a large residential hotel on West 102nd Street and Broadway. The building's first life as a hotel was architecturally evident in two important regards. The kitchen was literally a closet, and the bathroom was only accessible through the bed-room. As a result, when guests needed to go to the bathroom in the middle of the night, they had to walk through my room to get there. This added an element of pressure and suspense to the seduction scene I was hastily scripting on the brink of full consciousness. I was hard before I even got under the covers.

Like many gay men, I'd become adept at hiding my hard-ons. I turned my back to Jeff, got my shirt and pants off, kept my briefs on, and slid between the sheets, silently cursing the fact that he slept in his undershirt.

Jeff fell asleep and slept for several hours. My parents came quietly in and out. I pretended to be dozing.

By midnight, I had a mild buzz from the natural chemicals pumping through my body and brain, thwarted in their goal, flooding up behind a weakening dam. It got worse. Three hours later, vibrating from within, I was on the wildest endorphin rush of my life, luridly awake, my eyes tracing and retracing the sharp lines of Jeff's shoulders, the black hair visible in his armpits under his T-shirt, slope of the neck, hairy legs, hard chest, dark eyelashes—indescribable pleasure, the best drug ever. I had to have more.

Reassured by his slow and methodical breathing, emboldened by his lack of consciousness, I edged closer on the double bed. Jeff's smell was everywhere. He'd thrown his arms over his head; his face was turned away from me. My head pounded, and I watched his stomach gently rise and fall with every breath.

I moved so close I could feel his side against me, warm and firm. I brushed my arm next to his. His breathing changed slightly. I froze. He didn't move away. I put my hand on his chest. He didn't move. I kept my hand still for a few minutes, then ran my fingers lightly down to his stomach, brushed him with my nails, found the bottom of his shirt, stuck my hand inside. His eyes were open.

On my knees, I opened my mouth, tasted his skin, put my hands all over him, took in a sudden rush of air, held it, and became the man I was meant to be.

WE DIDN'T TALK much about it, other than for me to say that I had wanted to do it for a couple of months. At first, we said only what mattered.

"I knew you wanted it."

"Thanks for letting me."

Then, a few minutes later, I took words further than I should have. "I like your armpits," I said, and he answered, "Even if I liked somebody's armpits I'd never say I did." Then he left for Princeton.

With my parents still in the apartment, I closed the bedroom door and called Howard, getting instantly to the point: "I had sex with Jeff."

The following weekend, Howard and I went to a party thrown by some friends of mine from Haverford. At Howard's instigation, we both wore blue eye shadow. Around midnight, Catherine, our host, asked me, "Is there something you'd like to tell us?" "I think you get it," I said. By the end of October, I was out to all my friends.

The next step happened a few years later, when I came out in print. For a writer, this second coming out almost equals the first in nervous tension and liberating release. Setting your sexual deviance in type is a lot like setting it in stone. There's no turning back; you can kiss your campaign for the presidency good-bye. And thanks to the Industrial Revolution, not to mention twentieth-century marketing and distribution practices, you get to come out to tens or hundreds of thousands, even millions, of people at a single stroke.

A market-research firm once estimated that my particular audience was somewhere in the neighborhood of 100,000, if you counted the roommates and friends likely to take a look at every copy sold; I was writing for the *New York Native*. I also worked part-time as an editorial assistant at a public television station. A straight co-worker expressed astonishment that I was signing my own name in a gay paper, and I was indignant—until I realized that I still hadn't come out to my parents.

There they'd been, asleep in the next room as I'd licked the hairs on my best friend's stomach, and they still didn't know. My byline was appearing in every issue of a popular gay newspaper in the largest city in the United States. Every so often my name would show up on the front page. The paper was even being sold in the small bookstore/card shop in my hometown in western Pennsylvania, which meant that at least some people back home knew things about me I was still too nervous to tell my own parents. I resolved to break the news when they came to New York next.

We were seated in a fine Japanese restaurant in midtown awaiting yellowtail and fatty tuna. My mother lifted a spoonful of miso soup to her lips and I announced that there was a reason I had never mentioned girlfriends. The spoon appeared to hold itself motionless in front of my mother's tense face as I continued. The reason was, I said rapidly, I had boyfriends, not girlfriends, and I concluded in the subjunctive mode: I said I thought it was time they knew.

My sake cooled, full and untouched, on the table before me. I grabbed it and downed it. My father continued to eat his soup in silence, unperturbed. I'd have gotten a bigger reaction if I'd said the soup was rotten.

This was shocking. Having rehearsed the classic scene over and over in my head, I was now dumbfounded as one of the actors jettisoned my overwrought script and ad-libbed a much more true-to-life nonchalance. Then it dawned on me: He'd been reading books on human sexuality since I was an adolescent, books that had rested on his nightstand and lined our bookshelves for at least the last decade. Evidently, they had not appeared there by chance. My father already knew.

My mother took it a little less matter-of-factly, but then my mother always takes everything a little less matter-of-factly. The momentary look of anxiety was registered, by her as well as by me, but by the time the sashimi deluxe arrived it was all over.

Of course, they still don't know I had sex with Jeff while they were asleep in the next room. Most of my friends don't know it, either. Jeff doesn't know I'm writing this essay. And I'm acutely aware of all the details I'm leaving out. The lesson, I guess, is that there are always secrets, no matter how many you tell. Coming out is active: It has no end.

Photograph by James Cox Farrington

THE IMPOSSIBLE CITY

Michael T. Carroll

I WOULD HAVE to put the time down as the summer of 1976. I was twelve years old, just making the transition from sixth grade into junior high (now known as middle school). My brother, Greg, had made the switch two years before and would return each day with rumors of the abuse of plebeians by upperclassmen, the excitement still flashing in his wild but somehow trustworthy grin. The accounts I was most concerned with, the ones I got the greatest charge from, had to do with locker room procedure—specifically, how all the boys were required to strip to their skivvies and change into gym clothes in front of one another, then, after phys ed, depending on the coach you got stuck with, strip down completely and shower together, gang style. Junior high marked the switch from boyish games played in school clothes and sneakers to the rugged field of more sweaty, manly sports, supervised with military gruffness by instructors who could have doubled as drill sergeants.

"They might make you shower right there in front of them," Greg promised me, "if you stink bad enough."

"Well, I just won't sweat. Either that, or I'll play something else," I countered.

He laughed, providing me with the first bit of freshman cynicism I'd glimpsed in him, then gave me a look meant to confirm how weird I was.

"Gimme a break, butthead. You're not out there playing dodgeball, y'know, or Ping-Pong. You have to play the sport they make ya. And it's not like you're used to, running around the playground with all these choices. It's baseball for four weeks, everybody all together or else, and then it's—you're gonna love this—football for even longer. We played football for weeks and weeks in seventh grade."

Greg loved torturing me. He knew I wanted nothing to do with that sport (though I found the smell of pigskin pleasant after the guys' rough handling, evoking some masculine essence). It wasn't the potential accident or injury that worried me, but the idea of having to get naked for people. I was a short, skinny boy, slow to develop, sometimes mistaken for a girl. My brother was two years older and the picture of young, rugged maleness. His thick leg and chest muscles seemed to have evolved directly out of his childhood pudginess; he had strange shocks of dark armpit hair and the sketchier suggestion of hair filling in the wide, sinewy gap between his nipples.

During elementary school, Greg had wanted to be GI Joe. He'd collected each of the different versions of the foot-high plastic soldier, including Negro Joe, despite the fact we lived in the South and were white. (I was partial to the blond and to the stubbly haired redhead.) By the time he had collected every GI Joe uniform, vehicle, and other piece of combat paraphernalia, Greg turned twelve and decided that playing with dolls was for kids. He began to take scouting more seriously; sports became for him the means of getting in shape for a career in the army.

For me, getting out there for a good, hard game with the boys was terrifying. But with the fear came excitement. One coach was reported to be huge and pear shaped, his hair burred short and butch-waxed to stand on end like a jarhead's, who would spank out-of-line boys with a wood paddle before forcing them into the showers. He was single and, Greg said, had been accused several times of touching boys while they were naked. Then there was ABF (the Arlington Butt Fucker), who supposedly dwelled in a section of woods in our part of town and sodomized young boys passing through. That story caused me to start riding my bike alone into the small, hot pine forest.

My brother's best friend was our next-door neighbor Roddy, a tall (nearly six feet and still growing), skinny boy with pool-blue eyes and rich dark hair. He was the same age as Greg, fourteen going on fifteen, and played basketball a couple of hours each day on the other side of our brick wall, the bouncing ball against the cement driveway providing a metrical downbeat for taking in prose or a bass line as I sat in my bedroom reading or listening to Neil Diamond and America records. Sometimes I pulled back the curtain to wave to Roddy from my window. If he was alone (as he usually was), I went out to say hi in person. He'd toss me the ball and encourage me to shoot a few hoops, in order to lure me into a game of twenty-one.

Roddy moved about ungracefully, even clumsily. He was liable to lose his balance and fall, or unintentionally hurt someone with his enormous feet and long, swinging arms in the fray of bodies. For that reason, unlike my brother, he did not play on any school team. When he started moving in the driveway, the clamor of his huge slapping feet echoed off the concrete; the constant sound of the ball and his big-lunged breathing gave the impression of a giant galumphing in hot pursuit.

Despite my small size, I occasionally took up Roddy's challenge. It was a miracle I ever managed to get the ball out of his hands and dribble it past him through the gauntlet of flashing arms and ever-moving legs, or into the air for a shot. I could never hang on to it for more than half a minute; his gigantic hands prevented me from getting anywhere near the hoop. He'd grab the ball midair, clutch it with one hand, dribble out to the end of the driveway, and return seconds later, bouncing it around my legs, making a basket from almost any distance or angle. I stood by, instantly surrendering.

Playing football at school wasn't enough for some guys. Every afternoon during the fall, my brother and his friends would kick off in our street. These matches often resulted in bloody scrapes, twisted joints, and sprains which left them limping for weeks. My brother, who was also short, liked football and soccer and the rest of the team sports but did not play basketball. Only once or twice do I recall him going one-on-one against Roddy, and maybe it was starting here that they began to drift apart, Greg being unable to conquer or excel in that arena. On this court, Roddy always won. For all his lack of coordination out in the street with football—tripping on the curb, rolling in a bed of sandspurs on someone's unkempt lawn—he could smash the stockier, smarter Greg at basketball. Still, this disparity did not at first appear to affect their friendship.

My brother didn't care to spend much time with me, or even waste breath trying to make me go away. He had trained me to respond to his impatient sighs, which told me to get lost or else. I was not allowed to stick around when he and Roddy set off to camp or work on a fort they were building in competition with a group of rougher boys making their own hideout in another part of the woods. In time, Roddy wasn't welcome, either. Roddy seemed to grow an inch or two each year. The taller he got, the less I'd see him playing ball in the street with Greg and the others. My brother found a new friend, a senior at the high school Greg was about to enter.

Jeff was another new addition to our Jacksonville, Florida, neighborhood, which was then in rapid development. (Every time a house went up, it was all the builders could do to clear a space from the fund of pine woods at which they were busy chipping away; a new lot never remained vacant for long.) He lived on the opposite side of us from Roddy, who before long became the odd man out. Jeff had a couple of inches on my brother in height and was conventionally handsome. He owned a green Volkswagen bug with a CB radio. Soon Greg was asking my parents to buy him a CB, too, so he could qualify for a merit badge in radio communications.

It occurs to me now that my brother was searching for his own big brother, a guy he could look up to, if not too far. Jeff inspired Greg not to worry about doing better in school. Greg must have seemed all right to the older boy, who somehow didn't mind being associated with a freshman and didn't torture or pull rank on him. The new friends hung out in Jeff's or my brother's room, talking on Greg's CB to people all over town, pulling the guts out of Jeff's older radios to determine what was wrong or how to increase the range and wattage. Despite their age difference, Greg and Jeff at least could be equals in technology.

One day while they sat in my brother's bedroom working on the innards of a Magnavox, I overheard them using a catch phrase whenever one of them made a mistake touching the smoldering tip of Greg's soldering iron to the ailing PC board, delicate repair work that required a steady hand. "Duh, Roddy!" they would say, as if Roddy were there to mess them up, or, choking back a glottal stop of frustration, "Oops, I pulled a Roddy!" as if he were the patron saint of bumbling. On the street playing football or getting off the bus, when Roddy wasn't around, they might go into a caricature of a spastic, stumbling retard, aspirating like a freight train and stuttering, "Duh, Roddy!"—a display so grotesque you had never seen it anywhere else, not even in Jerry Lewis movies.

The worst part, and the hardest to report, is that I loved it. I worked out my own shtick, trying to impress them. After a football game, as soon as Roddy was gone from sight, I'd break into an imitation of a dweeb overcome by spasms and horrible coordination, tripping on the nearest lawn and slamming into trees. The slightest smile or laugh from Greg or Jeff was the morsel of approval I craved, and I was gratified if one of them joined in or echoed my performance with another "Duh, Roddy!" Then, alone in my room with my books and music, doing my best to entertain myself, I would listen to the rhythmic, bellowing *smack* of Roddy's basketball from the pavement into my wall, the thunderous *fwump* and *thump* of his feet landing on the cement after one more practice shot.

Junior high put me a school away from my brother and his crowd. There I met the only other guy in our neighborhood as unathletic as me. Mike was effeminate and quite thin, with a gentle way of talking, not like a girl but more mature, like a woman. He had dark, midnight-shadow eyes and lovely, thick eyelashes. Without trying to, he seemed to infuriate the other boys, who either resented him for his prettiness or were jealous of his popularity with the girls. He became the object of ridicule. His German last name rhymed with "fag-a-man," and everyone called him "Mike Fagaman" or just "Fagaman" behind his back.

Mike was in the eighth grade, halfway in age and class between my brother and me. We ended up having the same gym period, and so we were always in the locker room together. I was as obsessed as any preteen with my body's predicted maturing, though a part of me wondered if I wasn't just fooling myself. I regarded the male physique as the work of some divine genius. I was its most earnest secret admirer, given to prolonged staring and quick, furtive checks of my gym mates. I waited for a view of thickened, longer penises turning a shade darker with ripening, surrounded by a spray of pubic hair that didn't always match the color of the hair on the owner's head. I could have, if it weren't the wrong place to do it, gazed forever at the pendulous gonads that went by the thrilling slang of "nuts" or "balls"—thrilling because it described the anatomy in such basic terms, making it sound as everyday as eating, sleeping, sniffing your pits for smell, or taking a dump. Mike would unashamedly show his body to me in the locker room, knowing I was paying close attention to it, saying nothing. From the start I sensed a bond between us, one I could not name and then tried to deny.

We led two lives: a warmer, friendlier one in our neighborhood when the other boys were off playing ball or building forts, and a cooler, more self-conscious one at school, where all of us felt as if we were constantly being observed. Mike shared with me an interest in art, although his abilities were much greater. I always abandoned a project when the results were not instantly brilliant. One summer, my family had gone to the Smoky Mountains to visit an old college roommate of my father's, and I'd returned inspired to paint the rustic Appalachian hills and country roads, devoid of people, whose figures I could not draw or even suggest. I got bored touching in the pointillistic dots of green and dark hues of the background mountains, and quickly gave up. In contrast, Mike was bringing to life an entire world of his own imagining. *Star Wars* and a cheap television knockoff, *Battlestar Galactica*, were on the minds of a lot of kids then, and Mike was designing a space station, a free-floating city, its architecture, lifestyle, and culture all closely detailed with colored pencils. He'd show me a sheaf of drawings and excitedly discuss his plans to design cities in the future, his dark eyes searching over me.

All of the other kids, including my brother, and some of the adults, including my Calvinist father, told me I shouldn't hang around with that fairy. If Greg saw me talking to Mike or walking home with him from the bus stop, he'd give me hell. To me, Mike was special. But I worried about becoming a fairy myself. Maybe his personality brought out some latent effeminacy in me when I was with him. Around football-playing kids I was a wreck. Could they detect the earliest stages of fairyism developing? I monitored my manner and gestures, making sure they were nothing like a girl's. I must have succeeded in keeping the wraps on my sexuality, which part of me had always comprehended—or perhaps I was just too slight and kidlike to come off as either masculine or feminine.

Mike and I had a mutual friend in the neighborhood, a girl in my brother's grade who ignored Greg but not me. She had always accepted me as the younger brother my own brother didn't want. She protected me like an older sister would. Ann seemed to get a kick out of the team she, Mike, and I made together, yet she would gossip to me about Mike's being a fairy as if it were a fatal character flaw. Then, whenever I got too little-boy boring, she'd hang out with Mike as if they were best buddies.

Mike lived two doors down from Ann, and this proximity afforded her a close view of his after-school behavior while his parents were at work. At this point, I was only occasionally spending time with him, and then only under cover of our interesting and safe trio or in brief, shameful spells when his interest in drawing and his offer to show me his latest work, accompanied by the dead-on lock of his chocolate eyes, lured me into his house. I always glanced over my shoulder to make sure no one had seen me going in. Ann took a different interest in Mike than she did in me, reporting to me her observations as if she needed to hear herself repeat them in order to plan out her next move.

"Fagaman's started to smoke," she told me one day when she and I were sitting on the back of her mother's inherited Cadillac. She had recently started smoking herself, and one of her little bonds with Mike was to go behind someone's house, or into his when nobody else was home, and light up. She hid her habit from her mother by smoking at Mike's, where their cigarette smell blended with that of his parents. I tried smoking in order to fit in and couldn't stand it, but I was always welcome along for the ride, even if I said no thanks to a Kool or Salem Menthol. (They smoked only those feminine, mint-flavored brands.)

It wasn't long before I realized I was jealous of both of them. What transpired between them in the darkness of his family room, the curtains drawn against the sun? What weren't they telling me? What was I too afraid to ask? Alone with Ann, I called Mike "Fagaman"; when Mike mentioned her, I was cool as well. But I knew Ann was attracted to Mike, however much she criticized him behind his back. I sat in my room afternoons, unable to talk myself into going down the street to see them.

They began to spend all their time together, or hanging out as a sort of couple with a group of boys Ann liked from a few streets over who weren't clean-cut enough to play football with my brother's group or even be invited. Ann was not a hang-around-with-the-girls type. These boys made a world of immaculate suburban lawns a little seedier, and more interesting, by smoking cigarettes, drinking beer and whiskey, and getting high. None of this interested me. But the guys in the gang were certainly interested in Ann. Her enormous breasts had begun blossoming early and for a while seemed to be growing out of control; she'd confided to me that she'd recently gone up two bra sizes. I didn't quite know what the boys expected, or had already gotten, from her.

Mike, and his place in all this, made me curious. In gym class, I saw that he'd begun to mature. He had lots of delectable chocolate-brown hair under his arms and sprouting around his nipples and starting to fill in a trail between his navel and the waistband of his briefs, continuing downward, what guys called a "creeping Charlie." He'd become a sudden, sexy mystery to me.

My jealousy gradually turned to anguish. I spent my afternoons reading to fight off boredom and loneliness, listening to the thundering of Roddy's basketball. I was afraid to go out and get my ass kicked, afraid to try to be cool like Ann and Mike, afraid of facing truths about my world and the cartography of my longings. What I needed was a slow initiation.

That summer, Ann and her family went to visit her older sister, an air force wife living in Germany with her husband and their son. Mike seemed to spend less time with the rough boys. He was alone more, though if he missed Ann the way lovers miss their beloveds, he said nothing about it. Then my family went for our annual two weeks at my grandparents' farm in Tennessee. I spent my days with cousins in suburban Memphis malls, water-skiing behind my uncle's boat, digging weeds in my grandmother's vegetable garden and picking her peas and squashes, or enduring the stinging insects of Arkansas and Mississippi lakes on camping trips, and fed myself on the barbecued steaks and pork and packaged grocery store sweets of my relatives. I returned to Florida burnished by the sun along the arms, back, and face, and maybe a little less gangly. My hair was blonder.

Mike had spent part of his time going to the beach, but most of it housesitting for families away on vacation, mowing their lawns and cleaning their pools, then lying around in the sun. He was brown as a nut and confided to me that he had no tan line. ("All the houses have fences. Perfect for nude sunbathing.") The possibilities seemed endless to me, inspiring some of my hardest, most charged erections. A lot of my excitement was due to the development I saw in Mike: His shoulders were wider, his pecs well-defined, his abs enlarged from daily workouts with the lawn mower and all those long-handled pool nets and scrubbers. His legs were thin, but lightly touched with a soft-looking mess of brown hair. I was filled with violent envy for the sensual weeks he had spent on his own: *I* could have stayed home making money, reading, and watching TV (as I'd done anyway).

When I saw him later in July, Mike's attitude toward me was warmer. He smiled the entire time we talked and wasn't nervous or anxious for me to go home, the way he might have been if Ann were around and he knew they had a date in the woods with the guys. He was housesitting for a retired couple off with their children and grandchildren in Michigan until August. His parents were at work, and his sister, a few years younger, was at a Catholic day camp run by their church. We went across the street to look at Mike's recent drawings.

I stood in his bedroom, examining leaf after thick, bone-colored leaf, depictions of the space station lifestyle and Mike's streamlined designs for astral spires, turrets, gravitational parkways, and cylindrical hydroponic farms, spinning in orbit around the heart of his gleaming glass-arteried city—and sprang a hard-on. Mike was proof of what a little diligence and daily work could bring about: an entire world created by him and a beautiful, touchable body.

Mike looked directly at me, not turning away, and came closer. I could smell his adolescent sweetness, the kind I had brought on my hands to my nose many times after playing with my genitals, mingled with odors from other parts of his changing body. His armpit sweat, through the cutoff sleeves of his T-shirt, at first repelled me, but then he was pulling me down onto the neat, unwrinkled bedspread and pushing his face up to mine, still staring. His thick, girl-maddening mouth, smelling of cigarettes, opened to give me a sloppy, biting kiss; I could tell neither of us had gotten much practice from men. Our erections crossed like swords, and it wasn't long before we were pushing ourselves against each other. In an instant, he was rising to pull off his shirt, his shorts, and underwear, then standing with his beautiful tanned cock pointing at the ceiling. His pubic hair, growing so neatly above in a square, spread thickly along his thighs.

Now it was my turn to stare at him. He was even more striking naked than clothed, the proportion of upper to lower body so graceful, his torso strong-looking but smooth and rounded as it gradually narrowed to a slim waist and slender hips. No one would have guessed how mature his body really was, dressed in boy's clothes during the cooler winter weather. He was a wonderful surprise; in my family, the men were stockier and thicker in the waist and hips than most.

He smiled, moving slowly over me as his mouth approached mine for another kiss. I reached automatically to touch his dark chest, then slid to the edge of the bed, excited by the feeling of his nakedness. I sat up and started to undress myself. Mike came up behind me, touching my face and tugging at my clothes. I kissed his hand. He knelt down on the floor and began unhooking the brass fasteners of my overalls. As the straps came free and the front bib fell, he went for my shirt, pulling it over my head, dropping it somewhere near our feet. Another two strokes and the brass buttons on either side of the pants were released, the denim slid over my hips, thighs, down my legs. Then they were off, too, followed by my underwear. I was completely naked.

Mike nudged me back until I lay stretched out on the bed, then crawled on top of me a second time. We began rubbing our bodies together, using our cocks as a fulcrum, kissing and grinding. We ejaculated in a minute, mingling our come in the closed space between us. When he started to pull away, I got squeamish about the sticky mess all over my front, but he stopped and looked down without fear, as if he actually had done this before (I didn't ask). He continued to lift himself carefully, surveying the ick; the semen was so coagulated, he came away like the top of a pizza carton from a layer of molten cheese.

After he returned from the bathroom and toweled me off, I began to realize what people we knew would say about what we'd done. I could still smell the chlorine odor of semen as I pulled my T-shirt and overalls back on. I felt in a hurry to leave. Mike didn't get in my way to stop me.

Weeks passed; summer was over. I had plenty to think about, going into eighth grade. My brother and Roddy had made the leap into senior high, my brother's friend Jeff had gone away to college following graduation. The varsity soccer team kept Greg after school for practice every day. Although still fanatical about basketball, Roddy seemed to prefer shooting hoops by himself until runts like me came along and provided an easy triumph. Perhaps he just wasn't good enough for the team. I took no stock in such things, and never asked.

Roddy and Greg had had a falling out, for which I felt grateful. Afternoons, I'd stand near the end of Roddy's driveway watching him. Sometimes I'd bring a tennis racket and bounce a Dunlop ball up and down against the pavement, trying to keep it in motion while Roddy and I talked. We never discussed what had happened between him and my brother; he asked about Greg, mentioned having seen him at school, but went no further than that. We talked about things we'd never touched on before. Roddy inquired about my grades. He was aware of my bookish reputation even though we weren't in the same school. I wondered who'd told him, since I knew it wasn't my brother. Roddy did not seem put off by my being there. With Greg out of the picture, I saw clearly that Roddy had not been the one who wanted to get rid of me. He wasn't just out to whip me at one-on-one.

Roddy bounced the ball as he trotted in half circles and patterns of play, then tossed it in the air, nearly always making a basket. I forgot my spastic imitations of him and felt happy in his presence. He began to show off: A series of sudden twists, as if other players were close behind, hanging over his back and scaling up his impossibly high neck. Turns and leaps clear of imaginary guards and offense as he maneuvered toward the backboard, dexterously dribbling as he rushed a quick layup, took the ball back, bounced it hectically zigzag across the pavement, shot it long, made it or didn't, lunged forth to grab it again, bounce it a few more times, take it around the world for one more spin. He kept going, tireless. Finally, he stood at the far edge of the driveway, the toes of his scuffed white hightops touching the grass, his heels planted firmly on the cement, his back to the hoop, bending toward it like a spring flexing in an arch—and shot from the crotch, over his head and shoulders in a long, graceful arc to the basket, his face fixed, upside-down, on the result. A spectacular climax.

Sometimes he missed and sometimes he didn't, but I always stood by and looked amazed, laughing and hooting my praise. In truth, I had started to become impressed by something more. The protein shakes and extra orders of fries with his cheeseburgers had begun to make him more massive. His body was toughening up, his torso growing noticeably stronger. He was no longer gawky, but so large and athletic I thought I detected his body musk drifting across our adjacent driveways toward me. Those were quiet times between us. Once in a while, he would politely raise the ball and lift his eyebrows at me, an invitation to one-on-one. But he knew I'd learned my lesson and wasn't up for getting creamed by a giant that day, either.

Roddy's family were churchgoing Methodists and, almost out of defensiveness, as if to prove they could be every bit as pious as the Baptist majority in Jacksonville, they attended services three times a week and reserved their social calendar for other members of the congregation or their Methodist relatives. Sunday was a day of double worship, in the morning and the evening. On Wednesday night, Roddy, his parents, and his sister would jump into their station wagon after supper and head for church. Roddy was allowed to listen only to gospel music, and his parents didn't like him going to sexy movies or watching adulterous situations on TV, but by the time he reached high school, in a stroke of liberality, they permitted him to decide whether he would continue attending midweek services. After he got a job bagging groceries at the same supermarket where my brother worked (on different days), he ceased going.

On those Wednesdays he would head for the basket, and if I was at home and heard his thumping, I'd take my racket and join him with my own bouncing ball, waiting for the moment when his parents and sister pulled out of the driveway. Soon he'd tire and invite me inside for a Coke, to watch *Charlie's Angels*, an old sitcom, or a game show on TV. He never returned my stare with his big, tropical-pool eyes, nor told me to stop looking at him. I thought his ignoring my gaze was deliberate, conspicuous. Still, the silence was exciting.

We were getting to know each other in a way we hadn't been able to around my brother. I found out that, in the absence of Greg, Roddy had befriended a boy from outside our neighborhood, a member of the same CB operators' club my brother had recently talked my father into letting him join. Greg's replacement was a crazy, stringy blond with skin so pale, hair so wiry, eyes so direly corrected by bottle-thick glasses in nerdy frames, people mistakenly thought him harmless. He blew up toilets in the boys' and girls' rooms with cherry bombs, or chipped detailed close-ups of swelling cocks shooting a wad into hard masonry walls with a screwdriver. He cut classes to have breakfast at Dunkin' Donuts, devising alibis he knew were too preposterous to get him excused. He mooned teachers, folks driving down his street, shoppers in malls—anyone he could get a rise out of. He was just the kind of guy Roddy, son of staunch Methodists, was destined to buddy around with.

One Wednesday after basketball, Roddy and I were lounging in front of the family room television, talking about his new sophomore friend. Roddy lay along the couch in black knitted shorts which clung to his thighs and crotch and could instantly reveal a pubescent erection. His sweat socks were pushed down to his ankles, exaggerating the length of his legs. The hem of his shirt was up. He rubbed his belly and tugged at the hairs forming a mass across it. I sat in the matching chair directly across from him, my legs thrown over a stuffed arm, glancing furtively from the TV to Roddy, managing a few pro-longed stares. He lay lazily, half engaged with the plot and half in the conver-sation with me about the kid he said he knew was nuts and made him laugh but who came across as his idol.

"You know what he did? In the hallway, next to the lockers, last week?" Roddy paused and clarified himself. "To some girls standing there?"

"No, what?"

"Snaked 'em."

An idea of what he might mean twinged inside me, helped along no doubt by the sight of Roddy's hard-on poking up at the waistband of his shorts. I swallowed.

"What's that?" I asked.

Without looking away from the screen, he pulled down the front of his shorts and showed me his erect penis, pointing forty-five degrees in the direc-tion of the kitchen. It was quick, just a flash, but definite: the longest, thickest cock I'd ever seen. I had gotten only hints of its size before, outside on the driveway, where black polyester had kept it from view. He let the cloth drop back into place.

I sat mesmerized in the cushiony chair on my side of the den and focused on his crotch inside the pouch of cloth. Roddy kept his eyes on the TV, only once glancing over to survey my reaction. I let my mouth hang open and emitted a dumb-sounding "What?"—as though I hadn't understood, or needed confirmation.

He turned his head toward me, but otherwise lay as quiet and casual as before. I looked encouragingly back. He refocused on the TV. Then he pulled the front of his shorts down again, exposing himself longer this time. He was still hard and pointing.

I spent the next couple of years fellating that enormous cock, tasting the salty precome on the head but unable to get much past it: My appetite was far greater than my abilities. Sex would happen sporadically, reigniting unpredictably when the two of us found ourselves alone together. Then we made up for lost time. It always started haltingly, always wore the same unpremeditated guise it had that first evening. Once Roddy tried to enter me, using only tap water as lubricant; the pain shot through me so intensely, as he got barely past the tight ring of my sphincter, that I felt my insides splitting and spasming, trying to accommodate his wide reaming girth. Something inside me seized up; the breath flushed out of me. My head went blank. "Pull it out," I told him, more than either of us had ever said about sex. He did, grudgingly. I ran, naked and ailing, to the other bathroom in his house (his folks were at prayer meeting) and plopped myself onto the toilet, so sore that afterward I couldn't bear sitting on anything flat. I saw spots and fought a spell of fainting, terrified that I would come to and be condemned by angry church elders for seducing the older boy. Other times he asked me to suck him—fair enough, I loved that—but usually I got bored before I finished. It took a while just to stimulate that outrageous stick of flesh. Eventually, he tried to time me: "See how long you can go for" or "Just go two more minutes." The thrill of the covert kept me interested enough to begin asking for his cock. An idle fantasy would well up inside me, guiding me to go for it, or horny curiosity dreamed about during the day while masturbating (in the time when I used to read). At night, my thoughts were more poignant: I was in love with Roddy's oversized body, his big feet I kissed, the smelly pubic hair and fragrance of his genitals. By the end of that long year, we had tried it everywhere imaginable. In my bedroom. In front of the TV while my parents slept in another part of the house. In the woods where he and my brother had built a fort. In the kitchen, garage, backyard. Next to our dining room table. A couple of times, I took him in my mouth as I stood outside his window and he lay sideways on his bed facing me, rocking on one hip as he ran it in and out of my lips.

Although there was no visible evidence that Roddy was getting emotionally involved with me—I took making love as my job and showed it by planting my face between his buttocks—after so much time together, we actually, if awkwardly, started talking about it. "Do you and Fagaman do it?" he finally asked. Roddy had girlfriends, and besides, he professed to be a good Christian, if not always a practicing one. But Mike was a Catholic, quite lapsed after leaving parochial school, and went further against the small-town grain by wearing cannabis-leaf T-shirts, growing his hair long, continually smoking, and hinting he was "getting" a little on the side through the wild, rough boys he ran with. Getting it with girls, trying it with boys, while the tunes of Lynyrd Skynyrd and the classic rock of the late seventies played in the background. Mike's drug was marijuana, and hard liquor whenever one of his crowd could obtain it, which was more difficult for underage kids than getting grass. Roddy liked beer and was picking up on the back-to-country trend, buying Hank Williams, Jr., records and wearing a Stetson hat to the mall and movies. Then Mike's parents divorced and he moved with his mom and sister to another part of town. The change came suddenly; I don't remember any moving-day good-bye. Probably I was off in Tennessee and returned to find part of me slipping away. That fall, Mike was missing from school. He had transferred, someone said, or dropped out.

When I was sixteen, I got an unexpected call one evening. On the other end of the line was a familiar, smokier voice. Mike had not moved as far from our subdivision as I had thought; he'd just decided school was a drag and ditched it for a while. He was working full-time. His family needed the money and he had a car to pay for, but his job left plenty of room to study at night for his high school equivalency diploma. I was driving now, too. Mike invited me over right then, while his mother was out on a date and his sister was with friends at a slumber party.

The apartment complex he lived in was one block from our junior high; I was a sophomore in the senior high we'd never had the chance to attend together. Although I disliked school and was secretly jealous he'd been able to get out, I was no longer intimidated by the prospect of playing with the older guys. My brother and Roddy were about to graduate and go on to big changes, but some equally important changes were soon to occur in my life, though I wasn't really expecting any. I was bobbing along, nervous about the usual things teenage boys get nervous about, such as the future, but more and more oddly secure about liking boys, while ignoring the fact I still went after girls.

Mike looked fitter and more confident than ever; he had taken on the appearance of a more mature and handsome, virile young man at the age of seventeen. I was excited to see him, having been away from him and his futuristic sketches for nearly two years, biding my time with Roddy, who turned me on but whose bulk was overwhelming, his warmth and affection nearly nonexistent. What I needed, or most longed for, was to feel safe and secure in another boy's arms, satisfied by the hard force of his body against mine. Like some acolyte in Mike's Catholicism taking part in an important, edifying rite, I was young enough to feel the urgency of initiation. I awaited confirmation.

We exchanged simmering stares, examining each other for signs of our former selves, then embraced, lying across his new double bed and carrying on like long-separated lovers. Off went our shirts, smoothly, unashamedly. I touched his perfect, coin-sized nipples the color of turned copper, his hard, smooth chest. I asked him what he'd been doing to look so good. Working. I felt self-conscious about my own narrow chest and body, but when our pants came off and I smiled and showed pleasure at the sight of him, he looked at me admiringly. "You've gotten so big," he said, playfully reaching down to tug at me, then smoothing my cock and testicles more tenderly, lovingly, working up to the moment when he would eventually turn me over, wet me down from the bathroom sink, and gradually enter me. He stayed on top, grinding doggy style, and though it hurt it also relieved some of my doubt: In the future, I would ask for this, from whom I didn't know, again and again.

THE PASSAGE OF time since then seems unreal, as did those rolling days of fun underscored by a knowledge indelible as a visceral twinge that I was bound for something different from most of the guys I knew. At the end of that year, I started a twenty-four-month relationship with a girl. We would go on dates and French-kiss, hold hands, cuddle in my father's Pinto wagon, even discuss getting married. She knew about my sexual preference (a friend had told her) and assured me she understood; we could work out a special clause before the wedding. It never occurred to us, in those days just before AIDS, that jealousy or lack of monogamy could be the end of us. I loved her, I liked to hold her. But I wasn't drawn to her physically.

Roddy went on to become a police officer, as he'd always said he planned to, back when we were messing around on his floor under the banners of his favorite teams. Most of my knowledge of him comes by way of family friends. Years after he'd gotten married, I saw him in an open-air mall by the river in Jacksonville on one of my trips home. The city had become strange to me; I'd left it so many times, returning only briefly, that to come back again seemed like wandering. Then in his mid-twenties, Roddy had already begun to bald; the Southern sun had started to inscribe lines around his eyes and across his forehead. He had surprised me, and probably a few others, with his furtive boyhood fooling around. And life had in turn surprised him. He'd gone on to get what he'd wanted, but it cost him his youth. I'd heard he'd lost his first child to Sudden Infant Death Syndrome; maybe that was why he looked so grieved. I felt his scolding frown as I told his sister I was still single, did not have a steady job.

I went to a seedy Mafia-owned joint offering gays their only dance floor in town. I didn't see anyone I knew or wanted to know, and left, intent on a final eye sweep of the parking lot before getting back into my car. Toward the end of the night, guys often waited outside for last-chance pickings of the rejected or too hard to please. One of them, standing in the shadows near the door smoking a cigarette, called my name from the darkness. My middle name. (In the South, middle names are frequently used as nicknames by family, close friends, and neighbors. I had been called Todd.) I recognized the voice immediately: deep but gentle, a little fading Hollywood actress. It returned me to my old street, long since abandoned. I got closer, made out dim features, the sexy shape, and called his name.

"Mike?"

He turned toward the light and I saw the work he'd done on himself. He was quite manicured; if it had stopped there, he would have looked like the professional he'd once aspired to be. But he wore thick eyeliner and mascara, which made his already dark, distinct eyes seem twice their true size and dwarfed the rest of his still-tanned face, which had a shade of blush on each cheek. He'd turned out to be just what I'd been afraid of in those early years of keeping my distance from the feathery boy they called Fagaman.

I was horrified, confused by his act of vanity. His new look detracted completely from the masculinity, the dewy boyishness, I'd seen in him that first time we had sex. I felt alone again. And yet, part of me was thrilled to run into him after so many years.

We quizzed each other about what we'd been doing. Until recently, he'd been living in California with a lesbian wife. He'd married her to give them both a kid and now he had child support to worry about. His smile said he knew it would surprise me. He was working as an orderly in a Jacksonville hospital.

I hardly knew what to tell him about myself. I had done nothing so bold. In the end, I hadn't wanted to. I wonder what he thought of the life I described to him. We said good-bye a few minutes into our brief exchange, and I've never seen him since. I'll be grateful to him forever.

I hadn't started out to be a homosexual, to enjoy the bodies of other men, to forsake the acceptance of society for mere pleasure. And if I had, arrogance is the crib death of decision. Since I left home, I have tried and fought in vain for two relationships that didn't work out and I've resolved never to put myself above other gay men. What I work toward these days is survival in love, knowing the limits of any new design. When I think of my original hopes, I go back to Mike's careful sketches, his depictions of an impossible city: noble and very handsome.

DISNEYLAND

Norman Wong

WHEN I WAS growing up, the last Sunday evening of each month my family and I toured Waikiki. We had already seen the kung fu movie playing in Chinatown, held over from the previous week. Back then we did not go to many American movies. In Waikiki, Dad pulled Mom along when she remained too long in front of a jewelry shop window, examining the diamond, gold, and jade. She didn't care for the cheaper Hawaiian coral. "It's always in your mother's mind to buy something," Dad would say. He would steer us toward the beach, away from the crowds, the cars, and the street lamps, so bright and noisy that they robbed the romance from the white moon and the starlit black sky.

Dark silver waves crashed on the beach. "Beautiful," Dad exclaimed. Sand crunched violently beneath my sneakers, and in my head I could already hear Mom telling us to shake out the sand from our shoes before getting into the car. It was her only night off from the Chinese restaurant where she worked; Dad did not go to the factory on Mondays. They were not arguing, for a change. We walked halfway down the beach and then stopped, afraid of getting our shoes wet.

After a couple of minutes, Mom declared that it was time to move on, that we had seen enough water.

Dad retorted, "Well, let's go home then. I'm tired of looking at store windows."

We turned back. It was time to go home, to bed, to sleep, and to school tomorrow. Doom.

But before reaching the car, Mom cleverly detoured us through her favorite hotel lobby, the Sheraton's, with its three-ring fountain in the circular driveway, shooting up rainbow-colored water. In her eyes, I could see her imagining herself arriving with her luggage for a vacation away from us.

Inside the hotel lobby, a tropical-flower-print carpet covered the entire floor, and above, gigantic light fixtures, holding multiple bulbs, glowed like sunlight. Mom continued her window-shopping in the lobby, while Dad followed behind, the neglected child. I sat, sad and a little tired, on a circular green velvet lounge sofa, watching the tourists walk by. Beside me, my older sister, Cindy. Eventually, Dad caught up to Mom: the little boy reunited with his mother.

Holding hands, husband and wife again, Mom and Dad stepped up to the fancy entrance of the hotel restaurant, the House of Tiki, styled like an old Polynesian hut, with wood beams and a thatched roof of dried tea leaves. In front, a pool of goldfishes swimming, above which a rickety-looking wooden bridge led to the restaurant. Mom and Dad did not cross over but remained on the safety of the flowery carpet, studying the menu posted on a wooden plaque. I imagined them debating over what they would order, and then both agreeing how overpriced everything was. Dad would then begin to fantasize out loud about opening his own restaurant, what dishes he would serve, how much he would charge, all the people who would come. And then Mom would ask him where he was going to get the money to open this restaurant in the first place. Off the trees?

Cindy and I rejoined them, and together we all walked along the roped-off border of the swimming pool lounge where tourists swam in moonlit chlorinated water. Other tourists sat in rattan chairs under tiki torches. Fat Hawaiian men, moving from table to table, played their ukuleles and sang love songs. Cocktail waitresses, dressed in tropical-print cloths wrapped around their breasts and waists, served colorful, foamy drinks graced with miniature umbrellas and sweet, gold pineapple wedges. The tourists laughed and enjoyed themselves. It was time for us to go home. Our family vacation was over.

"I'M GOING TO Randy's to play poker," I told Mom as I headed for the door.

"Take the garbage with you to the Dumpster," she said. "And don't stay out too late. We're going to Ala Moana shopping center tomorrow. Early. Awake or not."

Shopping for college. I was leaving for the mainland the next weekend, the final weekend of August 1981. My playground would be Chicago, tall buildings, crowds, traffic, gigantic malls. Once there, Mom wouldn't know what I was doing, how late I was out each night.

At the Dumpster I produced from under my shirt my last porno magazine, a *Mandate*. I tossed it into one corner, the garbage into another; in case someone discovered the magazine, my family's garbage would not be implicated. Then I drove to Waikiki.

In Chicago, for the first time in my life, I would have my own room. (At home, I slept in the top bunk, above Cindy.) No longer would I have to masturbate in the bathroom, sitting on the toilet seat with a magazine in hand. Always, while in the bathroom, flipping through the worn, greasy pages (using Mom's Jergens lotion for lubricant), someone would knock on the door and ask why I was taking so long: *They* had to *au see* or *au nyu*. I'd aim for the toilet bowl, leaning forward, crouching down. Milky phlegm, curling and bobbing in the water. I'd flush the toilet twice afterward. When I masturbated in the shower I made sure to wash my come down the drain, sometimes even scrubbing the tub with Comet. When I found myself alone in the apartment, I would masturbate freely in my bunk, the magazine beside me, and ejaculate on top of a sheet of paper toweling placed strategically over my stomach. Afraid that someone would discover the stained paper towel in the garbage, I'd flush it down the toilet, the repository of my semen, the mother of my babies. It would be infinitely easier living on the mainland, alone with my secret.

As a teenager with a driver's license, I would return again and again to Waikiki, my parents' playground, secretly, alone at night, touring the hotel lobbies. I'd walk down the sidewalk path of the beach, onto the sand, to the edge of the waves, approaching and receding, daring to touch the water with the tip of my shoes.

I drove down Kalakaua Avenue, Waikiki ablaze. There were lots of traffic and crowds and no parking spaces. I did not want to park in a lot, afraid of someone's recognizing me. I drove several blocks away from the heart of the neighborhood, along the quieter Ala Wai canal. There I found a space. I would have to walk a few extra blocks, but what was the hurry? Where was I in a rush to?

Habitually, I walked to the International Market Place, a shopping arcade in the heart of Waikiki. I looked in the stores which sold pineapples, coconuts, and macadamia nuts, ready-boxed for shipping. I stepped in front of jewelry shop windows and picked out the prettiest pieces for Mom.

It was not yet ten. Still too early, I concluded. I went into a McDonald's, ordered a small Coke and fries, and sat in the smoking section. I salted the fries and squirted red ketchup on the paper liner of the tray. Automatically, I ate the fries, lightly dunking them first in ketchup. I was not even hungry. My father's Chinese food sat in my stomach. McDonald's was half filled with white tourists and local public high school kids out on a Saturday night. The local boys were tanned and wore shimmering rayon shirts and Levi's Angel Flights, a dark polyester-cotton blend dress pants which clung to their asses and thighs. Their hair, long past their ears and parted in the middle, was bleached lighter by the sun. At the beach they would grease suntan lotion in their hair. The Oriental girls wore tight dresses over their skinny bodies, along with high heels and makeup, looking like classy *gai* ("chickens," or whores). They were all on their way to the discos, located in the various fancier hotel lobbies.

Halfway through the fries, I began to worry about salty, greasy breath. I drank more Coke, swishing it in my mouth and between my teeth before swallowing. A cloud of cigarette smoke hovered above the table of boys and girls. In the mirrored wall I saw my own skinny acne-covered face, my spray-stiff black hair, parted to the side. I was considered a nerd in high school (an image I would change in college). I stopped myself from fixing my hair with my greasy fingers. Nothing would help it. I knew I was not pretty like the boys at the other table. I was alone, without a date on a Saturday night. I stood, picked up the tray, inserted its contents into the mouth of the trash receptacle, set the tray on top, and walked out of McDonald's. Outside, I passed the X-rated movie house, where a Hawaiian-looking man shouted to me in Japanese.

There was a corner in Waikiki, flanked by a tall white fence, behind which an enormous banyan tree rained down tentaclelike aerial roots and strings of bright white Christmas lights. White men entered through an opening in the fence. Loud music floated over the top. The white planks were fitted so closely together that a little boy could not fulfill a curious peek. When I was younger, Mom and Dad would usher me quickly around this corner. I assumed it was one of those places for tourists only.

I rounded the corner and saw the tall white fence. As I neared it, the music pulsated. My steps grew slower. I could feel Mom pushing me from behind to hurry on. Walking by the doorway, I stared up at the lighted marquee: HULA'S. I peered in but could see only a row of tall potted palms. I continued around the corner, past the men walking toward the entrance. They did not look at me. I went around the block, past McDonald's, past the fat Hawaiian man again—still imploring me to come into his theater—and back to the corner with the white fence.

When I was ten we had almost gone to Disneyland. It would have been our first trip to the mainland, my family's only true vacation. But at the last minute the trip had been canceled. The relatives with whom we planned to stay could no longer put us up, and we could not afford both plane tickets and motel rooms. Hopelessness overwhelmed my family more than usual as we unpacked our suitcase of the individual ramens, which we had planned to eat in order to economize. A few years later, I overheard Mom telling Dad about a co-worker whose daughter had been diagnosed with terminal cancer. The waitress mother planned to borrow money to take her daughter to Disneyland as a last hurrah before her death. Back then, when I weighed a terminal illness against a trip to Disneyland, I decided that I would have chosen to go to Disneyland, even if it meant having to die soon afterward.

Again I rounded the corner. The Christmas lights rained down from the branches of the banyan tree, bright like an amusement park. I walked under the lit marquee and imagined myself finally arriving at Disneyland.

The place was crowded with tourists and local men, a mix of *haoles* and Orientals. I headed to the bar under a thatched roof, a shack in the jungle, and produced a cigarette from my shirt pocket as I leaned on the wooden counter. I lit the cigarette, took a puff before ordering a Coke from the bartender, a *haole* dressed in a "Hawaii" tank top, sporting a dark mustache and bushy armpits.

"Lemon?" he asked.

"Okay."

The bartender served me and went to answer a customer at the other side. I looked around and spotted an empty stool beside the trunk of the banyan tree, beneath the white lights. Carefully and slowly, I walked over there, with the Coke and the lit cigarette. The *haoles* in the bars, both tourists and locals, wore mainly shorts and T-shirts or tank tops; their arms, legs, and chests, tanned or burned, mostly hairy. Their Oriental counterparts—Japanese, Filipino, and Chinese—rejected the "local" way of dress, opting instead for the more mainland look of khakis, polo shirts, or designer shirts with long sleeves rolled up neatly a quarter way, dressing more white than the *haoles* themselves. The locals were out on the town, their dark hair combed, sprayed, moussed, and/or gelled in place, their clothes ironed, their necks and wrists perfumed. These Orientals were looking for white lovers. I, too, was a want-to-be-white Oriental, dressed in khakis and a long-sleeved shirt, also in search of a white lover.

Finally, one candidate came over and stared at me, a clear drink in his hand. He swayed from side to side. "Got another cigarette?" he asked.

"Yeah, sure," I said nonchalantly, my heart racing.

I held the pack up to him. He picked out a cigarette, stuck it between his lips, leaned over, and attempted to light it off the cigarette in my mouth. I took mine and held it to his. After he was lit, he offered me his hand. "Tony."

"Norman."

"Nice meeting you. Aren't you hot, dressed in all those clothes?"

He wore swimming trunks and a tank top, which allowed him to show off the dark hairs sprouting behind his shoulders.

"Roll up your sleeves."

He reached over and attempted to unbutton my shirt with the hand holding the cigarette.

"Welcome to Hawaii."

I stood up from the stool and stepped back, afraid of getting burned.

He set his drink down, and a cold hand touched my face.

"You're so pretty."

He looked old, probably over thirty.

"What are you? Chinese? Japanese?"

"Chinese."

"I can always tell. *Ni hau ma?*"

"I don't really speak Chinese," I lied.

"Oh, you're one of those local boys. *Twinkie.* Yellow on the outside, white on the inside. Oh, well. How old are you?"

"Eighteen," I lied.

"Good."

"How old are you?"

"Don't ask."

He stepped closer to me and placed his hand on my waist. His breath smelled of vodka. He stuck his face into mine; his tongue emerged like an asp from a basket and licked my pressed lips. I tasted the alcohol.

"I want to make love to you, my pretty boy."

His hand had fallen below my waist to my skinny butt; he squeezed me. Again he attempted to kiss me, and this time I timidly opened my mouth. Two wet tongues touched; I wondered if Tony could taste the French fry residue in my mouth. I reached for my soda and finished it, then followed him out of the bar.

TONY WAS STAYING at the Plumeria Hotel, located behind the Sheraton, its entrance adjacent to the delivery dock of its grander, larger neighbor. The Plumeria's miniature lobby was furnished with a vinyl sofa, two matching chairs, a coffee table covered with tour brochures, newspapers, and a plastic potted plant. No three-ring water fountain, no chandeliers, no shops. The floral carpet was a plumeria pattern, a cheaper imitation of the Sheraton's. Off to the side was a coffee shop, with a white neon sign above its glass door declaring that it was open twenty-four hours. There appeared to be no one inside. A young, dark, petit Filipina dressed in a muumuu manned the reception desk. She leaned on the counter, reading a magazine. She looked up as we entered.

"How are you?" Tony asked.

She smiled, said nothing, and returned her attention to the magazine. Tony was probably the twentieth drunk guest to come in that evening. We rode the elevator up to the fourth floor.

There were two beds in Tony's room, both unmade. No balcony, just a couple of slatted-glass windows, cranked open to reveal the back wall of the Sheraton. The room smelled of coconut-flavored suntan lotion and the dank beach towels piled on the floor. Swimming trunks draped the wooden arms of the only chair in the room. Tony turned on the lamp on the nightstand between the two beds, then flicked off the overhead light. He sat on one of the beds, pushing the clothes on top to the floor, and patted the mattress.

"Why are you standing so far away?" he asked me gently.

He pulled off his tank top and began to unknot his swimming trunks.

"Come here," he ordered.

I slowly approached him. Thick, short, curly blond hair covered his chest, a forest surrounding two large, flat, pink nipples. He finished unknotting his shorts, lay back on the bed (his feet still touching the floor), and pulled his shorts past his hips and thighs to his knees. He kicked off his sandals; his shorts fell down around his ankles and he kicked them off, too. Sand lodged between his toes. He closed his eyes and resumed patting the bed, like a revived pulse.

I felt myself in a nightmare. His arms were outstretched like a mummy's. He opened his eyes suddenly and smiled sharp teeth, like Dracula.

"Take your clothes off," he told me.

Slowly I unbuttoned my shirt, imagining stripper music in the background. When the moment arrived to take off my shirt, I froze, ashamed of my skinny body. I reached over to turn off the lamp.

"Don't," Tony said. "I want to see your sexy body." I'd never thought of myself as sexy. I let the shirt fall off my shoulders.

My chest was whiter than Tony's. He reached out and took my hand and pulled me down on top of him. His tongue pried open my mouth. He kissed my ear and then my neck, hoisting me up so he could lick and bite my nipples. It hurt and tickled. His hand strummed my rib cage. He fumbled with my belt.

I stood up and pulled down my pants and underwear, letting them fall to the floor. I told myself to shake the sand from my pants before putting them back on. "Get naked!" he said. He pulled me back on top of him, positioned his hard dick beside mine, smaller than his; they rubbed abrasively together. It felt sore but nice.

He got up from under me, turned me over, climbed on my back, and inserted his dick in the space between my thighs, just below my ass. "Oh, that feels so good," he said to the back of my head. Warm cigarette breath touched my neck; my face smeared the sheets. He pounced on top of me, his hairy chest scouring my back. "Oh, that feels so good," he repeated. "Can I fuck you?" I craned my neck around to look at him. "Can I, ha?" Then he was gone, sliding down my back, nibbling my skinny butt, his hand spreading apart my cheeks, and then his tongue licking my hole.

I wondered if I had showered after my last shit. His tongue tickled the puckered lips and then attempted to pry them open. My muscles clenched. I did not want him to get in. It was dirty down there. But the instant I relaxed, his warm wet tongue got in, and I found myself swooning. A tingling sensation raced up my spine. "Oh," I exclaimed. "Oh."

He shifted his body back on top of me, his dick positioned at the entrance of my hole. My muscles clenched up again.

"Can I fuck you?" he asked.

"No," I answered. Then I asked, "Will it hurt?" I could only imagine that it would; his dick seemed too large to fit inside of me.

"Your first time to be fucked?" he asked.

"My first time," I answered shyly.

"My, my. I like being a boy's first time. A man wants to be a woman's first love, and a woman wants to be a man's last."

"Oh."

He began licking me on my neck, the tip of his penis pushing a little more forcefully.

"I don't think I want to do that," I said. "I think it'll hurt too much."

"Please," he said. "Just a little. I'll stop if it hurts too much. Please, just a little."

I hated when people made me feel guilty. Like when Mom complained, "All I do is work and clean up after you, boon san gee [American-born spoiled pig]." I did not answer Tony. I figured if he gets in, he gets in; then I wouldn't have let him fuck me, it would have just happened. If I planned to spend the rest of my life with him—or with any other guy, for that matter—I would sooner or later have to learn how to get fucked. He pushed harder.

"Ow! Stop!"

"Already? My tip didn't even get in."

"I'm sorry," I said, my face buried in the pillow in shame. "It's just that it's my first time. I've never had sex before in my life with anyone."

"So you are a virgin. I thought you were just making that part up to get me more excited." He rolled off me and reached for a pack of cigarettes on the nightstand.

Was sex over? In the lamplight, Tony looked even older than Dad. Dad has always looked the same age; he looked the same now as he did when he took Cindy and me to the beach and pulled us around in the water while we swam inserted in inflated lifesavers. Dad's skin was pearly white and soft, his chest hairless except for a few long black strands surrounding each of his baby brown nipples.

"You can remove your hand from your ass," Tony said, smoking his cigarette. "I'm finished, for now." He stroked his semi-hard dick.

"I think I have to use the bathroom," I said, sitting up from the bed, my arms crossed, covering my concave chest.

"It's over there." He pointed with his cigarette.

I got up, walked to the bathroom, and shut the door behind me. Before sitting down, I wiped the toilet seat with a few sheets of tissue. Damp towels cluttered the floor. There was sand all over the place. Why couldn't I have met someone who was staying at the Sheraton?

After a while, I realized that I did not really have to go, that it only felt as if I did, but nevertheless, I continued to sit. The bathroom had always been a haven for me, a private place to think things over (when I wasn't masturbating). It was the only place in the apartment where you could be alone. How I memorized the cracks and corners in the bathroom walls. Mom would also spend long stretches of time there, reading her Chinese movie magazines and novels. She kept the door cracked open in case she thought of something for us to do and had to tell us immediately. If I found the door closed I knew that she was probably upset with us.

I reviewed my present predicament: I was in a hotel room with a white man who looked older than Dad and who had just tried to fuck me. After a few more push-outs, my anus muscles relaxed. It was very late. Even though nothing had come out, I still wiped myself. I was like Mom that way—anal.

When I exited the bathroom another white man was sitting on the other bed. He had a beard and long hair down to his shoulders. He looked like Jesus.

"Tony," Jesus said. "I leave you alone for five minutes and you go dragging someone back."

I walked over to my clothes.

"Alan, Nelson. Nelson, Alan," Tony said, the sheet pulled up to his waist.

"Norman," I said to Alan, pulling on my underwear.

"Leaving?" Tony said to me. He turned to Alan. "It's my turn to have the room until five."

"Your turn. My turn. It's nobody's turn. It's late. I'm tired and I want to go to bed. We have a flight to catch tomorrow. Remember?"

They were leaving the next day. So soon. My affair with Tony was over. I would never see him again. I shook the sand out of my pants and slowly pulled them back on. Would I ever visit him? Instantly I felt melancholy.

"Look, you're scaring him off," Tony said. "Give me another hour, Alan." He squinted his eyes and smiled. The wrinkles multiplied.

"For ten dollars you get thirty minutes. I want to get something to eat downstairs."

"What happened to all your money?"

"Gone. Finished. *Pau.*"

"How do you plan to get to the airport?"

"In your cab."

"In that case, forty-five minutes."

"It's been nice meeting you, Nelson," Alan said.

Tony handed Alan a few dollars and Alan left the room.

"Have fun," he called as the door shut.

"Come here."

"I have to go."

"Come here." Tony patted the bed the way Dad had patted my butt to sleep when I was little. "Just one more little kiss, *sexy*." He pulled off the sheet and began to shake his semi-hard dick in my direction. "Come on, sexy baby. Just a little kiss."

I climbed back into bed.

AFTERWARD, WALKING OUT of the elevator, I found Alan reclining on the vinyl sofa, smoking a cigarette, his eyes closed, his legs crossed on top of the coffee table. The Filipina was now watching a small TV propped on the counter. It sounded like a police show. Gunshots fired. Alan opened his eyes as I walked past.

"Finally," he said. "I thought I would be sleeping here *again*." He put out his cigarette. "You're not staying the night?"

"No, I have to go home."

"Oh." He stood up and let out a big yawn. "I'm getting my second wind. Let's have a cup of coffee together." He got up and pulled me into the twenty-four-hour coffee shop.

Alan called across the empty dining room to the Filipina waitress, who looked like the sister of the woman in the lobby. "Two coffees." He led me to a window seat beside a box filled with plastic flowers.

"Decaf," I called to the waitress.

"Regular for me," Alan said. "I've poured so much into my poor body tonight that I don't think another cup of caffeine will matter."

The waitress arrived with two cups of black coffee, a bowl of miniature half-and-halfs, and two menus. After she left I picked up a menu.

"Are you having something to eat?" Alan asked.

"Maybe."

"I know I shouldn't," Alan said, picking up his menu. "But let's just see what they have here. Maybe something light. What are you thinking of having?"

"A kona burger."

"That's a little too heavy for me."

He lit another cigarette and blew a cloud of smoke at the window, which deflected back at me.

"What are you having?"

"Something light," he said again. "Maybe the Hawaiian French toast with coconut syrup."

Mom loved Hawaiian French toast, made with Portuguese bread. When Mom and I would go to a coffee shop together after her evening shift at the restaurant, she'd always order the Hawaiian French toast. She'd pay for the late-night snack with her wrinkled tip money.

After the Filipina waitress had taken our orders and left with the menus, Alan asked me, "What do you do?"

"I just finished high school," I said. "I'll be going to college next month. In Chicago."

"Oh. I have relatives in Chicago. It's a nice city. Big. Visited it when I was fifteen. It gets really cold there during the winter. Why do you want to go there?"

It's far away from my family. "Oh, I don't know. What do you do?" I asked Alan.

"I'm a waiter."

"At Tony's restaurant?"

"Is that what he told you? It's not his restaurant. He's just the daytime manager the last I checked."

"I think he told me he owned it."

"In his dreams. That's what he tells all of them. Mr. Entrepreneur himself. Oh, I'm sorry. I'm being mean. I don't even know you, Nelson."

"It's Norman."

"Norman, did you grow up in Hawaii?"

"Yes. And you?"

"I'm originally from Michigan—U.P., Upper Peninsula. I moved here ten years ago. But after a couple years in Honolulu, I wanted to move to an even smaller town, so I chose one in Maui. Been living there for the past four years and love it. Tony and I come to Honolulu a few times a year when we get the itch to be in a *big* city." He let the burning cigarette between his fingers come to a crash landing in the ashtray. "How old are you?"

"Seventeen."

"Statutory rape. I'm going to tell." He laughed. "Oh, don't look so scared. I'm not going to tell."

I wasn't scared. "How old are you?" I asked.

"Now, that's not nice," he said.

"How old is Tony?" I asked.

"He's old enough to be your father, you little chick. But I'm being mean again."

"Oh."

"He likes them young. He says it keeps him young."

"Can I ask you a question?"

"Only if I don't need to answer. Go ahead."

"When did you know that you were gay?"

"The day I was born!"

"I mean, when was the first time you slept with another guy?"

"I guess when I was around twelve. With my best friend and next-door neighbor, Jimmy Kelman."

"Oh."

"Boy love. And you? Don't tell me Tony's your first?"

"Yeah."

"Oh, my god. You are young. Did you tell him? He'd love it. How was it? Was he good to you? Did you guys do the *nasty*?"

"I don't think so."

"Are you okay? You look a little shook up. Some water? Water, please," Alan called to the waitress.

The waitress arrived with our food. She set down the plates, a bottle of ketchup, and a dispenser filled with coconut syrup. Alan proceeded to pour the thick, white, creamy syrup all over his French toast.

"I'm okay," I continued, picking up a French fry. "It's just that I'm only getting used to being gay. I'm just . . . coming out of . . . the closet."

"It's difficult," Alan said sympathetically, his mouth full of French toast. "My own mother still doesn't like it. Do your parents know?"

"No," I said. I stopped eating.

"Are you going to tell them before you go off to college?"

"No." I lost my appetite.

"Everything in its own time, that's what I say."

Soon he finished off the last bite of his toast and swallow of his coffee. I scraped the grilled onions off my untouched burger and reached for the ketchup.

"Are you going to eat your onions?"

"No. You want them?"

"Sure."

Alan reached over with his fork and scraped them off my plate onto his, into a sea of coconut syrup.

"Being gay isn't easy," he said. "It's not one big bar under white lights for the rest of your life, let me tell you. It's also a lot of hangovers, regrets, and 'Will he ever call me again?' "

He finished off the onions and then lit another cigarette. The waitress arrived with two glasses of water and a pot of coffee. She refilled our cups. I knew it was regular and not decaf.

"Anything else?" she asked.

"No."

She pulled a check from her apron and set it on the table. I picked it up and offered to pay, knowing that Alan didn't even have enough money to take a cab to the airport tomorrow.

"That's very nice of you," he said. "You don't know how broke I am. I owe you a meal. Next time you're in Maui, come by Mary's. Hamburger Mary's. It's right on the beach. You can't miss it. All the girls hang out there."

Tony walked into the coffee shop.

"So there you are. And you," he said to me. "I thought you had to go home. Moving in on my man, aren't you, Alan? Move over," he said to me.

I slid across the sticky booth toward the dusty plastic flowers.

"Don't be so possessive," Alan retorted. "We're just having a cup of coffee together."

"It always begins with coffee."

"Is it all right to go back to the room now, Tony?"

"Yeah, get out of here."

Alan looked at me and said, "It's been nice chatting with you. I wish you the best of luck on the mainland. See you in Maui." He offered me his hand.

As soon as Alan left the coffee shop, Tony asked me, "You want to come back up?"

"Alan'll be up there."

"We won't do anything, just sleep peacefully in each other's arms."

"I have to go home. I have to wake up early."

"Did I hurt you?"

"No. I just have to go."

"Your first time, huh?"

"Yeah."

"I'm your first. Wow. I guess I wasn't listening. It's just that you're so sexy that I got all excited."

"Oh. Thanks."

"You want some dessert?"

"No."

"How about some German sausage?"

"Huh?"

"I'm German."

"Oh." I thought Tony was white. German was white, I guessed. Under the table, he held my hand and guided it to his sausage, already hard. "You know you're very pretty."

I knew what he was doing, but then again, no one had ever called me pretty or sexy or anything nice before.

"I can't go back with you. My mother is probably wondering where I am."

"Just for a little while. I'll be nice to you. I promise. Please."

Begging. Guilt.

"With a cherry on top."

I left the money for the check on the table and followed Tony out. Back in his room, Alan was already in bed, naked and snoring, his butt shiny in the moonlight. In seconds, Tony slipped out of his tank top and shorts and jumped into his bed. He held his arms out to me. Again, I unbuttoned my shirt and pulled off my khakis and underwear; this time piling them on the chair, beside the damp trunks. Then I went to the bathroom to pee.

Trickle, trickle. When I was little, Mom would get mad at me for urinating in bed. Then I became permanently afraid of peeing in bed. I would often attempt to pee, even if I didn't really have to. Some fears you never outgrow.

Back in the room again, Tony lifted up the sheet for me to get under with him. We kissed. It tasted like coffee and cigarettes. He pushed my head downward. Other than Tony, Dad was the only man I'd ever slept with in the same bed. I wondered if Tony would pat my butt to sleep, like Dad did. I remembered the time when Dad freed my penis from my zipper. "It's all right. Stop crying." Tony's butt felt fleshy and moist. I held on for my life.

Afterward, I went to the bathroom to rinse out my mouth and attempted to pee again. When I returned to the room this time, both Tony and Alan were snoring. I got back into bed with Tony. There was only a little room for me, at the edge of the bed. Tony probably didn't even know I was there. When I slept with Dad, sometimes he would abandon me in the middle of the night, disappearing for hours. Only after he returned could I fall back asleep.

I slipped out of bed and dressed. Outside the hotel the sky was lighting up. I had to rush home, a newly converted vampire. In a few hours I would go with Mom to the mall to shop for a new coat for the mainland. It got cold in Chicago, colder than it ever got in Hawaii.

OUT-TAKES

Ron Caldwell

I.

ARE THOSE WHO read psychoanalysis destined to live it? I came out to my sister by a combination of wish fulfillment and a Freudian slip, which I used to think was the thing that stuck out from underneath my mother's dress.

Stacy dated a large lunk of a boy named Todd when she was a junior in high school, in 1983. He was the laconic type, a sphinx without a secret. I think he must have been either incredibly bored with us or incredibly frightened. Todd had dropped Stacy off after a movie. I assume they made out in the car for a little while, but not too long, since my father would most certainly have been peeking out the window of his darkened bedroom, waiting to pounce on the opportunity to accuse Todd of untoward behavior, or my sister of coming on to her boyfriend like a Jezebel.

I was home on a weekend visit from college. By the time Stacy came into the house, our parents and our little brother were asleep. I met her with a hug at the back door and we crept into her bedroom and talked until past midnight. She and Todd had gone to see *Psycho II* and she, having the most vivid imagination in our family, was still a little frightened. We had already opened up to each other in many ways; we'd even had long talks about sex. I was anxious that she should have more information so that she could enjoy herself but keep from getting pregnant, and hoped to mitigate whatever guilt she might feel. But that night we just talked about the movies, gossiped, and commiserated about life in our peculiar family.

We fell asleep on her bed. At some point, I rolled over in the darkness, put my arm around her, and said, "Tony, I love you with all my heart." She woke up in time to hear it, and didn't go back to sleep the rest of the night.

It was two months before Stacy was able to sit me down and ask what it meant, only telling me the story after she'd inquired whether I really was in love with Tony. She had no one in our tiny Bible Belt town of Atlanta, Texas, to talk with about it, but by then she had accustomed herself to the idea and was *fine* with it. But she didn't tell anyone else.

MY FAMILY MAY appear at the outset as typically East Texas, but I was born in Houston, lived there until I was ten, and went back as soon as I was old enough to go to college. We had urban roots. My mother's family was partly Jewish; I was raised in the Episcopal church, in some ways, for me at least, a much more liberal and liberating background than that of some of my friends in Atlanta, who were Fundamentalists.

From an early age I was aware of gay people. My parents had a close friendship with a male couple in Houston, and my mother's uncle is gay. It was not a difference that was of particular concern or interest, and did not carry with it, within my immediate family, any particular fear. That my parents expected, up till I was a young adult, for me to live pretty much the way they had goes without saying, but their attitude toward my sister's, brother's, and my sexual orientations, choices, and commitments was always accepting.

I've always been odd, and plenty of boys in grammar school called me "faggot" and "fruit" and "sissy" before I understood what the words implied; I could hear the hatred or revulsion, but not the meaning. I didn't mind being in love with Bobby Sherman, but I knew I wasn't supposed to tell anybody. When I was five and my father twenty-seven, I developed limp wrists and he became apoplectic (we used to worry about those elusive neighbors we never knew).

Although I had, on several occasions, brought my lover to my parents', they didn't figure out what our relationship was. Since they had moved after I graduated from high school, I didn't have my own bedroom; they would put us in one queen-size bed, something my parents would never do with my brother and sister and their significant others—not before marriage, at least. I don't know what they'd have thought had they found Tony and me humping in the den in the middle of the night.

When I was twenty-one and she forty, in 1984, I sat my mother down and told her everything, to keep her on my side—to preserve the banality of my homosexuality in her mind, the first step in really coopting her. I wrote about it shortly thereafter:

EXPLAINING THINGS TO MOM

No, I do not think that it is tragic
Or unbearably lonely, not
Fearful or sordid or unpleasant.

It isn't hardness or intrusion of
One into one crouched on knees,
Dug into mattresses, not all
Bitter, broken idols, weakness.

I hold her hand, we sit
On the sofa and I wonder
What "happy" has meant
To her and my father
For twenty-five years.
We don't have exactly
What they have, no . . .

Ours is a soft, gentle
Sameness: Let-us-touch-
At-every-point for a moment.
She must understand
The touch of a stubbled face
Burning across lips
At four o'clock in the morning.

Nowadays, if my mother calls after a guy has stayed the night, I'll roll over, pick up the phone, and tell her, with a giggle, what we've been doing—in general terms. (She's particularly amused by stories that feature handcuffs.) This does not seem to me to be strange, and she's not scandalized. There might have been a time when shock value was my motive, but I don't think that's the case anymore. She seems genuinely glad to know that I'm not keeping anything important from her. She is good and gracious and witty, and she seems to like my friends. She has never treated my misery at the hands of love with anything short of acceptance and compassion.

The official coming out to my father wasn't for another few years. I had finished my master's thesis, a book of verse, at Boston University. Dad had expressed a little curiosity about what I was writing, but I was for the most part reticent to share it with him. Part of this had to do with the rocky nature of our relationship, which had never been very good. From where I stood he was The Law, a disciplinarian at home and a policeman abroad; I was afraid of him and could not confide in him. When I was twenty, in a stupid argument over the telephone, I'd let drop that I was completely and utterly and hopelessly miserable and it was all his fault. With a cache of gay sonnets out in the world, though, I felt I had to tell him. So I did the safe thing: I wrote him a letter.

3-4 ii 88

Dear Dad—
    Here's a letter to serve as an introduction to my thesis, which I sent via Mom some days ago and asked that she have bound. I think the

printing came out pretty well. Though I have worked on many of the pieces for a long time, it still feels incomplete. I'm glad to have gotten it out of the way. Now I hope that I'll have some incentive to send some of them out and try to get published. We'll see.

All that business is secondary to the reason I'm writing today, which has more to do with the content of some of the poems. You're not naïve; I'm sure that nothing of mine that you have read or will read shocks you in the least, though you might be surprised to see how much of my private life has burst onto the printed page. That could be a little uncomfortable, since we've never spoken about many of the thoughts, feelings, and philosophies you'll find that I have often and, sometimes I hope, provocatively expressed on the pages of my thesis.

Working this business out—how much to reveal, when, to whom—has occupied me for a long time, not so much because of my own insecurities, as a total uncertainty about how my "audience" would react. That's something none of us can ever know, so it makes little sense to second-guess and worry. With this letter and my thesis in your hands (or at least in your house), you can see the culmination of that process: A very important part of my life—its past, present, and future—is my involvement with other men. It colors my ideas and actions; it is sometimes central, sometimes trivial and amusing, but it is always there. It is time, I think, to reconcile my public and private selves with who I am in our family.

If I were more optimistic (or maybe stupid or callous or crazy), I'd say that this shouldn't make any difference to you. We've lived with the reality of my homosexuality for a long time without expressing the fact. You and I want different things out of life, and play different roles. These things alone mean that there will be differences in the ways we understand and work within the world. That is not to say that there is any insurmountable misunderstanding, nor has anything negative come to light. Because of your perspective this may be a challenge, but you're not alone. I'm here to help make sense of it for you as best I can.

You should know that I take my sexuality for granted, as everyone should. It would be silly, painful, and wrong to deny it and pretend that I am or could be different from the way I am, just as it would make little or no sense to see being gay as the central issue in my life all the time. It is a political problem a lot of the time. Sometimes taking political stands is important—and I'm not afraid or embarrassed to speak out to ensure that I and others like me are accepted as worthwhile citizens, productive people, with all the rights anyone should have by virtue of being born into the world. And with no fewer responsibilities. I haven't the slightest desire to prove anything political to you. This is about your being my father and my being your child.

The other time when my being gay is most central to my life is when love is involved. Then there will be a discernible difference. In my still rather short life, I have only been in love with Tony, and our relationship has lasted—and faltered, sometimes—for over five years. When it has faltered, it has been because our personalities and inclinations have been stretched to the limit, not because of any inherent flaw in the way that we love. Love is generic, I think, and always boundless, no matter who the lovers are. And life for us is not bizarre—it's fairly calm and domestic. For men in love the major difference is that the rules for taking care of each other are not always apparent. Decency, respect, attention, and devotion are still the operative words, though. We just don't seem to have too many models for the way we conduct our lives.

Besides making the poems a little more palatable, I write to let you know that I believe that the responsibility for bringing all of this out into the open rests with both of us. I can't do it alone. I'm not particularly shy about being gay, but there have rarely been ideal moments to talk these things out. When we see each other, neither of us wants to upset the proverbial apple cart. I'm much less inhibited when I write than I am in person—I am more comfortable here on the page, without the tension and second-guessing. And I can express myself at my own pace.

I'm not afraid of your rejecting me—I know that would never occur to you. You have never wanted me to feel alienated. What I want most is for you to feel you know and understand me better. I hope you don't think that my being gay is bad, or even unusual. It just *is*. After some time and practice you may even champion the cause—inasmuch as it is a cause. Nothing has changed except my willingness to express this. I am the same man who was the Eagle Scout, trumpet player, acolyte, and opinionated little man you've watched grow. But perhaps I will be all the more real, complete. You've always expected a lot out of me. Well, there's a lot here—it just might not be what you expected.

If there is anything I can do to make this easier, any questions I can answer, please call or write, and don't feel like you should be inhibited, either. I'm not defensive—I want whatever respect I'm due, regardless of and including my sexuality.

I hope you'll be interested to some extent, and that we'll be able to talk about this openly and unashamedly. That may take some time. It's taken twenty-five years to write this letter. I'm certainly not rushing anything.

Thanks for your patience, attention, and understanding, Dad.

"Love has no position, / Love's a way of living, / One kind of relation / Possible between / Any things or persons," according to W. H. Auden, a poet whom [our parish priest] referred to last Christmas as "a notorious homosexual"—whatever that means. Take care.

Love,

Ron

My letter makes me squirm now. I should have been more casual and blunt—but I was so much older then. Nonetheless, it served its purpose. The night he read it, my father phoned right away. He told me about his own gay friends, a couple named Larry and Ben, whom he and my mother had been close to in the sixties; he said it didn't matter, that he'd thought for a long time I might be gay, and just wanted me to be happy. I still don't really confide in him, but there is an understanding between us. We have far to go, but my being gay isn't at issue.

My father did, however, ask me, when I came out to him, to hold off telling my little brother until he got out of high school. Dad thought Bret might have trouble understanding, that it might throw him into a tailspin and affect his work. That seemed reasonable and prudent, and I agreed.

Bret and I were raised in the same house, but under very different circumstances. Because of the seven-year gap in our ages, we hardly knew each other before he went to college. My sister, brother, and I had the same senior English teacher in high school, Ms. Trumble. In my glory days, I had been her champion ready-writer. (Oh, for half the *chutzpah* and a quarter of the feverish concentration I had then.) Those poor students who followed me, including Stacy and Bret, had to read and discuss my essays. I loved Ms. Trumble (and still do); she adored language and was a very witty woman who wore bold print blouses and A-line skirts. She was a divorced Roman Catholic, Mr. Trumble having run off with a younger woman.

Naturally enough, my sister and brother felt quite differently about her. But Bret was aware of how much she had liked me and, when he found out that some of my poems had appeared in a literary journal, he thought she'd like to see them. He took the journal from my parents' nightstand, slipped it into his knapsack, and drove off to school. English was first period; he had an in-class writing assignment. He gave the journal to Ms. Trumble, told her I had some poetry in it, and went to work. Later on in the class, Ms. Trumble thanked him and gave him back the journal. He returned to his seat, found my name in the Table of Contents, and flipped to this poem:

AN OTHER

Below his eye a bright blue vein—
Sleeplessness or age or nothing
But a variable to distinguish him
From others in a small way. Watching,
The composite is not half bad.
Twirl his hair through my fingers,
Close my eyes and sense the mattress
Rising up from the floor to meet us,
The draft blowing through the crevices
To chill our pasty feet. Then he does
The predictable expedient daring
Thing with gallant trepidation,
As if he were asking first, expecting
Denial. We have stood and embraced.
We have lain quite naked in full view
In the early light. We have walked

Arm in arm, forsaking nothing. It
Seems fine. Oh, but darling,
You are not the one to carry me
Through the day, not the one I would
Give up a good game of conversation
For. Some unsympathetic teacher
Taught me to look out for my spot
In a world-historical couple,
Not to settle for less: to find
The company of one who, with me,
Would land us in the pages of Dante,
Fiery passion and misunderstanding
In this world, and in the other.

Until that moment Bret had no idea I was gay. With the current of realization growing in his mind arose the terror of having brought me out to Ms. Trumble. It took us quite a few phone calls to get him through it. In the ensuing years, Bret's been my greatest political ally. He might have been even more pleased if I'd turned out to be African American, but my difference, such as it is, has been a touchstone for his own development as a good and gracious activist. I'm a very lucky man.

II.

I'm not sure I know exactly what "out" means. The queerer I get, the less I notice the abstract, though stark, contrast between myself and everybody else, and the less concerned I am about it. My being odd to the straight world is no longer new to me; by extension, what presumably links me to the millions of other people with whom I share this label seems less and less clear.

Coming out comes up all the time—on a date, when the moment of silence becomes unpleasant, because either too little or too much is happening over the dinner table. It's a convenient topic of conversation. On the other hand, I have no earthly idea what it means to be completely out, out of the closet. For a very long time, it seemed to me I didn't really have to come out at all, that somehow my mere aspect conveyed to the world that I was gay. As for letting most people in on the truth, sometimes all it takes is a certain intensity of focus in one's gaze, an indeterminate posture, a gesture. Sometimes, no matter how obvious I try to make it, the message doesn't get through. Sometimes one just has to make a little speech about it, or write a letter.

Maybe I am one of a generation that has not known the kind of oppression experienced by my—what shall I call them?—*forelovers*, those men who found themselves in the arms of other men and liking it. I have not been photographed in public often enough with another man in my arms.

I remember a meeting of the Rice University Gay and Lesbian Alliance held at the apartment of a graduate student or renegade faculty member, I'm not sure which, in 1982. Those were somber days. Something had begun to kill us, but we knew not what it was. One had to call a number to get directions about where the meetings took place. The members would consent to appear in the yearbook, but only wearing brown paper bags over their heads. I don't like paper hats. Brown doesn't become me.

I was very much in love with Tony, a tall, handsome, ultimately unfaithful tennis player my age who'd transferred from Sewanee under a cloud. He lived on the second floor of the dormitory and I could hardly remember having a life before I met him. Everyone at Rice knew we were lovers—they had all figured it out before it was clear to the two of us—but no one gave us any grief about it. Tony and I went to the Gay and Lesbian Alliance because we wanted to meet other couples and find out how to *be*.

The talk at the meeting was lugubrious. We all sat around in a circle and, instead of jerking off like we probably wanted to, each person related what it was like for him to come out of the closet. When it came my turn, I looked at the question, and at the men who had spoken before me, and thought that I, too, must answer. But I couldn't. I was either so well adjusted to my sexuality that I'd never seen the need formally to announce it, or I was so naïve that I didn't know the extent to which I was in denial. Granted, I had not yet told my family. My last girlfriend had found out through direct revelation, when she asked why I was being so distant and I burst out with it. She quickly took up with an intelligent but boring doofus with very long arms, reckless driving habits, and an extremely weak chin, who was cold on the question of marriage. But even boys on my hall, who seemed to me the most typical of macho American chemical engineering students, knew and didn't quake when we stood naked together in the communal shower. Tony and I were the subjects of gossip—which, if anything, I cultivated. As far as I know, we were not held up as objects of ridicule.

Once my father came to Houston with his friend Dennis, to the house I shared with Tony and a pair of straight friends. Dad and Dennis had a few hours to kill before they made some sort of business contact or connection. Dennis was wild in a conventional way; when he was away from his second wife, he liked to party. (No doubt that was how he'd met her, when he was on vacation from his first.) All the way down, Dennis had been insisting that my father, a devoted husband, go with him to Caligula XXI. My father didn't want to be a pill, but he didn't want to go unchaperoned to a sex club and leave open the possibility that Dennis would carry stories that weren't true back to Atlanta. Dad asked if I'd come along. I certainly did not want to, but there was pressure and bravado and nervousness. I convinced my lover to join us. At least we would have our own story to tell, I reasoned.

The four of us piled into a supercab pickup truck and drove out, out into the wilderness of strip malls that is South Texas, way out on the wrong end of Westheimer, to a large, irregularly shaped building hung with banners and plastic flags like the ones strung over used-car lots. We parked and went inside. Caligula XXI stank of smoke and drink and vinyl and Naugahyde and dust. Quite a few men stood around or were sitting, being served watered-down drinks by oddly unprepossessing women who looked not at all happy to be there.

Before long, Dennis ordered us a round of drinks, then began to wave a twenty-dollar bill at a heavy woman who looked about six months pregnant, with dimples and dark, sallow skin. She began to dance to the song that was already playing, jiggling her breasts in front of Dennis, wiggling her not insubstantial ass in his face while he laughed like an eight-year-old with his first porno magazine. When that ended, Dennis decided to procure a dancer for me. About five-foot-two and weighing at most ninety pounds soaking wet, she had the body of a prepubescent girl, with preternaturally small breasts.

Tony sat beside me, a hard, tense smile plastered on his face. The dancer ground her ass in my direction without actually touching me; she jiggled her small breasts in my face, wiggling and gyrating in various not very attractive ways (a comparable man doing the same things wouldn't have been any more appealing). The song was long and loud; at some point, Tony got up and ran out. Although I wasn't yet ready to make any confessions to my father and Dennis, I did whisper to the dancer that I was gay and ask her to stop. "Just relax," she said, "I'm almost done." When she finished, Dennis, the picture of macho glee, tipped her and ordered another drink. I went to look for Tony, and found him in tears in the parking lot.

Years later, I discovered that this had been the point at which my parents first spoke to each other about the possibility that I might be gay. Tony's reaction had been enough to convince them that *he* was. I think the incident was a marker of sorts. Although my father was not sure I was gay, he never afterward asked me whom I was dating or when I was planning to get married. My mother didn't tell my father after I told her—partly because she wanted me to tell him when I was ready, and partly, I think, because she wanted it to remain our secret.

Mostly, my coming to terms with—and bringing other people along in accepting—my sexuality seems to have occurred as a series of vignettes:

Marvin, a clerk at Sakowitz in downtown Houston, says I can borrow three pairs of theatrical tights if I tell him what I think about when I masturbate. I need the tights for a scene from *The Taming of the Shrew* we're doing in English class. I say, "Well, I think about sex mostly." "Do you ever think about men?" "Sure. I mean, sometimes. Doesn't everybody?" "No, not really, everybody doesn't." He suggests that we go and do something about it. I demur. He might have handed me the key to my sexual identity, but he was married; from my point of view at the time, he was old; I didn't like him. (Not that I wouldn't give in eventually.) A month later, Scott, my roommate, on the platform bed ten feet away, asks me if I've ever thought about having sex with a man. I had; we did. Seminal moment. We would have a close and turbulent sexual friendship. He would ask me to dress up as a cowboy. Later, he would suggest that I do myself in with a pair of single-edged razor blades provided by him. (I found out early that shared oppression doesn't guarantee solidarity.) The rest I've already told you.

My life is, I think, on a relative scale of human existence, pretty happy. I have many close friends who care about me and engage me in interesting ways. They form the backbone of my emotional life. Since I discovered that I am gay, sometime around my freshman or sophomore year in college, I have been involved—romantically, sexually—with men. For five years, I shared my life with Tony. We lived and traveled and planned and slept together, and it all ended rather badly, not unlike many complex marriages among bright and ambitious young straight people. I have dated lots of other guys, one for over a year; some of them have become close friends in their own right. Everyone I have gotten to know from the time I was nineteen or twenty has had full knowledge of my situation, and those who have been resistant have either been left behind or left me behind. Being gay is not something I worry about.

I can see no reason for my general attitude to change. The important things I wish for my life are things that I wish for the world: that it were kinder to those who have no one to hold them and listen to them; that people move from intolerance, not to tolerance but to full understanding; that rigid norms based on fear and inexperience be put away. It occurs to me that there is not only no harm in my being who I am, there may be good in it.

These days, I wear a ring in each ear. The word *gay* appears in my curriculum vitae quite a few times. I volunteer at Gay Men's Health Crisis. I don't have any trouble emoting. I write stories about men having sex with each other, poems about the love of men I have never been or am no longer involved with. I love to look at men's bodies, to feel them, to watch the way they react or respond to pleasure. My greatest role in the amateur theater of life: Queen Leer. Every time I fall in love with a man on the subway takes me farther and farther away from that elusive crystalline norm most people hold themselves up to or against, the way of life they defend so loudly that it sounds like they're protesting too much. Do I reserve some secret patch of ambiguity I can transgress against? Sure I do. But until the collective groan of straight life dies in me, I'll be outing myself—to myself and everybody else—all the time.

A N T

Scott Heim

I WAS SEVENTEEN when pornography first slammed my senses. I hadn't prepared myself. It was November 1983, and I'd arrived at a friend's election party in skinny tie, scarlet pants, bowling shoes—"punk," as yokels in my minuscule Kansas town termed it. Inside, twelve females and males huddled unchaperoned around a TV. The hostess had strategically placed vodka and scotch amid the card table's bowls of popcorn, cashews, cinnamon bears, and ice cubes molded into tiny donkey and elephant heads. Since no one cared about the election results, between updates we'd press the Play button on the absent parents' VCR. There it was, porn, scenes from a videotape a sandy-haired boy had rented. After a few minutes, most of the males present had centered pillows in their laps or swiveled to lie on the carpet.

That porn film became the room's volcano. We were stunned and burned by it, but helplessly immobile. Everyone fell silent; or, rather, the occasional laugh or crass opinion went unheard. I couldn't help but focus on one actor's penis. It seemed massive, unreal. The actress, Marilyn Chambers, stretched out on a pool table, leaned her head over its edge and planted the cock in her mouth. "Damn," someone said, "you can see it in her throat." The girls *oob*ed and *yuck*ed, but I pressed my pillow closer. I felt I'd been punched between the eyes, over and over and over. Would anyone notice I was aiming my attention on the actor instead of Ms. Chambers? After he came on her face, someone's finger stabbed the Stop button. We saw the latest precinct figures for Rice County, and I knew I'd returned to reality, to small-town Midwest teenage life, where tangible flesh-to-flesh contact didn't exist.

Later, home past curfew, I grappled with what I remembered of that flurry of sucking and fucking, those tits and cocks and cunts. I tiptoed through the living room. There, in a buttery vee of lamplight, I saw my mother, waiting up for me in the antique rocker she'd recently upholstered. The scotch glass glittered in her hand, resembling something pulled from a treasure chest. "You're late," she said.

During my high school years, my mother maintained a surprising level of trust and leniency. She often offered wise bits of advice, but remained misguided on any matter regarding sex. She was the woman who, years earlier, had answered my question about the homosexuals depicted on Anita Bryant's TV program with a deft, "Oh, they're bad people who live in cities and play with themselves a lot." She'd dismissed the evidence of my older sister's menstruation by explaining that she'd "cut herself down there."

Hmmmm. On that night, I knew my mother would inquire about the party. Half of me wanted to extricate myself from an explanation. The other half, in an uncharacteristic move, decided to sketch an outline of the film I'd just seen, to get my mother's reaction.

As expected, her opinion didn't deviate much from that of the females at the party. When I told a tamer version of the pool table scene, she muttered "Yikes," her favorite word. I explained how my male classmates appeared pale, flustered, fidgety. Then I slipped in the detail of the pillows. My stomach felt fizzy: It thrilled me to speak to my mother about sex, after all these years. "They obviously had hard-ons," I told her. "One kid practically whipped it out right there."

Perhaps it was the animation with which I described my male accomplices' reactions, the way I dwelled on their expressions, their exclamations, the fine tuning of their positions in that room. Maybe, with both of us drunk, my mother deemed it time for the shell of our conversation to crack. Or maybe, there in the dark room smelling of the wood stove and her cheap booze, she saw me as I might have appeared to an interloper, to someone other than family: a boy wearing red pants and bowling shoes, lip gloss, a haircut spiked and painted in a disarrayed bouquet. Whatever the case, my mother mustered the nerve for something she'd obviously been wanting to ask. "Scott," she said, her voice smoothed to a whisper. Her tone shut me up, hoisted my heart three inches higher in my chest. I felt it happening. "I'm going to ask you a question now, and I want you to tell me the truth."

I paused. *She knew.* "Is it what I think you're going to ask?"

She took a sip, finishing the scotch. "Probably so."

I looked away. "Then don't ask it," I said. The lamp seemed brighter, as if its bulb were bursting. I thought about sitting beside my mother, but didn't. Instead, I left the room.

I hobbled jelly-legged upstairs, then collapsed on my bed. The porn film seemed days, weeks ago. My mother had come so close to asking me, and I had demolished my chance. Here I was, unafraid to dress for school in space garb one day, Renaissance the next, yet I couldn't confess my sexuality to my mother. I was a total failure. I knew it would take something major, some bizarre circumstance or catastrophe, to get her to ask again, to get me to reveal myself. I fumbled with a record and lowered the needle, the volume soft, to usher me toward sleep.

BACK THEN, MUSIC governed my life. It still does, I suppose, but at seventeen, the bands I loved seemed so profound, every lyric speaking directly to *me*. I was floundering for an identity, and my favorite British New Wavers delivered it. A recurring memory shows me pogoing and lip-synching in front of my bedroom mirror. Mom would *knock-knock-knock.* "Can't you turn that crap down a little?" she'd ask. I never did.

I had three loyal friends, all girls. They were my partners in crime, and together we made a quartet of outcasts, the weirdos of Little River, Kansas. Traci, Deb, Lori, and Scott. With New Wave as accompaniment, we dressed in the thrift-store rags or garish costumes of our favorite bands. We wore makeup, a lot for the girls, a little for me. We dyed our hair; decorated it with feathered roach clips; spiked it with twisted pipe cleaners. (Deb's hairstyle saw the most metamorphoses that year; once, after applying a red food coloring rinse, she got caught in a rainstorm and wound up resembling Sissy Spacek in the finale of *Carrie.*)

Daring and outlandish, yes, but we were far from perfect. The girls were either considerably over- or underweight. We all had some feature most teenagers would deem unsightly: an upturned, porcine nose; spectacle lenses thick as Coke bottle bottoms; a forehead speckled with zits. And I was gay, although I'd yet to tell anyone. For Traci, Deb, Lori, and me, dressing as those British band members afforded the possibility that, instead of our enemies calling us "fat cow," "ugly bitch," or "fucking faggot," we might instead be called something like "weirdo" or "punk." Now *those* were names we could handle.

My status as hometown New Wave freak, then, was my first "coming out." I exposed myself as someone eccentric, nonconformist, unafraid to take chances. Not that it was hard to be distinctive in Little River. With a population slightly under one thousand, the community prided itself on a devotion to Sunday church services, school board meetings, and the random Main Street hootenanny, music provided by a local country-western outfit. My friends and I gritted our teeth and waited for graduation's inevitable deliverance. Until then, we were content to gather during lunch hour in the school gym to blast tapes of our latest records, our cowboy-booted classmates glaring as if we belonged among Satan's profane legions.

One of our favorite bands was Adam and the Ants. They wore satiny pirate pants, Spanish military jackets, Indian warrior gear. Their album *Kings of the Wild Frontier* seemed the appropriate sound track for our lives. When the group's leader, Adam Ant, sang about a "new breed" of outcasts who would "welcome tomorrow / instead of yesterday" and soar above the rest, I considered him spokesperson for me and my pals. Weekends, away from schoolmates, we would gawk at photos of the Ants, their tribal rhythms blaring from Traci's bedroom stereo's puny speakers. Then we'd dress up. I still have a photo of

Traci, hair spiked into a blonde crown, white lines crisscrossing her face like war paint. In another, I'm pouting at the camera, glittery silver stars trailing an arc from my eyelinered eye to my lipsticked mouth.

WHEN THE TIME came, Traci and I defected together. In 1985, we enrolled as freshmen at Kansas University, abandoning Little River for Lawrence, beginning the "next stage of our lives" so many parents and other well-wishers preached about.

Liberal KU rescued me from both Little River's oppressive atmosphere and my mother's whacked-out ideas about sex (she still hadn't asked that important question; I wasn't planning on telling her, anyway). After first semester, I began associating with other "freaks"—specifically, other New Wave devotees and, every now and again, queers. I remember the first time I met Brad, a dude who routinely played New Wave music at Exile, a downtown record store where he worked. He wore black skirts, makeup, crucifixes bigger than butcher knives. I complimented his outfits. In return, he gave me discounts on LPs, an easy avenue to my heart's sloppy center.

But Traci proved my true conduit to meeting other queers. She lived in Hashinger, the dormitory everyone gossiped about. It was the creative arts dorm. Its rooms hosted poets, musicians, actors, artists, lesbians, gays, vegetarians, punks and mods, Grateful Dead followers, and, rumor had it, witches. I visited as often as possible. My eyes wandered. Even my wildest appearances couldn't compare with Hashinger's finest.

Traci was with me, too, when I saw my first gay porn film. It happened in her eighth-floor dorm room. She and I crowded with her slew of new friends in front of a TV screen the width of a bread loaf's heel. When the horror movie grew boring, a guy headed for his room and brought back a shoplifted videotape. "Hey, let's watch this." We dimmed the lights, burned candles, trained our faces on the action.

If the Marilyn Chambers tape had punched me in the gut, this one—a William Higgins gem called *Big Guns*—removed my guts and shredded them. The movie left me breathless and slightly nauseated. It assaulted my senses, stunned me, and blurred my vision to such an extent I could only remember pieces of it when, alone in my room later, I tried to mold *Big Guns* into masturbation fantasies. An oily massage in a motel room; two guys suggestively aiming firearms at targets; a mustachioed dude propping a blond boy on a table and fucking him senseless.

Not long after *Big Guns*, I scheduled a time to tell Traci I was gay. She deserved the truth more than anyone, more than my family. I chose an evening while lounging in her dorm room, music thundering. I counted one-two-three. "Guess what?" She softened the volume, and I rested my head in her lap.

That night fit the mold of confession many are familiar with: the creepy-crawly stomach, the labored disclosure, her casual acceptance. Looking back, I wonder: How could she not have known? The pictures from our Little River High days, ordered chronologically in my photo album, make it obvious with a capital O. I still wince at them. Here we are, posing beside a sideshow at the Kansas State Fair. She's wearing her Adam and the Ants T-shirt. My arm's curled around her shoulders, taking care not to brush her breasts, and my spiked haircut's striped with blond and orange. I can almost hear the catcalls as the passersby watched us pose: "Faggot!"

AFTER SPRING SEMESTER of my sophomore year, I decided to remain in Lawrence. Traci packed up and returned to Little River for the summer. For the first time, I felt a strange solitude; without her, I lacked all hometown ties. Two friends and I found an apartment near campus, and to pay rent I monitored the front desk at one of the student dormitories. Some nights I'd work until midnight, others until four.

Returning from Pearson Hall, I'd drive the route that curved past the grassy hill overlooking KU's football stadium. On that road, at the pinnacle of campus, was the university bell tower. The Campanile, as everyone called it, stood tall and narrow, with flesh-colored brick and a white, illuminated tip, such an obvious symbol that people had stopped joking about it. On the sloping hill beneath it were oaks, cottonwoods, mulberry trees, lilac bushes, and an eerie pond still haunted, word had it, by a philosophy major who had drowned in the fifties.

As an innocent freshman, I'd been entranced by the drowning legend. Now I held a different fascination for the place. The Campanile had earned a sort of notoriety for being the main cruising ground for Lawrence queers. Since Lawrence lacked a gay bar, men both college age and older would congregate around the green stretch of land after midnight. They'd gather to chat outside parked cars. Sometimes they'd follow each other into the shadowy labyrinth of trees. Any in-the-know student could postulate what transpired there. Speeding from work, I'd see men cruising the sidewalks, leaning against oaks, outlined figures hunched in cars. I prayed no one would recognize me.

At the time, I was horrified by the thought of anonymous sex. My beliefs were nearly as absurd as my mother's explanations of homosexuality, years before. If I left my car, surely I'd be bludgeoned or knifed. A stranger's tongue in my mouth would no doubt result in disease. But my Campanile curiosity grew. When a friend bragged about the drunk fraternity boy he'd blown in the grassy field beside the stadium, I couldn't think of anything else for days. I started driving there every night, whether I'd been at work or not. Now, when I close my eyes and concentrate, those days seem eons away. I can't quite re-create that breathless first-time-cruising feeling: goose bumps inching up my arms, nervousness fidgeting in my gut like drugged moths, my New Wave tapes testing the volume of my car stereo.

That summer, Lawrence was blasted by thunderstorms. During a particularly potent one, I finished my shift at Pearson, hunched dripping behind the steering wheel, and beelined toward Campanile Drive. Just as I'd expected, the place was less populated than usual. The rain pounded, ceaseless, and in between windshield wiper swipes I looked into the laddered streetlight and saw the water shimmering against the sky. It was almost romantic. A few hundred feet from the bell tower's hill was a low-lit parking garage I'd occasionally witnessed dudes loitering around. *No one'll see me there.* I steered my car into the place and parked.

I waited two, three, four minutes. No one. Then, just as I was about to leave and recircle Campanile Drive, I noticed a guy in a green-and-white-striped shirt. He was hanging out under the garage's shelter. He had dirty blond hair, heavy on the bangs, and a smirk that made him more ugly than attractive. He trained his eyes on me. Behind him were the rows of trees that led toward the bell tower. Rain blurred everything beyond.

I must have taken twenty deep breaths before I'd generated enough nerve to leave the car. He nodded, and I nodded back. The rain trickled rivulets down my forehead and face. I ran a hand through my hair, my spiky haircut ruined, and marched straight for him.

I remember feeling cold, unfocused, my body racked with shivers so intense they felt like seizures. I remember leaning against the outside wall of the garage and closing my eyes. I remember him shuffling up behind me, snaking his hand around my body to rest on my stomach. In my half excitement, half terror, I grabbed the hand and boldly steered it toward my crotch.

He took over from there. He undoubtedly had some experience with cruising the Campanile, as he led me to a claustrophobic groundskeeper's closet built into the garage's side wall. (I've often wondered if he *was* the groundskeeper, as the room was unlocked.) With a twist of the doorknob, he pushed me in. The last thing I recall seeing after we stepped in were the green and white stripes on his damp shirt. He shut the door, and everything went black.

The room smelled of diesel fuel, fertilizer, the cut grass that crusts a lawn mower's blades. When the blackness draped us, things got serious. For some reason, I allowed him free rein over me; perhaps I believed he'd adhere to a fantasy I'd whittled from the blocks of pornos I'd seen since *Big Guns.* He didn't kiss me. Instead, he grabbed my shoulders, pushed me to my knees. His cock was already out of his pants, and he guided me toward it. I wrapped my mouth around it, thinking of the expert porn star blow jobs I'd witnessed and, maybe still, Marilyn Chambers on that pool table. While he fucked my face, I felt rain spattering me, baptismal. Then he began smacking me. He kept missing target, his hand striking my cheek sometimes, my ear or neck others, his blows unpredictable in the darkness. After the initial seven or eight, his hand made a fist.

Weary of that, he pushed me on my side. My head collided with a bag of some powdery substance which smelled like the chalk I used to line batter's boxes with before games, back when I was a twelve-year-old shortstop. It spilled and stuck to my wet hair. The guy fumbled with my belt and zipper. I knew what he was doing, but didn't fight him. He lifted me slightly, searching for his bull's-eye. When he found it, he fucked and fucked me, my head pounding against the bag of powdery stuff, little puffs making baby's breaths on my skin. After five or ten or fifteen minutes, he pulled out, came, dropped my now-unnecessary ass.

The guy wrenched open the groundskeeper's room door. Light and rain sliced in. I squinted and sat up. He was sprinting into the rain, back to his car or house or wherever, puddles exploding beneath his shoes. There's this image I carry: his green and white stripes blurring together, then disappearing. . . . I pulled my pants up and stood there, stunned.

I remember driving away, past the bell tower, the pond and its ridiculous hauntings, stories I'd once believed. I ended up at my apartment on Indiana Street. My housemates were sleeping, and I headed for my room, not bothering with lights. The storm drummed against my windows, creating an ambience that would have fit if I'd decided to hug my knees and cry. But I didn't cry. I remember thinking a little about my "experience," but perhaps not as much as I imagined someone would think after what had happened. I clicked the stereo on, slid an Adam and the Ants record from its sleeve, and dropped the needle. The vinyl was riddled with scratches from semesters of high school listening. I stretched back on the pillowcases my mother had embroidered, my band member heroes staring down from the walls. I tried to fall asleep as the record played. It didn't work, and I had to flip to side B before I drifted off.

I DON'T EVEN like the word *diary*. I envision clasped books with miniature gold keys diligently kept by adolescent girls with braces and tearstained cheeks. Yet mine was similar, a blank book with a blue-and-crimson cover, its narrow pages making it difficult to scribble in. I'd written economical versions of class experiences, nightmares I'd had, or butchered assimilations of Plath and Sexton and Lowell which would no doubt make me wince if I read them now.

But that's impossible, since I tossed the diary on a bonfire not long after Christmas that year. The reason: My mother had found the book in the guest room of the house where she and my stepdad were living. She surely skimmed through accounts of my feelings and experiences with boys. Probable examples: "What's-his-name has the most beautiful ass in the universe." "X and I jerked each other off in the Hashinger basement." "God, what I wouldn't give to service So-and-so." And, of course, the Campanile run-in. But by the time I'd jotted down that horror, it was a mere sketch, a "tame" version of what really happened, just as my version of the Marilyn Chambers film had been "tame," years before. Here's the way I imagine it: Mom, dressed in red and green for the holiday, fishes out said diary. Her gaze needles in, and Bingo! "Dear Diary: Tonight I went to the Campanile. This guy approached. We fucked in this gardening shed thingamajig beside the parking garage."

As we did every Christmas Eve, my sister and I had watched reindeer and snowman cartoons, ladling from a pitcher of eggnog Mom had spiked with brandy. At twelve-thirtyish, my stepfather retired. My sister followed later, slipping into one of the sleeping bags in the unfurnished guest room. But Mom and I stayed up, chatting. We clicked off the TV and watched the lazy wink of the tree's colors and, beyond the frosted window, the synchronic lights from neighbors' trees. A cross-eyed angel in a red foil dress, a joke family heirloom, peered down from her perch on the treetop. After a while, Mom's reminiscences

SCOTT HEIM

of Christmases past began to quiet and stall. I could tell something was up. I put my head in her lap, just as I'd done as a boy, as with Traci in her dorm room.

Whenever my mother tells me something upsetting or momentous, a piece of information she believes might make me argue or cry, her voice inches up half an octave, becomes the wheezy whisper of a frightened girl. Her voice adopted this tone recently, when the doctor diagnosed her with lymphatic cancer, her chances of recovery slim. Back then, her fingers stroking my hair, I felt her breathe deep, her stomach expanding against my ear. "Scott," she almost sang, "I did something that's going to make you mad."

When I asked what she meant, she blurted that she'd found my diary. I remember feeling erased at first, my mind a blank. I should have been furious, but I wasn't. I understood her meaning: not merely that she'd read what I'd written, but that she'd discovered my secret.

I remained lying in her lap. Three or four minutes passed, and I cleared my throat. "Was it a surprise?" I asked.

"No."

I thought of that election night, years earlier, when I'd shuffled through the house. I could still picture the way she'd appeared, her face's muscles slackened by booze. "I'm going to ask you a question. . . ." She hadn't actually asked it then. She still hadn't, but it didn't matter. Now it had been confirmed.

I forgave my mother's detective work which resulted in the diary find. Telling her the messy details about Mr. Green-and-White-Stripes seemed unnecessary now. Instead, I closed my eyes and concentrated on her fingers massaging my scalp, combing through to the ends of my hair. My mother loved me; it didn't matter if I was gay or straight. Why hadn't I understood this before?

The ultimate result of our discussion was that Mom and I would no longer hold secrets from each other. In the following days, she would confirm previously hush-hush details from her life, scandalous pieces and bits I'd overheard in her telephone conversations. She soon confessed the worst moments from her childhood, the fact that her father had sexually abused her and her sisters. She'd never loved my dad, and had married at eighteen only to escape her family and home. She even giggled through the revelation of her love of marijuana, the fact that "just last month" she had gotten stoned with my aunt.

I can't forget the way I felt that Christmas Eve: redeemed, as though everything could begin again. By the time Mom and I finished that night, her legs had numbed from the weight of my head, and our throats ached. It was almost dawn, the morning when we would crouch beneath the sequined tree, rip the paper off gifts. But we weren't a bit sleepy. Outside, the sun blossomed toward the horizon, and the room grew amazingly bright.

THERE'S ANOTHER PICTURE, taken only weeks after that Christmas Eve. My mother and I sit on the front porch of her house. Littered around us are dead leaves, chipped pieces of flowerpots, sediments of snow like crushed calcium tablets. She's wearing a red sweatshirt. In the wintry air her face is flushed, radiant. She has rinsed her hair with a sandy brown dye to cover the gray. The cancer is merely a seedlet inside her, if there at all. Her hand cups my knee. We're both smiling.

When I compare this photo to the picture of Traci and me at the Kansas State Fair, I can't help noticing the difference. The second photo shows a twenty-year-old boy, at last replacing the moody wraith from two or three years before. There's no mascara, and my hair has returned to its natural strawberry blond. My eyes look like photocopies of Mom's. And while I may be overinvestigating my smile or the glitter in those eyes, something else seems different from pictures taken prior to that Christmas: "as if a weight had been lifted"—or so goes the cliché. Yet that pretty accurately describes my expression.

Nowadays I telephone Mom once a month. The lines between New York and California are remarkably free of crackles. When we speak, our voices remain steady and brave, as if assured of complete remission. I don't mention friends who are sick, are dying, have died. Instead, I brag about my boyfriend. She details the antique carousel horses she paints and sells on commission. These are the things that make us happy now.

"Look pretty, have fun, be fearless" went a snippet of another Adam and the Ants anthem. Years ago, I would have deemed that a manifesto. Traci and the girls and I would have bellowed the lyrics, admiring ourselves in bedroom mirrors, locked out from our mothers. Those songs and clothes and attitudes provided our easy escape. They solved all problems, saved us. We would stay this way forever, and nothing bad would happen.

Funny, how faithfully I believed that then. I wish I still could.

THE CURE

Dennis Hunter

I.

I WAS BORN gay. Of course, I don't know that for certain—but I can say with confidence that I had become that way by the time I emerged from diapers, while my little mind was struggling to develop the most rudimentary tools of language and memory. Even as I learned to walk and talk and act of my own volition, I was exhibiting distinctly homoerotic behavior.

When I was four years old, in 1973, my grandfather worked as the towel attendant in a locker room at a large university in Norman, Oklahoma. He took me with him one day, and for the first time I saw a naked man, peeling off his sweaty basketball shorts and support strap. I stood gawking, transfixed, devouring the vision before me, until my grandfather came to fetch me. As he led me away, I craned my head around to stare at the man's backside, his butt jiggling slightly as he padded off to the shower. I was thunderstruck.

That same year, my grandmother caught me trying to kiss my grandfather's butt during our afternoon nap. I had recently heard the expression "kiss my butt" for the first time and wanted to find out what it was all about. Just as I succeeded in gently lowering the back of my grandfather's underwear and planting my dry, four-year-old lips on his hairy cheek, my grandmother stuck her head in the bedroom door. She emitted an abrupt and startled warning call, the sort of noise reserved for a dog's lifting its leg in the living room, preparing to water the houseplants. I looked up. She was pointing at me, her face twisted every which way with the scandal of what she saw, shaking her head frantically from side to side, making little *tut-tut* sounds. I released the elastic band of my grandfather's Fruit of the Looms and rolled over, dejected and ashamed of myself, not knowing exactly why. My grandmother never mentioned the incident to me, and to the best of my knowledge my grandfather never found out what I'd tried to do. But I can't remember being invited to nap with him after that.

At ten, I had two posters on my bedroom wall: Eric Estrada, shirtless and sweaty, flexing his muscles for the camera in front of his police motorcycle, a seductive grin on his face; and the Village People, arrayed in feathers and leathers around a large yellow bulldozer parked eccentrically in the middle of an outdoor café in Key West. I didn't have a clue that little boys weren't supposed to enjoy looking at pictures of a TV hero's naked torso; nor did I know who the faux macho musical group were, or what their songs "YMCA" and "In the Navy" were really about—or even what the word *gay* meant.

I'm not trying to turn my childhood into a case study; I wouldn't presume to say that everyone who is gay is biologically so, or even that my own homosexuality is wholly determined by genetics. I don't believe that the higher mathematics of human sexuality, full of variables and imaginary numbers, can be reduced to such simple arithmetic. Nor should it be. I am trying to give you an idea of how deeply, how primordially, my sexual orientation is rooted in my personality, and how many problems it caused me before I finally accepted the facts. From the time I was capable of conscious thought, I wanted what I was not supposed to want, and I punished myself for wanting it.

By the time I hit the skids of puberty and began to experience real sexual urges (as opposed to the cherubic affections of my childhood), I had been abducted into Berry Road Baptist Church, where, under the instruction of masters, I honed and sharpened my skills of self-punishment and self-deception. Now God was watching me when I went to the bathroom, eavesdropping on my mind, even monitoring my dreams, videotaping every sin I committed and jotting down every wicked thought, putting all the evidence in a great file to be used against me on Judgment Day. I prayed to Him to forgive me each time I masturbated, promising it would be the last—or at least the last time I would fantasize about men while I did it. Each time I broke my promise, my guilt was factored one step higher, increasing exponentially, driving me further into denial. If I could forget what I had done, then maybe God would forget it, too.

When I was about twelve, I began sneaking into my brother's room and rifling through his rather extensive collection of dirty magazines: *Playboy*, *Penthouse*, *Hustler*, *Jugs*—whatever periodicals he could purchase over the counter at the convenience store. Most of the pictures—naked ladies clad in silk and satin lingerie and high heels, oversized Kewpie dolls with superstuffed boobs and a strange compulsion to throw their legs in the air and pry apart their genitals with their fingertips—stirred no interest in me. But a few of the more daring publications, such as *International*, had started to feature layouts depicting men and women together, which—for some reason I couldn't at first figure out—aroused me a great deal. I stole several magazines and kept them for more frequent consultation. The layouts themselves were ridiculous; the men were always flaccid, which made it difficult to believe you were looking at pictures of people actually having sex. That was beside the point. Seeing a naked man in any kind of erotic context was enough to send me into a hormonal frenzy.

I never paid attention to the women in those pictures; my imagination fixed on the man: what his cock would look like fully erect; the way his butt muscles would squeeze together as he thrust into the woman; how his body would shudder, like mine, as that warm, familiar wave swelled up inside him. Then, just before I reached climax, I recalled that God was watching me, that He knew I was staring at the man instead of the woman, and a wave of shame washed over me. Abruptly, I forced myself to focus on the woman, to imagine climaxing inside her; somehow that took the sin out of it. I convinced myself that if I did this each time I masturbated, I would eventually supplant my unnatural desire for men with a natural desire for women. It never entered my mind to admit that I was a fag. I really didn't know what a fag was, except that it was someone wretched and ungodly, someone who would burn in Hell—and I knew I didn't want to do that.

As a teenager I lost my faith, leaving behind the Baptist church and becoming slightly less inhibited. I knew what a fag was now, and I knew for damn sure I wasn't going to be one. Not because they were sinners (that concept had ceased to hold much meaning for me), but because they were freaks and everyone hated them, a fate far worse than Hell. I had wrenched my mind free of the grip of religion only to surrender to the no less repressive, far less forgiving grip of society. The prying eye of God that had watched and condemned my sins for so long was replaced by the eyes of my peers at school, whose judgments posed more immediate dangers.

It became extremely important to monitor my behavior and ensure that I didn't show any outward signs of my inner conflict, even as that conflict was growing more violent, fueled by a constant accretion of testosterone and the increasingly unmanageable nature of my fantasies. I had long ago thrown away my Eric Estrada and Village People posters, sensing what they threatened to reveal about me. But now I was surrounded by real boys: boys I had gone to church with, boys in the neighborhood, boys who went to my school, boys at summer camp, boys who played basketball without their shirts on, boys who slept over and shared a pallet with me on the floor—even the boy who, to my unspeakable delight, jerked off on our living room sofa while I ogled him from around the corner. Temptation and opportunity were everywhere, but also the danger of being exposed. I couldn't stare at the boys on the basketball court for too long; I couldn't feel up the boy sharing my pallet until I was certain he was asleep; I couldn't let David Acker find out that I had spied on him. Once, I sat looking at a stolen *Playboy* with David, and seeing his face become flushed and ruddy, his breathing slightly irregular, his jeans bulge handsomely, was enough to get me equally excited. The difficult part was pretending it was the woman in the centerfold who had turned me on.

One sticky evening during August 1985, the summer between my sophomore and junior years of high school, I found myself in the gay cruising area of the local college campus just after sundown. I no longer recall what prompted me to ride my motorcycle at that hour to that out-of-the-way square. Perhaps I had heard about the place and wanted to see it for myself. Perhaps I was drawn there against my will, by the same instinct that carries a homing pigeon back to the place it started from. In any case, there I was, strolling aimlessly. And there they were, moving like spies, scanning one another furtively from across the street with a sense of purpose, a hidden motive I could only dimly comprehend. They stood near the bus stop, exchanged wary greetings, accepted a light from a stranger, walked slowly down one side of the street and back up the other, pausing to ask the figure beneath a tree for the time. Then the dimmer switch inside my head turned clockwise and a fuller understanding of what these men were doing dawned on me, slowly at first, but with increasing clarity. I was scared stiff, yet my curiosity was piqued. I knew I should leave—and I knew I had to stay.

Prime USDA sixteen-year-old chicken was not a commodity in great supply on that particular market, though the demand for it may have been as high there as anywhere else. Soon a man began to follow me. It was dark, he was too far away, my eyes were too shifty and timid for me to make out exactly what he looked like. I ducked into an alley formed by three buildings near the football stadium, with no way out but the way I'd gone in. Realizing my error, I leaned back against a wall and held my breath, hoping he would go away—but also, in spite of myself, hoping that he wouldn't. I had no idea how I was expected to act in such a situation, no idea what he might say or what I should say or what we would do if he did follow me. I realized the danger I had put myself in: He could have a knife, a gun. He could be a psycho, a cop. He rounded the corner and I was trapped.

I could see him clearly now: in his late thirties or early forties, spare tire, sagging face, thinning hair—everything hideous and unattractive to a sixteen-year-old. We exchanged awkward greetings. He asked me my name, where I was from, what I was doing—innocuous questions that seemed as caustic and insidious as those of an interrogation squad. The spotlight of his eyes burned into me. I did the only thing that seemed logical: I lied. Lowering my voice to make myself sound older, I told him the first far-flung, improbable tale that popped into my head. My name was George; I was an art buyer from Washington, D.C., in town on business with the university, purchasing some late-sixteenth-century paintings for its collection. The man nodded in assent, playing along, interested to see where the game was leading. He continued to ask questions and I continued to dig myself deeper into my wild story. Finally, I excused myself, saying I had to get up early the next morning to report to the president of the university.

I sped home, feeling that I had certainly been clever, using my wits to escape an unpleasant situation. But I wasn't satisfied. On the contrary, the stakes had doubled. I had acquired a glimpse into a fascinating subterranean world whose existence I had always suspected. I had come face-to-face with One of Them. Granted, he wasn't the most exemplary specimen, but now I knew for sure that They were out there. I could return whenever the urge struck me.

The urge struck me later that evening. I tried to sleep and couldn't close my eyes. A thousand little testosterone needles of curiosity pricked me. It was past midnight. I snuck out of the house and sped back to campus.

The square was busy. I no longer recall how I met Arthur Brown, although I remember other things about him quite clearly: Later that night, in his bed, Arthur gave me my first blow job. Then he gave me my second blow job. Then he gave me my third blow job. Arthur appreciated the fact that I was a virgin, and he swallowed everything I fed him greedily, as though he might never again have the chance to taste such a rare, sweet liqueur. I tried to reciprocate, but inexperience betrayed me and I choked on the sheer size of Arthur's equipment.

The sun was coming up when I got back on my motorcycle and rode home. Arthur made me promise to come see him again. I promised, but I knew that I would not go back. I had already determined that what had occurred that night would never be repeated. I thought that by allowing Arthur Brown to suck my cock I had worked some kind of ritual magic to exorcise the bad spirits that lived in me. To use a more secular metaphor, I saw those blow jobs as a kind of immersion therapy: I had confronted my fears *in extremis*, indulged the very desires that horrified me, and now I would be purged once and for all. I had stepped out of the closet just long enough to look around, then dashed back inside and slammed the door behind me. I resolved not to think about what had happened with Arthur. I went out of my way to avoid driving past his apartment or the campus cruising area.

My last two years of high school were a confused and harrowing time. After my experience with Arthur, I launched a new plan to drive away the demons, throwing myself into the effort with vigor. I managed to numb myself with drugs and alcohol, although marijuana often made me paranoid and a couple of acid trips brought me perilously close to the edge, peering with dilated eyes into an abyss where I lost all control over my thoughts, my feelings, my identity. I got myself that magic girlfriend, the one who was, finally, going to bring out the good boy in me.

I dated Joanne the last few months of my senior year. She went to another school, so I didn't have to see her every day, which probably kept the relationship going a lot longer than it might have otherwise. Joanne was smart, open-minded, and beautiful—everything that should have appealed to me. I even convinced myself for a while that it did. One night we told our respective parents we were staying at friends' houses and I took Joanne to the Holiday Inn. We ordered nachos from room service, got drunk, talked, watched TV. Then, when it couldn't be avoided anymore, we fumbled off our clothes and fucked, mostly missionary style. I was terrified. Terrified of Joanne's lithe, soft body, her pliant submissiveness, that tender pink rose she expected me to suck. Terrified and embarrassed and somewhat repulsed. But I forced myself to finish what I had begun. I came inside Joanne, the long-dreamt-of moment of glory which would cure me of my sickness and awaken in me the healthy, heterosexual boy who had been asleep all those years. Then I rolled off her; I'm ashamed to admit that, like a typical man, I have no idea whether or not she had an orgasm.

I took Joanne to my high school prom, the week before I graduated. We stood in my living room in pink chiffon dress and tux, my mother beaming with pride, cooing and taking snapshots. We rented a room again that night— I think maybe our parents knew what we were up to—but I couldn't go through with it a second time. I was searching desperately for an excuse to avoid sleeping with Joanne.

Meanwhile, in spite of all my efforts to change, I had fallen in love with my best friend, Kevin. I'd made gay acquaintances and friends and discovered there was really nothing wrong with them. I'd become a regular at midnight screenings of *The Rocky Horror Picture Show*. As it happened, Kevin and his buddies were going cruising after the prom in a rented limousine and had room for one more person. I left Joanne in the hotel room—alone, drunk, abandoned—while I went joyriding with Kevin. It was an appalling thing to do—and I knew it even then—but I had no choice. By the time I got back, she had passed out.

II.

That was the week it all went down: The planets aligned, the oceans swelled, and I shed my adolescent skin forever.

Graduation. To the glassy eyes of my family in the risers, the details were all in place: the cap and gown proudly worn, the principal's hand properly shaken. The embossed certificate had exchanged hands without being dropped. As I turned to walk off the stage, the flashbulb exploded, at just the right instant. It's all there in the picture:

My eyes are lit with it, so bright you can almost see the thought circling inside my head, over and over, a mantra: There's no turning back—an embarrassingly appropriate sentiment given its context, exactly what my family and principal expect me to think at this moment, and exactly what most of the eight hundred students around me are also thinking. But the sentiment doesn't mean quite the same thing to me as it does to the others. The appropriate conflicts are there, all the mundane hopes and fears of a young adult, the expectation that the best years of my life are yet to come pitted against the suspicion that I've already squandered them—joy and terror in equal proportions, two liquids dissolving into each other. But beyond all that is something else, something startling and unexpected. Under the hot, angry glare of the flash—an exotic heat that freezes this moment beneath a sheet of icy plastic—something is alive. It's moving; it refuses to stay frozen. It pounds against the thin wall of paper holding it captive, threatens to rip through the photograph and gush into the present. A secret wellspring has just broken loose, and inside, where I had grown dry, brittle, and bitter, I am filling up with cool, fresh water. For eighteen years I've kept it at bay; now I'm accepting the water. There's no turning back. I'm gay. Oh, Jesus, there's no turning back.

I had met Robert at a party a couple of gay friends had taken me to a few nights after the prom. Our attraction was obvious; I dropped a few hints, asked my friends to check into Robert's availability; within days, Robert was my first boyfriend. Joanne bowed out gracefully, saying she had seen it coming. Still, she joked, it was a bit humiliating to be dumped for a guy.

I wasn't with Robert long; we shared little beyond a fondness for drugs and dancing and sex (a recipe that seems to sustain many gay relationships). By the end of the month I had met Benjamin, at a party in Robert's apartment. We fell madly in love the moment we laid eyes on each other. Robert walked into the living room and found us dancing, grinding our crotches together spastically to the beat of Skinny Puppy's "Dig It." He bowed out less gracefully than Joanne. His face (like my grandmother's so many years before) twisted every which way with the scandal of what he saw. He chased everyone from his apartment in a fit of rage, then didn't speak to me for years. I couldn't have cared less. Benjamin and I were joined at the hip for almost two years.

I was still afraid to come out to my parents. By the time I had graduated from high school, they were long divorced. During college, purse strings were virtually the only threads that tied me to my father, but they held me tightly; I would fall a long way if he cut them. I lived in his house, ate his food, drove in the car he had bought me to the school whose tuition he paid. It was a comfortable and, at the time, necessary arrangement, and I understood clearly that coming out to him would jeopardize it. There was also the fear of physical harm. My father never hit me, in my recollection, but he threatened to quite often. I learned early to cringe at any sudden movement of his large, callused hands, his dangerous arms. He was full of strange, implacable currents of rage and bitterness which might boil over into violence at any moment. More important, his indifference, his coldness, had slowly, imperceptibly wounded me, more deeply and more permanently, I think, than his fist ever could have. It didn't make sense to me to endanger my lifestyle—and, perhaps, my person—for the sake of telling my father the truth about myself. What had he ever revealed to me about himself? I continued to hide my gayness, as I had always done, with the distinction that now I knew what I was hiding.

I use the word *hiding* in its fullest sense: It was never simply not telling my father my secret. It was hiding my dirty magazines, screening my phone calls, and, most of all, sneaking my boyfriend into my room after my father had gone to sleep. Every Friday night, Benjamin and I had muffled sex, with my father only ten feet away, on the other side of the bedroom wall. On Saturday morning, I would go into the living room and distract my father with awkward chat while Benjamin climbed out my bedroom window and slinked around the side of the house to my car.

After college, I lived in New York for two years, and my estrangement from my father became total. In 1992, I returned to Oklahoma to learn not that I disliked him, which I already knew, but that I had grown as indifferent to him as he had always been to me. I rejected altogether the notion that I was compelled by some obscure law of biology to love him, in spite of his faults, simply because he was my father. Those faults were my father, and I could find nothing else in him to love. Coming out to him seemed beside the point;

it would be like coming out to the mailman or the clerk at the grocery store, with whom I shared as much emotional rapport. Besides, couldn't he figure it out for himself after all this time? Still, I toyed with the idea of formally telling him, for the sake of putting it behind me.

One Sunday morning, he dropped by unexpectedly to see my new apartment. I had just begun dating Grant, and we were sleeping late. I threw on some clothes, shut my bedroom door, and received my father and stepmother in the living room. They sat stiffly on the sofa, looking nervously at objects in the room and making one failed attempt after another at conversation. I wondered if they were going to ask to see my bedroom, and I pondered the surprise they would find there—Grant lying naked in bed with a morning hard-on—but they didn't. And I didn't see the point in forcing it on them, or embarrassing Grant in that way. Hanging above the fireplace was a large photograph of me in hideous drag: emerald-green gown, chandelier earrings, sassy red wig, and far too much rouge. My father looked at it and asked me, "Who's the girl?"

I stared at him—I thought I might choke—but he was in earnest. I felt pity and I wanted to laugh, not at my father but at the irony of the situation. "She's just a friend of mine," I stammered vaguely, and changed the subject. I understood then why I will never come out to my father: He needs the wool that covers his eyes; like an Old English sheepdog, he'd go blind without it.

In the past couple of years I have stopped speaking to my father, but I remain fond of my mother and attached to her despite the distance that separates us now that I live in New York again. I was always Mama's boy, and my mother was the only member of my family for whom I harbored any true affection. Strangely, coming out to her felt more threatening than coming out to my father. There was no danger of violence or financial embargo, but the strings that tie me to my mother are heartstrings. I had something real to lose if she cut them.

One afternoon, she walked through my living room looking at the same pictures my father had noticed a few weeks earlier. I was putting away the groceries we had just bought.

"You have some pretty odd pictures on your wall," my mother said.

I stared at her, wondering how much she suspected.

"Dennis," she continued, "are you gay?"

I stood with a carton of milk in my hand, unable to believe that this was it. My mother was outing me. I swallowed the lump in my throat and said yes. She was quiet a moment.

"Well, I thought so," she said.

"You *did?*" I responded, incredulous.

"Yeah. I've kinda thought so for a long time now, ever since you were a kid, really."

My mother reassured me that it didn't make any difference to her whether I was gay or straight, that she would always love me, no matter what. It was more than I expected or hoped for, but somewhere in the back of my mind I felt cheated. This was an anticlimax. Where were the slammed doors and screeching tires, the angry, tearful late-night telephone calls? Where was the hurt, the denial, the bargaining? The final, bitter resignation? Where was my melodrama?

A few days ago, I told a friend who is also gay that I was writing my coming-out story.

"Coming out to whom?" Aaron asked.

"To myself," I said impatiently, the answer obvious.

Aaron looked perplexed. "Yeah, but to *whom*?" he repeated.

"What do you mean 'to whom'? To *myself*!"

Aaron paused a moment, then lowered his voice. "To yourself?"

It was the sort of exchange one might expect to have with a straight man, someone who had never undergone the painful process and therefore couldn't understand what I was saying. It made me realize that coming out meant different things to Aaron and me. Aaron had been raised in a far less repressive environment; he had never experienced the guilt and shame that were the bane of my adolescence. He couldn't conceive of coming out to himself because he had never been in the closet. For Aaron, coming out was a purely social event consisting of revealing to others something he had never hidden from himself.

For me, the event was almost wholly personal. The earthquake had to take place inside me. The process of coming out to other people, although frightening, was merely a series of aftershocks. The earthquake was accepting that I was not, after all, possessed by demons, that it was okay to want the things I wanted and to let myself have them. It was realizing that I was not, after all, destined to be wretched for the rest of my life, that the possibility of happiness lay in my hands. It was being born again, accepting the spirit in a way that I had failed to do at Berry Road Baptist Church. It was a cure, after all—the only cure—for the peculiar, but not altogether rare, malaise that cast its dank, tubercular shadow over my youth.

© Amy Timmons, 1987

JANUARY 18, 1989

William Sterling Walker

DON WAS TEN years older than me, in his early thirties, big and burly, with silver hair and, at various times during the year, a beard or mustache, or both. He liked to drink and tended to drink heavily. So much of social life in New Orleans revolves around food or alcohol.

I first met Don in September 1985, in a restaurant in the French Quarter where I waited tables. The restaurant was run by a gentleman named Kenny and featured home-style cooking (catfish and smoked ribs) as opposed to the gourmet Creole cuisine featured in most other establishments. Don had come down with Kenny from Natchez, Mississippi (Don's hometown), a couple of months earlier to help open the place and manage the bar. I was dating Kenny and fell into the job. When Kenny and I broke up that December, he fired me. By then Don and I had become fast drinking buddies.

We spent most weekends together, hanging out in bars and restaurants in the French Quarter and the Garden District or going to recitals or the opera. We took car trips through the Deep South and to the Gulf Coast, cruising rest areas along the route, stopping for a quick beer and pork rinds. Once we spent the night in a four-poster bed in a guest house in Natchez, telling bawdy jokes and dishing our friends until we fell asleep. I ignored any sexual tension between us.

One night a friend approached us in the Rawhide Saloon, on the rue Burgundy in the French Quarter. It was Bear Night, and men with facial hair got beers on the house during happy hour. I was sitting on Don's knee. We were both drunk and had our arms around each other, acting rather smoochy and fey. My friend asked me if I was Don's lover.

"With this piece?" Don answered. We were practically eyeball to eyeball, grinning. "You've got to be joking. That would be incest. Miss Thing here, she's my ugly stepsister."

I was his ugly stepsister and he was my greedy songbird.

DON WAS A tenor who had gone to New York in 1981 to build a career on the operatic stage. I'd listen wide-eyed to his stories of the piers and the bathhouses, and the Friday night feeding frenzy on Christopher Street, in certain bathrooms at Macy's, subway stations, and the Ramble. For whatever reason, he'd returned to Natchez in 1985. I assumed that Don was like Dorothy in Oz: drawn to the city but discovering there's no place like home. He told me he had come back because eccentricity was so highly prized in Natchez.

Within a year, Don began to pursue his singing career again. He had sung in church choirs in Natchez, Birmingham, and at the Church of Saint Mary the Virgin in New York (also known as Smoky Mary's—"Lots of smells and bells," he'd explain). In 1986, he became the paid tenor at a prominent Baptist church in the Garden District, in uptown New Orleans. He also sang elsewhere.

The Saint Charles Avenue Baptist Church was an anomaly—very High Church, with a distinct Anglican flavor, much like Smoky Mary's. The church had a number of queer deacons and deaconesses, all important members and respected New Orleanians. Don was quite at home there. He induced me to join the choir. The choir was good, with a good choral director. We sang everything from Negro spirituals to Bach chorales to plainchant and mighty hymns.

After Sunday services, Don and I rode the streetcar downtown to the French Quarter, where he lived, and had brunch: champagne cocktails and eggs hussard or eggs sardou. Then we romped through the bars, for tea dance. We were constant companions. In August 1988 we moved in together. We told each other everything, or so I thought.

Don was taken to the hospital by our friend Garold in 1988, the day after Christmas. He had participated in two church services on Christmas Eve, gasping for breath in the choir loft of Saint Dominick's, trying to sing "The Heavens are telling the glory of God." Doctors performed a bronchoscopy, and the next afternoon the worst was confirmed: Don had Pneumocystis carinii pneumonia, PCP.

I SOMETIMES WONDER how I survived the Reagan-Bush 1980s. I was apathetic about politics. I didn't even register to vote. As far as I was concerned, AIDS was still a far-off thing. I was putting myself through college, one or two classes at a time, semester after semester. I made a decent living working the night shift at a twenty-four-hour supermarket, which is to say that I was more or less financially independent of my parents. I hung out in the bars some mornings after work with the other nighthawks: hustlers, bartenders, strippers, denizens of the French Quarter (the bars never close in New Orleans).

In September 1985, when I met Don, I was taking a semester off from school, not so much to reassess my college career—I had been in school four years already and was only a third of the way toward graduating—as to recover from burnout. I was floundering, with little direction and no real sense of how to accomplish what I thought I wanted to do with my life, which was to write. I had only a vague notion of what that entailed. I half believed I was writing a novel. (I had written a novella in high school, in longhand in a blue spiral notebook.) Graduation was a finish line. But I wasn't totally committed to crossing that line, either.

New Orleans is great for an artist who has learned discipline someplace else; its laissez-faire attitude toward life can be a welcome respite, even a muse. But for a native, the feast days, the celebrations, usually bacchanalian in character, are not conducive to acquiring discipline and can be stultifying. That I never quit school is probably miraculous, considering how I tried to torpedo my academic career on numerous occasions. Don would always say, "Never underestimate your capacity for self-sabotage."

I REMEMBER NEW Year's Eve with such clarity.

I remember the condensation in the blue tubes between Don's teeth, in one of his nostrils, after they intubated him. It reminded me of breath on cold glass. The tubes made a gurgling sound as he wheezed. His lungs were filled with fluid. No voice. He mouthed words to me. I read his lips. The movements felt like *I love you.*

I remember the pale blue accordion tubes going to his mouth and nose. I remember the condensation. I remember his mouthing *I love you.*

VIOLET, DON'S MOTHER, sat on the square sofa of the Intensive Care Unit waiting room, in the same housedress she'd worn the day before. She had not left the hospital in three days. She looked physically haggard, but maintained a stoic tranquillity. Violet was in her sixties, and spry. Until her cancer, she'd worked in a child-care center. Her hair had fallen out due to recent chemotherapy, so she wore a gray wig. She found hope in everything. She kept telling her son, over and over, not to give up—a litany of *don't-give-ups.* Her faith shielded her against understanding we were on a deathwatch. She needed it. I, on the other hand, wanted it to be over. I wanted to rip the tubes out of Don's mouth and nose and let him go, let him not suffer any longer.

THE NIGHT AFTER he'd arrived in the hospital, Don whispered, through the oxygen mask.

"I fucked up."

I did not know quite what he meant. I guessed he thought he had waited too long to come to the hospital (a more immediate concern for me). He had been so insistent about not going to the hospital. I wondered why. Then it occurred to me that he had given up.

I allowed his comment to hang in the air too long. "No, you didn't," I finally decided to say. "You're pretty damn sick."

"They told you, didn't they?" he asked me.

That night I'd spoken to one of the ICU nurses, who'd told me that Don's chances of getting off the respirator if he stayed on it more than five days were next to nil.

"We're lucky Garold got you here when he did," I said. "You'll get better and come home."

I touched his face and sweaty hair.

I STOOD BY the fourth-floor window of Southern Baptist Hospital with my forehead pressed to the cold glass pane. A bus roared up Canal Street to the Cemeteries. It was raining; the lights of New Orleans smeared down the glass, melting in the cold dark. The line "Someone left the cake out in the rain" popped into my head; the song finally made sense to me.

"Does anyone want to work these jigsaw puzzles?" Violet drawled.

I told her no. She coaxed Garold and Martha-Joyce, Don's sister, and Lonnie, his new boyfriend, to help her work on a New England scene: red covered bridge, golden river, road winding off into the trees, leaves turning, no sign of human life—1,500 pieces. This was the hospital staff's idea of grief therapy, something to occupy the waiting. The television cabinet held an assortment of puzzles; in the three weeks Don was in the ICU, we went through them all, putting them together and breaking them apart on the square coffee table. It became a ritual.

I watched them fingering the pieces, turning each one over, comparing it to the picture on the cover of the box. I should be writing this down, I thought, with a detachment that scared me. But I didn't. I had to live through it first.

Garold asked me if I had spoken to my mother. He knew that I had been avoiding her since Don went into the hospital. We'd practically been living there. I didn't want to deal with any questions.

"You should call her, Sugar," Violet said to me. "You shouldn't let your mama worry about what you're doing or where you are."

"I don't know what I'm going to tell her about Don."

"You've just got to tell her," she said.

"I don't want her to worry about *me*," I said.

I wasn't afraid and yet I was. A few weeks earlier, a condom had broken when I was making love to my boyfriend, Paul. I was frightened, for him and for me. I'd always wash my hands after leaving Don's room.

Violet cocked her head toward me, which I read as a questioning gesture.

She thinks we're lovers, too, I thought. I went over to the sofa and sat down next to her.

"I'm very proud of Don," she said. "He's my baby and I love him no matter what. Your mama will love you the same way."

"You knew Don and I weren't lovers, didn't you?" I asked her.

Garold looked up at us from the puzzle.

"I didn't know," said Violet. "But that don't matter now. You need to tell your mama."

I HAD SHUNNED sexual intimacy with Don. Now, I almost regretted it. I sat in the yellow-brick corridor outside the ICU and cried. Cried and wished we had had sex. The yearning overwhelmed me, like a first love. This was something I could not explain to anyone. I had no vocabulary for the absurdity.

Later that evening I called my mother from the pay phone in the hall near the elevators and vending machines. As the phone rang, I thought of how I had been born in this same hospital twenty-five years before. My parents' machine answered. I left a message saying I was at the hospital with Don, looking after his mother, and that I would come over sometime in the next few days to explain what was going on, I couldn't tell her on the phone.

Afterward, Garold, Lonnie, and I drove to the French Quarter, to the rue Burgundy, and sat in the Rawhide Saloon, the scene of so many of my drunken revels with Don.

IT MIGHT HAVE rained the next night as I drove out to my mother's place in suburban New Orleans. During every holiday season of my memory, it seemed to have rained. If some details aren't factual, the impressions I'm left with are indelible. This could have been like a dozen other times I made my obligatory visit to the suburbs. I wish I could remember it as more than montage.

I remember my mother standing in her eggshell-wallpapered kitchen with the cream-colored appliances, aluminum sink, no-wax linoleum floors, and cherrywood cabinets. I thought I had missed dinner. I came into the kitchen and occupied myself with a stack of mail she always left for me in a ceramic bowl on the microwave. (Like half my friends, I still had mail going to my parents' house.) I shuffled envelopes: bills, Christmas cards, junk mail. I must have had something in my hands when I told her. I might even have shredded some piece of mail into a pile in front of me; I had a habit of doing that to cocktail napkins when I sat in a bar. I couldn't look at her. I heard distant rumblings, fireworks still exploding. My mother lives in a suburban war zone. I remember thinking, She must know why I've come. It made me more anxious.

She leaned against the kitchen counter in a blue turtleneck and black slacks, her auburn hair curled and sprayed like she was going somewhere, drinking Diet Coke out of a tall glass. The dishwasher hummed and churned and sloshed. My father was presumably napping with the television on in their bedroom.

"I've come over to tell you why I've been so scarce lately," I said.

"You left a message on the recorder about Don being in the hospital?"

"Don's on a respirator. He has the worst case of pneumonia his doctor has ever seen. He could hardly sing midnight Mass. He couldn't breathe. Garold, our friend, took him to the Southern Baptist the day after Christmas, when I was at work."

Be blunt, I told myself. *Get it out so that you have room to breathe.*

"He has AIDS. He's not going to live. I loved him. But he wasn't my lover. Paul is. What am I trying to say? I'm gay."

"I knew," she said.

How could she not have known? At nineteen I had lived with a man almost old enough to be my father and tried stupidly to hide the fact from her for two weeks. I'm sure this flashed through her mind at that moment, as it did mine. I suspected that if Violet thought Don and I were lovers, my mother certainly did. I imagined her thinking that I *would be* with an older man, though we never spoke of such things. All of my closest friends were older. I had been involved with my older lover for two years, although by the time I met Don I was almost exclusively attracted to younger guys, such as Paul, who was nineteen, unemployed, and spent four nights a week with me.

Often my mother would ask what was going on in my life, while avoiding the one topic. We had a de facto "don't ask, don't tell" relationship: You can share your life with me a little, just don't offer too much. I was complicit in this détente. It enabled me never to commit to anything.

She asked me about Paul. She had met him once, or I had let drop his name in conversation.

"I figured I'd wait until you asked me," I said. "I thought as long as you didn't, you must not want to know."

We both cried—I because I couldn't block out the flood of images from the hospital. My mother cried for other reasons.

"I always felt guilty about it," she said, "because it ran on my side of the family."

(Even today, my great-aunt and uncle and a cousin who were gay are never discussed. Last year, my grandmother and I were looking through old photographs and I asked her to identify one woman I did not recognize in a photo of my great-aunt taken on one of her excursions to Florida during the 1950s. My grandmother called her "That Woman.")

"It's ridiculous to feel that way," I said. "It's not like it's a birth defect. It's just something that happened. I've known for a long time, Mom."

Later, during dinner, one of my young nephews snagged a roll off my plate and took a bite from it, laughing. My mother, suddenly very practical and concerned, pulled me into her bedroom for a conference. Her voice, even in a whisper, seethed with anger.

"Don't let the kids eat off your plate."

"What?"

"How would you like me to tell your brothers?"

"What are you talking about?"

"AIDS."

She had this horrible expression on her face.

"I'm not worried about having caught anything from Don. We weren't sexual."

"What about sharing razors?"

"We never did that. It's plain common sense. Geez."

I don't remember how we left things that evening. I've blocked a good bit of it out. But I remember feeling rage.

MY MOTHER WAS the last person of importance I came out to, except myself. (She broke the news to my father.) Coming out to her seemed pointless at first. I still could not explain that I had loved Don, that this man had been so dear to me. Now I wonder how I could have expected her to understand when I was groping for answers myself. At the time it seemed important to explain how I came to know I was gay, that I'd sucked my best friend's brother's cock when I was seventeen, that I'd had a crush on him which ate me from the inside out. That the sight of Heath Barkley getting bullwhipped in prison in a scene from *The Big Valley* on TV had given me a boner when I was ten or eleven. That I'd wanted Steve the crop duster on *Petticoat Junction* to have his way with me. Or, even earlier, that seeing photographs of my parents' weekend trip to Biloxi with Lester and Nell, a couple they were once close to, pictures of the men in Miss Nell's black bouffant wig, with plastic cups under their shirts for tits and one wrist limp, eyes red from the camera's flash— that seeing photos of two young straight couples camping it up made me curious. I did not expect to accomplish anything by telling my mother, only to alleviate any worries she might have about me. I considered it my duty.

DON DIED ON Wednesday, January 18, 1989. He never left the hospital. He was thirty-five years old. His memorial service was held the next evening, at Saint Charles Avenue Baptist Church. The massed choruses of two churches, the New Orleans Opera chorus, and the New Orleans Gay Men's Chorus all sang. Garold and a tenor performed Malotte's "The Lord's Prayer" (Garold was the music administrator and chorus master at the New Orleans Opera). A member of our choir named David who was an accomplished flautist played Claude Debussy's *Syrinx*. I had never heard the piece before, did not know anything about it. I sat directly behind David in the choir loft facing the congregation, so close I could hear his breathing. The song from the flute rose from the silence.

I did not often see colors when I heard music; that kind of synesthesia was foreign, though I understood it as a concept. I listened to the flute, thinking, If there is any one thing that can capture Don's character, his spirit, his *presence*, it is this piece of music. Perhaps it was my memory coloring what I heard. I have listened to recordings of *Syrinx* since then, and can tell you I've never heard it played with such expressiveness again. But I couldn't tell you why.

After Don died, I packed his things to be shipped back to his family in Mississippi, and found the empty bottles of antibiotics he'd been taking for months, about which I'd known nothing.

HOW DO WE measure the effect someone has had on our lives? Trying to describe this is like trying to describe how music transports us. We are left with only the paltry renderings of its sublime effects, which is not nearly the same as feeling it. Perhaps it is because music and character are so evanescent, two equally ineffable things.

After Don died, there was only stillness. I knew I couldn't stay in New Orleans. I didn't know yet what to do about it. My closet was not so small as it was a succession of empty, windowless rooms, a labyrinth which allowed me to wander but not leave, a house that belonged to me and my family. We owned it, lived in it; but it was not a home. I was an alien in my own household.

This feeling hung in the back of my mind, even after I told my mother I was gay. I knew I had to hurry and graduate and leave New Orleans. For a long time, I imagined becoming Don in some way. This is difficult to explain, except to say that my hair became grayer and I found myself emulating the things he used to say. I thought of him constantly, saw his *doppelgänger* everywhere. This was how I grieved. But most important, I imagined leaving town.

The Christmas after Don died a snowstorm hit New Orleans—a rarity that far south—crippling the city and trapping me in the supermarket where I worked. After twelve hours, it finally stopped. I walked out on my lunch break to find the sky burdened with precipitation, heavy and brooding. About four inches of snow covered the parking lot. As I plodded across to McDonald's, I thought that the lanky kid who'd sucked his best friend's brother's cock was no longer me. That person no longer existed. I thought I was jaded, after Don.

Five years after Don's death, within days of my acceptance into graduate school in New York, I came down with a severe case of hepatitis A. I was housebound for the next four months; my mother and father took care of me. For medical reasons, I was given an HIV test, and spent three days with hovering anxiety, rehashing my every sexual encounter, knowing I must be positive, not knowing, doubting. Finally, the test came back negative.

EVERY TIME I smell new leather, it brings me back to those weeks I spent in the waiting room of the hospital where I was born and Don died. Some details are indelible. I had bought myself a bomber jacket for Christmas, and that cold winter of 1988–1989 I had it with me constantly. I remember New Year's Eve with such clarity that, for a long time, I forced myself not to remember. I closed off certain rooms. I would *not* write about some things.

Garold once suggested that it was because of anger: "You're pissed, William. You're pissed he left you."

Writing this down now is to make it all bearable, to diminish its power in some way. It has been seven years since Don died. I can no longer recall what he looked like in those weeks before—except that, when he went into a coma, I understood that he was no longer present. That was not Don. But still, I wish I could remember more than montage.

WHY DO WE assume that what we've forgotten is more significant than what we remember or are able to imagine? Why is that more truthful? We are the sum of our innumerable choices. We tend to think of time as linear, an arithmetic accumulation of moments. But sometimes it's more like ever-expanding concentric waves we move through, buffeted by the past and present. My soul is found in the past. It's not a single event, or even a string of incidents, but characters, and the awareness of characters. There are events on which other events seem to pivot, coloring everything that follows. This is a function of memory. It is what we think of when we feel something has been inevitable, *fated,* or when we contemplate the "roads not taken." Coming out is only part of the process, not the event itself. It must be part of coming into one's own. Because of Don's death, I came to the idea of a search. The search for what I've become, who I am. Call it my identity. The process is framed by Don's death and my leaving New Orleans. The discovery that I could simultaneously exist in the present and be detached from it was crucial to my becoming a writer. Most writers have one question they ask incessantly. Mine is: What is the nature of memory?

Unlike Paul, I did not keep a journal religiously—not until the winter after Don's death. There is much I have forgotten about that time. These are the things I remember.

EXPLAINING IT TO DAD

Rodney Christopher

MY FATHER IS at once a complicated and simple man. When he was twelve years old, he lost his mother, a beautiful, gracious woman who'd come to the United States from New Delhi. His teenage years were filled with challenges and uncertainty. But my father is strong-willed; he figured out how to fend for himself. He became a dental technician and, in 1956, on the advice of a trusted friend, enlisted in the air force when he was eighteen. To this day, my father carries with him the discipline he learned while serving his country. He believes strongly in working hard, being polite, following the rules, and "being a man." Like most people, he was not prepared to have a gay son.

I was born in January 1970 in Brooklyn, New York, and raised there in Prospect Heights and Crown Heights, two African/Caribbean-American neighborhoods. When I was two years old and my sister four, my parents separated and my mother weighed her options. She realized she would not be able to live with herself if anything happened to her children while she was off working and they were in someone else's care. That worry, combined with the lack of a high school diploma and the devastation of losing the life she'd dreamed of—raising her children with their father under one loving roof—led my mom to do as hers had done some twenty-five years before. She signed us up for welfare.

I grew up in a home filled with love and support. I had lots of fun as a child; my sister and I were close and spent a fair amount of time with our cousins. My father, while not living with us, was a steady presence in my life. Both my parents made sure of that.

School was a great place for me. I learned quickly, acted and danced well, and ran really fast. Teachers loved me, and I made many friends I still hold dear. At the same time, I jumped double Dutch better than my sister and many other girls on my block and at school. As I got older, I found it easier to make friends with girls. By the time I was in junior high, I was the only guy who knew when they had their periods and which boys they thought were the cutest.

Somewhere in my elementary school years, I discovered my attraction to other boys and men. A guy in my class, in another class, in my neighborhood, on TV, in a movie, or just about anywhere, would catch my eye and I'd feel a rush of excitement. I'd imagine what it would be like to touch him, kiss him, hold him. I knew it was wrong, or at least weird, to feel these things. After all, I'd never seen two men kiss on TV or in real life. Every image of love and sex available to me was of a man and a woman together. No alternatives seemed possible. Being a fairly quick study, I worked hard to suppress my desires, afraid that if I expressed them to anyone to whom I was attracted he would beat the living daylights out of me. I believed no one in my world would understand my feelings; but then, neither did I.

While I was quietly experiencing this inner turmoil, kids on my block and at school were calling me "faggot" more often than I like to remember. To maintain my sanity, I attributed it to their jealousy of my many talents. That's what my mother told me to think when I went crying to her.

My sister and I visited our father at his Long Island home every other weekend for most of our childhood. During my preteen years, I'd occasionally watch music videos with him. Whenever Boy George appeared on-screen, my dad would start speechifying: "Why would a man want to dress like that?" When George Michael, then with Wham!, appeared with rings in both ears in "Wake Me Up Before You Go-Go," my father droned on about what a sissy he was and how much he looked like a girl. Dad was warning me about what he expected from his son.

I attended Brooklyn Technical High School, a well-respected institution with an entrance exam requirement, where I was unhappy despite being at the top of my class. The school prepared its students well to become scientists, engineers, or mathematicians. I much preferred the arts and social sciences. I had wanted to attend the Edward R. Murrow High School, to study radio and television broadcasting, but the New York City computer system for high school applications managed to screw up and determined that three fourths of my junior high school graduating class did not live in Brooklyn. That glitch, which could not be corrected—or so we were told—made me ineligible for Murrow, and Brooklyn Tech ended up being the only school that accepted me.

In October 1985, during my sophomore year, I took the Preliminary Scholastic Aptitude Test (PSAT). The following April, I received an envelope in the mail which read "Are you bored with high school?" Intrigued, I opened it carefully. Inside were two brochures. The first asked, "Why wait to go to college?" It was filled with photos and anecdotes about Simon's Rock in Great Barrington, Massachusetts, a "college for high-school age students" (who begin their studies after completing the tenth or eleventh grade), all of which appealed to me. The second contained information about the college's DuBois Scholarship for minority students, named after the famous African-American activist and philosopher W. E. B. DuBois, who was born in Great Barrington. I applied for admission and financial aid, and was accepted for both.

I entered Simon's Rock as a freshman in September 1986. I was sixteen. While a student there, I worked ten to twenty hours every week at the switchboard and in the registrar's office, choreographed and/or performed dances every semester, sat on the Community Council as treasurer, then chair, was a resident assistant, played on the co-ed volleyball team, and worked diligently to graduate with a cumulative grade-point average of 3.75—all while developing some of the best friendships a person could have. Each year I was there, the student body ranged from 275 to 320 people, all struggling to find ourselves.

Five days after arriving on campus, I lost my virginity to a female classmate. (We're still great friends and laugh hysterically about the whole thing.) Not long after that, I learned through the grapevine that one of my male classmates whom I found interesting was bisexual. That night, I dreamed what it would be like to be close to him. I woke up in darkness and decided to go see him the next day.

I had difficulty focusing in class. Finally, I dropped off my books in my dorm, brushed my teeth, and headed straight to Russ's door. I took a deep breath. What if he wasn't there? What if his roommate was with him?

I knocked. Russ opened.

"Oh, hi, Rodney."

I was surprised he knew my name. We hadn't been in school for a month yet and had no classes together. He invited me in.

He was alone. We sat across from each other on the two beds in the room. After a few formalities, we discussed how we'd heard of Simon's Rock, what we thought of the place so far, what we might do after we left. I learned he was a talented writer and a real free spirit. I was fascinated. At last, I got up the nerve to ask if I could sit with him on his bed. Then I was embarrassed.

Russ took it in stride. "Sure," he said.

I had barely sat down again when I discovered we were playing with each other's hands. After staring nervously at our fingers intertwining, I looked up at him. We smiled. He leaned back on the bed, pulling me down beside him. We embraced. To control my excitement, I concentrated on his breathing. Soon we were breathing together. We fell asleep in each other's arms.

I woke up first. The sun had set. I checked my watch: We'd almost missed dinner. As I pulled away, he awakened.

"Where are you going?" he asked, grinning.

"To dinner . . . with you, I hope."

I sat and gazed into his eyes as he rose to join me, putting on his shoes. After tying our laces, he reached for my hand.

"May I kiss you?" he asked.

My heart began thumping all over again. I nodded. He leaned in and touched his lips to mine, very gently, then pulled away to look at me. I kissed him back, passionately. We separated, then got up and walked to dinner. I felt like I was floating off the ground.

It turned out his roommate's girlfriend roomed with the woman I'd had sex with. The rumor mill worked fast and furiously. I got scared and backed off from Russ. By the time I regained my courage, it was too late. But I knew after that kiss that my life would not be the same. I would dream about making love to a "crush du jour" and wake up in the middle of the night in a cold sweat. Luckily, by the end of my first year, I found some friends who were dealing with similar feelings, as well as friends who were confident about their heterosexuality and didn't find me strange because I was gay.

While the environment at Simon's Rock was supportive, having relationships on such a small campus was tough, especially when you weren't sure you were ready to be labeled either gay or coupled. I suspect that making commitments, especially those out of the norm, was simply too challenging for many of us because we were all so young. The fact that I was driven to be a super-student probably didn't help much, either. I never managed to have a successful relationship with a guy in college. But recognizing and accepting my gayness was crucial to my sanity. It meant an end to my inner turmoil. I was free to begin living my life without self-imposed repression.

Perhaps even more important was sharing my realization with the two people with whom I'd spent most of my life.

I told my sister first; I figured I could test out the news on her, since she rarely got upset. I think it was over the phone, sometime in January 1987. Angie was quiet, then asked if I was sure I wanted to tell Mom. I decided I'd wait until my next vacation. When the time finally arrived, it was a familiar scene: I was sitting on the floor in my mother's room, my back against her tall dresser. She was on her bed, watching TV. I think I asked her to turn off the tube, which let her know something important was about to be said.

I had thought for months about what I'd tell her. Would I remind her that she was supportive of one of her brothers, who is gay? Would I soften the blow somehow by saying I planned to have children? I told her I was bisexual, which wasn't exactly untrue; I still found the occasional woman attractive, even if it didn't always occur to me to act on those feelings as quickly as I would were she a he. I was still nervous about leaping into complete and total gayness. (I found myself in sexual relationships with three other women during my college years—although I admitted to them that I also had sex with men.)

Mom, like my sister, was quiet. But she was still my mom. She asked if I was being careful. Was I frequenting lots of late-night joints? "In Great Boring-town?" I responded. "Gimme a break!" We laughed. We cried. We hugged. I promised I would be careful about contracting "anything" and about offending anyone who was likely to off me because I was *like that*.

I had no idea how I would explain my sexuality to my father. I decided to avoid the subject.

In October 1988, during the first semester of my junior year, a day trip from Simon's Rock to New York City brought me into Greenwich Village for the first time in my life. I went with two friends to A Different Light, a lesbian and gay bookstore, and discovered *Other Countries: Black Gay Voices* (a journal of poetry, short stories, and essays by black gay men) and the tenth anniversary issue of *Black/Out* (the magazine of the National Coalition of Black Lesbians and Gays). Prior to reading those publications, the only images I'd had of black gay men were effeminate types, transvestites, and transsexuals, with whom I thought I had little in common. Learning that there were bright, articulate, thoughtful black gay men—some of whom I later found out were effeminate, transvestite, or transsexual men, an eye-opening reminder not to judge books by their covers—gave me courage to face life out of the closet.

Using my new black gay bibles and dialing 411, I found a New York City group called Gay Men of African Descent and began attending meetings while I was home from school on vacation. This led me to delve more deeply, and eventually to write about my discoveries for my senior thesis project. (When I returned to New York to attend graduate school, I became involved in GMAD, serving as assistant treasurer and then treasurer. I remain a proud member of the organization.)

During the last few weeks of my junior year, I found myself in a torrid affair with a guy which resulted in a huge hickey sitting proudly on my neck. As he had twice before, my father showed up at school on the final weekend to transport me and my things back to Brooklyn. Spotting the screaming purple monstrosity, my dad said proudly, "Looks like you've been having a little fun with these girls up here. You're being careful, right?" Catching my breath, I managed to reply something like, "Of course, Dad."

When he'd dropped me off three years earlier to begin my studies, my dad had pulled me aside, handed me a box of condoms, and said, "Make sure you use them." I remember being impressed by his effort to encourage his son to behave responsibly. But I couldn't help being amused as I found a double meaning in his words: not only "Be sure to use them if you have sex" but "Be sure to have sex, son." As each year passed, I'd struggled to find a way to tell him that only one had been used as he'd intended. Now, cruising down the highway in my father's new 4x4 Chevy Blazer after three years of learning and growing, suddenly the time had arrived.

As we approached a tollbooth, a sports car sped up and cut across us to get to the full-service booth. My father had to slam the brakes to avoid hitting the other car and ruining his own prized possession.

"Damn faggot!" he exclaimed.

I was shocked, frightened, and angry all at once. Before I could utter a word, my father concluded his speech.

"Creep! Can you believe that?"

I sat mute as we paid the toll and continued on our way. I knew I had to say something, I just didn't know what it should be. Okay, Rodney, I thought, here's your chance. He's not likely to do anything crazy on the road in his *brand-new car*, the one he's *always wanted*. Then I realized he could pull the car over and put me and my things out on the highway. I decided I should wait until we were closer to home to drop my bomb.

I remained silent, which was unusual (I am rarely quiet for more than five minutes). Time passed.

Finally, Dad said, "What's wrong with you?"

Before I could catch myself, I put forth a challenging yet diplomatic "I'd really prefer it if you wouldn't use the first of your two derogatory terms."

"What, 'creep'?" my father replied.

"No, the other one."

"'Faggot'?" he shouted.

"Yeah, that one."

"Why?"

My heart began racing—we were still a good seventy miles from home—but I had to give him an answer.

"Because a lot of people I know and care about would be really offended by it."

There, I'd said it. Well, sort of.

"What, are there gay people up there?"

"Yes, Dad."

"And they're your friends?"

"Some of them."

"Are there gay women, too?"

Demonstrating my cultivated pro-feminist stance on the world and gaining some confidence, I retorted, "Since when does 'people' equal *men*?" Admittedly, this was a tad obscure, which forced me to explain my point. We didn't stray long, however.

"Are there a lot of them?" Dad asked.

God only knows what possessed me, but I found myself saying "Well, it depends on who you ask. Some people think there are too many, others think there aren't enough."

My dad was dead silent. Snapping back into reality and noticing a sign for a town a good distance from Brooklyn, I made sure the conversation would not force me to reveal my secret just yet.

"Dad, what would you do if one of the guys you've been bowling or hunting with for years told you he was gay?"

"I don't have any gay friends."

"Yeah, but what if?"

"I would disassociate myself from him," he stated matter-of-factly.

I'd painted myself into a corner, and the walls felt like they were closing in fast. What to do? I decided I wasn't ready to spill the beans yet, especially if it meant my father was going to "disassociate himself" from me. I ended the conversation with something like "Dad, you and I will always disagree on many things. Let's change the subject, okay?"

We kept driving. As we left the highway for the streets of Brooklyn, I saw my birthplace in a new light. Run-down buildings with people still living in them. Dirty streets. Lots of liquor stores. Men on corners with bottles in paper bags. Kids sitting on stoops. Everyone seemed depressed. Suddenly, I felt depressed.

It must have been too long since I'd last spoken, because my dad looked over at me and said, "What's wrong now?"

"Why me?" I asked.

"What do you mean?" he responded.

"Why am I the one who got to move away and go to a really expensive school and all these other kids are still stuck here?"

"Well, Rod, for one thing you're smart and you worked hard in school. And you have *two* parents who love you."

I knew he was right. I felt really special, really loved, really *lucky*. As we got closer and closer to my home, I began to feel guilty. I had no right to be dishonest with Dad. I knew that he wouldn't want to hear what I had to tell him, but I couldn't allow myself to keep it from him any longer. He'd just told me he loved me. It might be tough for him, but he would handle this. He had to know, and it would be better for him to hear it from me. Besides, I couldn't believe my being gay had never crossed his mind.

Seemingly out of nowhere, I said, "Dad, I'm not sure I'm not gay." Somehow that was easier than "Dad, I *am* gay."

Dad paused, then began asking me questions about whether I had actually had sex with men and how long I'd known. And then we were parking the car. As we began unpacking the trunk, my father stood staring at me, mesmerized by the hickey on my neck. He looked disgusted with me. As much as that hurt, I understood. I'd disgusted myself for many years.

After we dropped off my things, Dad asked my mom and sister to join us in the living room for a "family meeting." I could not recall our ever having had such meetings before. My dad did not even live in our house.

Everyone sat down. I was so scared.

I don't remember the speech my father gave to open the meeting, but I do remember him asking me, "Why would you want to be gay when there's AIDS?" I paused to take the question in, then said (well, maybe I shouted), "Don't you get it, Dad? If I'm telling you I'm gay *in spite of* AIDS, it has nothing to do with a choice. I just *am* gay. And I've learned to accept it. I'm much happier than you could ever know."

My father sighed with exasperation, then turned to my sister for support. Angie has always been Daddy's little girl. As a rule, she doesn't like to argue and, while she's smart, she rarely takes positions on issues. My father seemed baffled that she had not joined him in trying to convince me I was making a big mistake. "Doesn't it bother you that people will call your brother all kinds of names?" he asked her. "Yeah, but he's still my brother and I love him," she responded—surprising everyone in the room. To this day, I am in awe of and thankful to my sister for her support at what easily qualifies as one of the most difficult moments of my life.

The family meeting didn't go on much longer after that. My father left, very upset. I barraged my sister with thank-yous. My mom, who had spent two years learning to accept my gayness, was worried. If his own father could not handle her son's sexuality, the rest of the world was bound to obliterate her child in no time. It took lots of conversations to convince her that she had taught me well how to avoid danger, and that I would do my best to take care of myself. It was 1989. I was nineteen years old.

LEAVING HOME TO attend college had been the beginning of a most important journey for me. I was suddenly free to be me, or at least to begin to figure out who I was. Thankfully, I discovered I liked myself and that I had a lot to offer to others. By age twenty, I had finally reached a place of inner peace. I respected that my father had tremendous difficulty handling the news of my homosexuality, and that he needed time to come to terms with it. I also knew that I had to try once more to explain my sexual orientation and my choice to be open about it to him. I sent him a letter.

May 7, 1990

Dear Dad,

I've been planning to write to you for some time now. We've been distant off and on for most of my life. We've always known that we both care about each other, but our differences have tended to rule our relationship. After being away for a few years, I began to notice some positive changes between us. But while our relationship was improving, I was also beginning to come to terms with who I am. That process has been anything but easy. For a long time I was so worried that if I told you what's been going on, all the progress we had made would be lost. Now that you know, we seem farther apart than ever. Dad, I am really sorry for that.

I need you to understand that my being gay is not a whim, and it's not something I "decided" to do. I've known ever since I was a little boy that I was different. I avoided it at almost every turn because, like many people in this world, I believed that sharing love (or lust) with those of my own gender was evil, sinful, unnatural. For a multitude of reasons, I no longer believe that and I have decided that unless I work to gain the rights of those who are not heterosexual to be treated like human beings, I will feel empty.

The main reason that I am writing to you—and perhaps the reason it has taken me so long to complete this letter—is to tell you why my senior thesis topic is "The Sociopolitical Movement of African-American Gay Men." By my junior year, I learned that I was not alone in being both black and gay. I spent my last undergraduate year researching and writing about the hundreds of black gay men across the country who, through organizations, are working to challenge blacks (mostly straight) and gays (mostly white) and society at large to understand the links between racism, homophobia, sexism, and poverty in an effort to better the world. I've experienced both racism and homophobia/heterosexism—the second more than the first. I've learned a lot; my thesis committee members (three professors), who like what I've done, have learned a lot; and I've produced over a hundred pages of written material!

However, I've been deathly afraid to tell you about any of this. I don't know if anything I say will help you understand why it was important for me to do this thesis. While Mom and Angie are not entirely comfortable with my gayness, they have been trying to understand. My thesis title will appear on the commencement program, and I don't know how you will be able to deal with that. I've come to the sad realization that you may prefer not to attend my graduation.

I would like you to come, Dad. If I earn a grade of "honors" on my thesis, I will be graduating *summa cum laude* (if not, I'll graduate *magna*—no small potatoes), and I'd like you to be there to see your son be perhaps the first black student ever in the history of his college to graduate with top honors. But I will try to understand if you don't feel that it would be best. Please promise me that we can get together soon so that we can try to talk about how you're feeling. Believe me, I know this is hard for you. I have many friends whose parents will not even talk to them. I'm really scared that it will happen to me, too. I don't want to lose you, Dad.

Love,

Rodney

I called my father on the day he received my letter. He said he was very disappointed in me, that my thesis topic was not an appropriate academic pursuit, and that he would not come to my graduation. He may even have said I had disgraced him, but I've managed to block out most of that conversation. I reminded him how important commencement was to me and that I would be the first person in his family to graduate from college. I told him I really hoped he could make it but that I'd try to understand if he didn't.

Although my thesis earned honors and I was graduated *summa*, my dad did not show up at commencement. I was deeply hurt, but I worked hard to overcome it. He did, however, attend my sister's B.A. commencement a few weeks later. When he arrived to bring us to the ceremony and noticed a recent photo of my mother and sister, he asked where it had been taken.

"At Rodney's graduation," my sister said.

Silence.

IT IS TRUE that time can make a difference. While my father and I never talk about my sexuality, we do talk. We continue to disagree on many things— gun control, welfare, the criminal justice system—but we manage to share and laugh about many things, too. I guess my father has come to realize that he has a son of whom he can be proud, that my sexuality is only a part of who I am, just as his is only a part of who he is. Maybe he'll never *understand* why his son is gay—neither will I, for that matter—but I'm sure thankful he hasn't disassociated himself from me because of it.

EXPLAINING IT TO DAD

As I grow older, I understand more and more how important it was and is for me to have my father in my life. A few years after I came out to him, he said, for the first time in a long time, "I love you, Rod." I cried for days. Now, every conversation ends with us being sure to say "I love you." He came to my last two birthday parties, at which my life partner was present. And, for the first time I can remember, I took him out to dinner for Father's Day, just the two of us. Despite his shortcomings, I'm proud of him.

Photograph by Veronica Chambers

THESE TREES
WERE ONCE WOMEN

Alex Chee

I KNEW MY mother would still love me if I told her I was gay, but I was unsure about my father.

"When I'm in a wheelchair someday," my father said to me once, when I was nine, "you'll take care of the family. You'll be the man then. You'll take care of me." I was accompanying him on a business trip by car. I remember sitting beside him as we headed southward to Massachusetts in the dark country night. Four years later, it was true: An accident had disabled him, paralyzing the left side of his body. "I won't live past forty," he used to joke to my mother. He was right about that as well. I was sixteen when my father died of complications from injuries sustained in the accident three years before.

That night in the car it seemed impossible, even ludicrous, that I could be a man like him. My father had become the tae kwon do champion of his international age group when he was eighteen. I have a photograph of him in an exhibition match, a brick splitting under his hand. As a child during the Korean War, he and his brother had stolen food from overturned supply trucks and carried it home on their backs. He'd worked his way through college in the States as a tae kwon do instructor. The captain of his college rugby team, he had run barefoot in the snow. He had gone on to become an engineer of the Saturn V rocket, and then a diver and oceanographer, even living underwater in the Tektite II experiment. He knew the exact location of the brain-spot on a shark's nose, and would disable them by punching the spot when they swam too close on underwater expeditions. He spoke Chinese, Japanese, Portuguese, Spanish, and Italian, in addition to his native Korean and his adopted English. My mother wore a fortune in jewelry during the poorest years of their marriage, due to his gift for poker. "You are descended from kings," he would say to me when I complained of prejudice at school. "One day they'll all be working for you." I believed him.

I am the oldest male of my generation, the forty-first, in a family that traces its history in an unbroken line all the way back to China, to Mongolia, to a first cousin of Genghis Khan. As a child, I was content for my father to be the man. He went hunting; he had seven rifles, including the one he had used during his mandatory stint in the Korean army, an ancient and cruel-looking thing. He took me to gun shows, where I could not conceal my horror; if he was disappointed, he did not show it. My aunts were quicker to point out my inadequate masculinity when I would visit my cousins and redo their Barbie doll outfits into more attractive and fashionable ones, but even they generally held their tongues while my father was alive. He laughed, his pride in me unfailing.

IN THE SPRING of 1990, I was in San Francisco, living in a gay neighborhood, working in a gay bookstore, interning at a gay magazine, and helping to organize a gay and lesbian writers conference. I was a member of the ACT UP/SF media committee, which meant appearing occasionally at press conferences and on television to talk about gay-related AIDS issues. I knew two straight people: my roommates, classmates from college, from which I had graduated the year before. I danced sometimes as a go-go boy at a queer bar in the Mission District, drove a motorcycle, and posed for a series of erotic photographs with a boy who worked at the café I frequented on a daily basis, a café that was, like the rest of my life, almost exclusively gay. For extra cash, which I needed almost all the time, I did makeup for gay pornographic films. My two best friends were an ingenious Tufts graduate named John and a gender illusionist named Justin. The three of us had abandoned using our real names with each other shortly after meeting, addressing each other instead as Betty (John), Glam (Justin), and Contessa (me).

One day, my mother called to tell me that she and my sister were coming for a week-long visit during my sister's spring break from high school in Maine. After I hung up the phone, I realized I had a month in which to come out to her, or else the San Francisco that I could show her would constitute that very small and commercial district downtown carefully delineated by the path of the famous trolley car—an area I had, in fact, never been to. Of my life in San Francisco, my mother knew only that I worked in a bookstore.

That was to be the spring my mother found out that her son and her daughter were both having sex with men. I had last spoken to her a month earlier, after she had found a condom in my fifteen-year-old sister's room and flown into a rage. My mother is usually completely unflappable. Her rages are storms appearing out of nowhere, so uncommon that we forget she has them; there is little to be done but to weather them. My sister had locked herself in her room and called me at work in San Francisco. While I rang up copies of *Mandate* and *Torso* and *The Lost Language of Cranes*, I spoke alternately with my sister and my mother on different extensions of their house phone and brokered a peace between them. I assured my mother it was not a bad thing that my sister was having sex with men safely on her own terms. I reminded my sister of our great-aunt in Maine, a writer who'd gotten pregnant and been forced into a marriage she didn't want, making her such a plague to her children and her husband that when she died they'd burned her unpublished work in an old oil drum in the pasture of our grandfather's farm. My sister related how my mother told her a story of a childhood friend, fourteen years old, who had become pregnant. The doctor had begged her parents to let him abort the child, as either the girl or the child would not survive the pregnancy. They refused, and the girl had died. I understood my mother's rage, and I wanted my sister to understand it also. It was as if she'd found my sister waving a loaded gun around.

"The condom is my fault," I finally said, explaining how, a year before, I had given my sister a lecture on safer sex. "I told her that if she was going to have sex with boys, nothing should go inside her unless it was covered in latex."

The conversation had taken place on a beach in Florida during a family vacation. On the first day I'd watched my fourteen-year-old sister field hungry stares from men fourteen to fifty-five as she rounded the hotel swimming pool, and I'd realized that the time had come for her to learn a few things. That evening, I'd taken her out by the fishing lagoon and explained how she shouldn't go anywhere with men she didn't know unless someone else knew she was going and the man knew someone else knew, how she had a right to say no to anything at any time, a right to make a man stop if he was hurting her, and a right to make him stop if he was just a plain bad lay. Then I'd told her about AIDS. "The rule with penises is that they are always covered, unless they're in your hand. And even then, if you have a hangnail, or any kind of cut or scratch, don't let come go anywhere near it." I'd outlined statistics that showed heterosexual teenagers were getting infected in greater and greater numbers and had become the fastest growing population of HIV-positive people in the United States, especially in rural and suburban communities. She'd paid close attention, accepting it all with equanimity. And then I'd told her why I was such an expert about men. "I'm gay," I'd said. "I know," she'd answered.

The bookstore was beginning to fill up; browsers in the AIDS section, which was right next to the register, were looking at me curiously. I'd been on the phone for over an hour.

"What you are telling me, Mom, actually makes me relieved," I said into the receiver. "It means she listened to me, and that she's going to survive the epidemic. She is not a bad child. She gets good grades, she does three hundred extracurricular activities, she hasn't shaved her head yet, and she doesn't do drugs. Other people are treating her like a sexual adult, Mom," I concluded. "You should be, too."

My mother came around quietly. She always listened to me. "We'll go to Planned Parenthood," she said, "and see about getting her on the Pill."

Pregnancy, not AIDS, remained her concern at that moment. She had once volunteered to liberate a friend from a marriage where the husband refused to use birth control. They'd had three children in three years; the friend was, at the time, twenty-two, as was my mother.

IN 1979, I announced to my mother that I was no longer going to be, as I'd often told people, the king of my own island when I grew up, but a fashion designer instead. In the seventh grade, my art teacher mounted a show of my designs in the breezeway at school. My mother attended, returned home, and suggested I try my hand at things that could be sold at the church sale. When my mother found my Gordon Merrick novels, she merely threw them away, she didn't chase me around the house like she did my sister. She threw away my copies of *Forth Into Light* and *The Lord Won't Mind*. She threw out a stolen copy of *Blueboy* magazine.

A year earlier, I'd watched from inside my grandfather's house as my mother burned my Uncle Stephen's pornography collection in an oil drum, perhaps the same one used for my great-aunt's writing. Occasional pages of cinder floated upward in the dark, somehow thin, smoke. My mother had discovered the magazines in my grandfather's garage. I was eleven, and an excellent reader, and though my mother burned every issue of *Penthouse* she found, it was too late. I already knew about fellatio, cunnilingus, multiple orgasms, homosexuality, and bisexuality. The stories were inside me, like all the stories I had read. She did not catch me in the act of reading, but, finding the magazines, she knew I had read them.

In those days, *Penthouse* subscribed to a swinger's mentality, that it was *all* good. Its letters section had stories under the heading "Boy/Boy-Girl/Girl," usually about threesomes gone strange. ("My wife wanted me to watch her have sex with another man. . . ." Or, better and more rare, "I was on a camping trip, getting to know my new brother-in-law. . . .") They electrified me. I drew on them for material a year later, when I invented pornographic stories for other boys who came to sleep over and play Dungeons and Dragons. As they squirmed around me in my family's dark basement playroom, I felt empty of everything but these burning, burning things. "He was walking down the beach," one of them went, "and she had just taken her top off to sunbathe. . . ." As I told the stories I traced lines across the bare backs of my friends, and felt like the world was blowing up.

MY MOTHER IS a feminist, and her life has been a series of escapes, geographic and social. Growing up in Maine, by her account, she was a meek and mostly obedient girl, a middle child who agreeably took care of her farm chores and her brothers and sisters. She went to school dances accompanied by her brothers, wore hand-me-down clothes from her cousins down the road, and was expected to be a farm wife. Her father's family, the Goodwins, have lived on the same farm for centuries, having settled there when the territory was called Massachusetts and George III was king. Her great-aunt Exerene, a drama professor at Colby College, took an interest in my mother and taught her posture, table manners, and how to make her own clothes. Exerene had never married. She'd traveled to Boston twice a year to buy her wardrobe, and encouraged my mother to travel. At twenty-two, a college graduate, my mother drove away in a car she'd bought herself, the first Goodwin to leave Maine since the Gold Rush.

I had often suspected Exerene of being a lesbian from the stories I'd heard about her—she lived with a female companion her entire life—but it wasn't only Exerene I thought of as I prepared to tell my mother. My father's side of the family has its own mysteries.

One is my aunt, named for a sister who died at birth the year before this aunt was born. In Korea, this is bad luck; the confused ghost, called back by its name, inhabits the body of the living child, crowding its soul. Whatever crowded her soul, this aunt, the eldest surviving daughter, was married off early in order to safeguard the future marriages of her younger sisters. On her honeymoon at Cheju Island, the Niagara Falls of Korea, she pushed her husband's flaming suitcase out to sea from the predawn beach and abandoned him while he slept. My grandfather had neglected to mention to the prospective groom that his betrothed was something of a pyromaniac, setting fires when she felt slighted. She once set fire to her parents' house when I was two, while I was napping in it. Apparently, a great deal of money was paid to quiet the husband, and my aunt was sent to Paris, to the Sorbonne. She never married again, obtaining a quiet divorce years later. She is currently a professor of French literature, a novelist, a member of PEN International, translating Proust into Korean—and one of my favorite relatives. Still as thin as a girl, she favors pomegranate colors and used to wear only clothes from a particular French designer. "I enjoy," she said to me on my most recent visit to Korea, "entertaining the foreign students." She hasn't set a fire in years.

My uncle is not one of my favorites. My father's youngest brother, he is often in poor health, the pollution of Seoul and his cigarettes both overwhelming his sensitive constitution. A resolute misogynist, he recently married a medical student, a very bright but passive young woman whom he forced to have a child, making her take a leave of absence from school. Now that she has resumed her career, he complains loudly about her deficiency as a wife. He loves their daughter across an abyss of disappointment, and takes care of her bitterly. He talks of wanting a son. During my last trip to Korea, he took me aside after we had finished working out together at his gym. I had noticed his profound disaffection from the task at hand, his attention to the other men. We stood in the marble lobby of the health club, surrounded by "greeters," women paid to wear traditional Korean garb and say hello to arriving visitors. "I used to be like you," he said. I suppressed a smile. "I used to hang around with artists and writers and go to parties in Tokyo, when I was at university there. But there comes a time when you realize your duty to your family and you settle down and get married." He seemed as robotic as the greeters around us mouthing "Hello" over and over again. The night before, at the dinner table, my grandfather had offered me any woman in Korea for my wife. "Anyone you want," he said, "you tell Granfi," referring to himself in his closest approximation of "grandfather." There were, it seemed, uncrossable distances between who I was and telling them about it, and this was apparently the way they wanted it.

When you are openly gay in Korea, your family declares you dead and holds a funeral for you. The family book lists you as deceased. Prayers are said for you once a year at the family shrine and incense is burned for your ghost.

The traditional exception to the funeral is the *mu dang*. Usually female, though often male, they are cross-dressing homosexual shamans who are actually expected to have same-sex lovers. The *mu dang* are go-betweens for the living and the dead, chosen by the spirit world as children. They are usually orphans or survivors of life-threatening illnesses, haunted by catastrophe until they accept their role. If you suspect some ancestor is making trouble for you, you go to a *mu dang* and find out how to appease him. *Mu dang* are not supposed to marry or have children of their own.

I felt headed more for a funeral than a conversation with the dead as the hour neared when my mother and sister would step off the plane. I spent my afternoon walks from my apartment to the bookstore staring into a puzzle: In a way, I expected my mother's response to my announcement to be like my sister's, acknowledgment rather than surprise. This didn't explain my dread, however. Then I realized, on one of these walks, that there was a silence I would be crossing, and that the silence was my father.

AFTER MY FATHER'S death, my mother would have moments when she grew quiet and drew inward, and it was clear she was consulting her memory of him, trying, in a way, to make him talk to her. She would watch me at something and say, "Your father used to do that." Once, in complaining to me of something my sister had done, she began her sentence with "Your daughter . . ." and I had to remind her that she was talking about my sister. We laughed. My father's death had been too sudden for her, and so I allowed this long game of remembering to occupy my memory of him. Out of respect for my mother's grief, I neglected my own.

There were times then that I wanted my father back, not just in the way that you long for someone dead to return to life but in very specific, active ways. I wanted his advice. I wanted him to show me how to wear a suit and tie, how to buy a car. I wanted a hug. I wanted his ferocity, the way he could change a room by walking into it. And now I wanted to know what he would say if I told him I was gay.

If you can teleport to the far mountain, a Ch'an Buddhist saying goes, then you should walk. Ch'an Buddhists advise against the use of magic, and so do I. For all my fascination with the *mu dang*, I didn't want to become one. I didn't want actually to speak with my father's ghost. I did, however, want to feel sure, when I went to speak with my mother, how my father would have responded, what he would have said, how he would have felt toward me. I wanted to know he would still love me. I wanted a way to consult him. What that would be, I did not know.

NOW MY MOTHER and my sister were coming to see me in California, on what I could only assume was meant to be a reconciliation trip for them. I had meant to write my mother a letter, or phone her in advance with my revelation, but instead I wound up calling her three hours before her flight. That way, I knew, she wouldn't cancel her ticket. We spoke briefly about their itinerary: two days in San Francisco, then a drive down the coast to Big Sur with overnight stops along the way. A car would be rented. I paused, then told her quickly, "There's something you need to know before you arrive." And while there was silence, it was not that silence of my father, but, rather, shock.

"You must have known," I said as she sighed heavily at the other end of the line.

"You raise your children and you hope for the best."

"The best you could hope for is that I'm happy," I said.

A long silence.

"You had to know before you came here, or there wouldn't be anything about my life I could show you."

She sighed again. When things were at their worst in my childhood, when she was working more than she was sleeping, when my father died, I remember sitting helplessly as my mother walked around the house, sighing. It was like a sudden thirst for air, as if she were so busy she'd forgotten to breathe, or the amount of air available in the world had shrunk.

We said good-bye and hung up. I had ten hours to prepare myself to see her.

My mother's love for us, her children, is something for which I know no easy metaphor. I have seen nothing care for its kind like she does. This was a bond between her and her mother-in-law. My Korean grandmother, upon meeting my mother with nine-month-old me in her arms, remarked on it instantly: "This one will never let her children go." It was a grief to my grandmother when her daughters convinced my grandfather to sue for custody of us during my father's convalescence. Despite their failure, my mother's anger at this has abated only slightly in the thirteen years that have passed since then. She took over my father's fisheries business, paid our bills, encouraged us to make the most of our bewildering talents with swimming lessons, music lessons, karate, choir, acting, drawing, the school newspaper. She sold the business properties in what was a record real estate deal for the waterfront of Portland, Maine, securing for us trust funds which provided for travel and private educations. She worked twelve- and fourteen-hour days, driving to visit my father in the hospital, then picking us up from our various activities. Her own genius eluded her then and eludes her still; she has no sense of it. Her husband had been the first person (besides, I suppose, Exerene) to make her feel that she could be larger than she was. Our genius, on the other hand, was front and center for her, and when we faltered, there were talks of how could we squander what God had given us. We owed it to life to be everything we could be—and life, that was her.

But my being gay was not something she had counted on, and so as I left to meet her, I resolved to be as gentle as possible. Then, in characteristic fashion, I forgot my glasses and had to drive near-blind to the airport, squinting in the dusk the entire way.

My mother and sister emerged from the gate quietly. The girl who had turned heads a year before now attracted what was, really, a rude amount of attention. Oval face, smooth dark hair, she had gained almost her full height and stood taller than my mother, looking me in the eye at almost six feet. Beside her, my mother glowed, as if light had gathered in her and was releasing slowly along the bright blonde mane of her hair and the white coronas at the centers of her navy-blue eyes. She was dressed in bright colors, with a gold chain from my father around her neck and her engagement ring and heirloom diamonds prominent on her hands. My sister was dressed in black.

I kissed my sister first, and then my mother. "You'll have to drive," I told my mother. "I forgot my glasses and almost killed myself getting here."

She smiled. I needed her still.

The fabric of the moment smoothed instantly, and our visit began.

WE WERE DRIVING a big white car, a Ford of some kind, unmemorable, with lots of legroom, the ocean on our right as we headed south. I kept feeling that the water would rush in and sweep us away. I would look into the rearview mirror to check the traffic and then see my sister, in a tight, cleavage-baring red top, reading the guidebook through black cat's-eye sunglasses. Both seemed impossible. The road kept bending away out of sight. There were clouds off in the far west, but plenty of sun here on the land.

My mother sat beside me, quiet. She hadn't liked San Francisco. She disliked the Castro, with its bars that opened before the restaurants opened for breakfast. She found the bookstore bewildering and my friends unnerving, if funny. She was thrown off her compass points, making it hard for her to know what to think of anything. I hadn't introduced her yet to the young painter I was dating, but then I hadn't introduced him to my friends yet, either.

The names of the places we visited that week were legendary to me from childhood: Carmel, Monterey, Big Sur. Santa Cruz. After leaving Maine in 1951, my mother had gone first to Connecticut, and then, a few years later, to California. Thirty-eight years later, so had I. I had attended college in Middletown, where my mother had taught grade school after graduating; she had gone to parties at the college. I had the feeling I was tracing routes I'd traveled already, in the womb. This particular day, we were on our way to Carmel, where we would stay at a cabin in the Asilomar State Beach national park.

We drove slowly through the park, a forest with a sandy floor. The wind coming through the leaves sounded like rustling feathers and smelled of eucalyptus and pine. Between the trees and the sea and the sky, the world seemed made of radiant sheets of blue-green, and we were quiet among them. Our cabin was a wooden, triangular structure, a giant child's abandoned toy in a shady corner of the park.

"I'm going to read," my sister said. She hauled her bag out of the trunk and set off for the cabin.

My mother and I looked at each other. "I need a walk," she said. She widened her eyes, imitating an expression of surprise. "Come keep your mother company."

The Atlantic had been the solace of my adolescence. When I was upset, and I often was, I'd take off on my bike for the shore; as we lived on a peninsula, it was never far or hard to find, and the road followed the coast. The Atlantic is a stern slate color, revealing nothing except in storms. The Pacific is deep blue, the ocean of my mother and father's love as they met and dated and decided to marry. I suspected she was remembering him, and this made me quiet.

My mother had not mentioned him. We had not yet directly referred to the matter at hand. As we walked north along Carmel's white sand beach and looked at the waves of the early-evening tide pulling out, I realized my mother's modesty was preventing her from bringing up her unhappiness with me. She wanted me to speak, so that she could. So I did.

"Do you mean to tell me you've traveled three thousand miles to see me and you aren't even a little curious? You don't have any questions?"

"I hate to see you wasting your life. You're a smart kid. But you never knew how to stick up for yourself. Never knew how to go after what really was yours. I wish you would."

I was quiet, ashamed for a moment of my job at the bookstore, of working for little better than minimum wage, eating burritos every day, living in a badly renovated Victorian with matted brown shag carpeting and sleeping on a bed I'd built myself. I thought I knew what my mother wanted from me: a son she could mention to her friends with ease. But I wanted to be a writer. I felt I needed to see the world beyond the Northeast and the suffocating possibilities I'd felt as a teenager. The suburban experiment frightened me. Cities were a comfort, and San Francisco was a Pacific capital. At the bookstore I got to see every kind of person, from the runaway teenage prostitutes I let use the bathroom to clean up a little, to the wealthy white man who came in with his young Thai boyfriend and ordered him around like a servant.

"Do you remember what you always used to say when I was growing up?" I asked. "'If I can't look myself in the eye in the mirror in the morning, it's not worth it.' You taught me to be honest with myself. When I'm honest with myself, I know I'm gay."

Clouds had drifted toward the shore, and we moved in and out of light and shadow as the sun set. The constant wind seemed to make my skin feel new. My mother searched the sand at her feet, an expression of insoluble bitterness on her face. No one likes to be quoted back to themselves, least of all by their children.

I may never know what exactly my mother was saying good-bye to then. Had she imagined me marrying? Did she think I was going to die in a few years?

As much as I think I know her, my mother offers surprises. She didn't fight me, didn't insist I reconsider or think of therapy, as she had when I was younger and angrier. She looked at me and smiled.

"I am happier," I said. "You always used to tell me how bitter I was, ask me when I would be happy. I'm happy now. Right? Look at me."

She turned away from me, then turned back. "Yes," she admitted.

"I am still your son, Mom. I am still the person you brought up. You just know more now. Didn't you notice how I never talked about my life? Didn't you wonder?"

She regarded me a moment, her lips pursed, as if she were seeing me all over again. She nodded. "You are," she said. "Still your grandmother's little brown berry."

We walked back to the cabin and found my sister asleep on her side, the book fallen from her hand. We covered her in a blanket and went to get dinner.

TWO WEEKS LATER I was standing in my shower at six in the morning, getting ready to go to an ACT UP demonstration at the Sixth International Conference on AIDS. I stood in the spray and tried to wake up. It was still dark out. I was humming something and I had no idea what it was. Eventually, I realized the music was something I had gotten from my father. It could have been an opera or jazz theme, or just a lullaby. He might even have made it up. I didn't know. I only had the memory of him humming it.

My father had loved my mind. He'd loved my rapid ability with words and my obsession with staying underwater. When I was four and we lived in Guam, he used to take me snorkeling on his back, both of us in masks. I would put my arms around his shoulders, my mask covering half my head, and he would turn to me and say, "We're playing dolphin now." And then we went down, his legs propelling us with graceful kicks.

My father and I went far away from Guam before his death, but I will always remember that water that once held us both, perforated by the light of the Pacific noon and the three thousand colors of everything he showed me there. His attitude was, here is the world, marvelous to see. Be marvelous in it. He mentioned being a man, but never what that would mean. This was his gift to me, the freedom to be something new, his reason for breaking from his family, race, and culture. But it has taken me some time to understand this. I know now that my father lives on in me, is a code deeply encrypted in me and rendering itself through me.

Before we had left Carmel, my mother, my sister, and I had toured the park again. We went down to the sea from a steep set of hills, forested by trees that seemed somehow to both reach and hide. The branches were dark and gnarled, and the leaves glittered like scales everywhere I looked. "These trees are beautiful," I said. "What are they?"

"Cypress," my sister replied. "They're a kind of cypress that only grows here, and according to Native American myth, these trees are women who lost their husbands at sea in a storm. The tribe here used to be fishermen, and the women came down to the water to greet the men and the men never returned. The gods took pity on them and turned them into these trees."

I didn't want to be alive without my father. I never had wanted it, and yet I was, and had been for years. I let myself cry in the shower. I turned the water off. No gods to make of me a tree, I had a great deal of walking to do. He would still love me, I thought as I stepped from the shower. And then, he still loves me. He loves me still.

MONEY TALKS

David Drake

I HAD A lot of secrets when I started performing on the community theater stages of Baltimore at age ten. Fused with whatever God-given talents I possessed were the fear, shame, rage, and ecstasy of being a sissy. However unexplained or unexamined, it was an energy that drove my life then as surely as it drives me today. The theater became a safe place where I was not only allowed to focus the energy of my queer delights and frustrations but encouraged to do it—applauded for it. In the controlled environment of an auditorium, behind the mask of a character, I was somehow free. And powerful. Ten years later, when I began pursuing acting as a career in New York, another energy entered the arena: money.

The business half of show business was never my motivation, the show half was. At first, getting paid to do something I loved was thrilling. The novelty wore off when the job-to-job struggle to make ends meet became a way of life. Still, putting a dollar amount to the commodity of my imagination taps into some very basic personal issues.

Money has a charged energy that makes me uncomfortable. The root of all evil? Debatable. Sin is not my issue. Worthiness is. Romantic legends of suffering artists have always appealed to me: Emily Dickinson waiting in white, never leaving her house in Amherst; Neil Sedaka missing "the hungry years"; Van Gogh chopping off an ear. Now, I'm a bit of a drama queen, but I draw the line at self-amputation. Then there are the individuals who received exorbitant sums for their artistic contributions. I was dazzled by the rich and famous, but they were always Other People. The ones who saw the unknown world as safe for exploration. The Ambitious Ones. The Promised Ones. The Straight Ones. (Or at least the ones who agreed to participate in the public perception of being straight.) I did not belong among those people.

This felt especially true in 1990, when I began writing pieces to perform myself. In an effort to combat my feelings of helplessness stemming from the overwhelming loss of friends and colleagues to AIDS, I joined ACT UP, an organization teeming with brilliant individuals contributing their medical, social, and political expertise to help change the course of the epidemic, if not end it altogether. I didn't possess these kinds of talents. But when a list was passed around asking people to sign on for "The ACT UP Talent Show," I discovered a way to contribute something as personal to me as the offerings of the activists who inspired me. Out of this grew a number of solo pieces chronicling my political coming of age as a gay man, developed in dozens of benefits. These proved so popular that a fellow activist offered to produce a full-length evening Off Broadway. Thus *The Night Larry Kramer Kissed Me* was born.

For most of the creative and managerial team, the show became an extension of our activism as well as a play. As the opening drew closer, money was low on the list of items making me nervous. That was my producer's territory. He wasn't nervous around money. As a matter of fact, he was terrific with the stuff. But investing in a play is one of the riskiest business ventures, so I wasn't surprised when he told me, three weeks before the first preview performance, that we still needed ten thousand dollars to capitalize the production.

"Give me twenty-four hours to think it over," I said.

That night I thought about it and thought about it. I called him back the next morning.

"I know where I can get it."

I'll call Dan.

Dan and I have been talking on the phone for several years now. That's how we met, as he lives in Baltimore and I'm in New York. To this day, I've never actually seen him, although I know he has brown hair and eyes, stands about six feet tall, weighs around 175 pounds. Goes to the gym. Single.

How do I know all this? He told me. And I believe him. Dan has no reason to lie to me, no reason to make himself out to be something he's not. Because Dan is straight. He's my stockbroker.

In 1988, I inherited a modest sum from a relative in Baltimore. The legacy was contingent on the money's staying with a local brokerage firm for a determined period of time. Our Maryland family lawyer set me up with the man who would handle my account: Dan. Our conversations were always business centered and friendly. Like so many straight guys, Dan referred to his out-of-the-office interests as matter-of-factly and easily as he did the bulls and the bears. Stereotypically, these interests were sports and girls. In Dan's world, one often leads to the other. That's how I found out he goes to the gym. When Dan asked if I worked out, I told him I did (the closest I ever came to an activity relating to sports). "Isn't the gym a great place to meet girls?" he responded unself-consciously. Since I happen to go to New York's gay ghetto all-male Chelsea Gym, I could honestly answer, "Yes!"

But irony was as far as I could indulge myself with Dan. When he, with baritone-sexy assurance, casually mentioned a night out with the guys, or a date, or an ex-girlfriend, I remained silent. I never mentioned a date, a boy-friend, a breakup. The street demonstrations where I screamed myself hoarse. The parades that marched pride into me. The vacations at Fire Island Pines. The young men I had buried. I was raised to believe that your private life is your private life. But as time passed, activism changed my way of thinking. In my conversations with Dan, I began sensing that my silence wasn't discretion. It was censorship. I wasn't protecting my privacy, I was keeping secrets.

Soon I would begin telling audiences seven times a week the intimate details of my experiences, which were rooted in my secrets. I didn't know then that for the next three years I'd be telling the stories of The Night Larry Kramer Kissed Me to tens of thousands of people around the world. All I knew at that moment in 1992 was that I had a show to get on. To do that, I had to tell Dan.

I picked up the phone and dialed Baltimore.

"Hi, Rosie, it's David Drake," I said to the receptionist who'd been transfer-ring my calls from the beginning. "I need to talk to Dan."

"How ya doin', hon?" She brightened with homey Baltimorese, a cross be-tween Cockney and Kentucky which makes most people cringe, but which John Waters and I adore. "Let me see where he's at. Hold a sec, hon."

The Muzak version of some Barry Manilow song oozed in my ear. Or was it the Beatles? (Who can tell? They all sound alike on Muzak.)

"Dave, hon?" Rosie cut in and told me Dan was just finishing up another call. I could either hold or he'd call me right back. I said I'd hold. This gave Rosie the chance to get an update on my career. "Sooooo . . ." she whispered with conspiratorial excitement, "how's the actin' going?"

"Good," I said, thinking I'd use Rosie as a litmus test. "I've got a new show coming up real soon."

"Congratulations, hon! We're all rootin' for ya! What's this new one about?" I paused. "About ninety minutes."

Rosie guffawed with a zealousness that comes when people not in show biz talk show biz with someone in show biz. But wait. What was that sound? A snort? Did Rosie actually let out a little snort? Oh, Rosie, honey, I thought, that Baltimore is really showing this morning.

"You are tooooo much." Rosie sighed. "Oops. I think Dan's comin' on. Hold a sec, hon. Break a bone!"

Leg, Rosie. Break a *leg*. More Muzak.

As I held, I could feel the anxiety rising in my throat from the pounding in my chest. My palms were sliding on the receiver. I felt as if I were eight years old again, waiting to ask my father for my weekly allowance, the one that would finally give me enough money to go to Toy Barn and buy Barbie. Ten years after I'd struggled out of the closet to my family and created a (mostly) openly gay network of friends and colleagues, I was shaking with fear.

Yes. I feared Dan. I feared him because he was straight. I feared his power, his position, his potential judgment. Feared the silence that would follow my confession. I feared he would begin making bad investments with my money because I was a fag. I feared he would not think the story I wanted to tell was worth the investment of any money, let alone my own, because he considered the issues of gay and lesbian lives of no value. Basically, I feared Dan was a Republican.

By the time he picked up on the line, I was not afraid. I was furious.

"Why have you kept me waiting this long?" I demanded.

"I'm real sorry, Dave. Didn't Rosie tell you I'd call you right back, so as not to make you hold?"

"She told me," I said. "Whatever. Listen, I've called because I want you to sell ten thousand dollars' worth of my portfolio and deposit it into my account. *Today.*"

"Okay," he carefully drawled. "Let's take a look at what would be best."

I had never been this aggressive with Dan. I had always been as cooperative and interested in the selections he wanted me to review before buying or selling as he had been with my opinions and suggestions. Now I was panting. My heart and brain were jumping with heat and energy and fear and rage.

"Dave," he quietly inquired, pulling my account up on the computer, "is everything all right?"

"Everything is fine," I clipped.

"We can get you this money today. . . ." he cautiously approached. "And I don't mean to pry, but, as a friend, are you in any kind of trouble?"

"Trouble? You mean like with the *law?*"

"Or," he whispered, "a girl?"

"Christ, Dan," I practically screamed. "I'm *gay!*"

"So . . ." He paused. "Is this for shopping?"

The phone slipped out of my hand, right to the floor—I was laughing so hard, I literally lost my grip. When I got it back to my ear, Dan's laughter was booming all the way from Baltimore, while he apologized profusely.

"I'm sorry, Dave, I'm really sorry. I know it was a cheap shot, but I just couldn't resist. You set me up, bud. You set me up!"

And I had set Dan up. I had set myself up as well. When we both calmed down, I told him what I wanted to do.

"Why didn't you tell me you'd written a play? What's it called?"

"The Night Larry Kramer Kissed Me."

"Who's Larry Kramer?" Dan said. "Your boyfriend?"

There was a lot of catching up to do.

COMING OUT TO Dan wasn't graceful, but it was necessary, not just to completing the capitalization of my play but to integrating the various energies swirling around my life, that small inheritance being the central force. It was the key unlocking the door to the secrets that held me back from living my life with a deeper sense of freedom, and from being as honest with my friends, family, and acquaintances as I strive to be in my work. The powerful energy of money, in this instance, helped to redefine my long-standing place of masked safety—the theater—into a place of unmasked truth and pride.

Dan was just one of the Prince Charmings who helped me along the path of the fairy tale that was *The Night Larry Kramer Kissed Me*. But he was the only straight one. Yet my fear of a straight man almost kept me from claiming power that was mine to begin with, artistic and monetary. Certainly there were elements of old shame and fear related to my father at work here. But that's another story. (My father, by the way, flew to New York to see the opening of my show. A framed poster of the play hangs in his den.)

Since I came out to Dan, our conversations have been filled with laughter and trust—and, I feel, my portfolio has reflected the strength of our bond. In 1994, I played a small role in the movie *Philadelphia*. Dan took a date the opening weekend. He called me the following Monday morning to tell me how moved he had been.

"It's a good thing the girl I was with wasn't a first date," Dan confided, "'cause at the end, man, I really cried."

I told him if it had been *our* first date and he'd cried at a sad movie, I'd have proposed marriage on the spot. (I love a man in touch with his feelings. Nowadays, anyway.)

Rosie filled me in on the rest. When the movie was released, *Premiere* magazine did a piece on me detailing the struggles of an openly gay actor in Hollywood. Dan cut it out and showed it to everybody in the office.

"It's hanging up on the corkboard above his desk," bragged Rosie. "You're his star client, hon, and everybody knows it. Just remember . . . we're *all* rootin' for ya!"

With Sir Ian McKellen (right), 1992, at a performance of The Night Larry Kramer Kissed Me

SEA LEVEL

Carl Phillips

PROVINCETOWN, NOVEMBER 1995.
Where most open, where seawall and brush of any to-be-reckoned-with size give out, they have lined the shore with what must be, given bits of tinsel still stranded among, flashing among the now-brown needles, so many discarded Christmas trees—heaped, then by wire bound down. Almost a year old, and yet the scent is still with them, strong enough to hold its own with the air's salt. I like the notion that what is dead, only a memory for most of the people already caught up in trying to catch up to the fast-approaching holiday season, can find a use in the life beyond it, a space in the world that says, *Yes, I will hold you.*

I have always loved a summer town in the winter, in what they call here the "off" season, or the dead one. I lived for many years in such a town and remember looking forward most to being able to see *things* again. It's why I've come here so late in November, strange month that finds its start with the dead, its end in the giving of all thanks.

Here are this afternoon's things. The water boatless, or only two-boated. The usual many of souls assuming, stepping out of, resuming the shells a life gives: glint of light or drown of it; seaweed in broken bits like distraction; barely seeable fish, a single skate whose moving remembers a scarf dropped and failing through air; birds, various but annunciatory all, of . . .

Of the general hunger too many know . . .

Of what thing *I* would know?

PRIOR TO ANYTHING like what is called "coming out" as a gay man, there was sex with other men. Naturally. As if knowing already the difficulties—the

328

baggage—that come with sexuality, morality, consciousness of and the recon-
ciling of the two, etc., the body tends to limit itself to the simpler instincts.
And I think hunger—for food as for the flesh—and the correspondent satisfaction that is the result of feeding that hunger—these are, of all our instincts,
the simplest. Close behind: fear, in the sudden thicket of danger (close behind
because hunger, pitched high enough, will inevitably override fear).

So. Sex.

I suppose everything is finally instructive, and that every lover is a kind of
teacher, but it seems especially significant that in each of my rather few forays
into the world of homosexual sex, I found myself—in bed, in a truck, on the
fallen steps of property entirely abandoned except by the weather and the
yard's unchecked strangle—with a professional teacher of one sort or another.
A medical school professor (I myself a mere college undergraduate at the time)
whom I would later cast, less than subtly, in a poem as Chiron, the mythological instructor to the hero Achilles in the art of becoming a man. Nearly ten
years later (and more than half of that into a marriage), a psychotherapist
whom I'd hoped could show me how to school my body away from what, as
it turned out, we both wanted. A conservationist, the first encounter with
whom began as a nature walk through the salt marshes where he instructed
school groups (and others, obviously) in the earth's fragility, in the need to
always take care. Granted, sex was the point in each of these meetings; the role
of teacher was, in each instance, immediately or almost immediately thrown out
the proverbial window. I learned, but in the way that any eager-enough, self-
motivated student will learn, despite a year in a classroom with a teacher who
either never could teach or, after years of steady burnout, has perhaps not lost
the gift but forgotten there once was one.

My wife of (eventually) ten years was not a teacher in the way these men
were, but I can see that relationship, too, as an example of student-seeks-
teacher. We were students together (and, ultimately, each the other's best
friend) at Harvard, having met there as freshmen in 1977, a time when I had
begun (but only barely) to question . . . not my sexuality but my hungers,
which I suppose I then wanted less to satisfy than to permanently undo. This
is not to say that when, at twenty-four, I married—never having lived alone
and, thanks to a graduate program after Harvard, never having lived in what
is called the "real" world, that world outside the academy—I married as a
means of erasing homosexual desire. Nor do I mean there was no love. There
was love. But I am reminded of the way in which a student with any genuine
zeal for learning (and a concomitant frustration with ignorance and/or the
unresolvable) loves a teacher—anticipatorily, I want to say. Already grateful
for the ease we have known clarity to bring. Already thankful for that clarity
that will come, surely, can't we already taste it, and isn't it sweet, for isn't that
what we were promised?

IT'S HARD TO imagine back, at this hour in high tide, to how bleak it was
earlier this morning, when the tide finding its lowest ebb meant also the

complete exposure of a usually forgettable (because unseen) world at the sea's floor. Tide flats, I think they're called, the generally exposed areas across which lie strewn the suddenly vulnerable lives of, oh, snails, worms that aren't earthworms (I suppose they are sea worms), tiny crabs, and things that seemed related to them—everything left helpless before the sun's indifference and the collective hunger of scavenger gulls whose hour this particularly is. Here and there a few fortunate creatures have found small pools of water between rises in the seafloor's surface. Brief seas, miniature havens, the pools say everything about how closely circumscribed hope or survival can be.

It's hard to imagine back, except on remembering one beaten and barely red anymore truck in the midst of where, normally, were feet and feet of water. Not only curiosity but human need brought me to walk across the tide flats to the truck. Isn't it human when anything—a lover's heart, a wound, a different world—has been exposed, to want to step inside of it, to know it, before we pass on to whatever's next (and usually predictable)?

He was kind enough, considering: one stranger to another.

As it turns out, he farms quahogs. ("Oysters I try each year—more luck with quahogs.") He led me to the netted-down beds he had seeded last year and, rummaging the wet sand, he drew several of the quahogs out—each a different size, each variously ready, or not quite, for market.

One was dead. The farmer pointed out a small hole toward where the shell's two halves came to a hinge. Apparently, there's a snail that drills through the shell, draws the meat out, and eats it, leaving the shell empty, the almost indiscernible hole the only sign that there has been . . . violation.

That was hours ago, now.

IN THE REALM of knowledge, the general (instinctive, I want to say) drift is toward the empirical. More precisely: Touch is always preferable to hearsay, no matter how often the latter may call itself Wisdom Gathered from Long Experience. (What does it feel like, that gathering, and how will we know unless we become the gatherers ourselves?)

Before I had touched a man sexually, I knew inside of me an attraction to other men. After I had touched a man sexually, I knew it not just inside but entirely. This, for some, is what will amount to a coming-out story.

But a stripping away of doubt as to one's physical attraction toward men is not, in and of itself, what I have found it to mean to be a homosexual man. On the contrary, the results of those physical attractions, the sexual encounters—predominantly (inevitably?) anonymous—with men before and, yes, during the last years of a marriage, had convinced me, not of my homosexuality so much as of my perversion, my abnormality—and of my revulsion from homosexuality *as I understood it*. But how else to understand it, in the absence of a societal openness that might have helped me overcome the fear of investigating the few books that did exist on the subject, or the fear of (what should have been easier) speaking up. In high school, college—sometime, anyway, before the pulling of at least one life, my former wife's, toward a disappointment none of which she deserved, all of which I might have prevented.

When I consider that I was born in 1959—am, in essence, a "child of the sixties"—I'm all the more surprised at my sense of society as closed to sexual openness. Certainly, if I recall correctly, the sixties were at least partly *about* openness, if not—in the face of a turbulence that seemed increasingly insurmountable—about a downright abandon that seems understandable (as I have always understood the ease with which the beleaguered crew of Ulysses at last yielded to the Lotus-Eaters). And if I was a child in the sixties, I was becoming socially and politically aware in the seventies, an era that, for all the bad press it sometimes receives, does seem to have brought women's rights and (to a lesser degree) gay rights more forcibly into the public view.

But the crucial difference, for me, was in being part of a military family. My father was a career air force man and, until I began high school in 1973, when he retired and we settled in Falmouth, Massachusetts, we moved annually from military base to military base, stopping to rest only in Germany, where we lived for four years—again, on a military base, which could have been anywhere. Germany was there, but how often did everyday life spill into it, given the nature of military bases? Worlds unto themselves, with housing, theaters, mall equivalents, restaurants, schools. One need never leave base borders—which is also to say one need never move outside the realm of military thinking. There was even a separate newspaper, the *Stars and Stripes*, in addition to the daily that each base generated.

Need I say, given the current hysteria surrounding the notion of gays in the military, that there was at no time any discussion of homosexuality in school? To be fair, there was little discussion of sexuality at all, and what little there was made it clear that heterosexuality was not just the norm but the only possibility. What did that make me, waking some mornings from disturbing dreams of lying naked and not fondling so much as fumbling with the guy who later in the day would again be Mr. Richie the algebra teacher?

Just to have heard—and been able to believe—somebody saying, *Yes, what you want, who you are—they're okay. . . .*

Instead—no; *therefore* (years later, of course): the windowless bars; downright frightening theaters for the showing of pornographic movies; other places where, if one was curious enough (or perhaps only that human), one could "stumble upon" live pornography on a stage, in a back room. At which point, haven't we come back to the empirical? Men as a matter of how many hands, this tattooed back, that cock, which ass, this one, whose lovely enough brow until dawn or the lamp's light am I forgetting?

THIS AFTERNOON, WALKING across town to the old dairy bar/seafood restaurant, I remembered a dream—or whatever to call what lies stationed between dream and nightmare—that I used to have often. Not of a house with windows, but of the windows themselves, alone, freestanding, no house unless air. There are two windows, one shutterless, the other with one shutter the blue that, could I have it, I think I could rest, I could want nothing. From the shutter a fish hangs, as it has done for days. I know this. I know its blue and green iridescence means finally rot and hunger, flies for scales. The fish hangs, its mouth gaping, as if wanting to say . . . who knows what? The dream ends.

It has long since ended.

The restaurant is one of those 1950s types, the pale green so many of the cars seem to have been, back then. Arrestingly bright plastic booths, paper plates only, and, for ambience, the usual nautica: fishing nets, wooden floats, buoys, a whale's forever-agape jaw one passes through to get to the counter and place an order. But the unique thing here, and perhaps my main reason for revisiting the restaurant, is the collection of deformed lobster claws. All is exactly as I remember: the back room as before, the same glass case inside it, and, inside that, the lobster claws, each mounted on its little cork stand, each variously misshapen, or lacking or hard-blessed with something extra, useless, half hindering (but only half), the size of each claw attesting to a life that, despite the body, for the usual number of years lasted.

I wept a little, when I saw them, I can't say why.

I wasn't sad.

WHEN I DESCRIBE as crucial to my understanding about identity my having been raised in a military family on military bases, I should add what was equally crucial: that I am the child of a biracial marriage. My father is black, from Tuscaloosa, Alabama; my mother, white, was born and grew up just outside of London, England, not far from the military base where my father, a young recruit in the 1950s, would eventually be stationed.

It's an interesting mix. I don't mean the black and the white of it. I mean that my parents, who, in getting married at all in so racially strained a time, could be credited with a certain rebellious, pioneering spirit, should at the same time have fashioned their lives within an institution not particularly known for the acceptance of nonconformity of any kind, least of all in the area of race. And my parents were clearly aware of the racism, no less common in the military than in the world at large. For this reason, my two sisters and I grew up in a very sheltered space, whose borders ended with immediate family. Few, if any, friends—of my parents, of us kids—entered the house. Evenings and weekends were spent among ourselves.

One way to look at this is with admiration for my parents' efforts to provide a sense of unity, of our family as a trustworthy refuge from a world that could not be relied on to give us the same shake, fair or otherwise, as the next—i.e., all-white—family.

The other view: Essentially, we lived in a tightly circumscribed circle called Family, that circle itself circumscribed by the circle called the Air Force Base, encircled in turn by that larger ring, the Military. Beyond that—as in the days when the world was presumed flat—who knew? Except a veritable sea of things nameless and better left unnamed.

"COMING OUT." "Come out of the closet." I think of a closet as storage space for what is so little used that it has been forgotten (an unfashionable tie, an old Hoover kept as backup should the new and improved model fail) or a place for what is very much and routinely useful (a broom, a favorite coat, the umbrella that still works) but not all-the-time enough to warrant regular display. I think sexuality—we are talking about identity at its basic level; before *Whose am I?* must come *Who and what am I?*—I think sexuality is neither of these things.

"To come out of one's shell" seems closer to, if not quite to be, the point. One's identity is a sort of shell, even as we can understand various aspects of identity to be so many shells we regularly step into, step out of. Now father. Now son. Now teacher. Now lover. Now beloved. Bottom. Top. Every role, as every body, entails an inhabiting of space. The shell image will serve.

Persona means "mask" in Latin. Mask: half a shell.

The shell image will serve, because it must. It had to. How else to explain, for example, that role of husband that I couldn't entirely call mine, or how explain away the more lurid lives that, I maintain, it was only partly myself living?

What is commonly called "coming out" I prefer to call a stepping into. We step into the shell that is finally and undeniably our own—that we entirely inhabit. This is not to say it isn't fragile, ultimately corruptible, necessarily impermanent. We are human; we do die, after all. But the right shell, stepped inside of, will at least be invulnerable to guilt about one's sexuality. Call that first moment of in-stepping, if you wish, a coming out.

FROM WHERE I am staying in this small harbor town at the tip of a peninsula, as we shift, all of us, routinely, toward dark, I can watch the lights as they raggedly come—not *on*, it seems, but *to*. The green light marks the stone jetty's single finger extended. There is a house. There . . . is another house. And of course the lighthouse two towns beyond these, but visible tonight.

"Lighthouse, tower of bright, distant witness" I once wrote in a poem from an earlier summer. But the lighthouse is witness to nothing, really, is only a tower proffering flat, unvaried warning, its lamp panning, like long habit, the now everywhere black, as for some somewhere findable gold.

I WON'T SULLY it. I won't. That's the way I used to think about my marriage. It's the way I meant to think about my body and then, always, forgot—until after, when it seemed that nothing could wash me clean enough. In this regard, to quote the poem from which the lighthouse description comes seems useful.

THE GODS

> It is not that they don't exist but that they are
> everywhere disguised, that no one space than another

is less fit or more likely:
the lighthouse, tower of bright, distant witness,

the same dull bird as before, still extendedly calling
where has every wing flown

—the sand, the salt grass.
Think of any of those times that they are said

to have assumed the slowing burden of flesh
and done damage; recall Christ, then (all over)

the boy you found lying restive
(among the sand, the salt grass),

naked—save for the words "breakfast included"
lipsticked onto his chest in thick, plum letters;

and that particular beauty that disarms first,
then attracts

(in which way he most resembled any bad road
collision from which the bodies have not yet been

freed, he resembled the bodies).
They are to any of our hungers as, once, the water was

to that Portuguese man-of-war that you can see
is collapsed now, stranded, useless to itself

against any mouth toward it and open.
They were equally to do with your saying no

and your saying no *not because of not wanting but*
Because, *you thought,* what else can it be, so much

wanting, except wrong? *Their forgiveness*
has never been to be sought: it will, or will not

befall us—you are not stupid, you know this.
As you have known, always, their favor: that it is

specific and can be difficult to see, it is that thin
and that clean. Easily it breaks, and it breaks clean.

I continue to be amazed at how densely packed with guilt and paranoia it all is: the equating of burden with flesh; the idea that the gods (read: judgment) are so ubiquitous that their gaze is inescapable—at all moments, the subject is observed. Even the sudden object of desire, a young man whose "included" breakfast promises to include his own ravishing self—even he is likely to be a god or the decoy of one. We can't know. In such a world, to arrive at the

ability to say no to random sexual temptation is less a matter of moral upright-
ness or self-discipline than of plain fear of . . . of retribution—something in
which we all seem to have been conditioned to believe, in one form or another
(even if that retribution is the nothing that is all the atheist is expecting). For
the space of the poem, fear wins out over hunger, but this moment of conquest
can only be temporary. Hence the other thing with which the flesh is here
equated: a damage that, given historical precedent, is to be expected. There is
a poem, in other words, which we understand to follow and provide the closure
to this one. But its predictability has bored us already. Why write it?

SUDDEN FIREWORKS, A treat I hadn't expected—though it *is* the day
after Thanksgiving, official start, I suppose, of one holiday season.

They shoot the fireworks over the water of this same harbor every July, but
that's in the midst of a tourist season that brings the town's population to
nearly ten times its "normal," off-season one, the streets so crowded, the harbor
that night so aglut with spectators that I've never bothered to join them in
the drunken fight for any view.

But *this* . . .

Alone in this house on the harbor, in a town that seems comparatively
deserted now, the watching of fireworks becomes an entirely different event,
almost as if I've never seen them before.

Something I haven't noticed before is the smoke left just behind the actual
bursting of the fireworks. I imagine that the cold has something to do with it,
the heat of the explosion lingering more visibly on the air's lowered temperature—that old phenomenon that, as children, we called *Look, I can see my breath.*

The other thing accounting for the visibility of the smoke is the moon, of
course. Not full; almost nothing, in fact. A shaving of light whose relative lack
of brightness, compared to the firecrackers' brilliance, somehow comes out the
winner nevertheless (confirming my long-held suspicion that what normally
seems only modest—even humble—if consistent can, when juxtaposed with
an excess of dazzle, find itself passing for that more elegant kinsman of the
humble, subtlety).

Tonight, anyway, the smoke of the fireworks is increasingly a more consider-
able thing to watch than the fireworks themselves. For whole minutes, the
after-smoke hangs in the air as if uncertain about the wisdom of rising. Then
it rises imposingly—into the air, across the water—and with what seems (for
mere smoke and no fire, anymore, behind it) an odd strength. The right wind
bears it away.

TO COME OUT, for me, ended up meaning to fall in love with another man.
To have sex with a man, as I have said, was to have the initial pleasure, sure,
of orgasm. Then, almost simultaneously—seconds after, at most—to find oneself deluged in the usual trinity of waves: guilt, fear, revulsion. The notion that

the body doing this cannot possibly be mine, or is mine for now only. When, when can I leave it?

It was unexpected. A cruise on the street four years ago, the sort of thing I had begun to fear could only become increasingly the norm for me. The cruise wasn't unexpected. (Why else was I standing outside a gay bookstore in Boston, all of me frozen except for the eyes that sought for questioning those of each customer coming, going?) Nor was the sex unexpected—that was presumably the point in repairing, immediately after having one's gaze at last met, to the men's room of the nearest hotel with the newfound stranger. But the sense (mutual, I'd later learn) of guilt surrounding the sex was different. This time, guilt stemmed not from a belief that the sex was morally wrong by society's standards but that it was for once not *entirely* the point. Something in this meeting made sex not irrelevant but *less* relevant, transcended the purely physical.

That is why, after the standard exchange of phone numbers, after my standard ride home on the subway that may as well have been powered by my sense of self-loathing (*a married man, a married man*), I did two things that were not standard—had never, in fact, happened before. I called the number I'd been given and I confessed to having deliberately given a wrong number, lest he should call and my wife answer. Now I gave my right number. I *wanted* to see him again, not for sex necessarily, but for what he'd (genuinely) asked for in giving me his number: the chance to meet for coffee and to talk. What other man had ever asked me for that?

At that moment I understood another definition for homosexuality, one that included—there seems no unsentimental way to put it—love.

The idea that love and homosexual sex could come together had certainly occurred to me, but on the level of fantasy. I'd neither read of nor seen any examples to prove the idea was any more than an unrealizable ideal. I could say that I found at that moment of falling in love with another man the shell—the life, really; the identity—that was mine, not in parts this time, but completely.

The man with whom I fell in love is the man I still happen to happily be with; but I do not mean to suggest that coming out must mean finding the so-called love of one's life. Doug was—to look at the situation in a manner less romantic—what might result were one to cross, say, a catalyst with a key or a map's legend. (Isn't this, now that I think of it, another definition for *teacher*?) This is why I can honestly say that I did not leave my marriage *for* Doug. When, two weeks after having met Doug, I told my wife that I was gay, it was because I had become able to do more than merely accept or understand (which had probably partially happened already) my homosexuality. I had come to know it as a core part of myself, about which there could be no choosing. This is also why, were Doug and I no longer together, I would not (contrary to my wife's continued belief—how much out of love, how much out of bitterness and an understandable fear of being alone?) return to the marriage. A realization of one's sexual identity is something quite different from an affair engaged in out of curiosity, boredom, spite—whatever the reasons commonly thrown up. Doug happened to remain in the picture, as they say, because that moment of my full knowledge of myself as a gay man happened to coincide with our falling in love. "Fate, fate, like a flag, like a novel," is how I have put it in a poem.

Most days, I simply smile and say *gravy*.

"THE SO-CALLED LOVE of one's life." Is that what I meant by "gold" when I wrote of a lighthouse's lamp as "panning the now everywhere black, as for some somewhere findable gold"? "Panning" as in scanning, the lighthouse as a gay man scanning the bar's darkness for the right body? As any genuine heart seeking its mate, who must be *out there* where we are not?

Yes.

No.

Just as: Yes, I did, and I didn't mean anything like being swept off of one's feet, as they say, in that bit about the smoke clouds suddenly carried off by wind. I didn't mean to equate wind with disease or violence and the clouds with the unsuspecting, unprotected, vulnerable flesh. And, yes, I did. It is the logic I mean in a statement such as "to come out is to finally step into, inside."

The travel writer Jan Morris, to a book describing her early awareness that she was a woman born inside a man's body (which is not, of course, the case with homosexuality, but is not unrelated to the homosexual who feels born inescapably inside a heterosexual model) and her gradual setting out on a journey whose merciful ending would be an understanding of transsexuality and a successful sex-change operation—to this book, Morris gives the title *Conundrum*. Nowhere else have I seen the word more beautifully applied, or more exactly.

THE WAVES ARE stronger on this morning of slow, reluctant leave-taking back to the city. The beach over and into which this small house stands is gone now, covered by the water that—if I didn't prefer the room's heat to the near-zero that would come with opening any door or window—I would hear more loudly meeting, beating up against, half burnishing, half stroking toward rot, the house's supporting posts that, for now at least, last.

From doors looking onto a deck and out to sea, the effect is of the house having finally separated from whatever held it to land and become a boat, moving steadily forward, not so much into and against an adverse current as aslant to one whose only pattern is indifference. Not fair and not brute, either.

Logic says that, if all of it holds long enough constant—current, wind, our little boat of a house and its not so little, almost willful drifting—we will eventually come out of this harbor that all our lives we have been told not to leave: this, the one safe place. And after that—as broad and as precarious, perhaps, to lean on as rumor—the sea. No oars, no handed-down-to-us wings, but—irrevocable, perilous, fraught, too, with joy—a life at last claimed: our own, for to steer with.

Photograph by Douglas Macomber

CONTRIBUTORS

Photograph by Jennifer Bishop

DAVID BERGMAN is the author of *Cracking the Code*, for which he received the George Elliston Poetry Prize, and *Gaiety Transfig-ured: Gay Self-Representation in American Literature*. He is the editor of *The Violet Quill Reader*, *Camp Grounds: Style and Homosexuality*, and the volumes *The Burning Library: Essays* (by Edmund White) and *Reported Sightings: Art Chronicles 1957–87* (by John Ashbery). In 1994, he succeeded the late George Stambolian as the editor of the prestigious *Men on Men* series of gay short fiction anthologies. His first volume, *Men on Men 5*, was nominated for a Lambda Book Award; his second has just been published. His work appeared in *Raritan, Kenyon Review, American Poetry Review*, the *James White Review, Men's Style*, the *Harvard Gay & Lesbian Review*, and other periodicals. Born in Fitchburg, Massachusetts, he is a graduate of Kenyon College and Johns Hopkins University. He now teaches English at Towson State University in Maryland and lives in Baltimore.

Photograph by Thomas Barbour

PHILIP BOCKMAN'S fiction has appeared in *Christopher Street*, for which he also wrote a column on gay issues; he was a frequent contributor to the *New York Native* from 1984 to 1991. After working as a typographer for two decades, he returned to school to earn a master's degree in social work from Hunter College, where he received the 1994 Goldfein Award for his professional paper on the effects of coming out on family dynamics. Bockman writes: "Having left the University of Michigan at the height of the antigay purges, I transferred to New York University and became involved in the Stonewall Riots and the actions that followed, working with Gay Activists Alliance and beginning to advocate for lesbians and gays as a teacher and writer. I worked with the Gay and Lesbian Alliance Against Defamation's (GLAAD) campaign for honest treatment of gays and lesbians in the media, writing hundreds of letters to the editors of major newspapers and magazines. In the late 1980s I joined the AIDS Coalition to Unleash Power (ACT UP) and began to write about AIDS; in 1990, I became a volunteer buddy team leader with Gay Men's Health Crisis (GMHC). Obtaining my degree from Hunter enabled me to work one-on-one with gays struggling with homophobia in several settings, including a facility for formerly homeless elderly people, some of whom are gay and/or have AIDS. In 1994, I joined the staff of the Institute for Human Identity as a therapist, and have helped to prepare a number of training guides for individuals working with people with AIDS."

CHRISTOPHER BRAM is the author of six novels: *Surprising Myself, Hold Tight, In Memory of Angel Clare, Almost History, Father of Frankenstein,* and *Gossip.* His short fiction has been included in *Men on Men 3* and *Aphrodisiac: Fiction from Christopher Street,* among other anthologies, and his essays have appeared in *Hometowns* and *Friends and Lovers.* He is the author of several screenplays, including two short films directed by his life partner, Draper Shreeve. A contributing editor for the *Lambda Book Report,* his book reviews, movie reviews, and essays also have appeared in *Christopher Street,* the *New York Native, Premiere, New York Newsday,* the *Advocate,* and the *New York Times Book Review.* Born in Buffalo, New York, he grew up outside Norfolk, Virginia, where he was a paper boy and an Eagle Scout, and was graduated from the College of William and Mary in 1974. He moved to New York in 1978, where he still lives.

RON CALDWELL is the author of an essay included in the anthology *Taking Liberties.* His poetry, fiction, interviews, and reviews have appeared in *Turnstile, Lynx Eye, Poetry Motel,* the *Harvard Gay & Lesbian Review, RFD, Christopher Street, Poultry,* the *GMHC Volunteer,* the *Gay Review, Gay Community News, FirstHand, Bay Windows,* and other journals. His collaborations with visual artist Lynne Caldwell have been exhibited in galleries in North Carolina and Washington, D.C. A native of Texas, he is a graduate of Rice University and the M.A. program in creative writing at Boston University, where he studied with Derek Walcott and George Star-buck. In the fall of 1993 he was a Writing Fellow at ART/OMI-Ledig House in Ghent, New York. He now lives in New York City, where he teaches writing at Marymount Manhattan College, works as a freelance editor, volunteers at GMHC, and participates in the Three Hots and a Cot reading series at the Cornelia Street Café in Greenwich Village.

© 1996 Markham McGill

MICHAEL T. CARROLL's 1992 short story "Afternoons" was the first gay fiction ever published in the *Chattahoochee Review*. Born in Memphis, Tennessee, he grew up in West Texas and in Jacksonville, Florida, and is a graduate of Florida State University and the creative writing program at Bowling Green State University. He writes: "I got interested in writing after reading Fitzgerald and Capote, to name just two. I wrote a novel when I was thirteen and sent it off to one publisher, who of course rejected it. In high school I wrote more novels of no interest whatever, and thought I would be chiefly a writer of young-adult novels like S. E. Hinton, though I had no gritty or even interesting experiences (save for a few sexual ones) to write about. I grew up in a conservative, Baptist-dominated Southern community but enjoyed a number of gay encounters with other boys. I continued writing straight-oriented fiction, not at first considering gay subject matter. After flop-ping in my first college (a local state university branch who'd given me a scholarship on the strength of their award to me for a full-length screenplay I'd written in high school), I kicked about, started at another local college, dropped out again, then finally got serious at Florida State. I met my first real boyfriend there, another writer who shared a lot of my interests. We later went off together to graduate school in Ohio, he as a writing student and I as a literature student. I couldn't get into a writing program anywhere. I continued teaching, stayed the course, and finally was admitted to the MFA writing program at the same school the following fall. Much later, after that and another boyfriend, I went to Yemen with the Peace Corps, then to the Czech Republic. I am now out of the Corps and living and writing in Paris."

© 1996 Amy Steiner

ALEX CHEE's short story "Memorials," written while he was attending Wesleyan University, was published in the 1990 an-thology of work by student writers, *Literature of Tomorrow*. His poetry has appeared in *Interview*, the *James White Review*, and *XXX Fruit*; his journalism and reviews in *Out/Look*, *Outweek*, the *Advocate*, *Out*, and the *San Francisco Review of Books*. An MFA Graduate

Opportunity fellow at the Iowa Writers Workshop in 1992–93, he is the recipient of a Story Magazine Short Short Fiction Award, a Holt, Rinehart & Winston short fiction prize, and a Paul Horgan Short Story Award. Born in Rhode Island, Chee spent his childhood in South Korea, Kuai, Truk, Guam, and Maine. He now lives in New York, where he is at work on his first novel, a collection of short stories, and a book of poems.

RODNEY CHRISTOPHER spent time in 1993 and 1994 as a writer and performer for Basic Black Productions, a small theater group he co-founded. His writing has appeared in *BLK*, a national monthly newsmagazine for black lesbians and gay men, and in *Soap Opera Weekly*. He hopes one day to write for soap operas. "I'd like to use the medium to teach people that they are more often alike than different, and to encourage them to ask themselves tough questions about the long-term disadvantages of maintaining the status quo," he writes, admitting, "Of course, I also love romance, long-lost siblings, split personalities, and other classic soap plots." Born and raised in Brooklyn, Christopher holds a bachelor's degree in social sciences from Simon's Rock College and a master's in urban policy analysis and management from the New School for Social Research. Since 1992, he has worked for Nonprofit Facilities Fund, which provides loans and technical assistance to New York City nonprofit groups for planning, acquiring, and maintaining their facilities. He now lives in Manhattan with his life partner, Greg McCaslin.

SAMUEL R. DELANY has published twenty-three volumes of fantasy and science fiction, four other volumes of fiction, and nine volumes of nonfiction, including critical studies of literature and a memoir, *The Motion of Light in Water*. He began his career in 1962 at the age of twenty with the novel *The Jewels of Aptor*. Since then he has received four Nebula Awards and two Hugo Awards, the highest honors for science fiction writing, as well as a William Whitehead Memorial Award for Lifetime Contribution to Lesbian and Gay Writing. His 1975 novel *Dhalgren* caused a sensation due to its graphic, sympathetic portrayal of both hetero- and homosexual behavior and is considered by many to be the most controversial science fiction novel of its decade. Delany was born and raised in Harlem. Since 1988 he has been a professor of comparative literature at the University of Massachusetts at Amherst. He lives in New York.

© *Greg Gorman*

DAVID DRAKE has contributed articles to the *Advocate*, *Theater-Week*, and *Details*. He is the author and original performer of *The Night Larry Kramer Kissed Me*, for which he received a *Village Voice* Obie Award. One of the longest running one-actor plays in Off Broadway history, *Larry Kramer* has received over thirty productions in nearly a dozen countries, and the published version was nominated for a Lambda Literary Award. As an actor Drake has appeared in the feature film *Philadelphia*, among others, and on the New York stage in *Vampire Lesbians of Sodom*, *Pageant*, *The Boys in the Band* (at the WPA Theater), and *A Language of Their Own* (at the New York Shakespeare Festival). Born and raised in Baltimore, he now lives in New York, where he is editor-in-chief of *POZ* magazine.

© *Shelley V. Smith*

PHILIP GAMBONE is the author of the short-fiction collection *The Language We Use Up Here*, which was nominated for a Lambda Literary Award, and the novel *Pushing Off*. His short stories have appeared in more than a dozen magazines and anthologies, including *Men on Men 3* and *Men on Men 6*. His essays, reviews, and feature articles have appeared in *Bay Windows*, the *Lambda Book Report*, the *Advocate*, *Frontiers*, and the *New York Times Book Review*; and his essays have been included in the anthologies *Hometowns*, *A Member of the Family*, *Sister and Brother*, and *Wrestling with the Angel*. He is currently working on a collection of interviews with gay and lesbian writers and a novel set in Naples, the city of origin of his four Italian grandparents. A former fellow at the MacDowell Colony, he hosted *The Word Is Out*, a series of twelve hour-long radio interviews with gay and lesbian writers that aired in Provincetown, Massachusetts, and lectures frequently about writing and gay literature at colleges and universities around New England. A native of Massachusetts, he now lives in Boston and teaches at the Park School in Brookline and in the writing program at Harvard, where he has received two Distinguished Teaching Awards.

© 1995 *Walter Briski, Jr.*

BRAD GOOCH is the author of five books: the biography *City Poet: The Life and Times of Frank O'Hara*; *Jailbait and Other Stories*, selected by Donald Barthelme for a Pushcart Foundation Writer's Choice Award; a book of poems, *The Daily News,* and two novels, *Scary Kisses* and the *Golden Age of Promiscuity.* His writing has appeared in the *Paris Review, Partisan Review, Bomb,* the *New Republic, Harper's Bazaar,* the *New Yorker, Vanity Fair, Out, New York,* the *Los Angeles Times Book Review,* the *Nation,* and *American Poetry Review.* He has received awards from the New York State Council on the Arts and the Academy of American Poets. Born and raised in suburban Pennsylvania, he is a graduate of Columbia University. He teaches English at the William Paterson College of New Jersey and has lived in New York City since 1971.

ALLAN GURGANUS is the author of *Oldest Living Confederate Widow Tells All,* which won the Sue Kaufman Prize from the American Academy of Arts and Letters. His book of stories and novellas, *White People,* was awarded the *Los Angeles Times* Book Prize. A recipient of grants from the Ingram Merrill Foundation and the National Endowment for the Arts, Gurganus recently won the National Magazine Award for a novella published in *Harper's.* That work also appears in *On Tattered Wings,* a group of short novels. Gurganus studied painting at the University of Pennsylvania. Following military service in the Vietnam War, he worked with Grace Paley at Sarah Lawrence College and with John Cheever and Stanley Elkin at the Iowa Writers' Workshop. He has taught writing at Stanford and Duke and is "emeritus" faculty at Sarah Lawrence. Gurganus's political essays appear on the op-ed page of the *New York Times.* He has spoken against homophobia and censorship on the *MacNeil/ Lehrer News Hour.* A native of North Carolina, Gurganus recently returned there; he lives in a village of 4,500 souls.

SCOTT HEIM is the author of two novels, *Mysterious Skin* and *In Awe,* and a book of poems, *Saved from Drowning.* His short fiction has appeared in *Christopher Street* and *Kansas Quarterly* and been included in the anthologies *Waves* and *Discontents.* His poetry has appeared in *Santa Monica Review, Midwest Quarterly, Arshile, Wisconsin Review, Chiron Review, B-City, Mudfish, Silverfish Review, Yarrow, Brooklyn Review, Pacific Review,* and other journals. A recipient of a Whitcomb Award for fiction and a Carruth Award for poetry while a student at the University of Kansas, he holds master's degrees from there and from Columbia University. He writes: "I was born and raised in central Kansas. As a kid, my major interests were baseball, horror films, Bigfoot, and UFOs. I was a spelling bee champion, announcer at a softball complex, and general teenage mess." He now lives in New York City.

ESSEX HEMPHILL was the author of *Ceremonies: Prose and Poetry* and two collections of poems, *Earth Life* and *Conditions*, and the editor of *Brother to Brother: New Writings by Black Gay Men*. His poetry has been published widely in journals, and his essays have appeared in *High Performance, Gay Community News,* the *Advocate, Pyramid Periodical, Essence,* and other periodicals. His work has been included in the anthologies *Tongues Untied, In the Life, Gay and Lesbian Poetry in Our Time, Art Against Apartheid, Men and Intimacy, The Poet Upstairs, High Risk, New Men, New Minds,* and *Natives, Tourists and Other Mysteries*. The recipient of fellowships in literature from the District of Columbia Commission for the Arts and the National Endowment for the Arts, his work is featured in the black gay films *Looking for Langston* and *Tongues Untied,* and he narrated the black gay AIDS documentary *Out of the Shadows.* Born in Chicago, he died of AIDS complications on November 4, 1995. "The *Other* Invisible Man" is part of an as-yet-unpublished autobiography completed before his death.

ANDREW HOLLERAN is the author of the novels *Dancer from the Dance, Nights in Aruba,* and *The Beauty of Men;* a book of essays, *Ground Zero;* and a monthly column in *Christopher Street.* His work has also appeared in the *Village Voice, New York, Frontiers,* and *Wigwag.* A graduate of the Iowa Writers' Workshop, he was born in Aruba, the Netherlands Antilles, and now lives in North Florida.

DENNIS HUNTER's short fiction has appeared in the *Church-Wellesley Review* and *Blueboy* and is included in the anthology *Discontents.* His essays have appeared in the *New York Press.* Born in Wiesbaden, West Germany, he grew up in Norman, Oklahoma, where he attended school from first grade through college. He now lives in New York City, where he is currently at work on a novel and a book of autobiographical essays.

© 1995 Susan Arnott

STEPHEN McCAULEY is the author of the novels *The Object of My Affection*, *The Easy Way Out*, and *The Man of the House*. His stories, articles, and reviews have appeared in *Gay Community News*, *Bay Windows*, the *Boston Phoenix*, the *New York Times Book Review*, *Vogue*, *House and Garden*, *Details*, *Vanity Fair*, *Harper's*, and *Travel and Leisure*, among other periodicals. Since 1987 he has taught creative writing at the University of Massachusetts in Boston, Wellesley College, Harvard University, and Brandeis University. He now lives in Cambridge, where he is working on a new novel. He writes: "After dropping in and out of a variety of graduate programs (English Lit., Education, Psychology, etc.) and working for many years as a travel agent, I realized that what I most wanted to do was write fiction. I signed up for several creative writing courses at adult education centers, but always felt uninspired or intimidated, usually both. One term, I unintentionally signed up for a class in writing nonfiction. By the time I realized my mistake, it was too late to switch into another class, and I decided to stick it out. I had no interest in writing nonfiction, but given the topic of the course, I found it necessary to make my stories as convincingly 'real' as possible. For some reason, this exercise provided the right combination of elements—confession, lying, gossip, exaggeration, etc.—and for the first time, I felt as if I had a grasp on the process of writing and a sense of my own voice. I wrote my first novel as part of the requirement for a degree from the Columbia University writing program. It was published shortly after I graduated and gave me the opportunity to pursue writing and teaching as a career."

Photo by Michael Marsland

J. D. McCLATCHY is the author of three books of poetry, *Scenes from Another Life*, *Stars Principal*, and *The Rest of the Way*; a volume of criticism, *White Paper: On Contemporary American Poetry*; and four opera librettos, *A Question of Taste*, *Mario and the Magician*, *Orpheus Descending*, and *Emmeline*. He is the editor of the anthologies *The Vintage Book of Contemporary American Poetry* and *The Vintage Book of Contemporary World Poetry* and of the quarterly journal the *Yale Review*. His work has appeared in the *New Yorker*, the *New York Times Book Review*, the *Paris Review*, the *New Republic*, *Poetry*, *Partisan Review*, the *Washington Post Book World*, and *Saturday Review*, among others. He is the recipient of fellowships from the Guggenheim Foundation, the National Endowment for the Arts, and the Academy of American Poets, an Award in Literature from the American Academy of Arts and Letters, and the Melville Cane Award from the Poetry Society of America, and has been named a Literary Lion by the New York Public Library and a Chancellor of the Academy of American Poets. Born in Bryn Mawr, Pennsylvania, he is a graduate of Georgetown University and Yale. He now lives principally in Stonington, Connecticut, where he is at work on a fourth collection of poems, *Ten Commandments*. (Photo courtesy of the Office of Public Affairs, Yale University.)

KEITH McDERMOTT is known primarily for his work as an actor. He played a title role in *Ignatz and Lotte*, cited by the *Village Voice* as one of the best independent films of 1995, and has worked frequently with Robert Wilson, the world-famous creator of theatrical spectacles. On Broadway, he starred with Richard Burton in *Equus*. He has played leading roles in many Off Broadway and regional theater productions as well as a pivotal role in the film *Without a Trace*. Born in Texas, he studied at the London Academy of Dramatic Arts after graduating from Ohio University. He now lives in New York City with his lover, the painter Eric Amouyal, and is currently at work on a memoir and a book of short stories. Aficionados will recognize "Larry" as Larry Kert and *Company* as the show he was starring in when he and Keith first met.

TIM MILLER has been writing solo theater works since 1980. After writing "How to Grow Fruit" for this anthology, he developed it into a full-length performance piece, *Fruit Cocktail*. Miller made headlines in the United States when he successfully sued the National Endowment for the Arts for withdrawing a grant under political pressure. A founder of Performance Space 122 in New York City, he is also the artistic director of Highways Performance Space in Santa Monica, California. He teaches in the graduate theater department at UCLA and conducts performance and writing workshops throughout the United States and abroad. Born in Pasadena, California, he has lived in Venice Beach since the mid-1980s.

MICHAEL NAVA is the author of a series of mystery novels featuring a gay Chicano criminal defense lawyer named Henry Rios, *The Little Death*, *Goldenboy*, *HowTown*, and *The Hidden Law*, for which he has received four Lambda Literary Awards, and *The Death of Friends*. He is the co-author, with Robert Dawidoff, of *Created Equal: Why Gay Rights Matter to America*. His essays have been included in the anthologies *Hometowns*, *A Member of the Family*, *Friends and Lovers*, and *Wrestling with the Angel*. At seventeen, he left his family's home in Sacramento, California, for Colorado College, where he wrote poetry and earned a degree in history. After graduating he spent a year in Buenos Aires, studying and translating the poetry of Ruben Dario. He entered Stanford Law School in 1978, graduated in 1981, and practiced law in Los Angeles for fourteen years. He now lives in San Francisco, where he still practices law and is working on *Unlived Lives: The Memoirs of a Misfit*.

Photograph by Douglas Macomber

CARL PHILLIPS is the author of two books of poems, *In the Blood*, winner of the 1992 Samuel French Morse Poetry Prize, and *Cortège*, which was nominated for a 1995 National Book Critics Circle Award. His work has been published widely in journals including the *Yale Review*, *Atlantic Monthly*, and the *Paris Review*, as well as in anthologies including the 1994, 1995, and 1996 editions of *The Best American Poetry*. As a child of a military family, Phillips moved almost annually from air force base to air force base in the United States and Germany, until finally settling on Cape Cod, Massachusetts, in his high school years. A graduate of Harvard University and the University of Massachusetts, he taught high school Latin for eight years before attending the creative writing program at Boston University. He subsequently took a teaching position at Washington University in St. Louis, returning to Harvard in 1995 as a visiting professor in English and American literature and language. He now divides his time between St. Louis and Provincetown, Massachusetts, with his partner, Doug Macomber.

© John R. Ellis

DOUGLAS SADOWNICK is the author of a novel, *Sacred Lips of the Bronx*, which was nominated for a Lambda Literary Award, and the nonfiction study *Sex Between Men: An Intimate History of the Sex Lives of Gay Men Postwar to Present*. A chapter from his novel was included in *Men on Men 4*. His articles have appeared in the *Advocate*, the *Los Angeles Times*, *Genre*, *High Performance*, the *New York Native*, and the *L.A. Weekly* (for which he received a GLAAD award for excellence in reporting). Born and raised in the Bronx, New York, he attended Columbia College and is currently enrolled in the graduate program in clinical psychology at Antioch. He served as co-chair of the Eighteenth Street Arts Complex and has also been a performance artist. He has lived since the mid-1980s in Venice Beach, California.

Photograph by Jean-Pierre Bonin

ED SIKOV, a film historian, is the author of *Screwball: Hollywood's Madcap Romantic Comedies* and *Laughing Hysterically: American Screen Comedy of the 1950s*, as well as the *American Cinema Study Guide*. His work is included in the anthology *Friends and Lovers*. His film reviews, features, and media criticism have appeared in *Architectural Digest*, the *New York Native*, and both the U.S. and British editions of *Premiere*. Born in Natrona Heights, Pennsylvania, he earned a Ph.D. from Columbia University and has taught courses in film there, and in film and gay and lesbian culture at Haverford and Colorado Colleges. He has lived in New York City since 1979 and is currently at work on a critical biography of Billy Wilder.

Photograph by Gene Bagnato

DR. CHARLES SILVERSTEIN is the author of *A Family Matter: A Parents' Guide to Homosexuality, Man to Man: Gay Couples in America,* and *Gays, Lesbians and Their Therapists: Studies in Psychotherapy*, and the co-author (with Edmund White) of *The Joy of Gay Sex* and (with Felice Picano) of *The New Joy of Gay Sex*. His essays and professional papers have been published widely in journals and anthologies. He is the founding director of the Institute for Human Identity and Identity House in New York City, and the founding editor of the *Journal of Homosexuality*. It would not be exaggerating to say that his work—as a personal therapist, through the institutions he has championed, and as a writer—has had a positive influence in the lives of countless individuals, gay and straight.

MATTHEW STADLER is the author of three novels: *Landscape: Memory, The Dissolution of Nicholas Dee,* and *The Sex Offender*. His work has appeared in *Christopher Street, Mirage Periodical, Grand Street,* the *New York Times, Rocket,* the *Stranger, Wiederball, High Times,* and the *Village Voice,* and has been included in the anthologies *Men on Men 4* and *His*, among others. A graduate of Oberlin College and Columbia University, he has received grants from the Ingram Merrill and Guggenheim foundations and is the recipient of a Whiting Writers Award. He is a co-director of the Rendezvous Reading Series in Seattle, where he was born and has lived since the late 1980s. He is now at work on his fourth novel, *Allan Stein*, concerning the nephew of Gertrude Stein and a painting by Picasso.

WILLIAM STERLING WALKER is completing a book of short stories centering on the lives of people in and from New Orleans. His stories have appeared in *Men's Style* and *Modern Words*, and his nonfiction in *Brooklyn Bridge*, *Lesbian and Gay New York*, *Les Amis* (the listening guide for the classical music radio station of the University of New Orleans), and in the 1992 season program of the Utah Opera. A native of New Orleans, he is a graduate of the University of New Orleans and the MFA writing program at Brooklyn College. He now lives in Brooklyn, New York, with his lover, the artist Jeffrey Dreiblatt.

EDMUND WHITE is the author of five novels, *Forgetting Elena*, *Nocturnes for the King of Naples*, *A Boy's Own Story*, *Caracole*, and *The Beautiful Room Is Empty*; a book of short stories, *Skinned Alive*; a collection of essays, *The Burning Library*; *States of Desire: Travels in Gay America*, and *Our Paris: Sketches from Memory*, with drawings by his late lover Hubert Sorin. His *Genet: A Biography* received the National Book Critics Circle Award and the Lambda Literary Award. He has also received fellowships from the Ingram Merrill and Guggenheim foundations, and an Award in Literature from the American Academy of Arts and Letters. In 1993 he was made a Chevalier de l'Ordre des Arts et Lettres of France. He has taught literature and creative writing at Yale, Columbia, Johns Hopkins, and New York University, and served as executive director of the New York Institute for the Humanities. Born in Cincinnati, he has lived in Rome, New York City, and, since 1983, Paris, except for two years in Providence, Rhode Island, when he was a full professor of English at Brown University. He is currently at work on *The Farewell Symphony*, the third installment in his trilogy of novels portraying gay life in America from the 1950s to the present. In 1996 he was made a member of the American Academy of Arts and Letters.

© DM Reznik

NORMAN WONG is the author of *Cultural Revolution*. His stories have appeared in *Men's Style*, *Kenyon Review*, the *Asian Pacific American Journal*, and the *Threepenny Review*, and have been included in the *Men on Men 4* and *Men on Men 6* anthologies. Born and raised in Honolulu, he is a graduate of the University of Chicago and the writing seminars of Johns Hopkins University. He now lives in New York City's East Village and teaches fiction writing at the Writer's Voice.

© Mariana Cook

PATRICK MERLA was the editor of *Christopher Street* magazine from 1978 to 1979 and the *New York Native* from 1984 to 1988. In that capacity he worked with virtually every important contemporary gay writer from Edmund White to Larry Kramer and discovered and gave first publication to countless others including Christopher Bram, Douglas Sadownick, and Matthew Stadler. Merla has also been an editor at *Saturday Review* and the *SoHo News*. He is the author of *The Tales of Patrick Merla* as well as literary essays and book reviews in numerous publications. A lifetime resident of New York, he is currently the fiction editor of *Men's Style* magazine.

THE FOLLOWING BIBLIOGRAPHY was compiled by Richard Labonté of A Different Light bookstore using suggestions from the contributors to this anthology as a beginning. No attempt has been made to be comprehensive. It includes works that deal with the coming-out experience in some way or provide a picture of the life of gay men that could be useful to a person in the process of coming out. Most of the books listed are in print; a few out-of-print titles worth tracking down are also included. In most cases, the publisher and date of the original edition are cited for historical context, although individual titles may now be in print from other publishers, usually in paperback editions.—P.M.

AUTOBIOGRAPHY, BIOGRAPHY, MEMOIRS, LETTERS, POETRY

Aarons, Leroy. *Prayers for Bobby*. HarperCollins, 1995.
Ackerley, J. R. *Hindoo Holiday*. Viking, 1984.

———. *The Ackerley Letters*, edited by Neville Braybrooke. Harcourt, 1975.

———. *My Father and Myself*. Harcourt Brace, 1968.

———. *My Dog Tulip*. Fleet, 1965.

SELECT BIBLIOGRAPHY

[Alexander, Jeb, and Dasham, C. C.] *Jeb and Dash: A Diary of Gay Life 1918–1945*, edited by Ina Russell. Faber & Faber, 1993.

[Auden, W. H.] *Auden*, by Richard Davenport-Hines. Pantheon, 1996.

[———.] *Auden in Love: The Intimate Story of a Lifelong Affair*, by Dorothy J. Farnan. Simon & Schuster, 1984.

[Baldwin, James.] *James Baldwin: A Biography*, by David Leeming. Knopf, 1994.

[———.] *James Baldwin*, by Randall Kenan. Chelsea House, 1993.

[———.] *Talking at the Gates*, by James Campbell. Viking, 1991.

[———.] *James Baldwin: Artist on Fire*, by W. J. Weatherby. Donald I. Fine, 1989.

Beam, Joseph, ed. *In the Life: A Black Gay Anthology*. Alyson, 1986.

[Beard, James.] *The Solace of Food: A Life of James Beard*, by Robert Clark. Steerforth, 1996. (Originally *James Beard: A Biography*. HarperCollins, 1993.)

Bell, Arthur. *Dancing the Gay Lib Blues*. Simon & Schuster, 1971.

Bory, William. *Orpheus in His Underwear*. Cythoera, 1993.

Broughton, James. *Coming Unbuttoned: A Memoir*. City Lights, 1993.

Burke, Glen. *Out at Home*. Excel, 1995.

[Capote, Truman.] *Capote: A Biography*, by Gerald Clarke. Simon & Schuster, 1988.

Chandler, Kurt, ed. *Passages of Pride: Gay and Lesbian Youth Come of Age*. Random House, 1995.

Chase, Clifford. *The Hurry-up Song*. Harper San Francisco, 1995.

Clarke, Lige, and Nichols, Jack. *I Have More Fun with You Than Anybody*. St. Martin's, 1974.

Cooper, Bernard. *Truth Serum: Memoirs*. Houghton Mifflin, 1996.

Corn, Alfred. *Autobiographies*. Viking, 1992.

———. *All Roads at Once*. Viking, 1973.

Cory, Donald Webster. *The Homosexual in America*. Greenberg, 1951.

Crisp, Quentin. *The Naked Civil Servant*. Holt, Rinehart & Winston, 1968.

DeCaro, F. A. *A Boy Named Phyllis: A Suburban Memoir*. Viking, 1996.

Delany, Samuel R. *The Motion of Light in Water: Sex and Science Fiction Writing in the East Village, 1960–1965*. Arbor House, 1988.

Dew, Robb Forman. *The Family Heart*. Addison-Wesley, 1994.

Dlugos, Tim. *Strong Place*. Amethyst, 1992.

———. *Entre Nous*. Little Caesar, 1982.

Doty, Mark. *Heaven's Coast*. HarperCollins, 1996.

Drake, David. *The Night Larry Kramer Kissed Me*. Anchor, 1994.

Driberg, Tom. *Ruling Passions*. Stein & Day, 1977.

Duberman, Martin Bauml. *Cures: A Gay Man's Odyssey*. Dutton, 1991.

————. *Midlife Queer*. Scribner, 1996.

Eighner, Lars. *Travels with Lizbeth: Three Years on the Road and on the Streets*. St. Martin's, 1993.

Feliz, Antonio A. *Out of the Bishop's Closet*. Alamo Square, 1992.

[Finland, Tom of.] *Tom of Finland: His Life & Times*, by F. Valentine van Hooven III. St. Martin's, 1993.

Fleming, Mickey C. *About Courage*. Holloway House, 1989.

[Forster, E. M.] *E. M. Forster: A Biography*, by Nicola Beauman. Knopf, 1994.

[————.] *E. M. Forster: A Life*, by P. N. Furbank. Harcourt Brace Jovanovich, 1978.

Fricke, Aaron. *Reflections of a Rock Lobster: A Story About Growing Up Gay*. Alyson, 1981.

Fricke, Aaron, and Fricke, Walter. *Sudden Strangers: The Story of a Gay Son and His Father*. St. Martin's, 1992.

[Genet, Jean.] *Genet: A Biography*, by Edmund White. Knopf, 1993.

Gide, Andre. *Corydon*. Farrar, Straus & Giroux, 1987.

————. *If It Die . . .* Penguin, 1950.

Ginsberg, Allen. *Journals: Early Fifties, Early Sixties*. Grove, 1977.

Glaser, Chris. *Uncommon Calling: A Gay Christian's Struggle to Serve the Church*. Westminster John Knox, 1966.

Gooch, Brad. *The Daily News*. Z Press, 1977.

Goodman, Dean. *Maria Marlene . . . and Me*. Shadbolt, 1994.

Greene, Julien. *Restless Youth*. Marian Boyers, 1996.

————. *The War at Sixteen*. Marian Boyers, 1993.

[Griffes, Charles Tomlinson.] *Charles T. Griffes: The Life of an American Composer*, by Edward Maisel. Knopf, 1984.

Gunderson, Steve, with Bawer, Bruce. *Of House and Home*. Dutton, 1996.

Gunn, Thom. *Collected Poems*. Farrar, Straus & Giroux, 1994.

Hart, Jack, ed. *My First Time: Gay Men Describe Their First Same-Sex Experience*. Alyson, 1995.

Harteis, Richard. *Marathon: A Story of Endurance and Friendship*. Norton, 1989.

Hartland, Claude. *Story of a Life*. Grey Fox, 1985.

[Hay, Harry.] *The Trouble with Harry Hay*, by Stuart Timmons. Alyson, 1990.

Heath, Gordon. *Deep Are the Roots: Memoirs of a Black Gay Expatriate*. University of Massachusetts, 1992.

Helms, Alan. *Young Man from the Provinces*. Faber & Faber, 1995.

Hemphill, Essex. *Ceremonies: Prose and Poetry*. Plume, 1992.

————, ed. *Brother to Brother: New Writings by Black Gay Men.* Alyson, 1991.

Holobaugh, Jim, with Hale, Keith. *Torn Allegiances: The Story of a Gay Cadet.* Alyson, 1993.

Isherwood, Christopher. *Christopher and His Kind.* Farrar, Straus & Giroux, 1976.

Johnson, Fenton. *Geography of the Heart.* Scribner, 1996.

Jolly, James, and Kohler, Estelle. *Gay Letters.* Marginal, 1995.

Kantrowitz, Arnie. *Under the Rainbow.* St. Martin's, 1996.

Katz, Jonathan Ned. *Gay American History: Lesbians and Gay Men in the USA.* Crowell, 1976.

Kennedy, James. *About Face: A Gay Officer's Account of How He Stopped Prosecuting Gays in the Military and Started Fighting for Their Rights.* Carol, 1995.

Kirkup, James. *A Poet Could Not Be But Gay.* Peter Owen, 1992.

Kirstein, Lincoln. *Mosaic: Memoirs.* Farrar, Straus & Giroux, 1994.

————. *By, With, To & From.* Farrar, Straus & Giroux, 1991.

Kopay, David, and Young, Perry Deane. *The David Kopay Story.* Donald I. Fine, 1988.

Louganis, Greg, with Marcus, Eric. *Breaking the Surface.* Random House, 1995.

Lundun, Ace. *The Closets Are Empty, the Dining Room's Full: An Autobiographical Legacy.* Ponderosa, 1993.

[Mann, Thomas.] *Thomas Mann: Eros and Literature,* by Anthony Heilbut. Knopf, 1996.

Mass, Lawrence. *Confessions of a Jewish Wagnerite.* Cassell, 1995.

[Matlovich, Leonard.] *Matlovich,* by Mike Hippler. Alyson, 1988.

[Matthiessen, F. O.] *Rat and the Devil: Journal Letters of F. O. Matthiessen and Russell Cheney,* edited by Louis Hyde. Alyson, 1978.

Maugham, Robin. *Escape from the Shadows.* McGraw-Hill, 1973.

[Maugham, W. Somerset.] *Willie: The Life of W. Somerset Maugham,* by Robert Calder. St. Martin's, 1990.

[————.] *Maugham: A Biography,* by Ted Morgan. Simon & Schuster, 1980.

McClatchy, J. D. *The Rest of the Way.* Knopf, 1990.

————. *Stars Principal.* Macmillan, 1986.

————. *Scenes from Another Life.* Braziller, 1983.

McNeil, John J. *Freedom, Glorious Freedom.* Beacon, 1995.

Merrill, James. *A Different Person: A Memoir.* Knopf, 1993.

Milam, Lorenzo. *The Cripple Liberation Front Marching Band Blues.* Mho & Mho, 1992.

[Milk, Harvey.] *The Mayor of Castro Street,* by Randy Shilts. St. Martin's, 1988.

Miller, Merle. *On Being Different: What It Means to Be a Homosexual.* Random House, 1971.

Mixner, David. *Stranger Among Friends.* Doubleday, 1996.

Monette, Paul. *Becoming a Man: Half a Life Story.* Harcourt Brace Jovanovich, 1992.

SELECT BIBLIOGRAPHY

Morgen, Kenneth B. *Getting Simon: Two Gay Doctors' Journey to Fatherhood.* Bramble, 1995.

Nardi, Peter. *Growing Up Before Stonewall.* Routledge, 1994.

[Nicolson, Harold.] *Portrait of a Marriage,* by Nigel Nicolson. Atheneum, 1991.

Norse, Harold. *Memoirs of a Bastard Angel.* Morrow, 1989.

[O'Hara, Frank.] *City Poet: The Life and Times of Frank O'Hara,* by Brad Gooch. Knopf, 1993.

Other Countries: Black Gay Voices. Other Countries Collective, 1990.

O'Toole, Lawrence. *Heart's Longing.* Douglas & McIntyre, 1995.

Pallone, Dave, with Steinberg, Alan. *Behind the Mask: My Double Life in Baseball.* Viking, 1992.

Peck, Scott. *All-American Boy.* Scribner, 1995.

Perry, Troy. *The Lord Is My Shepherd and He Knows I'm Gay.* Nash, 1972.

Perry, Troy, and Swicegood, Thomas L. P. *Profiles in Gay & Lesbian Courage.* St. Martin's, 1992.

Phillips, Carl. *Cortège.* Graywolf, 1995.

————. *In the Blood.* Northeastern University, 1992.

Picano, Felice. *Ambidextrous.* Masquerade, 1995.

————. *Men Who Loved Me.* Masquerade, 1995.

Pitcher, George. *The Dogs Who Came to Stay.* Dutton, 1995.

Preston, John. *My Life as a Pornographer and Other Indecent Acts.* Kaysak, 1995.

————, ed. *A Member of the Family: Gay Men Write About Their Families.* Dutton, 1992.

————, ed. *Hometowns: Gay Men Write About Where They Belong.* Dutton, 1991.

Raphael, Lev. *Journeys & Arrivals: On Being Gay and Jewish.* Faber & Faber, 1996.

Reed, Paul. *Savage Garden: A Journal.* House of Lillian, 1994.

Reid, John. *The Best Little Boy in the World.* Ballantine, 1993.

Rorem, Ned. *Knowing When to Stop.* Simon & Schuster, 1995.

————. *Setting the Tone: Essays and a Diary.* Coward McCann, 1983.

————. *The Paris & New York Diaries 1951–1961.* North Point, 1983.

Saks, Adrian, and Curtis, Wayne, eds. *Revelations: Gay Men's Coming-Out Stories.* Alyson, 1994.

Schneebaum, Tobias. *Where the Spirits Dwell: An Odyssey in the New Guinea Jungle.* Grove, 1988.

————. *Keep the River on Your Right.* Grove, 1969.

Schuyler, James. *Collected Poems.* Farrar, Straus & Giroux, 1993.

Sherman, Philip. *Uncommon Heroes.* Fletcher, 1994.

Sledge, Michael. *Mother and Son*. Simon & Schuster, 1995.

Spencer, William, ed. *In the Beginning: True Tales of Coming Out from the Pages of Guys Magazine*. Firsthand, 1993.

Steffan, Joseph. *Honor Bound: A Gay Naval Midshipman Fights to Serve His Country*. Avon, 1993.

[Stoddard, Charles Warren.] *Genteel Pagan: The Double Life of Charles Warren Stoddard*, by Roger Austen. University of Massachusetts, 1991.

[Strachey, Lytton.] *Lytton Strachey: The New Biography*, by Michael Holroyd. Farrar, Straus & Giroux, 1995.

[Symonds, John Addington.] *The Memoirs of John Addington Symonds: The Secret Homosexual Life of a Leading Nineteenth-Century Man of Letters*, edited by Phyllis Grosskurth. Random House, 1984.

Thompson, W. Scott. *The Price of Achievement: Coming Out in Reagan Days*. Cassell, 1995.

Trillin, Calvin. *Remembering Denny*. Farrar, Straus & Giroux, 1993.

Vidal, Gore. *Palimpsest: A Memoir*. Random House, 1995.

Vining, Donald. *A Gay Diary 1975–1982*. Pepys, 1993.

———. *A Gay Diary 1967–1975*. Pepys, 1983.

———. *A Gay Diary 1954–1967*. Pepys, 1981.

———. *A Gay Diary 1946–1954*. Pepys, 1980.

———. *A Gay Diary 1939–1946*. Pepys, 1977.

———. *How Can You Come Out If You've Never Been In: Essays on Gay Life and Relationships*. Crossing, 1986.

[Waddell, Tom.] *Gay Olympian: The Life and Death of Dr. Tom Waddell*, by Tom Waddell and Dick Schaap. Knopf, 1996.

[Wescott, Glenway.] *Continual Lessons: The Journals of Glenway Wescott 1937–1955*, edited by Robert Phelps and Jerry Rosco. Farrar, Straus & Giroux, 1990.

[Welch, Denton.] *The Journals of Denton Welch*, edited by Michael De-la-Noy. Dutton, 1984.

[———.] *Denton Welch: The Making of a Writer*, by Michael De-la-Noy. Viking, 1984.

[White, Patrick.] *Patrick White: Letters*, edited by David Marr. University of Chicago, 1996.

[———.] *Patrick White: A Life*, by David Marr. Knopf, 1991.

[White, T. H.] *T. H. White: A Biography*, by Sylvia Townsend Warner. Viking, 1967.

[Whitman, Walt.] *Walt Whitman's America: A Cultural Biography*, by David S. Reynolds. Knopf, 1995.

[———.] *Walt Whitman: A Life*, by Justin Kaplan. Simon & Schuster, 1980.

[Wilde, Oscar.] *Oscar Wilde*, by Richard Ellmann. Knopf, 1987.

[Williams, Tennessee.] *Tom: The Unknown Tennessee Williams*, by Lyle Leverich. Crown, 1995.

[————.] *Tennessee Williams' Letters to Donald Windham 1940–1965*. University of Georgia, 1996.

[Wilson, Angus.] *Angus Wilson: A Biography*, by Margaret Drabble. St. Martin's, 1996.

Windham, Donald. *Emblems of Conduct: Coming of Age in the Depression-Era South*. University of Georgia, 1996.

Wojnarowicz, David. *Close to the Knives: A Memoir of Disintegration*. Vintage, 1991.

Wooley, Robert. *Going Once: A Memoir of Art*. Simon & Schuster, 1995.

FICTION

Ames, Jonathan. *I Pass Like Night*. Morrow, 1989.

Arenas, Reinaldo. *Old Rosa: A Novel in Two Stories*. Penguin, 1989.

Argiri, Laura. *The God in Flight*. Random House, 1995.

Arlen, Michael. *Young Men in Love*. Doran, 1927.

Baldwin, James. *Another Country*. Dial, 1962.

————. *Giovanni's Room*. Dial, 1956.

Barr, James. *Quatrefoil*. Greenberg, 1950.

Beachy, Stephen. *The Whistling Song*. Norton, 1991.

Bills, Greg. *Fearful Symmetry*. Dutton, 1996.

————. *Consider This Home*. Simon & Schuster, 1994.

Birman, David. *The Book of Billy*. Pluto, 1993.

Bookbinder, Bernie. *Out at the Old Ball Game*. Bridgeworks, 1995.

Bradley, Marion Zimmer. *The Catch Trap*. Ballantine, 1984.

————. *The Heritage of Hastur*. Daw, 1975.

Bram, Christopher. *Almost History*. Donald I. Fine, 1991.

————. *In Memory of Angel Clare*. Donald I. Fine, 1989.

————. *Surprising Myself*. Donald I. Fine, 1985.

Brodkey, Harold. *Profane Friendship*. Farrar, Straus & Giroux, 1993.

Brown, Forman (writing as Richard Meeker). *Better Angel*. Alyson, 1987.

Brown, Todd D. *Entries from a Hot Pink Notebook*. Washington Square, 1995.

Campbell, Michael. *Lord Dismiss Us*. Putnam, 1968.

Campo, Rafael. *The Other Man Was Me*. Arte Publico, 1994.

Camus, Renaud. *Tricks*. Serpent's Tail, 1996.

SELECT BIBLIOGRAPHY

Capote, Truman. *Other Voices, Other Rooms*. Random House, 1948.

Chabon, Michael. *The Mysteries of Pittsburgh*. Harper, 1988.

Chambers, Aidan. *Dance on My Grave*. Harper, 1983.

Cocteau, Jean. *The White Paper*. Macaulay, 1958.

Coe, Christopher. *I Look Divine*. Random House, 1988.

Cooper, Bernard. *A Year of Rhymes*. Viking, 1993.

Corbin, Steven. *Fragments That Remain*. Alyson, 1993.

Cruse, Howard. *Stuck Rubber Baby*. Warner, 1995.

Cunningham, Michael. *Flesh and Blood*. Farrar, Straus & Giroux, 1995.

———. *A Home at the End of the World*. Farrar, Straus & Giroux, 1990.

———. *Golden States*. Crown, 1984

Curzon, Daniel. *Curzon in Love*. Knights, 1988.

D'Allessandro, Sam. *Zombie Pit*. Crossing, 1988.

Davis, Christopher. *Joseph and the Old Man*. St. Martin's, 1987.

d'Hondt, John. *The Bunny Book*. GLB, 1991.

Duane, Diane. *The Door into Fire*. Dell, 1979.

Duplechan, Larry. *Blackbird*. St. Martin's, 1987.

———. *Eight Days a Week*. Alyson, 1985.

Ferro, Robert. *The Blue Star*. Dutton, 1985.

———. *The Family of Max Desir*. Dutton, 1983.

Ford, Charles Henri, and Tyler, Parker. *The Young and the Evil*. Obelisk, 1933.

Forster, E. M. *Maurice*. Norton, 1971.

Fox, John. *The Boys on the Rock*. St. Martin's, 1984.

Friedman, Sanford. *Totempole*. Dutton, 1965.

Fritscher, Jack. *Some Dance to Remember*. Knights, 1990.

Gabriel, Eric. *Waterboys*. Mercury House, 1989.

Gambone, Philip. *The Language We Use Up Here*. Dutton, 1991.

Gervais, Paul. *Extraordinary People*. HarperCollins, 1992.

Gide, Andre. *The Immoralist*. Cassell, 1930.

Gilgun, John. *Music I Never Dreamed Of*. Amethyst, 1989.

Greene, Harlan. *What the Dead Remember*. Dutton, 1991.

———. *Why We Never Danced the Charleston*. St. Martin's, 1988.

Grimsley, Jim. *Dream Boy*. Algonquin, 1995.

SELECT BIBLIOGRAPHY

Grumley, Michael. *Life Drawing*. Grove, 1991.

Hale, Keith. *Cody*. Alyson, 1994.

Hallasy, Paul. *The New York Trilogy*. Downtown, 1990.

Hansen, Joseph. *Jack of Hearts*. Dutton, 1995.

———. *Living Upstairs*. Dutton, 1993.

———. *A Smile in His Lifetime*. Plume, 1989.

Hardy, James Earl. *B-Boy Blues*. Alyson, 1994.

Harris, E. Lynn. *And This Too Shall Pass*. Doubleday, 1996.

———. *Invisible Life*. Doubleday, 1994.

Heim, Scott. *Mysterious Skin*. HarperCollins, 1995.

Henderson, William Haywood. *Native*. Dutton, 1993.

Holland, Isabelle. *The Man Without a Face*. Lippincott, 1972.

Holleran, Andrew. *Nights in Aruba*. Morrow, 1983.

———. *Dancer from the Dance*. Morrow, 1978.

Hollinghurst, Alan. *The Swimming-Pool Library*. Random House, 1988.

Hsien-Yung, Pai. *Crystal Boys*. Gay Sunshine, 1995.

Hufford, Charles. *The Toy Soldier's Heart*. Carter, 1995.

Isherwood, Christopher. *A Meeting by the River*. Simon & Schuster, 1967.

———. *A Single Man*. Simon & Schuster, 1964.

———. *The World in the Evening*. Random House, 1954.

———. *The Berlin Diaries*. New Directions, 1946.

———. *Prater Violet*. Random House, 1945.

Islas, Arturo. *Rain God*. Avon, 1991.

Katz, Jonathan Ned. *Coming Out: A Documentary Play About Gay Life and Liberation*. Ayer, 1975.

Killian, Kevin. *Shy*. Crossing, 1989.

Kirkwood, James. *Good Times/Bad Times*. Simon & Schuster, 1968.

Klein, Adam. *Medicine Burns*. Serpent's Tail, 1995.

Kluger, Steve. *Changing Pitches*. Alyson, 1989.

Knowles, John. *A Separate Peace*. Macmillan, 1960.

Kramer, Larry. *The Destiny of Me*. Plume, 1993.

———. *The Normal Heart*. Plume, 1985.

———. *Faggots*. Random House, 1978.

Lambert, Gavin. *Norman's Letter*. Coward McCann, 1966.

SELECT BIBLIOGRAPHY

Leavitt, David. *While England Sleeps.* Holt, 1996.

———. *The Lost Language of Cranes.* Knopf, 1986.

———. *Family Dancing.* Knopf, 1984.

Lefcourt, Peter. *The Dreyfus Affair.* HarperCollins, 1993.

Leventhal, Stan. *Skydiving in Sheridan Square.* Masquerade, 1995.

———. *Mountain Climbing in Sheridan Square.* Banned, 1988.

Linmark, P. Zamora. *Rolling the 'Rs.* Kayak, 1996.

Lynn, Elizabeth A. *The Dancers of Arun.* Berkley, 1979.

Mamet, David. *Edmond.* Grove, 1983.

Manley, Joey. *The Death of Donna May Dean.* St. Martin's, 1992.

Martin, Kenneth. *Billy's Brother.* Gay Men's, 1989.

Maupin, Armistead. The Tales of the City Series. Harper.
 Sure of You, 1989.
 Significant Others, 1987.
 Babycakes, 1984.
 Further Tales of the City, 1982.
 More Tales of the City, 1980.
 Tales of the City, 1978.

McIntosh, Harlan Cozad. *This Finer Shadow.* Lorac, 1941.

McLaughlin, Christian. *Glamourpuss.* Dutton, 1994.

Merlis, Mark. *American Studies.* Houghton Mifflin, 1994.

Mishima, Yukio. *Confessions of a Mask.* New Directions, 1958.

Mordden, Ethan. *How Long Has This Been Going On?* Villard, 1995.

———. The Buddies Trilogy. St. Martin's.
 Everybody Loves You, 1988.
 Buddies, 1986.
 I've a Feeling We're Not in Kansas Anymore, 1985.

Munoz, Elias Miguel. *The Greatest Performance.* Arte Publico, 1991.

Parker, Canaan. *The Color of Trees.* Alyson, 1992.

Peck, Dale. *Martin and John.* Farrar, Straus & Giroux, 1994.

Peters, Fritz. *Finistere.* Farrar, Straus & Giroux, 1951.

Phillips, Thomas Hal. *The Bitterweed Path.* Rinehart, 1950.

Picano, Felice. *The Lure.* Masquerade, 1996.

———. *Like People in History.* Penguin, 1995.

Plante, David. *The Catholic.* Atheneum, 1985.

Price, Reynolds. *The Promise of Rest.* Scribner, 1995.

Purdy, James. *Malcolm*. Serpent's Tail/High Risk, 1996.

Quinn, Eric Shaw. *Say Uncle*. Dutton, 1994.

Raphael, Lev. *Dancing on Tisha B'av*. St. Martin's, 1991.

Read, Kirk. *Lovevision*. Kirk Read, 1995.

Rechy, John. *City of Night*. Grove, 1963.

Reidinger, Paul. *Good Boys*. Dutton, 1993.

———. *Best Man*. Alyson, 1989.

Reinhart, Robert. *Walk by Night*. Alyson, 1994.

———. *A History of Shadows*. Alyson, 1985.

Renault, Mary. *The Last of the Wine*. Pantheon, 1975.

———. *The Persian Boy*. Pantheon, 1972.

———. *Fire from Heaven*. Pantheon, 1969.

———. *The Mask of Apollo*. Pantheon, 1966.

———. *The Charioteer*. Pantheon, 1959.

Rodi, Robert. *What They Did to Princess Paragon*. Dutton, 1994.

———. *Closet Case*. Dutton, 1993.

Russell, Paul. *Boys of Life*. Dutton, 1991.

Sadownick, Douglas. *Sacred Lips of the Bronx*. St. Martin's, 1994.

Salinger, J. D. "Seymour: An Introduction," in *Nine Stories*. Little, Brown, 1953.

Scanlan, Dick. *Does Freddy Dance?* Alyson, 1995.

Selvadurai, Shyam. *Funny Boy*. Morrow, 1996.

Siman, Ken. *Pizza Face, or, The Hero of Suburbia*. Grove, 1991.

Spanbauer, Tom. *The Man Who Fell in Love with the Moon*. Grove, 1991.

Stadler, Matthew. *Landscape: Memory*. Plume, 1991.

Stein, Eugene. *Straitjacket & Tie*. Ticknor & Fields, 1994.

Vidal, Gore. *The City and the Pillar and Seven Early Stories*. Random House, 1995.

Vilmure, Daniel. *Toby's Lie*. Simon & Schuster, 1995.

Warren, Patricia Nell. *The Front Runner*. Wildcat, 1994.

Weiner, Steve. *The Museum of Love*. Overlook, 1995.

Weir, John. *The Irreversible Decline of Eddie Socket*. Harper & Row, 1989.

Welch, Denton. *In Youth Is Pleasure*. Dutton, 1986.

Weltner, Peter. *Beachside Entries*. Five Fingers, 1990.

White, Edmund. *Skinned Alive: Stories*. Knopf, 1995.

———. *The Beautiful Room Is Empty*. Knopf, 1988.

———. *A Boy's Own Story*. Dutton, 1983.

Whitmore, George. *Nebraska*. Grove, 1987.

Windham, Donald. *Two People*. Coward McCann, 1965.

Wojnarowicz, David. *The Waterfront Journals*. Grove Atlantic, 1996.

Wong, Norman. *Cultural Revolution*. Persea, 1994.

Yourcenar, Marguerite. *The Memoirs of Hadrian*. Modern Library, 1995.

———. *Alexis*. Farrar, Straus & Giroux, 1984.

Zilinsky, Ursula. *The Long Afternoon*. Doubleday, 1984.

ADVICE

Adair, Nancy, and Adair, Casey. *Word Is Out: Stories of Some of Our Lives*. New Glide/ Delta, 1978.

Babuscio, Jack. *We Speak for Ourselves*. Abingdon, 1991.

Barber, Karen, ed. *Testimonies*. Alyson, 1994.

Bauer, Marion Dane. *Am I Blue? Coming Out from the Silence*. HarperCollins, 1995.

Berzon, Betty. *Setting Them Straight*. Plume, 1996.

Blumenfeld, Warren. *Looking at Gay & Lesbian Life*. Beacon, 1993.

Bohlin-Davis, Odell, ed. *Breaking Silence: The Coming Out Letters*. Xanth, 1995.

Brimmer, Larry Dane, ed. *Being Different: Lambda Youth Speak Out*. Franklin Watts, 1996.

Califia, Pat. *The Advocate Advisor*. Alyson, 1991.

Clarke, Lige, and Nichols, Jack. *Roommates Can't Always Be Lovers*. St. Martin's, 1974.

Due, Linnea, ed. *Joining the Tribe: Growing Up Gay and Lesbian in the '90s*. Anchor, 1995.

Ferrante, Tony, and Jacobson, Paulette. *Letters from the Closet*. Tzedakah, 1994.

Flood, Gregory. *I'm Looking for Mr. Right But I'll Settle for Mr. Right Away*. Brob House, 1990.

Ford, Thomas Michael. *The World Out There: Becoming a Part of Lesbian and Gay Community*. New Press, 1996.

Heron, Ann, ed. *Two Teenagers in Twenty*. Alyson, 1995.

Herrman, Bert. *Being Happy Being Gay*. Alamo Square, 1990.

Hodges, Andrew, and Hutter, David. *With Downcast Gays*. Pink Triangle, 1974.

Isay, Richard. *Becoming Gay: The Journey to Self-Acceptance*. Pantheon, 1996.

Jay, Karla, and Young, Allan, eds. *After You're Out*. Pyramid, 1975.

———. *Out of the Closets: Voices of Gay Liberation*. Douglas, 1972.

Kissen, Rita. *The Last Closet: The Real Lives of Gay and Lesbian Teachers.* Heinemann, 1996.

Leong, Russell, ed. *Asian-American Sexualities: Dimensions of the Gay and Lesbian Experience.* Routledge, 1995.

Loovis, David. *Gay Spirit: A Guide to Becoming a Sensuous Homosexual.* Grove, 1975.

Manasse, Geoff, and Swall, Jean. *Making Love Visible.* Crossing, 1995.

Marcus, Eric. *Is It a Choice?* HarperCollins, 1993.

McNaught, Brian. *On Being Gay.* St. Martin's, 1988.

Price, Deb. *And Say Hi to Joyce.* Doubleday, 1995.

Remafedi, Gary, ed. *Death by Denial.* Alyson, 1994.

Romesburg, Dan, ed. *Young, Gay and Proud.* Alyson, 1995.

Signorile, Michelangelo. *Outing Yourself.* Random House, 1995.

Silverstein, Charles. *A Family Matter: A Parents' Guide to Homosexuality.* McGraw-Hill, 1978.

Silverstein, Charles, and Picano, Felice. *The New Joy of Gay Sex.* HarperCollins, 1992.

Silverstein, Charles, and White, Edmund. *The Joy of Gay Sex.* Mitchell Beazley, 1977.

Singer, Bennett, ed. *Growing Up Gay/Growing Up Lesbian.* New Press, 1994.